REBEL KING

BOOK ONE

HAMMER OF THE SCOTS

Carolyn Hale Bruce

REBEL KING
BOOK ONE
HAMMER OF THE SCOTS

Chronicles of Robert de Brus, King of Scots

A NOVEL

Charles Randolph Bruce
&
Carolyn Hale Bruce

AHEAD OF THE HANGMAN PRESS
2 0 0 2

AN
AHEAD OF THE HANGMAN PRESS
BOOK
PUBLISHED BY
BRUCE & BRUCE, INC.

Copyright © 2002 by Charles Randolph Bruce & Carolyn Hale Bruce

Published and Distributed in the United States by
Bruce & Bruce, A Virginia Corporation.
PO Box 64007 Virginia Beach, VA 23467-4007

www.robert-de-bruce.com

FIRST EDITION

Library of Congress Control Number: 2002092630

Hardback: ISBN 0-9721674-0-4

Paperback: ISBN 0-9721674-1-2

Manufactured in the United States of America

Cover design and illustration and character drawings by Charles Randolph Bruce

To Our Mothers

Map of events 1306 - 1307

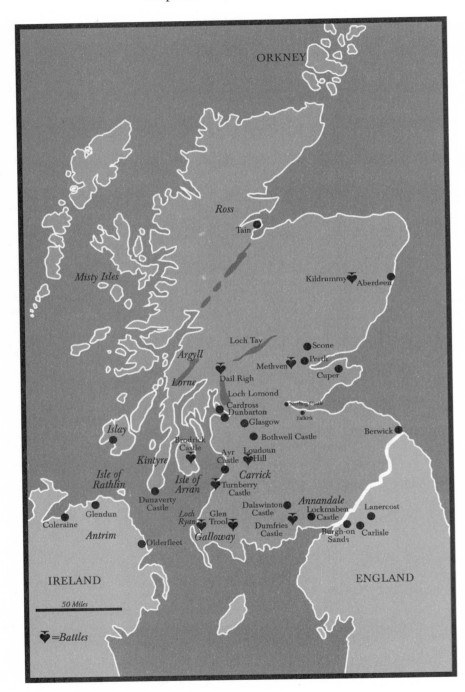

LIST OF ILLUSTRATIONS

ḣiꜱꜱоꝛісаꞁ васꝀɡꝛоυио

It is said by some that Robert de Brus, King of Scots, achieved his kingship by sacrificing his principles, and vacillating back and forth between English sovereignty and Scottish independence for his own personal benefit. But, did he?

Perhaps it would be judicious at this time to present a bit of the extremely convoluted and often conflictive history of the relationship between the Scots and the English. Necessarily, this is but the barest explanation of why the two peoples who have so long shared a small island have often been at odds with each other, even though many of their familial and traditional roots extend deep into the same European soils. Our readers must forgive our brevity, for we would otherwise be writing a tome the magnitude of an encyclopedia, so complex is this exciting, tragic, comedic, romantic, and bloody story.

Kenneth MacAlpin, in 844 A.D., united under his leadership many of the disparate tribes of the land that is now Scotland, and his descendants ruled the kingdom for generations.

Duncan I, distant nephew of MacAlpin, ascended the Scottish throne in 1034 and achieved immortality, of a sort, by being murdered six years later, an event which is now and forever shall be dramatized in Shakespeare's play *MacBeth*. The overly ambitious MacBeth was himself deposed in 1047 by Duncan's son, Malcolm III, and the MacAlpin line continued upon the throne through the Norman invasion of the England in 1066. That occurrence and the marriage of Malcolm III to Margaret Atheling, an English noblewoman of Saxon heritage (later canonized by the Roman Catholic Church), brought an influx of English and Norman customs and thought to Scotland.

Interestingly, it was in the horde that accompanied William "The Bastard," Duke of Normandy, in his conquest of England that the first Robert de Brus, a Norman knight from Brix (near present-day Cherbourg, France), arrived in England.

Since earliest times, English kings had tried to exert suzerainty, or feudal superiority, over the Scots. William, ever after 1066 called "The Conqueror," cast an eye toward Scotland six years later, and Malcolm III submitted rather than war against far superior forces. To cement the deal, Malcolm sent his son Duncan to live at the English Court as a hostage. Though it was a lovely existence, and beneficial in wealth and power for the young Scottish prince (and his successors), it was nevertheless "pampered captivity."

Malcolm's youngest son David married a very wealthy English-woman, Matilda of Huntingdon, who possessed a great deal of land. When the Scottish throne subsequently came to him, King David I then owned large, rich tracts in England. As was customary, he paid homage to the England's King for the land, which duty was perverted by subsequent English kings to denote Scottish acquiescence to their supremacy.

Malcolm III and Margaret's great-grandson, King William the Lion, after being defeated by the English in Northumbria, recognized England's Henry II as his liege, or feudal lord, in the Treaty of Falaise in 1174. Fifteen years later, however, this vassalage was relinquished by Richard Coeur de Lion, who, in order to finance a crusade, sold the vassalage back to the Scots for 10,000 merks and Scotland was once again independent.

William the Lion's son Alexander II began his reign in 1214. His rule proved to be one of the longest continuous periods of Scottish prosperity, and in fact, carried forward after his death through the abbreviated reign of his son, Alexander III. England, meanwhile, suffered devastating civil war. Much of the nobility rose up against King Henry III, and all concerned suffered widespread destruction and carnage

Robert de Brus, "The Noble," was laird of Annandale and a grandson of Scotland's King David I. During the English civil war, he raised an army of Scots and fought on the side of the English monarchy. A great defeat befell the royalists at Lewes in 1264, and Lord Robert's army was massacred by the rebel cavalry. He was captured, along with Henry III and his twenty-five-year-old son, Lord Edward. The Scottish laird's son, also named Robert, hastened to England to ransom his father, as was common practice among the warring nobility. The surviving peasantry of a losing army on enemy soil were most often, as in this case, hunted down and killed, if not by the opposing army, then by the local populace.

At age thirty-three, Lord Edward succeeded Henry III on the throne of England, and two years later, another Robert de Brus was born. It is he who is the subject of the following story. Grandson of the laird of Annandale Robert de Brus, "The Noble," and son of Robert de Brus and Marjorie, countess of Carrick, the infant was born close to the line of Scottish succession, and was thus fated to become King Edward's mortal enemy.

While the baby Robert grew into a handsome, strong boy, Edward, nearly forty years old, strove mightily for order and good government in England. Among his many admirable achievements, Edward, in his middle years an able administrator and a courageous warrior, established regular meetings of Parliament and yielded to that body the right and task of levying taxes within the realm.

When the boy Robert was less than ten years old, Edward brought the principality of Wales under his control by warring on Llewelyn ap Gruffudd, the "last true Prince of Wales," and his brother David, settling the affair with the Statute of Wales in 1284. Edward gave the country and the title "Prince of Wales" to his newborn son, Edward, who would one day succeed him on the throne.

It was Edward's great desire to encompass the entire island under his crown. However, familial concerns prevented his warring on Scotland, for Edward's sister Margaret was married to Scotland's King Alexander III, making the entire island a "family" holding.

Alexander III outlived Margaret, and their two sons and one daughter. The latter, having married the king of Norway, was queen of that land at her demise. She left one very young daughter, also named Margaret, who was heir apparent to the Scottish throne. Having no living children the Scottish king sought to remarry and produce another, preferably male, heir, and so espoused a young French woman, Yolande de Dreux, granddaughter of King Louis VI. Late on the evening of March 18, 1286, having met with his councilors at Edinburgh, and having drunk far too much, Alexander headed home to his bride of just six months. Against advice, he set out into a wild storm, and was found dead next day at the bottom of cliffs along the River Forth near Kinghorn.

The powerful men of the land, the churchmen and the nobility, swore fealty to the only living descendant of Alexander III, Margaret, the "Maid of Norway," as their lady and future queen. They also pledged that, should they fail to guard Scotland and keep the peace for her, they would be excommunicated from the church by the Scottish bishops.

Scotland's government was then temporarily placed into the hands of Guardians who pledged to do nothing that would diminish the country's independence, or harm the royal "dignity." After establishing an interim government, the Guardians put royal officers of the land on notice that they must, within twenty-four hours of being alerted, have knights and soldiers owing military service to the crown ready to do battle to protect Scottish liberty and royal interests. Late in the year, they also sent a mission to King Edward to ask his advice and, should it be needed, protection for the sanctity of the Scottish nation.

The wheels of government turned slowly. In July 1290, Scottish emissaries, negotiating with England and Norway, completed the Treaty of Birgham, an agreement stating that the "Maid of Norway," heiress to the Scottish throne, would, at the proper time, marry the five-year-old and only surviving son of King Edward, also named Edward. Approved not only by the Guardians, but the bulk of Scotland's empowered society as well, the treaty went into great and specific detail to ensure that Scotland remained a free and independent entity and in no way a vassal to any other. Edward signed the treaty in August 1290.

Too late. By that time (actually the previous June), Edward had taken over Scotland's Isle of Man, in the middle of the Irish Sea, which was of strategic importance to him, and put that part of Scotland "under his protection" without a word to the Scottish authorities. This was months before the Guardians received news that the child Margaret, the "Maid of Norway," had died at Orkney on her way to Scone to be crowned, and had been taken back to Bergen for burial. Her sudden death left no obvious successor to the crown.

In the ensuing confusion, a dozen others desired the vacant throne, but two strong Scottish aristocrats laid claim to it. One was John de Balliol and the other, Robert de Brus, "The Noble." Both descended from David, earl of Huntingdon, younger brother of Scotland's King William the Lion. Earl David had no surviving sons, but his three daughters had male descendants.

John de Balliol was the grandson of the eldest daughter, Margaret. Robert de Brus was the son of second daughter, Isabel, and thus one generation closer to Earl David. He also had acquired the prerogative that gave him the support of seven Scottish earls having the authority to elect a king. However, argued de Balliol, his grandmother being the elder sister, primogeniture ruled, as it had in England (but not Scotland) for the two centuries since the Norman conquest. Ah, but Robert de Brus, in 1238, had been made heir presumptive to the Scottish throne by King Alexander II before he had a son to inherit the crown. And thus it went.

Unable to decide whose interests were stronger, the argument threatened to incite civil war among the various factions, and at length, the many rivals agreed to have a "disinterested" party make the decision as to which of them held the strongest claim. Their chosen arbiter of "The Great Cause" was Edward, king of England.

Edward's queen and greatly beloved wife of 35 years, Eleanor of Castile, died that winter, an unhappy event that did not favor the Scots, as Eleanor had given Edward a softer, more reasoned approach to many things. After her death, his ambitious iron will was unrestrained.

The following spring (1291) Edward invited the Scots to meet and talk with him on the English side of the Tweed, assuring them that crossing the border would not put them in a lesser negotiating position. They no sooner arrived than he demanded suzerainty over Scotland, and backed it up with an army gathered from England's northern shires. The Scots requested time to consider his demand, and then sent him a formal, polite, but firm, letter of refusal saying that they had not the power to grant such rights. Only the Scottish king had such power, and even if they agreed, it would not be binding. Edward dismissed the reply as not "to the purpose."

However, Edward eventually did receive from the Scots, including de Balliol and de Brus, his temporary overlordship of the kingdom; the physical control of Scotland, its castles and strongholds (tantamount to suzerainty); and the power to make the final decision regarding the succession to the Scottish throne by his presidency of a special tribunal set up to weigh each candidate's claim. The Scots competitors for the throne, wanting to be in Edward's good graces, agreed to the demands (however illegally), and to abide by Edward's decision, even though he retained rights to be a competitor for the throne himself! Fealty was sworn to Edward by virtually all Scots of any import, the castles were surrendered, the elected Guardians resigned to be re-appointed by Edward, and Scotland became, for all practical purposes, an English protectorate.

For their part, the Scots obtained his promise that the English king would surrender possession of the kingdom to the rightful king of Scotland within two months after the new king was crowned, and that he would make no further claims against the country.

Thus it was that Edward became chief lord of Scotland, and the Scots were to rue the day.

The matter of Scottish royal succession went quickly before a legally established court, in which arguments were heard from all competitors. For a year and a half, much posturing and figurative beating of breasts went on, especially between the two primary claimants, each trying to convince the court that, for various reasons, his was the stronger, more valid claim. Arguments dragged on until November 1292, at which point things drew rapidly to an end, and the de Bruses were privately informed that de Balliol had been chosen the rightful heir.

On November 7th, the aged Robert, The Competitor, resigned his claim to the crown in favor of his son, then earl of Carrick, and his heirs. Perhaps it was thought that the claim should be passed down to prevent its being lost in the event of the elder Brus' unexpected death. That was well, except that the Countess Marjorie, mother of the future King Robert, had predeceased the claim's transfer by some months. Her widowed husband had not the mettle of The Competitor, and on November 9th, he deftly sidestepped the responsibilities thrust upon him by relinquishing the claim and the earldom of Carrick to the title's rightful heir, his eighteen-year-old first-born son, Robert.

The new earl was a canny youth and fully realized the injustice that had befallen his family and his country at the hands of Edward of England, but there was then nothing to be done. Thus, on November 17th, the court made public its decision. The last day of the month, St. Andrew's Day, 1292, John de Balliol was crowned at Scone. None of the de Bruses swore fealty to Scotland's new king, considering him usurper of the throne rightfully theirs. This dichotomy of loyalties would later place them at war with their homeland.

English law of primogeniture had supported de Balliol as heir, but, many felt and many yet feel that Edward preferred de Balliol because he was younger, less knowledgeable, more malleable, and could thus be more easily turned to favor whatever Edward desired for Scotland. In the words of Barrow, "It is true [de Balliol] was not a forceful man and certainly no match for Edward."

The king who had theretofore always dealt with the Scots legally and usually fairly, may have, indeed probably did, plot to acquire the kingdom as his vassal state, having declared at the time of Queen Eleanor's funeral his intent to subjugate Scotland as he had Wales. Evidence suggests that he encouraged a small number of civil disputes, properly decided by Scottish courts, to be afterward appealed to his justice.

Edward's first counter-decision came on December 22nd, after which four Scots magnates and others forwarded a petition pleading that he abide by his agreement to preserve Scottish laws and customs, and that no Scottish lawsuits would "be dealt with outside Scotland." The last day of the month, Edward abrogated all commitments made to the Scots during the interim between the reigns of Alexander III and John de Balliol. He further asserted his intention to hear any appeals brought to him, even unto summoning the King of Scots before his court, if he so chose!

King John, having sworn fealty to Edward before the crowning at Scone, and under great pressure from Edward to do so, also issued pronouncements freeing the English monarch from any and all obligations he might have agreed to during the time of the Guardians, including the Treaty of Birgham. Thus, Edward joined other English rulers who had repudiated promises made to the Scots. Edward, in his own mind, was rightfully empowered to be overlord of Scotland, and he continued hearing complaints against legal decisions by Scottish courts. Edward's rules for settling such complaints, as he had stated, required the King of Scots to appear in person before the English parliament to explain the reasons for the said decisions, and other, equally repugnant stipulations. Summonses for such appearances by King John were properly ignored, but eventually, John de Balliol relented, and late in 1293, finally went before the English parliament.

King John initially showed "courage and dignity" in responding to a body that treated him shabbily. He stated that he could not answer before an English court on matters affecting his kingdom without consulting with his own advisors, the "responsible men" of Scotland. However, savagely berated by Edward (who was apparently vicious) and threatened with losing his three principal towns and castles for being in contempt of court, de Balliol's personal courage wilted and he submitted to Edward's feigned superiority. As Scotland's king, de Balliol thus submitted his kingdom to Edward's vassalage.

It was obvious to both the Scots and the English that King Edward had succeeded in placing a "yoke of servitude" upon the "fickle and unstable" Scots, and the English felt it just. Their king had subdued and annexed the Welsh state and defied King Philip of France, and the Scots had undeniably shown great weakness and vacillation in their dealings with Edward, even before King John had been enthroned. However, the independent-natured Scots soon saw the irresolute King John as Edward's puppet, a situation they found intolerable and dangerous. He was soon labeled "Toom Tabard," or "empty tunic," by many of his countrymen.

Perhaps taking advantage of Edward's preoccupation with things at home, King Philip IV (called " Philip The Fair") of France confiscated Edward's French duchy of Aquitaine, in response to which Edward angrily renounced his homage to the French king. He entered into discussions with the leaders of Germany, northern Spain, and many of the Low Countries, and soon formed an alliance that would effectively surround France. The English king forbade communications with the Continent sans royal permission, and ordered King John to exert similar control in Scotland. This raised the ire of many of the landed and titled

Scots, who, like the American colonists of a later time, saw that the English king was treating them more like vassals than free men.

Next, the English military was ordered to report for overseas duty at Portsmouth, from whence they would embark for war in France. Edward sent the Scots an order for King John, along with "ten earls of Scotland, and sixteen barons, headed by James the Stewart and Brus of Annandale, The Competitor, [then] eighty-four years of age" [Barrow] likewise to report at Portsmouth. No longer even giving pretense that Scotland was a sovereign nation, Edward was behaving as reigning monarch. Giving excuse on top of excuse, the Scots (who were in no mood to give overseas military aid to the English king) failed to show.

In August, Edward called for the Welsh to report for service, and made the error of arming them prior to embarkation. Within a month, the whole of Wales was in revolt against him, capturing and destroying his castles and creating a great deal of turmoil. The Welsh halted Edward's winter offensive by attacking and seizing his baggage train.

While the Welsh were warring on Edward, Robert de Brus, The Competitor, laird of Annandale and grandfather of the future Scots king, died at Lochmaben on Good Friday 1295. His son and heir was then in Norway, having escorted his daughter Isabella to be wed to Norway's King Erik. It would be autumn before he returned to take up his new responsibilities.

Many discontented Scots, taking note of the rebellious Welsh' successes, determined that neither would they stand idly by and be taken over by the English. In early summer, due to de Balliol's apparent lack of competence and their distrust of his resolve, the Scots held a parliament at Stirling and, though not deposing him, removed governmental control from King John. On July 5, 1295, they elected a "Council of Twelve" to take command and prepare the country for inevitable war with Edward.

By October, a Scottish mission to France had negotiated a renewal of "The Auld Alliance," between France and Scotland. Scotland agreed to invade England if Edward left home for the Continent, and the French pledged to furnish aid or create diversions if the English invaded Scotland. Neither side would make a separate peace, and the whole treaty would be crowned by the marriage of King John's son Edward de Balliol, who was guaranteed to be heir to the throne, and King Philip's niece, Jeanne.

In a separate agreement, the two countries joined with Norway, in spite of King Erik's formerly amiable relations with Edward, and formed an alliance more or less surrounding England.

In order to resist English intentions toward Scotland, word went out for the Scottish military to hold inspections of arms and equipment, a prerequisite to a call to assemble. That order soon followed, and the Scots landholders who were ready to do battle against Edward gathered with their knights at Caddonlee, near Selkirk, and prepared to do battle to the south as had William the Lion in 1173. Among nobles holding lands in Scotland and remaining loyal to the English king were the de Bruses. As a result, many of their neighbors considered them unwelcome and, like the Tories of the American Revolution, they, along with English citizens, were banished from their lands, their homes, and even religious orders in Scotland. Annandale, home of Lord Robert de Brus, was given to the earl of Buchan to be used as headquarters for attacking Cumberland.

Meanwhile, the war in France went poorly for Edward, who was unable to cross the Channel and lead his armies in battle due to the dangers to his crown closer to home. English coffers were being drained and there were disastrous losses in the field. Yet, in spite of their drubbing in France, his armies were gaining experience that would prove invaluable once the upstart Scots met them on the battlefield.

Thinking they had little to fear from Edward's defeated armies, the Scots blindly headed toward disasters of their own. Edward is said by Barrow to have stated, "What matter if both Welsh and Scots are our foes? ... let them join forces if they please. We shall beat them both in a day." Edward demanded that the Scots relinquish, until the end of the war with France, the castles of Berwick, Roxburgh, and Jedburgh, all along his border. He further ordered the Scots not to allow any French or Flemish to enter Scotland, to which they replied they would welcome whom they pleased. But Edward had only begun to fight.

Under his edict, Scottish-held lands in England were seized, and six months later, Scots in England were arrested; even the toddler son of Sir William Douglas was taken into custody! Full-fledged war began in late March 1296, when the Scots burned their way from Annandale to Carlisle. There they were repulsed, ironically, by the lord of Annandale, Robert de Brus, then in command of Castle Carlisle, and his son the earl of Carrick. The invading Scots' greatest success at Carlisle was the burning of half the town, after which they withdrew back to Annandale.

Edward was far more successful at attacking Berwick-on-Tweed, Scotland's largest and wealthiest town, taking it on first attack. Only 30 Flemings fought to the death, perishing when the Red Hall was burned with them inside. But, it was what happened afterward that shows Edward's extreme brutality. It became one of the darkest events in English history.

After the town lay prostrate before him, Edward ordered that none beneath the rank of knight be spared. The murdering of the helpless men, women, and children of the town went on for days, until the local clergy were at long last successful in begging mercy from the English king. It is estimated that between ten thousand and twenty thousand Scots were slain, so many that their bodies became a "dangerous nuisance" and were hastily thrown into the sea or buried in deep pits. Edward then established his "capitol" at Berwick from which defeated Scotland would be governed.

The Scots raided and burned numerous small villages, churches, and monasteries in Northumberland, and some said they set fire to a school building resulting in the deaths of two hundred young scholars. Whether the schoolboys were murdered or not is in doubt, but the burning of the village and the priory of Hexham, as well as other towns, is factual.

Inexperienced in pitched warfare, the Scots' main armies were met at Dunbar in late April by those of Edward under the command of John de Warrene, earl of Surrey (and father of the wife of John de Balliol - another control Edward had thought he held over the Scottish king). Having laid siege to Dunbar Castle, the tough English forces turned to meet the oncoming Scots (who actually held the more advantageous position). Seeing the movement, the unseasoned Scots got the notion that the English were withdrawing and, relinquishing the high ground, gave chase... only to find their well-formed foe awaiting them. In short order, the Scots were overpowered and fled the area looking for safety in Selkirk forest, some forty miles distant. The Scots soldiers of foot suffered heavy casualties, and great numbers of the "important" persons of Scotland were captured. It was a crushing defeat for an army ill prepared to fight a modern war.

Subsequent Scottish resistance was slight, and in some instances non-existent. One-by-one, the castles fell until, by mid-summer, King John and the Comyns had fled northward and sued for peace. Edward informed the hapless de Balliol of what must be done to achieve cessation of hostilities, and meanwhile, went about the business of securing his captured land. He toured the country, proving his victory to the masses, while looting the wealth of Scotland's royalty. Among his trophies were "regalia and a mass of plate, jewellery [sic] and relics, including the Black Rood of Saint Margaret, the holiest and most venerated relic in Scotland." He then had the Stone of Destiny removed from its place in the abbey at Scone and sent to Westminster Abbey as a gift to his personal patron, Edward the Confessor.

King John, thoroughly defeated, gave Edward all that he had asked:

a servile confession of rebellion, renunciation of the Scots' treaty with the French, and, on July 10, 1296, abdication. The blazon of his royal arms was stripped from his tabard, thus completing his humiliation before his own and the English peoples. The ex-king was sent south to the Tower of London, but was soon granted quarters near his home. The more prominent Scots leaders, including the Comyns, were sent to England, some to the Tower, while others were imprisoned in various castles throughout the more distant parts of England and Wales.

Robert de Brus, son of the Competitor, having been promised the Scottish throne in return for the de Bruses' support during the uprising, instead received only Edward's disdainful query, "Have we nothing else to do but win kingdoms for you?"

Back in Berwick by late August, Edward had his parliament draw up an ordinance for the English governance of the captured land, making himself direct lord, but not eliminating Scotland as a separate entity. He required that fealty be sworn, again, and a fairly complete list of those so doing can be found on a formal document called the "Ragman Roll." (The term "Ragman," as used here, was possibly derived from the Old Norse "ragmenni," meaning "coward," and comes down to us today as "rigmarole," or, useless, confused statements or nonsense.) Those who had not rebelled also swore allegiance, including the de Bruses.

Notably absent from the list is the family of landholder and vassal of the Stewart, Malcolm Wallace, and his brothers, John and William. Perhaps they were not of enough import to be included on the Ragman Roll, or perhaps, they refused to pledge their fealty. Those who did not take the oath were declared outlaws and stripped of possessions and inheritances, and forbidden to possess weapons of war.

Edward then considered the whole Scottish matter settled, and after setting up English administrators, left that unhappy country, making the comment, "He who rids himself of shit does a good job," and returned his attentions to his war against the French. Many Scots, however, held nothing but animosity toward the English and their over-lordship, creating a cauldron in which an undercurrent of rebellion continued to simmer just beneath the surface. It would not be long before the lid blew off.

With most powerful Scots imprisoned or out of the country, Scotland's leadership fell to the likes of Robert Wishart, Bishop of Glasgow and one of the old Council of Twelve. Another was one of the most powerful landholders in Scotland, James the Stewart, canny and less fiery than Wishart, but nevertheless holding no love for Edward of England. Perhaps, then, it was no coincidence that the next uprising came under the leadership of William Wallace, a long-time friend of

Wishart, and under the patronage of the Stewart, on whose land he lived. It has been suggested that Wishart and Stewart may actually have plotted Wallace's revolt of the following year.

Wallace was known to be a daring warrior and still carried his five-foot long sword. Educated beyond his station by an uncle who was a priest, Wallace came to the fore in the spring of 1297, after some grumbling of discontent arose in the west highlands and violence erupted in Aberdeenshire and Galloway. In May, the English sheriff of Lanark, William de Heselrig, having failed to trap William Wallace at the home of his wife, Marion Braidfute, had Marion and her family slain and the house burned. Wallace avenged the murders the next night by returning with a small band and killing every Englishman in Lanark. Moving stealthily, he started in the home of the Sheriff, whom he woke and personally dispatched with a dagger to the heart.

Aided by the turbulent Sir William Douglas, Wallace next attacked the English court at Scone, routing the justiciar and acquiring much plunder. This effectively ran most English north of the Forth to ground.

Wallace turned to the English garrison at Ayr. His uncle Sir Reginald Crawford had been sheriff of Ayr, and was tricked to his death by being solicited to confer with an English judge named Arnulf. They were to meet in a large building near town, which became instead a place of massacre. About three hundred Scots, entering in ones and twos to attend the meet, were hanged from the rafters as they entered. Then the building was cleared and used as English barracks.

Wallace again attained vengeance. In the night, he and his men surrounded and set fire to the barracks, slaying any who escaped the flames. He then took Castle Ayr and, from its walls, hanged Arnulf.

About the time Wallace "raised his head," Andrew Murray (son of Sir Andrew Murray, Lord of Petty, deposed [by the English] Justiciar of Scotia and a wealthy baron), escaped from a captivity suffered after the Battle of Dunbar. He gathered fighters from around Inverness and captured Castle Urquhart. Within three months he controlled Inverness, Elgin, Banff, and other northern castles formerly held by the English. King Edward sent the Comyns, John of Badenoch and John, earl of Buchan, to join those yet loyal to him in quelling the disturbances in the realm's northern reaches. However, the earl of Buchan crossed to the side of the rebels.

Among others joining this rebellion, interestingly, was young (aged twenty-two) Robert de Brus, earl of Carrick. Kicked out of Scotland for siding with Edward against John de Balliol, his family had regained its holdings after the English conquest for the same reason. As far as

Earl Robert's father was concerned that support existed yet, in spite of Edward's broken promise of the Scottish throne.

The bishop of Carlisle, however, suspected the true loyalties of the younger de Brus and coerced him into taking a special oath of allegiance to the English crown, which he soon rightly abrogated as being given under constraint. "I must join my own people [the men of Carrick] and the nation in which I was born," he is quoted as having said to his father's knights while trying, mostly in vain, to convince them to join him in the revolt.

With those he did persuade, de Brus managed to relieve Castle Douglas, under English siege and defended by the Lady Douglas and her twelve-year-old son, James. From that day, James Douglas would follow Robert de Brus to the death, and beyond.

Irrespective of his success at Douglas, the untried de Brus was no better at war than were Bishop Wishart and the Stewart, who met a larger and better equipped English contingent of well-trained mounted troops at Irvine and immediately asked to negotiate terms for surrender. Many interpreted that as a ruse to give Wallace time to continue his successful activities. The talks dragged on, and in a late July letter to King Edward from Hugh Cressingham, the situation was described in direst terms. Most Scottish counties were no longer under Edward's control because his "keepers" were either dead, holed up, or in Scottish hands. Cressingham is quoted as saying, "And in some shires the Scots have appointed and established bailiffs and officials." The Scots, in other words, were taking back their country and establishing home rule.

Submission at Irvine contained a special demand upon Earl Robert de Brus, who did not submit with the others. Robert had married very young, and his wife, Isabella, daughter of Donald, earl of Mar (a friend of Robert's late grandfather, The Competitor), died in 1296 while giving birth to their daughter, Marjorie. To meet the terms of his capitulation, Robert was ordered to surrender his only child as a hostage. He had not done so as of November of that year, and there is no evidence that he ever submitted or surrendered the infant.

In late August, Wallace and Murray joined forces. Edward's commanders, Warrene and Cressingham, moved on Stirling with one thousand heavy cavalry and a host of nearly sixty thousand English and Welsh infantry, arriving September 9th. Wallace and Murray formed their army of about ten thousand north of Stirling Bridge, which spanned the Forth about a half-mile beneath Stirling Castle. Between the two was a high road through plowed fields and meadows, totally unsuitable for deploying cavalry. There the river formed a horseshoe bend and flowed on both sides of any advancing army, which could only cross the narrow bridge two riders abreast.

After much unsuccessful parleying between Earl Warrene and several Scots (including James the Stewart), who said they would try to "pacify" their countrymen, the Englishman finally sent two friars to Wallace, seeking capitulation. His reply came back a veritable slap in the haughty English face, "...we are not here to make peace but to do battle to defend ourselves and liberate our kingdom. Let them come on, and we shall prove this in their very beards."

Cressingham, the penny wise and pound foolish English treasurer, had sent home reinforcements to save money, and now used the same logic in urging that the coming battle go forth immediately. Sir Richard Lundie, who had gone over to the English at Irvine, proposed a delay, that he might cross the river at a tidal ford near Kildean and maneuver his forces to a position behind his fellow Scots. Apparently distrustful of the turncoat and confident that his superior numbers would carry the day, Warrene ordered his army across the narrow bridge the next morning, September 11th.

Wallace and Murray watched patiently until a sufficient number of English troops, both horse and foot, had crossed the arch. They then rushed in to cut the invading army in twain. Among those who made it to the north bank of the river was Cressingham, the niggardly treasurer, who charged into the Scots spearmen and was killed. Those yet on the south side had no way to help the advance party, but watched as they were cut to pieces. Warrene, seeing his command losing severely, fled in haste all the way back to Berwick. Out of the forests, James the Stewart and the earl of Lennox led their commands down upon the English supply train and the fleeing enemy troops, killing great numbers and capturing horses and wagons in the marshes south of the river.

Success at Stirling was not lightly won, and among the sacrificed Scots was Andrew Murray, whose lingering death came in November.

With no way to re-supply, the English garrison in Stirling Castle soon surrendered. A wildly popular win for the Scots, the Battle of Stirling Bridge was no crushing defeat of the English, though to be sure, the English nose was well bloodied by the victory of mostly afoot and untrained Scots peasantry over the primarily professional and highborn English cavalry.

The political situation in Scotland reverted to its previous form, with John de Balliol, still held in England, as king, and all else as it was before his abdication. Murray, while he lived, and Wallace, throughout, never attempted to claim the throne or be anything more powerful than guardians of the kingdom and commanders of its army.

Wallace led raids into Northumberland in October and November, and ferociously retaliated against the English in border areas, making all fear his appearance on the horizon. Some of the undisciplined rabble in his command crossed the line between warfare and atrocity, plundering and pillaging at will with none to stop them. It was not until winter that the Scots returned north without having captured any major castles on either side of the border, save Stirling, but with plunder to divide amongst themselves.

Warrene and Sir Robert Clifford attempted a half-hearted counter-offensive in December, but the relatively minor damage they did amounted to the burning of ten towns, and the slaughtering of many Annandale peasants. They also freed Roxburgh and Berwick of Scottish sieges before retiring for the winter. Edward, then on the continent, sent word to hold off on any major campaigns until he arrived to lead such. Wallace spent the interim trying to train and prepare his soldiers and increase their number, knowing that Edward would strike with heavy blows come spring.

According to an English source at the time, William Wallace was knighted prior to the end of March 1298, by "one of the foremost earls of Scotland," which Barrow goes on to surmise was probably either Buchan, Carrick, or Lennox. He contends that Wallace earned this honor at the Battle of Stirling Bridge. Wallace was also elected sole Guardian of Scotland and commander of the armed forces. However, while the powerful men of the kingdom may have admired and supported Wallace and wished him success, they were reluctant to take orders from a commoner. They would have to do so if they joined the fray, and so the hereditary leadership of the kingdom failed to lead, or even to follow, and left to Wallace their country's freedom.

Edward prepared to invade Scotland with an impressive army of two thousand mounted and twelve thousand foot soldiers, though the vast majority of the latter were from Wales and Ireland, and their commitment to Edward's war with Scotland was dubious. As for the English populace, they had taken the defeat of England's finest at the hands of Wallace as an almost personal affront. Their appraisal of the Scottish leader was based on hatred, resentment, fear, and titillation, as baseless rumors spread about his despicable character and horrendously cruel deeds.

In early July of the following year, Edward marched on Scotland, catching neither sight nor sound of Wallace and his army. To his dismay, he found Berwickshire and Lothian burned and deserted, and his supply ships delayed at sea, save a few that brought mostly wine. With no way to feed his soldiers other than foraging in that devastated land,

Edward sent Bishop Bek's force to capture three Scottish-held castles in Lothian, which he was unable to accomplish until after the arrival of some English grain ships.

Edward's force, however, was yet starving, and in order to quell their hunger and lift their spirits, he ordered they be given some of the wine. A debacle followed in which the intoxicated Welsh instigated brawling and several priests were killed. In response the English knights charged into the Welsh troops, killing eighty and scattering the rest.

Threatening to join the Scots, the Welsh stayed away from camp until word came with Patrick, earl of Dunbar, and Gilbert de Umfraville, earl of Angus and an Englishman, both of whom had always supported England, that the Scots were just thirteen miles away, near Falkirk. The army regrouped to meet them the following day, July 22, 1298.

Lacking cavalry and having only longbows, Wallace was at a severe tactical disadvantage. His spearmen were set in place on the side of a solid hill with heavy woods behind them, and faced southeast across a loch that was more of a marshy bog. They were grouped into four schiltroms of perhaps as many as two thousand men, each holding a long, metal-pointed pole or spear toward the outside of the circular group, making the whole much like a huge and deadly quill-laden beast. Into the turf around the schiltroms had been driven wooden stakes, roped together, and between each were stationed Wallace's archers under command of John the Stewart. What cavalry he had, contributed by the Comyns and others, Wallace held to the rear.

Eager to be about their business with the Scots, the English commanders refused to delay until their men had eaten, as Edward suggested, and instead, moved forward in the direction of what was ostensibly but a small brook separating them from their enemy. Reaching the loch, the first army circled the swampy obstacle by heading west, the second, east. The Scottish cavalry, for the most part, panicked and deserted the field without making contact with the enemy. A few notable exceptions remained and took part in the battle, including MacDuff of Fife, who was killed leading his men.

The English professionals systematically picked apart the Scots' preparations. They first attacked the archers in between the schiltroms, killing almost all of them, from their commander Sir John the Stewart on down, leaving the schiltroms separated and vulnerable. They fought valiantly, but the spearmen suffered such a merciless rain of arrows, crossbow bolts, and stones, that the outer rings of the schiltroms began to gap. Soon there were not enough replacements to move out from the center; the English cavalry charged into thinned and faltering ranks and annihilated the Scots, killing hundreds if not thousands more.

Wallace and other Scots magnates escaped and fled to "castles and woods." It is unknown whether or not the young earl of Carrick was among those who participated in the Battle of Falkirk, but when Edward later arrived at de Brus' estate, he found the town empty and the castle destroyed, burned on Earl Robert's orders.

Falkirk, though not a vanquishing of the Scots, was the undoing of Sir William Wallace. From that point his fortunes steadily declined, as he had only his military prowess to thank for his rise in society, and that reputation rested primarily on his success at Stirling Bridge. Having been greatly encouraged by that success, the influential Scots' faith in Wallace was now shattered, and they realized their freedom was going to require their own active participation and sacrifice. As for Wallace, he either was removed or resigned as Guardian of Scotland, and the following summer left for the continent to work in the interests of the realm.

Edward was driven out of Scotland, not by the Scots, but by famine and the discontent of his commanders. Prior to exiting the kingdom, he successfully wrested Lochmaben, home of Robert de Brus, lord of Annandale, from Scots who apparently supported the rebellion more strongly than did the laird. Returning in September to Carlisle, Edward found the Scots had been there before him and taken his supplies, leaving him with insufficient food for his already hungry army. Nonetheless, he swore to return the following year, and commenced bestowing Scottish lands upon his supporters, claiming that the properties' rightful Scottish owners had forfeited them by their disloyalty to him. It was true that most of the Scots had closed ranks to defend themselves and Scotland against the English interlopers, and most would eventually pay dearly for their patriotism.

Before December 1298, Robert de Brus of Carrick and John Comyn, the younger, of Badenoch were elected joint Guardians of the kingdom. They continued to act in the name of King John and upheld the acts of Wallace while he was Guardian. Edward was unable to mount an offensive to the north the following year, and the Scots used the providential gift of time to appoint their own administrators and officials wherever they were needed, to collect taxes and to gain additional power in the Scottish church. England still held many castles in southeast Scotland, but for the most part, the Scots controlled the rest of the country.

At the intercession of Pope Boniface VIII, King John was released from captivity in July 1299, but Edward would only surrender him to papal custody. Thus, de Balliol was removed to the Continent and held in a papal residence.

In August, William Lamberton, having replaced the late William Fraser as Bishop of St. Andrews two years previously, arrived from his mission to France to find de Brus and Comyn setting out on an ambitious raid south of the Forth. He joined them, as had the earls of Buchan, Menteith, and Atholl. Sir Malcolm Wallace, brother of William, was there in the de Brus contingent.

Deciding against attacking heavily defended Roxburgh, their original target, the Scots left Sir Ingram de Umfraville with troops and any locals who might be persuaded to join the effort, and raided as far as the environs of Edinburgh. But, an English spy among them was sending back military and other pertinent information to his master, Robert Hastings, constable at Roxburgh.

In a missive to King Edward, Hastings described a fissure between de Brus and Comyn during a council the Scots held August 12th. He reported that Sir David Graham lay claim to the lands and goods of Sir William Wallace for his having left Scotland without the Guardians' consent, to which Sir Malcolm objected on grounds that his brother's work abroad was for the good of the kingdom. The two drew daggers upon each other. Graham being in Comyn's retinue and Wallace in de Brus', the argument was quickly reported to John Comyn, who took de Brus by the throat and the earl of Buchan, a Comyn supporter, turned on neutral Bishop Lamberton, accusing them both of plotting treason. Future troubles between the two men might have been settled mortally at that point had not the Stewart come between them.

A report that Sir Alexander Comyn (brother of the earl) and Lachlan Macruarie were warring on fellow Scots in their district, burning and despoiling the region, arrived in timely fashion, sobering and unifying the opposing camps. Agreement was made that Bishop Lamberton would become the principal captain and remain in control of all the castles. He was also elected third Guardian of Scotland in an attempt to buffer the de Brus-Comyn factions. Afterward, the council participants took their respective followers and returned, each to his bailiwick.

For the next few months the joint Guardians tried to make things work among them, holding the government together with dogged determination while starving the English out of Stirling. There was talk of a truce between England and Scotland to be negotiated by King Philip "The Fair" of France, to which the Guardians seemed amenable. Edward, having his own troubles at home, was virtually rendered incapable of charging north after the Scots as he would have wished. Eventually the English in Stirling surrendered, after which they were permitted to return safely home.

So it was that the Scots set about governing Scotland and recapturing the English holdings along their border. The southwest region would be first, and de Brus was greatly influenced in his decision to resign as a Guardian by this campaign; after all, his father, lord of Annandale and always Edward's supporter, still resided there. His decision may have been made partially due to threats of attacks by the men of Galloway upon his northern Carrick lands. Whatever the cause, Robert de Brus did resign before May 1300, leaving Bishop Lamberton and John Comyn as joint Guardians. Sir Ingram de Umfraville, kinsman of Balliol and supporter of Comyn, quickly filled De Brus' vacated position.

King Edward, having gathered a suitable force for the first time in nearly two years, marched that summer from Carlisle to Annan, and afterward to Lochmaben, still held by the English. From there he moved the ten miles to Scottish-held Caerlaverock Castle and laid siege to it, bringing up battering rams and catapults, effecting the castle's demise in short order and hanging many of the Scots defenders.

Rolling west into Galloway, Edward held a two-day meeting with the earl of Buchan and Comyn of Badenoch. The Scots demanded the restoration to his throne of John de Balliol, recognition by Edward of de Balliol's familial succession thereto, and the return of English estates to the Scots from whom Edward had seized them, else they would defend Scotland against him as long as possible. To all this Edward was adamant in his refusal, and the war continued to rage.

After a small skirmish by his foragers at a glen along the Cree, Edward moved his army there and, with archers and three brigades of horse, faced off against Buchan, Comyn of Badenoch, and Umfraville, each commanding a horse brigade. When the English moved across the tidal basin at ebb tide, the Scots fled in such a panic that some even left their horses and took flight on foot into the wilderness. The English horsemen were not prepared to fight in such terrain, and the bulk of the Scottish army escaped.

Though he captured two prominent Scottish patriots, Sir Robert Keith and Robert Baird of Strathaven, Clydesdale, Edward was disappointed that he had not been able to thrash the Scottish army into submission. On top of that, the Archbishop of Winchelsey was finally in receipt of the previous year's missive from Pope Boniface VIII, excoriating Edward for his invasion of Scotland, a sovereign, Catholic country, and demanding that the whole matter be submitted for papal adjudication. The Pope and Philip of France also supported the Scots' demands for a truce, and the declining, elderly monarch finally agreed to one, but lasting only until the following May (1301).

The new combination of joint guardians was no more workable than the previous one, and at some point before May 1301, all three of them resigned to be replaced by one man, Sir John de Soules. Older, and neutral in the de Brus-Comyn affair, de Soules was a great patriot and an active Guardian, mounting renewed efforts to return King John to his throne.

It was during this time, also, that Edward prepared to lobby the papal court in an attempt to prove his suzerainty over the Scots, bringing in proofs of the several times that the Scots earls swore fealty to Edward. He further claimed that he was in "full possession" of Scotland, which was untrue, as the Scots pointed out, because he controlled not one of the twelve bishops' sees or the twelve dioceses in Scotland, but merely portions of the St. Andrews and Glaswegian dioceses. The Scots mounted a vigorous counter-claim culminating in a request that the Pope forbid Edward from making further war upon Scotland. Edward had no intention of abandoning his war, but the Scots' pleadings did manage to get their king released from the custody of Rome and, thanks to King Philip, residing in his family's ancestral home, Bailleul-en-Vimeu.

Edward aimed to capture Scotland with a two-pronged attack, the one army to be in command of his son Edward, Prince of Wales, the other and larger under his own command. The prince was to take the southwestern lands, and the greater glory, so his father hoped. But, while the prince held cautiously to the Solway coast, the Scots, commanded by de Soules and de Umfraville, attacked Lochmaben in early September and threatened the king's forces at Bothwell, all the while maintaining an awareness of the prince's whereabouts. Though Edward captured Bothwell in late September, and the prince had earlier helped in capturing de Brus' Turnberry Castle, the English sovereign and his son met to winter at Linlithgow without having damaged the Scots' fighting ability. In January 1302, Edward agreed to a nine-month truce.

This date more or less coincides with the desertion of Robert de Brus to the English side. Hitherto he had been on the side of the patriots of Scotland, but at some point that winter, he surrendered to the English and, as was his father, became a supporter of King Edward. There are multiple reasons that may have prompted his turning, not the least of which was that de Brus may have found it loathsome, continuing to sacrifice his Carrick followers, family, and heritage for the failed monarchy of de Balliol.

Rumor was that de Balliol would return with a French army. Even if such an event was successful in returning the irresolute king to the

Scottish throne, it did not bode well for the de Bruses, the auld enemies of de Balliol.

Also, Robert's father was an old man and ill, and may have wished his son to seek peace with Edward, who, he would have been convinced, would be the victor over the rebellious Scots. The elder de Brus would have seen that, if the rebellion failed and his son were running against Edward, he would lose everything, titles, lands, honors, and probably his life. And it stands to reason that the father would also want to live out his own remaining time at peace with his king *and* his son.

Further, it is conceivable that the fact that Robert married his second wife that same year had much to do with his decision. His bride, Elizabeth de Burgh, was the daughter of the earl of Ulster, Richard de Burgh, one of King Edward's most trusted and valiant champions. In addition, Elizabeth was a niece by marriage of James the Stewart, another tie de Brus would have wanted to strengthen.

However, though recently pledged to support Edward, it is interesting to note that Robert de Brus sent a letter to the monks at Melrose Abbey in March 1302 that effectively weakened his usefulness to the English king. Apologizing for having called the monks to service in his army when there had been no national call up, the earl of Carrick pledged that, henceforth, he would "never again" require the monks to serve unless it was to "the common army of the whole realm," for national defense.

More serious to Scots freedom than the loss of de Brus was the loss of support from King Philip and subsequently, Pope Boniface. Philip's feudal host lost severely at Flanders against the nationalists he was warring on there, and he became too involved in his own difficulties to care about the Scots. He had also created a schism between himself and the Pope, whose support for the Scots faded without Philip's influence. It seemed that Philip had such a full plate in Flanders that he was willing to sign with Edward a peace treaty excluding the Scots, an act that the Scots knew would spell their doom. A powerful delegation, including even de Soules, went to Paris that autumn to try to head off such an event.

In November 1302, when the temporary truce between the Scots and the English ended, Edward delayed calling up his army until spring. Over that winter, however, he sent Sir John Segrave and a mounted force of three brigades of knights on a scouting expedition into the area west of Edinburgh. They were ambushed by Comyn and Simon Fraser, who had ridden all night to meet them.

The Scots attacked the lead brigade and captured the severely wounded Segrave. Though the second brigade later rescued their leader, the Scots were exultant at their success, which mounted a short time later as they captured the new tower at Selkirk. Their successes, however, were rendered useless in May 1303, when King Philip, formerly a great advocate for the Scots, signed a peace accord with England and omitted any consideration for the Scots.

So it was that Edward began his campaign, cleverly sailing siege engines and specially constructed pontoon bridges up the coast from King's Lynn to the Firth of Forth. Having ability to get over that body downstream and obtain direct access to Fife meant that he would not have to cross that infamous, in his view, narrow bridge at Stirling. The castle there was then in rebel hands under Sir William Oliphant, who declined to surrender. No matter. There would be time for Stirling.

Leaving Newcastle in early May, Edward led his army to Roxburgh, Lauder, Edinburgh, Linlithgow, and across his floating bridge to Perth by mid-June. From there, it was to Cupar, to Arbroath, and to Brechin, where in latter July he laid siege to the castle being valiantly defended by the garrison commanded by Sir Thomas Maule. Maule was killed August ninth, and the castle fell. Edward moved on to Kinloss Abbey by way of Aberdeen, Banff, Cullen, Rathven, and Elgin. Turning back south, he was in Dunfermline by early November and made his winter quarters at the abbey there.

Early in 1304, Edward sent a raiding party under the command of Segrave, Clifford, and William Latimer, who put to flight the forces under Fraser and Wallace west of Peebles. Losing heart, all of the Scots leaders of significance surrendered to the English in February except Wallace and Fraser, and de Soules who was yet out of the country. Safe passage home from France was given John Comyn, earl of Buchan, James the Stewart, and Ingram de Umfraville, and the bishops Lamberton of St. Andrews and Crambeth of Dunkeld.

Surrender terms were negotiated by John Comyn of Badenoch, who refused to surrender unconditionally, but asked that prisoners of both sides be released sans ransom, and that Edward agree there would be no reprisals against or disinheritance of the Scots. The laws and liberties of Scotland would be as they had been in the day of Alexander III, and any that needed alteration would be with the advice of Edward and the advice and assent of Scotland's responsible men. Though not all that was asked, final surrender terms were not unreasonable or greatly brutal. (They may be seen in the Ordinance of September 1305.)

Excepting William Wallace and John de Soules, it seemed that all would be forgiven... after some of the more famous leaders were exiled from Scotland for various periods of time. And 'forfeited' estates could be recovered by payment of fines levied in amounts deemed appropriate for each individual's betrayal. Inheritances would continue as they always had, allowing the landed nobility to pass titles and properties to their progeny in normal fashion.

De Soules remained abroad, refusing to surrender; Wallace was still at large in Scotland and, unlike all the earls, lords, and bishops, refused to pay homage to Edward. Edward needed to make an example of someone, and, by refusing to capitulate and accept his country's occupation and elimination, Wallace was the unfortunate focus of Edward's lingering hatred. The Scot would be granted no peace unless he put himself "utterly and absolutely in (Edward's) will." Further, it was decreed that The Stewart, de Soules, and Ingram de Umfraville could not return home or anyplace else where Edward reigned until Wallace was "given up," and Comyn, Alexander Lindsay, David Graham, and Fraser were actively to seek Wallace's capture. The king's dispensation of English justice toward them would depend on how exhausting were their efforts. He who gave the greatest effort would be held in highest regard.

It was thus inevitable that Wallace should fall into Edward's hands.

Robert de Brus, lord of Annandale, succumbed to his lingering illness in March 1304, leaving his lands and title to his eldest son. Thus, at thirty, Robert de Brus, earl of Carrick, was now also lord of Annandale and held vast lands and homes in England as well as Scotland, including a house in London. He was also guardian of his young nephew, Donald, earl of Mar, and for him kept the castle at Kildrummy.

In May, having contained most Scottish opposition, Edward again turned his attentions to Castle Stirling, laying siege with great determination. Asked by Oliphant if he might ask de Soules whether he had permission to surrender or must hold the castle, Edward refused, saying, "If he thinks it will be better for him to defend the castle than yield it, he will see." Recently remarried, the old tyrant may have felt he had something to prove to all the younger men in his army, or perhaps just to his youthful bride. At great risk to himself, Edward actively participated in attacking the castle walls, nearly getting himself killed in a foolish display of bravado.

For the better part of three torturous months, under terrible bombardment and in spite of the use of every siege engine Edward could bring to bear upon the courageous defenders, they held. When they could no longer, they offered to surrender unconditionally, but Edward refused to accept. He would first bombard the castle with 'The Warwolf,' his new catapult of extraordinary size and power. After a day of horrific punishment, the destroyed castle was allowed to submit, and about fifty men surrendered. Unlike the courteous and respectful surrender and safe withdrawal that had been granted the English garrison at that same castle in 1299, the Scots' surrender drew Edward's threats to disembowel and hang them. Having been dissuaded from carrying out his threats by the Scots' humiliating degradation and the reasonings of his subordinates, Edward instead sent them south to prisons in England.

Robert de Brus, earl of Carrick, and William Lamberton, bishop of St. Andrews, witnessed on June 11 1304, the heroic efforts against overwhelming might by their besieged countrymen at Stirling. The two great patriots, who had so long fought for their country's freedom, made a pact that bound them, each to the other, in "friendship and alliance against all men." If one should break the secret pact, he would forfeit to the other the sum of ten thousand pounds sterling, a veritable fortune. Though both had already surrendered to the English, the pact indicates deep patriotism and commitment to their future perseverance for the Scots people and their freedom. All around them death, desolation, and despair bespoke volumes about the suffering inflicted by the now lost war. None of that memory would leave them in their lifetimes.

Now, Scotland lay defenseless. Edward, in his usual methodical and logical way, went about absorbing her into his kingdom. Homage was again paid to Edward by all the "responsible men" of the *land* (not the *realm*) of Scotland, and a parliament was held in May 1305 to elect those who would meet later in the year with the English parliament for the establishing of a constitution for captive Scotland.

John of Brittany, nephew to Edward, was to head up the subordinate government of Scotland and control the castles of Roxburgh and Jedburgh. Justices were appointed in pairs of one Englishman and one Scot. Militarily strategic localities were controlled by English sheriffs and constables, but most others were by Scots. The castles of Stirling and Dumbarton were the only good castles commanded by Scots, with their leaders being William Bisset and Sir John Stewart of Menteith, respectively. A council was formed to advise the king's nephew/ lieutenant, and among those were Robert de Brus, John Comyn, and Bishop William Lamberton. For all the apparent participation by Scots in the government, however, the English held the real power, and Scotland was a vanquished nation.

While all this took place, William Wallace was finally captured near Glasgow on the third day of August 1305. He was delivered to the English by retainers in the service of Sir John Menteith. Wallace easily had been the most hunted man on the island for years, but especially for the previous eighteen months.

Being first routed circuitously through the countryside of his beloved Scotland, his legs bound beneath his mount, and no doubt wondering why no one loved him enough to put an arrow through his heart, he was taken to London August 22nd for "trial." He was led through the streets of the city the following day in what can only be termed a "parade" before great masses of derisive and scornful Londoners.

Bringing into fruition a boast Wallace was alleged to have made that he would one day wear a crown at Westminster, a laurel leaf "crown" was placed upon his head for the crowd to jeer. He was then indicted on charges of treason, murder (of the sheriff of Lanark, who had butchered Wallace's wife and her family), war atrocities, convening Scottish parliaments, and instigating the renewal or maintenance of the Scots' "Auld Alliance" with France.

Wallace, who once again stated truthfully that he had never been a liege of Edward nor of England, denied the charge of treason, but affirmed the others. The verdict on all counts was a foregone conclusion, the penalty to be exacted particularly horrible and devised by King Edward, himself.

William Wallace was tied to a sledge behind a horse and dragged for over four miles so that he might be displayed in captivity to the people of London, finally arriving at the Smithfield elms. He was then hanged, removed while yet alive from the gallows, disemboweled, and decapitated. His heart and other organs were burned and the headless body quartered. The severed head of Sir William Wallace was displayed upon London Bridge, and the towns of Newcastle upon Tyne, Berwick, Stirling, and Perth each received and exhibited one of the corporeal quarters.

Rather than frightening others away from Wallace by taking such savage, bestial revenge on the Scot, Edward created a martyr, a larger than life hero whose unfair and inhuman execution settled poorly in the Scottish psyche and imbued their hearts with the yearning for justice and freedom for which Wallace himself had fought those seven long years. Rather than settling the "Scottish question," Edward had wrought enmity that would hound him the rest of his days, and haunt his memory for centuries beyond. In the words of Barrow, his cruelty showed him to be "small and mean," compared to his victim, the noble Wallace.

The following month, on the fifteenth, the parliament met with the Scots representatives to carve out the new constitution, The Ordinance of September 1305. In the midst of listing punishments to be meted out to other Scots, Edward ordered Robert de Brus, earl of Carrick, to put his castle, Kildrummy, "in the keeping of such a man as he himself will be willing to answer for." Barrow asserts that the placement of this item within the document suggests plainly that Edward suspected Robert's loyalty.

Earl of Carrick, lord of Annandale, and holder of massive estates and residences in both Scotland and England, Robert de Brus had a great amount of wealth and privilege. He also had a large family about which to be concerned. In addition to his wife Elizabeth and daughter Marjorie, there were his brothers, Edward, Alexander, Thomas, and Nigel, sisters Christian, Isabel (queen of Norway), and Mary, and his nephews Thomas Randolph and Donald, earl of Mar. If he declared for the throne, he would throw the country into yet another bloody uprising, and if he failed, he would be sacrificing everyone and everything he knew.

And yet, his country was not free...

HAMMER OF THE SCOTS

*King Edward
of England*

JANUARY 18th 1306
A LONDON CASTLE OF KING EDWARD OF ENGLAND

The short, spindly legs of the Earl of Gloucester's Keeper of the Wardrobe carried him as fast as they could down the dim, torch-lit passageway toward the sleeping rooms of noble visitors and their servants. He pulled his robe tighter around his sleep clothes, shivering and looking fearfully in both directions to see if the drowsy guard was paying attention to him, passing with his small candle lantern.

The keeper had been roused from his warm bed quickly and the malodorous scent of his frosty night breath followed in his wake.

His nervous fingers formed a fist as the keeper reached a heavy but small wooden door recessed into the stone wall. The timid fist tapped on the door, prompting ferocious barking from a dog within the room on the other side. The keeper's shaking increased all the more.

"Quiet, dog!" commanded a sleepy, rough voice. The dog was stilled.

Though he greatly feared to do so, the timid keeper knocked again. There was a long silence.

"What?" roared an angry voice as the heavy door suddenly swung open to reveal to the keeper a much larger man, silhouetted black by the light from a glowing fireplace within. The man in the room could see little in the dark hall, and so took the old man's hand and lifted it and its lantern toward the little keeper's face to get a better look. The fearful man took a full step back as the lantern came toward him. He then tightened his courage enough to speak to the towering form.

"Y-y-you are Robert d-de Brus, Lord of A-a-nnandale, Milord?" asked the little man, his voice soft and shaky, his eyes as large and round as an owl's in his ashen face.

"Aye! What is it, man?" answered Robert in a more civil tone, realizing the lesser man's nervousness and seeing the pair of spurs in the old man's hand.

"My... my lord and master... the Earl of G-Gloucester... instructs that I b-bring these things to you, uh... 'for what you have done for him yesterday,'" recited the old man, and he held out his hand, offering the spurs and a single shilling. He then darted his eyes warily toward the dozing guard.

Robert understood and kept his voice low.

"Now? At this hour?" he questioned, bending down a bit to step through the door, out of the light and into the cold passageway, his dog at his heel. He pulled the door all but closed and took the gifts from the steward's hand.

This was a large man, fully six-and-a-half feet tall. His rugged features shown dark and indistinguishable against the gray-white of the shirt in which he had been sleeping, along with long, woolen trews. From a wide belt around his neck a great claymore hung, its full weight on his body as he leant against the wall to examine the spurs and the coin in the wan light from the lantern.

Robert's dog growled and sniffed at the keeper's robes, causing the man much fright.

Robert reached down with his left hand and gently grabbed the mouth of the large, sleek, yellow-gray hunting dog, an obvious signal to the disciplined dog to remain quiet. Frowning, Robert studied the items the keeper had brought and tried with little success to wipe away the drink induced sleep-fog from his brain.

"If I may, Sir," said the chilled keeper, turning the coin in Robert's hand to the obverse, "...point out the fine portrait of our beloved King Edward."

"Damn!" exclaimed Robert half aloud. The meaning of the symbols then instantly crystallized in his mind.

Now knowing what was afoot, Robert abruptly folded the silver coin back into the keeper's hand. "Have this for yerself, good man... and... tell yer master that he has my deepest gratitude."

"Thank you, sir," replied the old man smiling broadly, and he tucked the treasured coin into his robe. With one quick bow, he then left the way he had come, his lantern light soon disappearing with him as he hurried off into the black hallway.

Robert and the dog re-entered the room. The smell of overindulgence in a bad combination of fine wine and too-quickly-made whisky permeated the heavy, still air. He shut the door and slammed home the iron bolt.

On the large bed in the middle of the room were several lumps under the piles of covers, and one booted foot dangling limply off the near edge. In the fireplace along the left wall, the waning glow of a few embers threw orange-tinted light but a few feet, and all else seemed absorbed into all but complete darkness.

Robert took the sheathed five-foot sword from around his neck and with it unceremoniously whacked the closest lump in the bed, as he forcefully whispered through clenched teeth, "Get up, Edward!" The lump yelled a muffled obscenity.

Edward de Brus poked his smarting and sleepy head from under the covers and looked quizzically at Robert, who was quickly getting fully dressed. "Robert, ye're out of yer mind!" said Edward angrily. "'Tis the middle of the night!"

"We've got to get out of here, fast!" replied Robert in a low but determined voice.

As Robert continued to dress, Edward sat up against the bed's head-board and yawned. "I'm too damn tired an' drunk," he slurred, and laid back against a large pillow and closed his eyes.

"Ye're going to be too damned dead, if ye don't move, little brother!" growled Robert, trying to get him to realize the gravity of the situation. "Shake Thomas up there, too!"

"But, ye don't know that for a fact, do ye Robert?" asked Edward, tucking himself back under the warm covers and trying to ignore his tormentor.

"Believe me… they're comin' for us," said Robert. Standing on the close side of the bed, with his sword as lever and Edward as fulcrum, he rolled Thomas Randolph, sleeping on the other side of Edward, com-pletely off the bed and onto the floor, blanket, booted foot and all.

"What the hell…?" groaned the huge hulk of a man.

"Who? Who is comin' for us?" questioned Edward, raising himself up on one elbow, ignoring Thomas's disoriented struggles on the floor.

"That idiot king! And soon!" replied Robert. He pulled a couple of wool blankets from the bed and rolled them up.

Thomas finally sat up. His enormous full-bearded head peered, bleary-eyed, across still covered Edward to Robert, who was obviously preparing to leave.

Thomas reached under his shirt and found his wineskin, uncorked it and gulped a good drink. The head of a thin young woman suddenly appeared behind Thomas' and seemed no less dizzy than his own.

"Look, Robert, Thomas had a wench tucked to him!" exclaimed Edward in a surprised tone as he sat up in the middle of the bed.

"So he did," replied Robert. "We *must* go... *now!*"

"How do ye know this?" asked Edward, insistently returning to the original subject.

"Know what?" queried Robert as he threw a pouch over his shoulder.

"That they're comin' for us," said Edward, somewhat exasperated.

"Spurs and a twelve pence, spurs and a twelve pence!" His older brother said absently. Robert then signaled for silence, having heard approaching footfalls and voices talking quietly in the passageway beyond the door.

"Here come the sons-a-bitches now!" said Robert, strapping his claymore belt around his waist and quietly unsheathing the blade. "Ye had best get yer little arses out of bed! And put on everything ye own, 'cause it's as cold as..."

"Cold as the bitches in this damn castle..." interrupted Thomas. Then, realizing the drunken maid leaning on his back seemed a bit miffed at what he had said, he managed a kind of crooked, drunken smile. In a much more patronizing voice he added, "... except, of course, my wee darlin', ye are the exception."

She seemed satisfied as she laid her head on the back of his broad shoulder.

Suddenly, a sword pommel in the hand of the king's guard hammered a thundering knock on the heavy wooden door, and the dog again leapt up and barked fiercely until Robert signaled him to stop.

Edward's suddenly sobered eyes widened as he leapt out of bed and quickly began to stuff his things into his shoulder pouch.

"What do ye want?" asked Robert indistinctly, pretending to be sleepy.

"Open this door! I have a warrant for the arrest of Robert de Brus, lord of Annandale and earl of Carrick, and Edward de Brus, knight!" shouted the captain of the guard from the passageway.

The woman panicked and began to shriek uncontrollably.

"I can't stand screamin' women!" yelled Thomas, still without his wits about him, putting his hands over his ears. Grimacing at the sharp noise, he climbed back into bed and, like a child, covered his head with the last remaining blanket.

Robert moved close to the door. "Ye're upsettin' our women in here, man," he said. "I'm sure ye have made a mistake."

The sword pommel knocked all the louder.

The woman squalled all the more.

The dog growled at the door from his place at Robert side; his teeth bared and the fur along his spine standing erect.

"Open the door in the name of Edward Plantagenet, by the grace of God, King of England, Wales, and Scotland!" commanded the captain, even more forcefully.

Robert's face tightened as he said mockingly to himself, "Ach! He's done it now... King of England, King of Wales... King of Scotland!... 'king' of naught but his own arse!"

By this time, Edward was dressed in as many clothes as he could find and had his pouch packed full. He strapped on his claymore and drew it.

"A'right... a'right... just a minute!" said Robert through the door to the captain.

"Shut that wench up, Thomas!" barked Edward, his long arm pointing in the direction of the incessant howling.

Thomas stuck his head out from under the cover. "How?" he asked.

"Knock her in the head, if ye must!" Edward hissed.

Thomas picked his sword up from the floor and raised it high. As he did, the woman's nerve-wracked, over-indulged senses gave way and she passed out into a blissful, silent stupor.

"That worked better than I thought it would!" commented Edward.

Thomas reached his big arm around her and pulled her into the bed with him. Beginning to come to herself, she giggled witlessly as Thomas rolled on top of her under the covers. Thomas grunted.

In the passageway the captain motioned to four of his men to move forward with the heavy, oak log battering ram suspended on stout leather thongs.

Edward threw the contents of the night bucket into the fire causing a steamy, vile smelling vapor to rise from the fireplace, damping the embers and filling half the room with eye-stinging smoke. His claymore at the ready, he took a position on the hinged side of the door.

"Better move back a wee bit," Robert said in hushed tones to Edward, "or when that door comes flyin' open, ye won't be worth a damn."

Edward immediately obeyed his older brother, whose wits seemed clearer than his own.

Thomas and his wench were still laboring under the cover, and sighs and moans of ecstasy accompanied by giggles and drunken laughter were the only sounds the captain heard when he put his ear to the door.

"They're havin' an orgy in there!" said the captain under his breath. "We're 'bidin' out here with arrest warrants and they're in there havin' a damned orgy! What manner of men are these Scots?"

Scowling at the thought of such disrespect, the captain turned to see his men's faces grinning at each other. Catching sight of him put more stoic countenances upon them.

"Knock it down!" barked the captain, angrily. "We'll teach these damned Scots some respect for English might!"

The ponderous log swung back, and the four guards, their muscular arms wound tightly with the thick leather straps from which it swung, heaved their weight with the sway of its forward motion, and with great force slammed the sharpened end into the door. The door held.

Robert and Edward flinched. Randolph jumped around and peeked out from under the covers. The woman started to scream again, but one stern look from Thomas and she thought better of it.

The ram hit the door the second time and the door's hinges loosened, slightly.

Robert quickly and quietly pulled the iron bolt back.

On the next swing the unbolted door was slammed with such force that all four of the guards strapped to the log were flung headlong into the room with it, and didn't stop until they had plunged into and collapsed the footboard of the bed.

A fifth guard came through the door with his sword drawn. Unable to see through the nauseating smoke, he stopped but a foot away from Robert while waiting for his stinging eyes to adjust to the lower light. Robert pulled his dirk and, in the same motion, silently slit the hapless fellow's throat. Already dead, the guard made a gurgling noise with his own blood as he fell to the cold, worn stone floor at Robert's feet.

The guard captain remained in the passageway, a torch in one hand and papers in the other, ready for presentation upon the subduing of the Bruses. This would be over quickly and he could then return to his own hearth.

One of the sprawled guards was getting unsteadily to his feet when Edward tapped him on the shoulder and said in a disarming manner, "Hello, friend, I'm Edward, but I'm *not* the king."

The muddled guard was temporarily amused at this jest, but gathered his wits enough to lay hand on his weapon, at which Edward brought his claymore up from its low angle at the man's feet and cut deep into his crotch. The guard groaned in surprised agony and fell to the floor.

Another guard got up with his sword drawn and saw Robert in the shadows beside the door. He was short work for the massive Scot.

With horrific growls and devilish teeth, Robert's dog was cruelly attacking a third guard, and the fourth had been knocked unconscious when his head struck the bed.

Not realizing that the mortal moans and groans were those of his own men, the captain strolled casually through the open door, his torch above his head, and stared into the stench and smoke of the dismal gloom. His stinging eyes adjusted to the light just as the last man fell. He was suddenly immobilized as Robert reached with one powerful hand and clenched his fingers tightly, but not fatally, upon the captain's throat.

The suddenly worthless warrants fluttered to the floor with the torch following.

"Pick up the torch," said Robert as he eased the captain to his knees.

The captain could do little else except what he was told and, completely under Robert's control, he groped around the floor for the wooden handle.

"I better go, wee darlin'," said Thomas to the woman as he crawled out of bed in a short woolen shirt that fell just to his buttocks. Oblivious to his state of nakedness, he gathered all of his clothes and weapons under his arm. "See ye when I'm next 'round." He received only peaceful, if drink induced, snores for a reply.

Seeing the dog still struggling with one of the guards, he sauntered unsteadily over and said, "This wee pup too mean for ye, is he?"

"Get him off! Get him off!" cried the guard, his sleeves in tatters, his legs nearly devoured by the looks of them.

"Oh, for sure," replied Thomas as he balled up his great fist and clouted the guard squarely in the forehead, knocking him cold. The dog let go and trotted off to stand by Robert. "All ye had to do was lie still, Laddie," Thomas explained to the unconscious soldier.

"Bet he'll not beg ye more, Thomas," snickered Edward.

"Don't mind if he does," said Thomas with a grin, picking up a shirt that had fallen from his arm.

"'Tis a long way to the stable," said Robert calmly, still holding the captain by the throat. "It won't take long before they realize something's gone wrong here."

Turning to the captain, he whispered, "I'm goin' to loose yer neck, now, but my dirk will make short work of ye if ye don't go straightaway to the stable holdin' that torch high. Do ye ken what I said?"

The captain, unable to speak, nodded his head as best he could and Robert released his hold, at the same time pricking the skin on the man's back with his dirk to let the captain know it was really there, though he had sheathed his sword.

"Let's walk," said Robert to his captive. Then to Thomas he advised, "Best wake yer men on the way out."

"Sure, Uncle," replied Thomas, trying to fit a long woolen tunic over his huge body and his large sack of clothes.

The procession went hastily down the passageway toward the courtyard door. Across the cobbled bailey stood the stables.

Thomas, stumbling awkwardly over the bodies, followed the diminishing light of the captain's torch. He grabbed another torch from its holder along the passageway wall and ran on, stopping only to pick up various pieces of clothing occasionally dropped from his overloaded pouch.

Just before reaching the courtyard door he came to a door under the staircase, and pounded on it with the butt of the torch. Fireballs went flying as he opened the door, let out a war whoop and yelled, "All ye bastards that don't want to die tonight had better drop yer peckers and get with me!"

He then continued his stumbling run after Robert, the captive, and Edward, as six men ran into the passageway after him, carrying and dragging with them what clothing, blankets, and weapons they could.

"Thomas hain't no subtle soul, is he Robert?" puffed Edward in the cold air while trying to keep up with Robert's longer stride. The guard captain was fairly trotting to stay up with them and prevent being prodded by Robert's dirk.

"Nobody's goin' to think he's sneakin' up on them," replied Robert, glancing around. "Get our horses, Edward," he ordered as they entered the stable, "…and stay away from those big destriers; we need the fast ones for Thomas' men."

About then came a stream of expletives from Edward that would have singed Robert's beard, if he'd had one. "What is it!" he demanded.

"Aaagh! I've stepped into a pile of manure!"

"Ye've been in worse, tonight. Here comes Thomas with another torch," said Robert. "Just turn all the stalls out; we'll need the cover."

Thomas came trotting up to Robert, hard panting and grimacing in pain. "What is the matter with ye?" Robert asked the son of his half-sister.

"Too much whisky and runnin'," Thomas said, holding his belly. He doubled over to relieve the stress on his abused gut, and the torch went with him, catching the hay on fire.

The captain's eyes widened, as he realized that his last hope of arresting the Bruses was gone.

"Damn!" said Thomas as he looked at the mounting flames. "Get that put out!" he ordered his men, who were just stumbling into the stable area.

"Forget it!" barked Robert. "We've got to get out of here, fast, and that will keep the locals busy while we leave!"

"I don't remember where my horse was," groaned Thomas, still in pain.

"It don't matter," yelled Edward as the flames mounted. "Just grab one and throw a saddle on it."

Many of the horses were beginning to panic and some were running out into the courtyard.

"FIRE!" hollered a terrified voice beyond the stable walls.

"We're about to have company, then!" said Robert, and he threw the captain to the ground and sheathed his dirk.

Thomas had his horse saddled and, just as he mounted, he dropped another shirt. "Damn it!" he lamented in the cold night air. "That's one I'll be missin' 'fore the morn." The freed captain picked it up and handed it to him.

"Thank ye," said Thomas, surprised.

The captain shrugged in obvious defeat.

"Ye want to go with us?"

The captain smiled a resigned smile and shook his head. "My liege is my lord Edward... I'm no Scot. And besides, you'll not get far."

"If we don't leave now it will be too late!" ordered Robert, mounting the horse his brother had saddled for him. He pulled his claymore from its sheath.

Those in the courtyard saw in the light from the hay fire dancing silhouettes of panicked horses and nine horsemen who rode amongst them. In the effort to mount a brigade to fight the fire, no one noticed who the nine were, or which way they headed once outside the castle gate.

Guided only by moonlight now, the Scots rode full-tilt across the ice and snow laden landscape north, toward Scotland.

• •

An hour later, in a small anteroom near King Edward's bedchamber, the monarch of England was not in good humor.

"Why?... Why?" echoed through the night. "Does God not love His king?" he loudly lamented as he sat with his back to the desk, looking at the blowing snow through the small, warped windowpanes.

"Why is it, when I ask for the heads of my enemies to be delivered unto me, I am suddenly surrounded by bumbling idiots..." his voice rose to a shriek as he vented his wrath. Having exacerbated his chronic respiratory problem, a progressive illness that none of his physicians had yet been able to arrest or cure, he began to cough spasmodically. At the age of sixty-eight years, Edward was a dying man who had yet much to do to secure Scotland for the Plantagenet name before he died. His effort toward including the kingdom in his realm had already earned him the sobriquet, "The Hammer of the Scots," and was a baneful task he nevertheless enjoyed performing.

"...And captains who have bungs for wits?" continued the monarch once he had recovered himself. On the other side of the desk, the poor unfortunate guard captain was still being held on his knees by two of the king's own.

"I would have rejoiced to awaken to the news of one of my dungeon cells having been filled with those Bruses," he said rubbing his sleep deprived eyes, "but, I got that not. I got my stable burned, instead. I got my guards whittled up like so much firewood, instead I... GOT... NOTH-ING, INSTEAD!" He regained his composure and added derogatorily, "Nothing except a cowardly captain."

He suddenly stood up beside the chair, turned and put his hand on the back of it. There was no doubt why he had acquired the name 'Longshanks,' for he was more than six-and-a-half feet in height, much of that due to his exceptionally lengthy legs. For all his loftiness he lacked physical substance, being a thin sort of man with a thinning dark brown beard surrounding piercing blue eyes and a long nose.

"Your sentence, Captain," the king declared, then mockingly stopped. "Oh! Yes, that's right! You have not had your little say, have you? A'right, out with it!"

The captain merely looked at the king, knowing the lengths of cruelty to which he could stretch his imagination in the ways of torture. He prayed silently to himself for a sentence of a quick death, then bowed his head once more.

"No words?" mocked 'Longshanks', adding coldly, "That was perhaps the wisest choice you have made tonight, Captain!"

The king once again was wracked with coughing and its force caused him to double over until his head was rested on the top of the chair back. After a long pause he again brought himself up to his full height, looked down upon the kneeling captain and pronounced sentence. "You, Captain, shall know the bite of the rope on your neck... and your creator... by the dawn," he whispered.

Thank you, God, thought the condemned captain as he was dragged from the room. There would be no protracted death.

King Edward stifled more coughs until the door to the chamber was closed, and only his personal valet heard the ensuing fit.

Edward Brus

JANUARY 26th 1306
IN SCOTLAND, JUST ACROSS THE BORDER

The snow in the wintry field was at mid-calf and still blowing in the cold wind where Robert stood with drawn bow and set arrow. His brother Edward sat his horse about twenty yards back and watched intently. From his saddlebow hung six freshly killed hares.

The warm vapors of the horse's breath poured from his nostrils into the cold air as he dug through the snow to reach the earth beneath in search of food of his own. Edward held the reins of Robert's horse. It quietly whinnied as Robert loosed the deadly barb.

"Did ye get him, Robbie?" asked Edward. His voice was hushed, absorbed by the snow that softly crunched beneath Robert's rag wrapped boots.

When he approached the hare, Robert saw that his arrow had found its mark through the shoulder. The hood of his heavy cloak fell back exposing his reddish locks and four-day growth of beard to the bright sun as he held his still-kicking quarry above his head in answer to Edward's question.

"This makes seven!" shouted Robert. "Large as they are, 'twill be enough."

Edward rode up to Robert, took the carcass by the hind legs, and tied it with a leather thong onto the string that held the other brownish-white, heavily furred rabbits. "These hares are far better clothed for the weather than are we," he remarked.

Robert mounted his horse and turned it toward camp at a walk. Edward caught up with little effort and rode beside him, neither of them speaking for a short distance.

"Why is it?" asked Edward at last.

"Why is the hare better clothed?"

"Nah," Edward grinned. "Why is it that ol' 'Longshanks' suddenly turned on us?"

"Ye don't know?"

The younger man thought a moment and shook his head. "Nay. I know not. We were just there, at his own invitation, and without so much as a cross word from him or us, he wants to hang us. Don't make sense to me."

"Our 'king' got impatient," explained Robert. "He had planned to have the five of us brothers there at once, and hang us all from the same gallows."

Edward rolled his eyes in disbelief.

"I thought" continued Robert in reverie, "as long as brothers Thomas, Nigel, and Alexander were not around, we were safe... wrong, dead wrong, I was."

"But Robbie, that still don't answer the *why* of it," insisted Edward, prodding his horse to keep up with Robert's. "We're on his side."

"Ah, but Edward fears us," Robert explained. He and his brother pulled their hoods tighter around their faces to shield them from the wind and stinging snow. "We five, and the Comyns, are all continual threats to him as long as we are alive. He's illegally set himself up as 'King of Scotland'" he said distastefully, "and rules, not by the grace of God, but by the corruption of might. And though he may have her body, yet he knows he shall ne'er have her heart... not e'er."

"Politics! Too much for me," growled Edward.

"Well, fancy this for politics, little brother," said Robert in all seriousness. "I have an agreement with 'The Red' Comyn that says when King Edward dies, he will support my kingship with his considerable influence, and arms if need be, and he, in turn, will get my lands."

His brother stared in disbelief, "Ye're givin' up yer lands?"

Robert shrugged, "Aye. But as king, all lands in the kingdom will be of profit to me."

"Aye," said Edward, fairly sure he understood.

. .

A few minutes later the two men arrived at their small camp on the edge of a wood. It was tightly surrounded by woven 'wind-break' sticks and brush on two leeward sides, and heavy evergreens on the windward side. There, two of Randolph's soldiers were constructing debris shelters, and another was tending the horses near the edge of the compound. Two more warmed themselves at the camp's large fire, having brought wood to feed it. In spite of the activity in camp, the men all had to fight continually against frozen toes, fingers, and noses.

Edward lifted the seven hares from his saddlebow and handed them to one of the men close by the fire. It would be dark by the time they were cooked.

"Ye don't mind fixin' these up for a little supper, do ye?" asked Edward with a smile.

"No, Milord." Not at all!" replied the hungry soldier as he hastened to his task. First he untied one of the long-legged carcasses from the thong and strung it up by the hind legs on a low-hanging tree branch. He cut the fur from around the tied legs and with no more effort than removing his own trews, pulled the skin off, leaving just the silvery pink flesh underneath. Slitting the creature down the underbelly, he paid no heed to the thin vapors rising from the fresh cut, nor the rich red blood, and quickly detached entrails making stark, contrasting patterns in the snow. Immediately, the dog appeared and sniffed the bloody mass, then seized it and went to a nearby area to eat alone.

"How come the dog always eats first?" asked another of Thomas' soldiers to the skinner.

"Have at it on the next one, if ye want to fight the dog for it," answered the busy man without pausing. "I'm waitin' for the cookin' to happen, m'self. Now, take this and put it on a stick over the fire. And have a care ye don't drop it!" With that, he proceeded to dress the next kill.

Robert unsaddled his horse, tied him in the line and left the blanket on him until, with a handful of soft dry grass, one of the men could briskly rub the horse down. This was done nightly, or whenever the group made camp, though to be sure, there was not much sweat to be found on the horses or their riders in the sharp coldness of this night.

"Rider comin'!" yelled the soldier on watch.

With his claymore drawn but held low, Robert watched the incoming rider slowly ride toward their camp, his free hand raised to let them know that he meant them no harm. Though the colors the rider wore were mostly beneath his heavy cloak and not easily recognized, Robert knew them to be those of John 'The Red' Comyn.

The rider seemed harmless enough, but the campers poised for action as the fellow drew closer.

"He's alone," said Edward, scanning the trail behind the intruder. The camp relaxed and everyone went about what he had been doing.

Thomas, who had been gathering firewood among the near trees, dumped his armload upon the pile near the fire. "This should hold us for the night," he said to Edward.

Edward nodded in agreement.

"Who's the rider?" asked Thomas, wiping his hands on his heavy woolen kirtle, then warming them by blowing his hot breath into them.

"I don't know, but he hain't goin' to hurt us none. There's only one of him," said Edward.

"Aye," Thomas said with a grin as he stepped outside of the camp perimeter and raised a hand to greet their mystery guest before he got inside.

"Hello in the camp," loudly said the squat little man as he rode up.

"What brings ye to our company on such a bitter eve?" asked Thomas with feigned gruffness.

Robert's dog growled at the hostility in the young man's voice, and left his dinner to sit beside Robert.

Suddenly filled with uneasiness, the man said, "Yer pardon, Sir. I but saw yer smoke as I was passin' by on yon road and bein' as it's a'most sundown, I thought to ask if I might join yer camp for the night."

Thomas took hold of the horse's reins and looked at the stranger sternly. The rider grew nervous and started for his short sword.

Without a blink, Thomas twisted the horse's head so that the beast was forced to go down, spilling the rider into the snow. Before the interloper could recover, Thomas stepped hard on the man's sword hand and asked, "What did ye think to do with that little dagger ye were goin' for, eh?"

"Nothin'... n-nothin', I swear," whined the sprawled man. "I hain't g-got but t-t-tuppence, but ye can have it if ye will only spare me!"

Thomas looked at Robert who signaled to let the frightened fellow go.

"Nay, we intend ye no harm, little man," said Thomas changing his entire demeanor. "Ye come hungry to our camp, did ye?"

"A-a-aye sir, aye, t-t-that was my reasonin'," stammered the little man.

"Looks t' me like ye hain't missed much grub," teased Thomas patting the man on his rounded belly.

"And what's this?" asked Edward, coming up to the already nervous and suspicious man and inspecting a black and white pony hide pouch around his neck.

"'Tis nothin', Sir," replied the man. "I-I am simply a messenger of plain dispatches of most c-common origins."

Robert approached the messenger and said "So, ye haven't et yet?"

"No, Milord, I hain't," said the man, removing his hat before one he recognized as the group's superior, "...a-a-and I would be most obliged if I might take supper with ye good gentlemen tonight. I have naught but bread for my supper, but I shall share it gladly for a bit of the meat I smelt a'cookin." With that he pulled a round loaf from his saddlebag.

"We're havin' spit-cooked hare," said Robert softly to the man.

"I like hare cooked just about any way at all," said the smiling messenger, now feeling more confident in Robert's attitude.

On the other hand, Edward couldn't believe the outgoing hospitality that his brother was providing the stranger... obviously just somebody's thrall on an errand. Robert motioned for one of the soldiers to retrieve the visitor's horse and tie him with their own.

"Don't unsaddle him!" ordered the messenger. Then, realizing he had no right to give orders, added deferentially to Robert, "I'll just have to saddle him up again in the mornin', Milord."

Edward protested, "Ye oughtn't do...." Robert interrupted, "As the messenger wants... he shall have it."

"Aye, as he wants," Edward agreed reluctantly.

The campfire threw flickering shadows against the dark backdrop of winter trees as the small band of campers ate their meager, but welcome supper. Robert, Thomas, and Edward huddled together on a log close to the fire, and the messenger, not far away, his message pouch placed with his weapon against a tree. The other men, having eaten, were milling around, tending to chores, setting the perimeter pickets before sleep.

Thomas tore a leg from the last hare spitted over the fire. He reached behind him and scooped up a handful of snow, put it into his mouth, then gnawed on the stringy leg.

"'Tis good eatin'," remarked the messenger, and he rolled himself up on one cheek to allow a particularly long and loud fart to escape.

"I'd rather sleep under the horses than around that one," whispered Edward to Thomas as he covered his nose with his sleeve.

Robert finished a piece of a back and was giving his dog the bones, when he said of the messenger, "Don't worry about him, Edward. He'll be gone with the mornin' dawn."

"None too soon for me," replied Edward.

The messenger tossed a bone in the fire.

Edward threw the blanket from around his shoulders, jumped up quickly and kicked the bone out of the fire. "Damn it, man! Don't ye know that bones in the fire stink about as bad as pissin' on it?"

The messenger jumped to his feet in instinctual challenge, then realized Edward was at least a head and a half taller than he, and so, stepped back.

"I must go scite," announced the cowed messenger as an excuse to withdraw from the conflict, and he started walking toward the woods.

"Make sure ye're a long way from camp when ye get shed of it!" said Edward angrily as he resumed his seat on the log.

"E'en after four days at the king's table, this, my friends, is far better than royal English dinin'," said Thomas, trying to change the subject.

"The only thing better than a free meal, is a free meal ye've gotten for yerself," chimed in Edward.

"Aye," agreed Robert, watching from the corner of his eye as the messenger disappeared into the woods. Satisfied that the man was out of sight and hearing he said quietly to Edward, "Hand me that pouch, will ye?"

Edward was puzzled, but quickly obeyed his brother.

In the firelight, Robert unbuckled the flap on the pouch and looked inside.

"Damn!" he said after he broke the seal and read one of the two messages, for he then knew what the second one contained. Robert replaced the message in the pouch, re-buckled it and handed it back across to Edward. "Put it back," he said coldly. Both kinsmen were puzzled at Robert's sudden attitude change.

Seeing the messenger coming through the line of evergreens back into the camp, Robert whispered to Edward and Thomas, "Think of somethin' funny to say."

"Uh... uh... oh... and remember the time in the tavern, we had those three wenches, Thomas?" asked Edward.

"Aye! I do! We weren't a bit cold *that* night, not after they crawled in the bed with us. That is, until we found they were beset with vermin and we had to go scrub ourselves raw in the river!"

All three of the men were laughing heartily as the messenger returned to his place at the base of the tree and sarcastically said, "I'm glad to see all of ye men are havin' a good ol' time here, while I was freezin' bare- arsed over yonder in the woods, so I was."

Robert answered, "Come now, Messenger. We only wish to spend a pleasant evenin' and have a sound sleep, for we've far to go on the morrow. We've only just come from Carlisle this day." Robert leaned back on one elbow and asked, "Where did ye say ye were from?"

"I didn't say, Milord," replied the little man as he sensed himself becoming the center of attention. "My own home is fair near to Dumfries, but I come this day from Dalswinton Castle."

"What? Now, isn't that a coincidence!" continued Robert, not believing it was that easy to get information from him. It was obvious the simpleton enjoyed bragging a little, and Robert pressed further. Not wanting to be blatantly inquisitive, Robert said aloud, but pretending to have asked the question of himself, "I know some folk around Dumfries and Dalswinton..." Then, not able to come up with a definite answer, he said, "Ach, probably some wench, eh, Nephew?" and slapped Thomas on the shoulder.

"Aye," Thomas went along, "or the gaol keeper!" The three laughed raucously, again, continuing to play the game for benefit of the messenger.

"I carry a message for the King, himself," blurted the messenger, feeling left out and needing to play his trump card. With one filthy finger, he pushed a piece of rabbit off his chin and into his mouth.

The three kinsmen stopped laughing and stared at the dumpy little man. Robert wanted more. "I thought ye said ye were carryin' only ordinary messages, and here ye are carryin' a message for ol' 'Longshanks' himself!"

"Aye... none other," basked the little man in his newfound grandness as he pulled the last of the meat from the spit and bit off a great chunk.

"Dalswinton... Dalswinton... Who do we know, Robert, would be holed up in that Godforsaken Dalswinton?" asked Edward, at last understanding the pretension.

"I doubt that ye would know," vaunted the messenger, "the one who sends me to the King." He was most impressed with his master's prominence.

Robert could stand the game no more. "Could it be Sir John 'The Red' Comyn?" he asked as he stood up to tower over the little fat messenger. Totally cowed, the fellow shrunk back against the tree and gagged on the morsel yet in his maw. The gold and yellow flashes of the fire accentuated the fear in his eyes as he saw the resolute anger in Robert's. He didn't know what he had said or done to alter the direction of the winds that now blew against him.

With no appetite for finishing the last bit of rabbit, he threw the bones, but toward the dog, not into the fire this time. He then wiped his sleeve across his mouth and started to gather his pouch and sword to himself. "Well, good men, I should be on my way now," he said meekly with a twitching smile. "I thank ye for the supper..."

Bending closer to him, Robert said ominously, "Oh, but ye must stay the night with us. A body never knows what manner of danger might confront a lone rider along this road... late at night."

Sweat beaded on his forehead as he tried to talk himself free, "Oh... I'm sure there's no one to harm me on my way tonight, Milord."

"But, we'll not hear of yer leaving our warm fire for the cold trail. Better ye should stay in our company, where there are men with stout arms to protect the King's messenger," Robert asserted through clenched teeth, pulling his claymore and facing the dark in mock "defense" of the man. "Nay, ye'll go nowhere, this night," Robert said, turning back toward the messenger. "Ye stay put!" With that, he re-sheathed his sword and strolled to the other side of the compound, followed by Thomas and Edward.

The messenger fingered the black and white pony hide pouch as the thought of running went storming through his head, but the desire for survival kept him fastened to the tree.

Robert, Edward, and Thomas stood huddled on the other side of the fire out of earshot of the messenger. Thomas' men were bedding down on their pine branches and grass tufts, and didn't realize the unfolding circumstance.

"'The Red' Comyn has betrayed me!" Robert confided to the other two. "I trusted him, and he has betrayed me in the worst possible way."

"If he's at Castle Dalswinton," said Thomas, "go confront him. Ask him his purpose."

"Aye... then ye can cut off his head," said Edward crossly.

"I have no point in takin' his life," replied Robert. "He could be of great worth in a war against England. His family ties spread more than half the breadth of Scotland."

"Then ye must go see what he's about, Robert," advised Edward.

"Why not," said Robert pensively. "I'll send a messenger to John requestin' a meetin' in a fortnight. That will give us time to think this through ere we meet with him."

Quietly the messenger slipped the pouch belt over his head and onto his shoulder, having mustered almost enough nerve to make a run for it while his host was occupied.

"Are ye trustin' enough to meet with him, Robert?" asked his nephew.

Robert looked at Thomas intently. "Let the message read: '...to meet at Greyfriars church, close to the castle.'"

"Holy ground should be a neutral enough place," nodded Edward.

"What about the English garrison at Dumfries?" asked Thomas, thinking of the possibility of a trap.

"Aye," Robert concurred. "We'll be in Lochmaben in the morning,' and from there we'll send the message to Lord Comyn."

The saddled horse in the line reared up as the messenger suddenly climbed on his back.

"Look! He's gettin' away!" shouted Edward. The little man wheeled the startled horse and spurred him into the darkened landscape. The other men in the camp scrambled to their feet and grabbed their weapons.

"If he gets off, its all of our lives," shouted Robert.

Edward stopped a passing soldier and grabbed his bow; the archer instinctively passed him an arrow. Edward notched the arrow and since he could no longer see his escaping target, shot it toward the hoof-beats. The soldier, a good man at his art, supplied another arrow, and another. As fast as Edward could loose one shaft, the next awaited his fingers. Finally, when he had put a half dozen arrows into the night in the direction of the fleeing messenger, a short scream echoed through the winter night. At least one arrow had found the messenger, and the sound of his body hitting the ground was of great relief to Robert.

"Fetch that horse!" commanded Edward to one of the soldiers, who swung up on the bare back of his own mount. "Bring him back here and take that damn saddle off him! And get that pony hide pouch back here, too!" The man set out into the snowy darkness.

Thomas Randolph walked over and stood beside Edward and philosophized, "That horse probably wouldn't have reared if he hadn't been sore from keepin' the saddle on all the time," adding, "Our messenger would be alive right now if he hadn't been so damnable lazy."

"And stupid," Edward answered. "If he'd only kept his mouth shut instead of braggin'..." He shook his head.

Elizabeth Brus

JANUARY 27th 1306
THE CASTLE AT LOCHMABEN

"Sound the alarm! Sound the alarm!" The watchful guard's stout voice fell upon the courtyard. "The laird is home! The laird is home!" Almost instantly, a small kitchen bell in the courtyard pealed repeatedly for the next few moments, to alert the household that the lord of the castle was near and approaching.

In her apartment within the innermost reaches of the castle's keep, a woman's heart leapt with joy, and, eyes closed, she offered a little prayer of thanksgiving before busying herself with preparations for her husband's arrival.

Quickly and quietly, she issued instructions with the precision of a battlefield officer, and with a minimum of turmoil, sent servants scurrying about to welcome home their master in proper fashion.

It was midday when Robert de Brus led the small band of men as they emerged from the tree line and crossed the fields that, in summer, grew much of the food for the inhabitants of the castle. Now, the ground was frozen hard and snow-laden, with hardly a footprint to be seen. By the time the party crossed the drawbridge and reached the castle gate, it was being held wide open by servants already prepared for their arrival.

Robert rode his horse into the courtyard, smiling and greeting all, but the one he was most anxious to see was his wife Elizabeth, to whom he was deeply devoted. Elizabeth de Burgh was the daughter of the most loyal Irish military leader in King Edward's court and, when Edward had been wooing the de Brus family to remain by his side four years earlier, he had so favorably approved of the marriage between Robert and Elizabeth that he had generously hosted their wedding.

At last Robert's ardent eyes found her standing in the doorway of the keep, a tall, shapely woman of elegant stature, clothed in finely detailed apparel of the best Scottish wool, a shawl wrapped tightly about her to prevent a chill. Seeing her sunlit form outlined against the dark interior he suddenly realized how greatly he had yearned for her in his absence.

As beautiful as e'er, he thought, and he kicked his mount to draw nearer to her side. The dog followed behind his master for a short way, then went in search of a warm place to rest.

"Well come, Milord," her familiar voice came to his ears like soft music.

"I thank ye, Lady de Brus," he responded as he reined in his horse and sat drinking in her beauty. For a moment, they held the pose, each excited merely at the other's nearness. Elizabeth spoke first, again.

"How was the gatherin'?" asked Elizabeth. "Does 'Longshanks' entertain as lavishly as when Eleanor lived?" she asked, smiling the warm smile for which Robert had longed beyond reason to see.

Robert gladly returned the smile and leaned on the saddlebow. Not wanting to discuss the king's attempt to arrest them before he had even dismounted, he jested instead, "Milady... these days, his hospitality runs as thin as his person."

They both laughed and probed the depth of each other's eyes.

Robert suddenly was serious and silent, then said softly, "I've been gone only a few weeks, but I did miss the sight of ye."

"But I've not missed the likes of ye, Laird Robert," she said teasingly, her flirtatious smile giving away the lie.

Robert chuckled gently and dismounted. A groom appeared beside him to take his reins and lead the horse toward the stable. Robert bounded up the steps to join Elizabeth, drawing close enough to smell her sweet breath as it left her flared nostrils. He took her hand and touched it gently to his lips before he led her through the doorway into the keep and shut the door behind them.

• •

"He sure is quick to disappear when Lady Elizabeth is around," remarked Edward to Thomas Randolph. The two young bachelors watched enviously from the backs of their mounts as the couple's quiet greeting unfolded.

"Ye know, Eddie lad," said Thomas thoughtfully, "That puts me in mind of a kitchen maid with long blond hair and..."

"Ye'd better not be talkin' about her that I think ye're talkin' about!" threatened Edward with an angry frown.

Thomas laughed his big raucous laugh and slapped Edward on the back so hard that he almost fell onto his horse's neck.

"Thomas, ye're purely a dart in my arse," growled Edward, adding appreciatively, "but, it's a'right 'cause ye've proper saved it more times than one."

His nephew was briefly embarrassed, and so smiled and lowered his head a bit. He then said heartily, "Let's find Sarah of the kitchen!"

The two rowdies dismounted, and, their arms around each other's shoulders, left their horses standing in the courtyard while they went off across the square in the direction of the kitchen, kicking drifts of snow and telling each other lies that neither believed.

The courtyard door to the kitchen creaked slowly open as the lusting duo peeked around the room slyly. "Sarah," they both called in a teasing, childish way. "Sarah," they called again.

"She's gone! Anyways, ye should leave her alone," scolded an older woman from within the kitchen as she forcefully kneaded a large lump of bread dough on a heavy wooden table she had scattered with flour.

"Gone! Gone where?" asked Edward, crestfallen.

"She has gone to visit her cousin in Dumfries!" lied the woman.

"And just when will she be back?" demanded Thomas, suspecting the lie and continuing to look about.

"When she comes back!" announced the woman sharply, giving the dough a loud couple of slaps.

"Ye two!" barked Sarah loudly as she turned the corner into the kitchen from the keep, her shapely body not being denied expression even in her heavy winter clothes.

"She's back!" said the betrayed old woman, retreating quickly into the shadows, not that either of the young men would have noticed.

"What are ye two doin' here?" the comely young woman shouted even louder.

"We're livin' here, remember?" said Edward with a sly smile on his face. "We just came by for... a couple of yer hot biscuits!" he added, pointing to a pan of freshly baked breads.

"Aye," agreed Thomas, grinning broadly. "One of yer hot biscuits was what I wanted, too!"

Sarah picked up a heavy iron skillet from beside the fireplace, poised the pan above her head and set her feet wide, preparing for action as her anger built. "Ye two have the nerve of Satan, himself!"

"Well, what about them biscuits?" asked Edward most seductively.

"Ye're unbelievable!" cried Sarah as she charged the two men, chasing them out the courtyard door and sending them sliding into the snow with her greasy skillet-bludgeon swinging all the while, "Get none around here this time, ye two won't!"

A young peasant man hurriedly followed her through the door, having come to see why she was yelling so. He looked at Edward and Thomas sitting in the snow, put together what had happened, and laughed. He then pinched Sarah on the backside, to let them know that he now had claim to her affections.

"Stop it!" she said angrily to the man, and she hit him on the chest with her small fist. But, to spite the two in the snow, she raised herself up on tiptoes and kissed the fellow on the mouth. She then looked back at Edward and Thomas with a "so there" expression. Pushing the grinning young man backward into the kitchen, she followed on his toes and closed the door behind them.

"Guess he's gettin' all the hot biscuits now," said Thomas, dolefully.

"Aye," Edward agreed as they disappointedly picked themselves up. "And I was so looking forward to getting' some," he said to his companion. The two retrieved their mounts and led them off toward the stable.

. .

"Have ye a leg of mutton or a loin of boar around anywhere, woman?" asked Robert hungrily as they walked into the great dining hall in the center of the keep. He had changed from the dirty clothes he had worn on the trail, and now appeared freshly washed and comfortably clad, but as yet unshaven. "I'm altogether tired of eating rodents. And so's the dog."

The dog raised his head from his paws and yapped as if to agree. He lay on a pallet placed for him in front of the huge fireplace, one of two that attempted, with limited success, to heat the enormous room in winter. Though the servants had lighted a fire in each as soon as they were alerted to his approach, Robert found that in order to be warmed by the roaring blaze, he had to sit at the end of the vast table, nearest the fire.

When the laird was not at home, his lady and family members took their meals in a private dining room nearer the kitchen. It was smaller and easier to heat, and thus more comfortable and more conserving of the winter's fuel supply.

"Stay here and rest yerself, Milord," offered Elizabeth, "A proper banquet is bein' prepared for ye, and 'twill be ready in a short time." She kissed his mouth tenderly before disappearing down the passageway into the kitchen to see that her instructions to the staff were carried out to her satisfaction.

"Hello-o-o, My Lord Robert!" came a youthful male voice from above Robert's head. The lord of the castle looked in the direction of the voice, and there, two stories up on one of the balconies overlooking the dining hall, was Robert's youngest brother, nineteen-year-old Nigel. Beside him stood sweet-faced little Agnes, a year Nigel's junior, lovingly holding his arm.

"Come down, little brother, and let me look at ye!" shouted Robert. His voice echoed around the great, cold, empty room.

"I shall join ye presently," replied Nigel. "Agnes insists on re-working her hair before dinner." Agnes smiled.

"Ach, we're but family here," returned Robert, attempting to convince the girl to forego taking the extra time.

"But she wants to make sure she will be well accepted into the family, Robert," answered Nigel, his long black curls falling forward as he leaned over the rail to be better understood.

"I suppose ye still fancy her then, do ye?" grinned Robert.

Agnes blushed and put her graceful little hands over her face.

"With all my heart, Milord Brother," replied Nigel, looking at Agnes.

"Then she has nothin' to fear from us, I'd say," returned Robert.

The two merry young lovers disappeared behind the railing as Robert, having warmed up rapidly by the huge fireplace at his back, doffed his hooded overgarment, threw it on the bench and sat beside it.

It is certainly good to be home, thought Robert. He ran his fingers across the wood of the table, worn smooth by generations of use, and remembered for some moments his family's history by those boards, times most often happy. By contrast, he recollected as well the delectable smoothness of Elizabeth's soft skin.

A rotund old woman hobbled to the table with a small bowl of apples tucked tightly to her large breasts. "Milady asked that I bring these to ye, Milaird, so that ye do not starve ere the meal is ready," she panted, and set the bowl on the table in front of him. "Be needin' a wee bit of wine to wash that down, will ye?" she asked as she curtsied and turned to leave.

"Aye," said Robert, "perhaps two wee bits."

"Very good Milord. I shall be back soon."

Robert watched the plump old woman walk purposefully across the room. She had been with his family at least half his life and always took estimable care of her responsibilities around the household.

Within a short time, as Elizabeth had promised, a small feast was spread across the great dining table. Although only mid-afternoon, it was overcast and little light from outside penetrated this deeply into the keep. Thus dozens of candles were lit and placed on or near the table, and, with the fires, made for a cheery glow all around.

Robert remained at the end of the table with his back to the fire and shared his bench with Elizabeth. Nigel and Agnes sat to Robert's left, followed by Marjorie, Robert's twelve-year-old daughter by his first wife, Isabel de Mar, who had died giving the girl life. Robert's brothers, Alexander, the Glasgow dean and acclaimed scholar, and young Thomas, had arrived in the hall and were seated to his right.

Edward and his strapping nephew Thomas Randolph sat also on Robert's right, but at the far end of the table, where they had a better view of the kitchen traffic in the luscious form of Sarah. Occasionally, the two would giggle between themselves, and drink more wine. Sarah teased them unabashedly from afar when her boyfriend wasn't looking. The rest of the table did their best to ignore their puerile dinner mates.

"Pass some of that meat this way, Brother Nigel," said Thomas, who, for all his youth, was a large-boned man and strong as a destrier. Nigel cut a sizable portion and passed it, impaled on his dirk blade, across the table to his brother, who took the meat in his hand and continued to eat heartily.

"Ye've gone unshaven, Robert," remarked Elizabeth quietly, breaking a piece of bread off the loaf and handing it to him. "Do ye intend to grow yer beard, again?"

"Aye, I'm thinkin' on it, her husband affirmed, holding onto her fingers momentarily as he received the bread from her hand. "Do ye mind it?

Elizabeth looked at his face critically, then answered, "I always liked it shaped to yer face, ye know."

"That makes it unanimous...the dog likes it, too!" teased Robert, and they all laughed. The dog lay near the fire and continued to gnaw on a fleshy bone in ignorant, contented bliss.

"Milaird, please tell us of the king's festivity. Was it a very grand affair?" asked Agnes, shyly.

"Aye, Lass, 'twas very grand, and colorful. There were jugglers and musicians, and an excess of food and drink," Robert answered. "The hall was filled to overflowing of the knights and their ladies," he turned to Elizabeth and added, "and King Edward expressed his regrets that ye had not accompanied us there. I also wished ye had been with us... until Edward sent his wee 'gift'."

"What did ol' 'Longshanks' have for ye?" asked Thomas Brus.

"Been surprised, ye would, little brother," replied Robert, nodding his head and arching his eyebrows.

"Speakin' of 'Longshanks', do ye remember, Robert," Thomas Brus interjected, "in the battle at Stirlin', when he was showin' off for that new young queen of his, how he rode up so close to the wall, shoutin' orders to his men and such, that he 'most got a spear right through him?"

The men all laughed at the shared recollection, though few of them had been there.

"And then," he continued, "'bout got a boulder dropped on his head, and his horse reared and threw him to the ground?" They laughed all the more.

"Aye. We all thought he was near to meetin' his maker, that day," laughed Robert with the rest of the table.

"A toast, Brother. In thanks for yer safe return this day," declared Alexander, as he stood and raised his cup held above his head.

"Ye don't know how that is appreciated," said Robert, joining him.

The other men stood and raised their cups in silent thanks, then drank... all except Thomas Randolph and Edward, who were preoccupied with their silliness.

After getting their attention by rapping his empty cup on the table, Robert chided, "Air ye not drinkin' to our safe return?"

Both sat at drunken attention, though swaying a bit. From the kitchen door, Sarah could see what was happening and covered her mouth to stifle her snickering.

Edward was suddenly and unexpectedly serious, and rose to his feet with his cup sloshing. "Aye, we should, 'specially since we had to sneak out from under ol' 'Longshanks'' nose... and... and left a few widows behind in the doin' of it, too."

Not to be outdone, Thomas Randolph jumped up to chime in, "*And there was 'The Red' Comyn's messenger who went missing last night in the forest yonder, don't forget.*"

For a moment, everyone was shocked into silence. Elizabeth fastened her wide eyes on Robert, who looked in reproach and grimness at his two drunken magpies before meeting his wife's steady gaze.

Just as he opened his mouth to explain to Elizabeth, the youngest spoke.

"Oh, Father!" exclaimed Marjorie, her eyes tearing and wide, "Ye could have been killed!"

Elizabeth continued to look at Robert and wondered why he had not told her. He knew by the look on her face that she wondered, and that he would have some explaining to do.

Robert pushed his plate back and leaned heavily on the table, "This is the tale, and I don't think ye're goin' to like it, but I have a weighty decision to make."

"Are we goin' to war?" asked Nigel excitedly. Agnes squeezed his arm in chilled fear.

"I pray not," said Robert softly, "but neither can I let devouring jackals rule our blessed Scotland."

Robert told the table the entire story of the last few days, his agreement with John Comyn, Comyn's apparent betrayal, and his intention to meet with Lord John in two weeks in hopes that they could, face-to-face, put aside misunderstandings and, in his words, "work together toward the freedom of Scotland."

The happy homecoming supper suddenly turned into a solemn one. No one spoke; the only sounds came from the fire and the small movements of the diners as they went through the motions of finishing the remains of the meal.

Elizabeth, neither eating nor drinking more, said not a word but quietly left the table and retired to the solar of the castle. With a heavy heart, Robert dutifully sat with his kinsmen a while before he followed.

"What's wrong with Elizabeth?" asked Edward of his brooding companion once Robert was out of hearing.

"Not interested in bein' queen, I guess," returned Thomas Randolph, draining his cup, again.

. .

The crackling embers and occasional flare from the fireplace in the solar cast dancing shapes on Elizabeth's nude torso as she disrobed to the hips and sat on the hearth to wash herself, a bowl of steaming water in front of her. She had sent her handmaiden to bed after the woman had prepared hot water for her bath.

Startled, she jumped a bit when the door pushed open without a knock. She had not expected Robert to leave the dinner so soon, but when she realized the intruder was he, she returned quietly to her bathing.

Her husband removed his claymore belt and laid it on the table along one wall.

A faint glow from the last of the winter sunset highlighted the tiny frosted windows on either side of the rack of ten-point antlers which served Robert as a sometime clothing tree. He hung his kirtle on one of the points.

Tired, worried, and more than a little affected by drink, Robert walked across the room and looked down on Elizabeth. He pushed the heavy chair close to where she was sitting and perched himself on the edge to drink in Elizabeth's sensual beauty.

She failed to pay heed to him, continuing her bath as if he were not there.

Even in his pleasure at watching her, Robert sensed her quiet anger at not being told sooner of the dangerous trek and how they had managed to save themselves. A long, awkward pause stood between them until at last he said gently, "'Tis good to be home, my darlin'."

"'Tis good to have ye home, my husband," she replied genuinely as she rinsed the soap from her shoulders. The warm water poured tiny rivulets down her body and disappeared into the robe she had around her waist and across her legs.

Robert's eyes danced excitedly as he reached out less than an arm's length and touched Elizabeth on one bare nipple. She responded as she had dozens of times before, with chills of excitement. She took his large callused hand in hers and laid her face against it.

"What are ye doin', Robert?" she fervently asked.

"I think I'm havin' a passion for ye, woman," remarked Robert, somewhat perplexed.

"No, I mean, why are ye even thinkin' of takin' the crown? There are damned few of the other earls that will support ye; *ye*... who could certainly, if ye wish, live however ye please and pay tribute to no man... except a kind nod to ol' Edward on rare occasion. And ye know it!"

"Can we talk about this later?" asked Robert, leaning his face into her sweet smelling tresses.

"'Tis botherin' me now," she replied pulling away from him, but slightly, and turned to look directly in his eyes. That was one of the things that so attracted him to her in the first place, her honest, open gaze.

Robert exhaled heavily, then explained further. "There were papers found on William Wallace when he was captured last year. I don't know what they contained, but Edward hasn't been the same toward me since. 'Tis too late to laze around the manor as does John de Balliol in France, and not give a farthin' for my homeland!" He stared at his hands. "John Comyn bein' a Celt, I thought he would support me..."

"Ye thought Lord John would do any more than suited his own greed?" She was incredulous. "And ye are surprised that he betrayed ye?"

"Aye, purely disappointed," he said, looking longingly into the fire.

He had no equal in battle, but he still has a wee bit of his innocence intact, she silently observed.

Elizabeth smiled as she stood in front of the chair where he sat and dropped her robe to the floor. He held her tight across the middle and she ran her fingers through his hair, then cupped his face with her hands and turned it toward hers. Their lips touched. Their passion supplanted all else.

John "The Red" Comyn
Lord of Badenoch

FEBRUARY 10th 1306
LORD JOHN COMYN'S CASTLE OF DALSWINTON

The early morning sunshine played about the small study in a rainbow of colors as it filtered through the man-sized stained glass window and onto the table, whereon laid an open book, a candle, quills and an inkpot.

Forty-two-year-old John 'The Red' Comyn, earl of Badenoch, was sitting at the table with his back to the kaleidoscopic window. Lord Comyn was, perhaps, the most powerful man in Scotland, being not only a candidate for the throne by birth and having a network of kin through many of the clans, but also because of his vast personal holdings in lands and castles, which were spread across Scotland and England.

"'The wolf' will be howling for my blood if he has discovered that which I fear he has," mused John Comyn metaphorically to his uncle, Sir Robert Comyn, who lounged in a stout little chair across the table from him. Sir Robert was temporarily governor of Dumfries castle, some nine miles to the south.

"Ye fret like a wench in labor, Nephew," teased the elder but less commanding man. "Do ye really think because yer messenger has not returned from England that Robert de Brus has somehow taken hold of him?"

"Do not underestimate this man, Uncle," retorted John Comyn abruptly, "He is not like us! Winning 'freedom for Scotland' is becoming a religion with him."

A thoughtful moment of silence hung between them until Robert

Comyn spoke, "I still think the Brus, yer so-called 'wolf,' mad though he may be, has not the inclination to sink his teeth deeply enough to kill."

Turning his back to his kinsman, John pondered the situation carefully, contorting his face as he ran the gamut of emotions: fear, resignation, puzzlement, until finally he said, "If he has found me out, I shall just lie to him! Deny any knowledge of it. Such has worked before."

John turned around and continued his thought. "I'll... I'll say the papers were stolen... and my privy seal. 'Tis... a... a forgery!" He forcefully pounded his fist against the book on the table and accidentally spilled the ink, which flowed to the edge and splattered onto the floor.

Robert Comyn thought this to be an omen, and saw the black liquid to be tears of prophecy. A tingle of fear traversed his spine.

After a moment more he spoke, "Yer life will depend on yer judgment, here and now, John. I am more experienced than ye, by virtue of age if naught more, and I counsel ye not to let yer avarice for Brus' lands kill ye."

"The king knows me to be recently loyal to his causes," bragged John Comyn." And gettin' rid of Robert de Brus for him..." he paused thoughtfully "*and* for me... would consolidate my position in a single stroke." He looked at his companion, "And, that, it seems, is a calculated risk that I am obviously willing to take." Then he added confidently, "Anyway, I will meet him at the Greyfriars church, tonight, as he has requested."

"I am not in agreement with ye on this, John!" objected Robert Comyn. Then, receiving a stony glare from the younger man, he acquiesced, "But, I will do as ye ask."

"Ye be there with men, and if the meet goes against us, ye signal them to fall upon the Brus and his entourage and kill them all."

Roger Kirkpatrick

FEBRUARY 10ᵗʰ 1306
GREYFRIARS CHURCH NEAR DUMFRIES CASTLE

"Robbie, I see men in arms hidin' in yonder wood," cautioned Christopher Seton quietly to Robert Brus. The two led an armed procession that included Edward Brus, Roger Kirkpatrick, James Lindsay, and twenty horsed knights, down the snow-covered trail toward Greyfriars Church.

"We're near up on the kirk," replied Robert, pulling his hood tighter to his face against the biting cold wind. "They would be John Comyn's men, waitin'."

Christopher Seton was husband to Robert's sister, the Lady Christian; Kirkpatrick and Lindsay were old friends from skirmishes with the English several years before, and about the same age as Robert. Having heard of 'The Red' Comyn's deceit, they had individually joined Robert's contingent, each for his own reason.

"They seem to be greater in number than are we," added Christopher, "but it is hard to see with the sky growing so quickly black." He looked at the heavy winter clouds amassing to blot out the dwindling light from the sun, which had already set.

"It matters little," insisted Robert. "They'll not attack us for fear of our havin' John trapped in the abbey. Besides, I don't expect trouble."

"Would ye not think them pure assassins?" asked Christopher.

"I wouldn't fancy John Comyn to be that stupid," retorted his brother-in-law. Realizing that Seton missed the point, he continued. "If he were to assassinate me, or t'other way 'round, it would furnish Edward Plantagenet with reason to arrest and execute the survivor for murder, thus riddin' himself of us both. I'm sure John has realized that. Else he is not the cunning man I think him to be."

The troop rode up to the holy building and, with the quick eyes of experienced warriors, took a survey of the situation. Everything looked normal in the gathering dark. There were two horses standing near the four-foot-high, gated fence that surrounded the entrance to the crumbling church.

Light from the candles within made its small windows glow with a yellowish hue that reflected softly off the stone steps, polished smooth by the tread of the faithful generations.

The mounted knights took positions along the front as Robert, Christopher, Roger Kirkpatrick, who wore a cloth band over the eye he had given for Scotland, and James Lindsay dismounted.

They made their way up the steps and through the main door of the kirk. Edward Brus and Thomas Randolph stayed outdoors and in command of the knights. The dog waited on the steps, preferring to remain outside in the threatening elements rather than enter the church.

In the vestibule, Robert doffed his hooded cloak and handed it to James Lindsay, who laid it on a nearby table. Robert's upper body armor shone brightly under a loosely worn tunic.

Christopher chose to retain his cloak and, alongside Robert, went through the heavy wooden door into the sanctuary.

. .

Hearing the door open, John Comyn, standing before the high altar, turned gracefully to greet Robert as one would hail an old friend. "Ah, the Earl of Carrick has arrived! I hope yer journey was an uneventful one, Lord Brus," greeted John with a wide smile.

"My kinsmen and I, and even my dog, would prefer to be at home by the fire on my own hearth," replied Robert with solemn aspect as he walked toward the spot where John Comyn waited, his uncle at his side.

Not wanting to inhibit the meeting, Christopher Seton stopped a few paces back from the three men, that they might speak privately. He noticed, nearly out of sight to one side of the altar, two curious friars watching the unfolding events, but nothing else moved within the unheated room, save themselves.

As Robert looked upon John's smiling, friendly face, a quiet rush of anger filled his being, but he held his countenance.

"What be this matter ye were so anxious to meet with me about?" asked John, taking the high ground of innocence in his arrogance. Robert turned to Christopher, who reached under his cloak to expose the distinctive black and white pony-hide pouch his brothers-in-law had taken from the corpse of John Comyn's late messenger.

John's eyes betrayed his knowledge of the all too familiar packet.

"It must have been his second day on the trail when yer messenger came upon our camp and could not resist the warm fire and a hand-out supper," related Robert. Christopher calmly withdrew the contents from the pouch and, striding forward, handed them to Robert.

"What is this?" asked John, feigning ignorance.

"This," said Robert coldly, "is our agreement, the same in which ye agreed to support me for the throne and I, in turn, would surrender all my lands to ye."

Robert Comyn, only a few feet behind John, moved closer as a sign of loyalty to his nephew.

His malevolently flashing eyes piercing the older man's courage, Robert Brus gestured for him to back up, and the Comyn obeyed.

"I ne'er received yer lands," said John turning his head away from Robert and toward the altar. He rested his open palms flat down on the top, a disarming gesture, perhaps to hide his deception, perhaps to pray. He now knew that his plan's worst possible outcome, and his most deeply held fear, had indeed become manifest.

"And I am not yet crowned," replied Robert. "However, that bears not on the crux of the matter at hand."

"Which is?" asked John, inwardly scheming to escape the trap.

"I offered support for yer attaining the crown of Scotland, with me to receive yer lands in return," asserted Robert. "But, ye chose instead to have my lands... and relinquish yer claim to the crown to me, as witnessed by yer hand and seal upon this agreement." Though outwardly calm, he all but trembled with rage.

"Aye, that was the agreement," replied John, who prayed that Robert did not also have his letter to King Edward.

The friars noiselessly peered out from their hiding place, their fear growing as the tension between the two men increased.

Robert said not a word as he revealed the dreaded second document in the pouch, the letter to King Edward.

'The Red' Comyn took the parchment from Robert's hand and looked at it briefly, then shouted in a somewhat shaky and overly surprised voice, "This be a lie!" He looked at it aghast, to make Robert think it came to him as a shock. "Someone plots against us and attempts to create distrust and overthrow our strategy... someone who forged my privy seal... someone..."

"No one but ye is responsible," interrupted Robert with barely controlled anger, "Yer messenger, lyin' dead in the snow these past two weeks, no doubt has been et by the wilderness, and ye think I have not the evidence to know these things?"

"Dear Robert, ye have obviously misread my intentions..." John gasped as his nervous fingers danced against the jeweled grip of the dirk he wore strapped around his waist.

"Would ye now draw yer blade against me?" barked Robert gruffly.

Robert Comyn shifted fearfully as he crossed his arms in front of his chest, thinking he could act faster from that position if need arose.

Christopher Seton stood firm but alert.

"Robert," implored John, seeing that the time for dissuasion had gone from him, "it is only that ye have not the mind, nor the heart for properly administerin' a government... or for dealin' with the quarrels of the earls and clans. 'Tis true that there are few who can hope to equal ye on the battlefield, but I..."

"Ye had the choice to be king and 'administer' the government if ye thought I was not capable. And the clans are pretty well ungovernable in any event. Nay, John, ye saw a way to claim my lands... and perhaps the crown as well," the Brus said through gritted teeth. "Whatever ye claim yer reasons to be, now that ye are caught, the fact of the matter is ye lied and ye betrayed me! Aye, and Scotland!"

With eyes darting toward Robert Comyn to see his demeanor, 'The Red' Comyn breathed deep in anticipation of action, giving away his next move. As he drew his dirk Robert Brus stepped back, pulling his own. Comyn's attack was strong but wild, and Brus easily sidestepped the ill-planned foin.

The elder Comyn looked at Christopher to see if his intention was to join the fight, but Christopher held his position.

John regained his balance and came at his adversary once more.

With battle-hardened instincts, the Brus grabbed John Comyn's blade arm, pushed it outward and struck with his own dirk at Comyn's torso, piercing the man's armor and went deeply into his upper chest and shoulder.

The Brus removed his blade from the stout hold of Comyn's armor, but once retrieved, the dirk was lowered, having done its work.

John staggered back and fell against the high altar; he tried to hold himself up but slowly slumped to the floor, leaving a trail of blood across the front of the chantry.

"Ye have killed him!" cried Robert Comyn aloud in disbelief.

"He is not dead," growled Robert Brus, "See there, he yet moves."

"Avenge me, Uncle!" whispered John through bloody teeth, "Avenge me!"

"Aye!" said Robert Comyn, and with a single stroke unsheathed his sword and struck Robert Brus full upon the chest with all his might.

Caught off balance, the Brus fell backward and struck his head hard against the floor. For a moment, he lay there stunned, unable to move.

Having such advantage, Robert Comyn moved over the immobile Brus and raised high his sword to serve the killing blow, sarcastically spitting, "And this to ye, 'King' Robert!"

"Uncle! Behind ye!" cried the wounded Red Comyn. Robert Comyn turned to see the blade of Christopher Seton flash in front of him.

It was his last vision.

With the speed and agility of the experienced young knight that he was, Christopher had swung his dirk across the throat of Robert Comyn and killed him instantly.

"Ye bastards! Ye sons of cur bitches!" shouted Lord John as he lay bleeding at the foot of the altar. His uncle's body had fallen close enough that blood of both men mingled on the floor.

Christopher did not reply but went straightaway to Robert Brus' side and helped him to a sitting position.

"We must leave," whispered Robert to Christopher, who was retrieving the bloodied documents.

"Will ye live?" asked one of the two friars, who came from their hiding place and knelt before John to comfort and, if necessary, to shrive him.

"Aye! I will!" sputtered John angrily, splattering the friars with speckles of his blood, then shouted loudly at Robert, "I will live... to see yer rottin' bones in their grave, Robert de Brus!"

"To horse!" ordered Robert quietly as he pushed unsteadily through the heavy door into the vestibule where Roger and James were waiting.

"What was said about yer grave, Robert?" asked Roger steadying his friend. "Have ye killed 'The Red' Comyn?"

"I think not!" barked Robert angrily, "Else why does he continue to scream bloody curses!" With that, Robert swung his cloak about his shoulders and, followed by Christopher and James, walked outside to join his waiting knights.

Roger Kirkpatrick stood a moment, listening to the howling curses and blasphemy from within the sanctuary, and determined that John Comyn meant what he said about seeing Robert in his grave. He turned on his heel and opened the stout door into the bloody scene.

The two friars, thinking they, too, might be murdered, were helpless to do anything more than close their eyes and cross themselves, as Roger unsheathed his dirk and opened John Comyn's gurgling throat.

After wiping the blood off his blade on John Comyn's cloak, Roger sheathed his dirk and reached for his money pouch. He withdrew two coins and dropped them on the altar, crossed himself and said to the two friars, "Pray for me, brothers, and for them, too. Sinners all."

Sinner or no, when he came out of the church and down the few steps to Robert, his one good eye gleamed. "'Tis done," he said. "Neither his curses nor his threats shall fret ye more."

Robert stood next to his horse and clung to the saddlebow to regain his strength and sense of balance. His head was throbbing as if struck by mace at the end of a strong arm. He was silent a moment, then somberly said, "'The Red's' death changes all. Mount up lads. We're for takin' Dumfries castle." His lieutenants looked from one to the other in mild surprise.

"When?" asked Roger finally, as Christopher, Edward, and Thomas Randolph stood close to be within earshot of the conversation.

"Yon men of the Comyns' don't yet know their lords are dead," said Robert across his saddle to the group. "Else we would be well bloodied by now. As long as we have this benefit, we'll use it. Ride out slowly from here toward the castle. Once there, if all is as I suspect, we'll hasten across the bridge and through the gate, and secure the castle."

"Robert, are ye mad? We are no force to take a castle," objected Edward. "We are but a little party of twenty-six men and a dog!"

"Aye," his brother agreed, "but we are a little party of twenty-six men and a dog... and the weapon of surprise!"

. .

Within a mile's ride Robert and his men rode through the barbican, across the drawbridge, and up to the secured gate of Dumfries Castle. The castle guards, knowing Lord Comyn had ridden to meet Lord Brus, and seeing the Brus banner in the torchlight at the gate, opened it straightaway, thinking their lord followed.

The "little party" rode into the interior courtyard.

Sir Richard Siward, the English constable of Dumfries, hastened forth on foot and greeted Robert Brus with an appropriate bow. "Well come, Lord Brus," he said.

"Thank ye, Sir Richard. 'Tis most hospitable for ye to open yer castle to us. But, I fear we must abuse yer hospitality, as we are takin' this castle as our own," replied Robert with a smile, hoping to prevent bloodshed.

The confused constable stood silent for a moment, looking at Robert's face and waiting for further explanation. With none forthcoming, Sir Richard twisted his face up with curiosity and stammered, "I-I-I am afraid I do not understand, Milord."

"Surrender yer castle, man!" commanded Robert sternly as his knights revealed their drawn swords.

Sir Richard's eyes widened as he at last realized the situation. He immediately wheeled around and ran through the courtyard crying, "Kill them! Kill them all! They are come to take the castle!"

Robert signaled to his men, and they immediately repositioned themselves near the outer walls throughout the courtyard, as a large, clanging bell sounded the alarm. The garrison being alerted, half-dressed English soldiers began pouring into the courtyard from their barracks quarters.

Robert's dog jumped ahead of his men and so struck the first blow, that upon the leg of the nearest oncoming Englishman.

"Fire that door!" ordered Robert to a nearby knight, pointing toward the wooden barracks.

A magnificent horseman, the young knight spurred his mount toward a hay cart standing at the far end of the enclosure, beyond the barracks door. Leaning out of his saddle until he could almost touch the ground, he caught the handle of a pot of gudgeon grease and threw it into the cart. As the tallow spread down through the dry tinder, the young warrior cut across the way, snatched a torch from the hand of a fleeing serf and, wheeling around, jabbed it into the greasy mess, igniting it instantly.

He next grabbed the handle on the front of the cart by which the serfs pulled the transport from the field and dragged the growing fire headlong at the doorway, throwing the already emerged Englishmen into panicky flight. The cart smashed into the open door and wedged itself tightly between the jambs, trapping the remaining soldiers inside.

Few of the English scrambled out under the burning cart and through the mounting flames. One who did was aflame when he reached Robert, who quickly put the fellow out of his agony.

Those soldiers left inside were only interested in removing the blazing cart and escaping the rising inferno. Besides, they had no way of judging the strength of their enemy or their placement in the fire-lit courtyard, and so were none too interested in combating anything other than the flames.

Edward Brus had given a war whoop and spurred his mount forward into the onrushing English foot soldiers, thus leading the Scottish knights into the thick of the fray. His battle-ax hacking whatever head or body was within reach caused Thomas, just behind him, to use great care not to get too close to Edward's wild swings.

Robert was suddenly engaged by another of the defenders and brought him to the ground with a one-handed slash of his claymore.

Several of the guards stationed on the wall above them began to shoot bolts from their crossbows into the now brightly lit courtyard, catching one of Robert's knights through the neck, and another through the ribs beneath his arm as he raised it to deflect a blow from a battle-ax. Both men died instantly.

Robert wheeled his mount to shield himself from this new onslaught, when an arrow from a long bow pierced the heart of one of the wall guards, and pitched him forward into the square.

"I have no archers," thought Robert, his eyes searching the courtyard for the source of the responding arrows as another crossbowman toppled from the wall, an arrow through his thigh. With no shelter on the open walkway, the others took refuge in the corner towers and continued to target the assaulting Scots, but to far less effect.

An English guard, in the thick of the fight on the ground and seeing that Edward was the single greatest threat to him and his comrades, heroically rushed between the long arcs of the battle-ax swings and viciously stabbed Edward's horse.

The horse reared and screamed in pain, almost throwing Edward Brus into his enemies, and after staggering back a few steps, the animal fell, with Edward still astride, onto the hard-frozen ground.

Claymore in hand, Thomas dismounted between his fallen comrade and the English and set to defending Edward, who lay motionless with one leg trapped under his mount.

Thomas was at once beset by a guard with a lance, and another followed just behind the first. The first man's blade was near Thomas' throat almost before he had both feet on the ground. As he dodged the extended weapon, the lance caught just the side of the young noble's face and, pushing his helmet off, fairly severed half his ear.

Thomas hardly noticed the injury, grabbing the passing lance and using the momentum of the charging soldier to pull the man directly into the line of the claymore. He then delivered a hefty blow across his adversary's neck, separating the man's head from his body.

The second fellow, seeing the fate of the first, withdrew.

"My God!" bellowed Edward as he came to his senses looking into the eyes of the decapitated head, laying beside his own. "What happened?" he cried and began trying to pull himself up with his elbows, only to find his leg pinned fast.

"Nothin' of import. I just saved yer wee arse again," smirked his nephew, turning back to the battle. He realized the resistance was quickly dwindling; those not actively involved were seeking places to hide. "Better get up fast if ye want to fight more, Laddie!"

"Nay, Thomas," commanded Robert as he approached the two from out of the smoke. "Let them retire. They're done."

"Armed riders a'comin'!" shouted Sir Christopher who stood watch near the gate.

"Get the portcullis down! Close and bar that damned gate!" commanded Robert, but Christopher was already doing so.

He dismounted and released the brake on the portcullis gear, and the heavy grate rumbled to a thundering stop as it seated itself firmly in place. By then the knight was laboring one of the huge iron-studded doors to a close. To his surprise, a young peasant from within the castle joined him as he closed the other.

"Thank ye, lad" grunted Christopher, straining at his task.

"Nay, Sire. Thank me not, for I'm a Scot, same as ye," replied the youth.

"For sure ye are, m'lad," replied Christopher, and the two pulled the great drawbars into place. "For sure ye are," he repeated.

"Get this beast off me," yelled the still struggling Edward. Thomas returned to where his friend lay and, with heroic effort, pulled on the saddlebow of the dead horse, rolling him just enough for Edward to pull his leg free. Scrambling to his feet at last, Edward looked solemnly at the poor dead creature and shook his head before going on to recover his claymore and return it to its scabbard.

Across the bailey, Robert removed his helmet and, bloodied sword in hand, walked his horse to the center of the bailey and hollered, "Turn out the constable!"

Sir Richard Siward finally stirred from behind a barrel where he had timidly hidden during the clash. "Here... Lord Brus," he said in a voice barely audible.

"*Now* yield yer castle, damn ye!" demanded Robert, eyes flashing in anger that so many had to die to get the man to listen. He put the cold point of his crimson blade squarely upon the frightened man's Adam's apple.

The constable raised his trembling hands and, after getting his voice to work, yelled with tears streaming down his cheeks, "Relinquish your arms! All that hear, fight no more! Milord Brus... holds... Castle Dumfries!" Slowly, the English came out of hiding or ceased fighting, and threw down their weapons.

The blazing barracks lit the surrounding courtyard near bright as day as the more enterprising of the soldiers trapped inside used their weapons and hacked their way through the back wall. Choking with smoke, confused and dazed, they surrendered without resistance.

While the injured among the young knights tended their wounds, others herded the vanquished Englishmen together and allowed them to minister to their own.

"Better they used their axes and blades on the wall than on our heads," remarked Edward, limping obviously as he came to Robert's side.

"Aye," Robert agreed, then looking about, changed the subject.

"Brother, I would have ye find me the bowman who saved our lads from the bolts of the wall sentries," he pointed to a gathering crowd of the castle inhabitants. "He is one, perhaps more, of them, I should think."

"Aye," obeyed Edward as he strode painfully away toward the curious and apprehensive crowd, which milled about, but avoided the armed Scots when they could.

The drawbridge, still down, suddenly shook with a thunderous roar. The returning Comyn horsemen, having charged through the open barbican gate, supposed the portcullis to be open as well, only to find it closed tight against them. "Hold! Withdraw!" shouted the captain of the contingent, reining in his own great stallion. "Withdraw!"

The narrow bridge allowed no room for the heavily armored, mounted men to stop so quickly, much less turn around, and those behind the forward troop found themselves in collision with them.

A number of the still-mounted knights fell into the moat with much cursing and great splashes, the weighty metal of their protective armor drawing them all the way to the miry bottom, from which many never rose.

Sir Christopher, hearing the commotion on the other side of the gate, rushed up the stairs and into the gatehouse to peer down at the pandemonium on the drawbridge. Seeing the calamity, he broke into uproarious laughter, so much so that the men on the drawbridge were even more unnerved and thrashed around in greater panic, sending more of them off the sides onto their drowning mates.

He suddenly ceased laughing when an arrow whizzed through the air and struck the window casing next to his face before falling harmlessly to the floor. "Who among ye got an arrow off in that madness?" rhetorically asked Christopher of the men on the bridge. They were still unable to control their mounts and get wheeled around in the tight quarters.

Adjudging that the hapless fellows on the drawbridge were of no present danger to the conquering Scots, Christopher quickly lost interest in the spectacle. Returning below, he found Robert and several knights with a battering ram gathered around the door to the castle's great hall. Christopher walked across the bailey to stand beside Robert, asking as he approached, "What wee creature have ye caught behind this door, Rob?"

"Damned English judges, Edward's own, who sit in judgment of Scots! I mean to have them leave, or give them a taste of what they can expect in hell!" said Robert pointing his flaming torch toward the door. "I'll surely roast them like the swine that they are if they do not come out!"

Inside the large room were six judges, appointed by King Edward, who had held court there that day. Before retiring for the evening, they had feasted in the great hall and, calling for strong libation, had drunk too much. Brus' contingent had arrived at the gate while the justices were yet at table, telling each other uproarious tales and jokes and wishing there were agreeable females in attendance, that they might show them English prowess in the art of making love. Alas, there were no maids about, even to give an occasional pinch, and one of the diners had just decided that the smooth-faced young lads who waited their table would suffice, when the great clamor arose in the courtyard.

Within moments, one of the scullery vassals had run in from the kitchen and shouted, "The castle is under attack by the Earl of Carrick!" At that, the Scottish lads had bolted the room and disappeared.

Running to the front of the hall as fast as they were able in their overly sated condition, the justices had viewed the carnage through the smoke and dust, and grew ever more sober and afraid. Their position, should the castle be taken by Brus and his men, was precarious at best. Like one watching the hangman approach, they stood in dread as the English defenses crumbled, knowing all the while that the result would not be favorable to them.

Thus, they sought to fortify themselves in their hiding place, and pushed as much of the heavier furniture against the door as they could move. Then, having nothing else heavier at hand than their own fat, sweating bodies, pushed themselves hard against the piled furniture.

"Have ye yet tried the battering ram?" asked Christopher, pointing to the four knights and the ram.

"Aye, we hammered it a couple of times. It's ironbound oak... and thick. Tough work to batter in such a door, so I'm thinkin' we'll just set it afire and let the flames do the deed for us," replied Robert loudly enough that it could be heard from behind the door. "We are in no great hurry."

"'Tain't a good thing, killin' English judges, Rob," advised Christopher quietly, putting his arm on Robert's shoulder.

"Aye," agreed Robert, "Nothin' of this night's adventure has been good for English relations."

"They're close by the door. Ye can hear them whimperin' and cryin'," said Christopher with his ear to the door.

"'Twould be them, a'right."

"Pray, let me handle this for ye, Laird Robert," replied Christopher, bowing.

Robert looked quizzically at Christopher then passed the torch to him.

"Ye might want to send some stout Scots to see to ol' Comyn's men, piled on the drawbridge!" shouted Christopher. "They'd be easy pickin's for those crossbows we just captured."

Robert threw up his hand to acknowledge that he had heard Christopher as he turned and walked toward the open bailey. There he sighted Constable Siward, trussed by his hands, shivering in the cold atop the barrel behind which he had hidden near the burning guard barracks.

"Come with me!" demanded Robert, grabbing the constable by the collar and jerking him to his feet.

"We goin' to hang him?" asked Edward as he hurriedly limped to Robert's side and walked with him.

"Nay, not yet, little brother," replied Robert, forcing the stumbling man toward the gatehouse. "He has advantage to us still."

Up the circular steps went the three men, one fairly dragging another and the third following, until they came to the upper chamber of the gatehouse, the constable's personal quarters. The constable's wife, abed with the covers pulled up to her eyes, shrieked in alarm as the men entered her bedchamber.

"Fear not woman! We want only yer window overlookin' the bridge," Robert stated flatly. She pointed to two small stained-glass windows as she clapped the other hand across her mouth in an effort to stifle her screams.

Edward opened the window as Robert got close to the constable's ear and sternly whispered, "John 'The Red' Comyn and Robert Comyn lie in yonder church, dead! Advise these men to take the bodies back to Dalswinton, tonight, and await further orders, for Robert de Brus, earl of Carrick, holds Castle Dumfries."

Sir Richard relayed the message nervously, but almost verbatim. The captain of the remaining troops understood and, his command greatly reduced in strength, complied.

"Ye did well, Constable," said Robert, removing the bindings from the exhausted man's wrists. "Just stay here with yer woman and no harm will come to either of ye."

He and Edward started to leave the room, but Robert turned back, adding, "Don't bother boltin' yer door. We'll have need of ye on the morn." As the stalwart pair closed the door behind them, the constable fainted dead away.

Returning to the bailey, Robert and Edward found Christopher holding the six judges in a huddle, still in their robes and wrapped in blankets, shivering in the frosty night wind outside the castle's church.

"I see they've chosen wisely," said Robert.

"Being such insightful and sage justices," Christopher said mockingly, "they soon came to realize that their stand against us would be foolhardy and wasteful of their own lives, especially after my men entered the hall through the kitchen and surrounded them."

The three of them roared with laughter, much to the chagrin of their captives.

None of the judges spoke out in their own defense, not yet knowing what the Scottish barbarian had in store for them, but revenge weighed heavily on their minds.

"Give them one hour here, then put them in yonder oxcart and send them on their way. And wrap them well and amply provision them, for I want them to report to 'Longshanks' feelin' fit and mean," ordered Robert. To Edward he said, "Send those English soldiers and mercenaries on foot with the six of them. Meanwhile, set a guard. See that all is secure. Then we'll meet in the Great Hall for food and drink and talk of a plan."

Later, as the judges' oxen took their first steps toward London, dragging the heavy cart through the gate, the vanquished party expected little kindness from the Scots along the route, many of whom had at least one family member or neighbor who had fallen victim to the prejudiced verdicts. They would have no friends until they entered England, days hence.

"These are the ones ye wanted, Robert," announced Edward, shoving two young men through the door of the Great Hall and to the front of the table, where Robert leaned his head heavily on the palms of his hands in meditation.

"What?" questioned Robert, looking up into the dirty faces of two ill-kempt, shabbily clothed youths, but not yet understanding the intrusion. The boys, not knowing what was afoot, started looking for a quick way out of the hall.

"The ones that took care of the crossbowmen on the wall," reminded Edward. "Ye said ye wanted to know who they were."

"Ach, of course," remembered Robert in a tired voice, his head still throbbing from the blow it took earlier at the church. "I wanted personally to thank ye, and all the other loyal Scots who helped us, tonight. Ye have reason to rejoice, for tonight we have made the first blow for an independent Scotland."

"Thank ye, Milord," said the larger of the two, who grinned snaggle-toothed at the nobleman.

The second of the two young men stepped forward and said nervously, "Yer Lairdship, we know nothin' about the doin's of the nobles. We are simple people. But, we are not English slaves! Show us a way to a life without the English, and we will follow where ye lead."

Robert again bowed his head, his eyes fixed on the single candle in front of him. "Dear God! What have I wrought upon these people?" he worried under his breath.

"Thank ye, men," said Edward, realizing Robert's state of mind. With a couple of hearty slaps on their bony young backs, he assured them that their fight for Scotland's freedom would need the likes of such superior bowmen, as he ushered them out the door.

Robert was still fixated a few minutes later when Roger Kirkpatrick walked in and sat across from him at the table. His presence stirred Robert from his black thoughts, and he said, "I see ye're no worse for wounds than when last we talked, Roger."

Holding his mighty hands out in front of him and looking up and down his forearms, he said loudly, "They might have got my eye, way back, but they hain't caught up with the rest of me yet!" With that he laughed boisterously and pounded the table. Then, he demanded, "Where's the food?"

"Comin' directly," answered Robert, as Edward Brus and James Lindsay entered noisily, followed by Christopher Seton and several of the knights who had not yet been posted. "Gather 'round, men!" Robert waved. "Let us share a drink to our victory!"

Or a terrible, bloody disaster, he added in his thoughts.

Roger and one of the knights poured wine from the half-empty bottles left by the departed judges. Soon, every man had a cup and stood close to Robert and Edward, hearts pounding in anticipation of the coming effort.

"To victory!" shouted Edward excitedly. The assemblage held their cups high and drank deeply of the intoxicating contents. Several more rounds were poured and drunk, and soon the shouts were louder, the boasts greater, the impending struggles all but won.

About then, the kitchen doors swung open and a great roast pig was carried into the room by the head cook of the castle and his helper. Lesser cooks and pages followed carrying spit-cooked geese, cheeses, breads, fruit pies, and more bottles of wine.

Robust cheers went up all around from the hungry Scots.

It was a feast that had been a gift, hurriedly, but deliciously, prepared by fellow countrymen and gratefully accepted by the warriors. Most of it came from stores laid in by the English for their stay, and that made the victuals taste all the sweeter.

"See that the sentries are fed," asked Robert of one of the attending cooks.

He bowed, "'Tis being done, Milaird."

Robert nodded, whereupon he said quietly, "Leave us to our repast, then, and know that yer efforts this day have fueled to her service those who love Scotland." He then turned to the bounty before him and his comrades, some of whom were already partaking ravenously of the largesse at the candlelit table.

"Hold, lads," he said, "let us offer up thanks for God's bounty before we forget 'twas His hand provided it."

Roger growled under his breath, "And all the while, I thought it was left for us by the English!" A couple of young fellows guffawed, but Robert's stern visage soon quieted them, and they bowed their heads when he did. The soldiers' grace was short and plain, there being no priest attending, and the men gladly accepted its end with a ragged chorus of "Amens."

Robert wearily sat at the table and a plate of food suddenly appeared before him as if by magic. Even before he took his first morsel, the men's thoughts had turned to the morrow.

"What now, Robert?" asked Edward, looking up from gnawing on a large portion of meat, his face and hands shining with the fat of the pork.

Robert paused to wash down a mouthful of the succulent meat with a draught of wine. "First, James will go back to Lochmaben and tell the family of the events of this night," said Robert, directing his conversation toward James Lindsay. "Elizabeth and each of our brothers must be told of these events, so if any have wandered elsewhere, track them down, James. It is sure the Comyn family will look to strike us back hard and fast for the killin's at Greyfriar's." He threw his dog a bone still heavy with meat. The dog caught the gift in mid-air and retreated to his place nearer the fire to enjoy it.

"Aye, I will leave on the dawn light," replied James before swallowing the remainder of the wine in his cup.

Robert pushed back trenchers and food with his forearm to clear a spot on the wooden table, dipped his finger in his wine, and began to draw a map.

"We're leavin' Roger in command here, in Dumfries," he explained as he put a drop of wine from the tip of his index finger in the middle of the open space on the table. "There are three English controlled castles that keep us from the Firth of Clyde, here," to the left of the single drop he roughly drew in the western coast for a hundred miles. "Then, from the Orkneys and Ireland, where our kin and friends abide, here and here," he left droplets at each, "we can get supplies and reinforcements."

He glanced around the table at all the earnest young faces and said simply, "This we must control."

"We takin' them other castles?" asked Edward.

"Aye, we must, " said Robert soberly. "'Tis our only hope."

"There are only twenty of us who can fight," protested James.

"And a dog as good as any three Englishman like those we met tonight!" added Robert. They all laughed. When they had again grown quiet, he spoke. "But there are many stout men in just this castle, alone... and in the village, who will join our little band," surmised Robert.

"I don't like to mention this, Rob, "said Christopher, leaning into the group, his face grave," but ye are runnin' against yer luck to think that ye will be cheered by the people."

"How so?" asked Edward, somewhat affronted.

"Because we killed on holy ground," answered Robert, "and Christopher is right."

Roger sat down the table from Robert, making the same low growling noise he always made while he ate. The growl stopped as, for the first time since he took up eating of this banquet, his one eye looked up from his plate. The thought had never occurred to him that this brave night's work could end in sudden failure.

"Christopher and I will ride to Bishop Wishart in Glasgow," Robert decided. "We... I will accept all responsibility and ask for the church's forgiveness, for the liberty of our Mother Scotland."

"Aye," agreed Christopher. "The Scottish clergy are sore afraid of being crushed under the heel of the English Crown, Rob. 'Twould be well judged also to pledge the independence of the church, to hold them sided with ye."

Robert nodded, and put his finger into his cup. "Edward, and Thomas of the cropped ear," this generated a snicker among his men and a grin from Thomas, "...will rally an army and meet us..." he pushed his finger, with a fresh drop of wine, in a circular motion to indicate another site on his table map, "...there, near Ayr, in three days time. Ayr will be the first of our objectives."

"Ayr it is!" shouted Thomas. "We'll get ye the meanest bunch of Scotsmen that e'er swung a stick, Robert."

Edward agreed, his heart pumping so hard already that he could hear the blood rushing in his ears, in anticipation of what they were about to undertake.

"Then we shall leave on the dawn with James," said Robert. He drained the last of the wine from his cup and retired.

FEBRUARY 18th 1306
WESTMINSTER IN LONDON

"You surely took yourselves a leisurely journey!" uttered Edward sarcastically to the six judges standing before his throne. They were clad in dirty, raggedy robes and carried a bit less weight than they had when they left Dumfries seven days earlier.

Indeed, they had covered the distance between Dumfries and London in remarkable time, considering that their escort of soldiers had disappeared to make their own way back to England, the cart and almost all of the supplies had been stolen, and the ox had been roasted before they even reached the Scottish border.

Five of the judges found some refuge from the king's wrath by hiding behind the more corpulent body of the sixth as they cowered before their sovereign. They dared not take the time for a proper bath and clothes change when they arrived, for they had urgent news for their king.

"Sire," offered the largest of the judges, who was forced to assume the roll of spokesman by virtue of his forward position in the timid group, "we were taken at Dumfries Castle by a great and numerous horde led by the traitorous Lord Robert de Brus, earl of Carrick."

As his dumbfounded peers nodded in agreement, he continued with somewhat greater courage, "We have barely, and only with great bravery and daring, escaped with our lives, and have risked all to come before our most gracious liege," at which point the fleshy liar bowed as low as he could manage, "to bring our beloved sovereign information of the utmost importance!"

"LIES!" interrupted Edward stridently. "Fabricated lies! Anyone can look at this great mass of quivering flesh before me to see that there be not a single piece of backbone amongst the lot of you!"

He continued until he took a deep coughing fit. It racked his bony frame so ferociously that everyone then in the court wondered if fate had lent a hand to their being present to witness the coughing death of their monarch that day. They were, however (and some would say, greatly), disappointed that he regained control, his shoulders heaving as he struggled with his affliction.

He spat on the polished stone floor, wiped his mouth with a linen cloth, and continued his thought as if he had not lost a moment of time between. "Do you think that in these latter days I have not received dispatches from the north, brought by messengers who arrived from Scotland *days* ahead of you?"

The judges stood, silent and sweating, not knowing what response would please their king, or at least assuage his anger.

"In fact, I have yesterday received a missive from Lord Brus himself, claiming the castle... and the entire kingdom of Scotland!" he shrilly hollered at the judges. "What say you to that? Not only that little piss pot of a castle, but the whole damned country!"

His voice grew so high pitched that it seemed he might emit a womanly screech, but he managed to calm himself enough to sit quietly for a moment.

'Lord' Robert shall soon be no more, he thought. I shall see to that in short order.

He smiled a malignant little smile, unnerving everyone.

The quaking judges remained silent, and as motionless as they could manage, while Edward coolly peered at them across interlaced knuckles, mulling over the situation and the ramifications of his next move.

"How dare they throw out *my* judges," rhetorically questioned the king. "How *dare* these rebellious, snotty little Scots occupy *my* castle!?"

The massive wooden arm of the throne supported Edward's elbow as he leaned his head over and rested it on his open hand. His long, bony fingers moved across his brow, his fingernails digging deep into his forehead in prideful anguish as he successfully stifled another round of coughs.

He looked with disgust upon the shaking judges.

Then, suddenly as dispassionate as he had been rabid, he dismissed the judges with a simple wave of his hand.

The frightened six realized their luck and swiftly backed out of the throne room, bowing all the way. The king had decided he could not punish them for Robert Brus' success without heaping laurel wreaths upon Brus' head, and that he would not do.

After a long silence, during which he seemed lost in thought, King Edward motioned to Sir Fulco Ballard, his steward, to approach the throne. The man neared the throne and bowed low without saying a word, awaiting the king's desire.

"Send for the Earl of Pembroke," ordered the king.

"Yes, Milord," replied the steward.

Sarah

ϹΟΑRϹḋ 15ᵗʰ 1306
LOϹḋϹΟΑBEN ϹΑSϹLE

"Everybody's off to Scone, this morn," said the cook in a matter-of-fact voice, while she stirred the embers of the fire getting ready to bake two more loaves of bread. She rounded them expertly into floury brown lumps and placed them on the oven's hot stone floor for baking, as she had done almost every day of her life since she was a young girl.

Sarah sighed wistfully and continued to pack up some of the stores from the recently taken English castles, plus turnips and grains saved from the local fields, for the cook wagon that she would not be accompanying on the trip to Scone.

The chill early morning air could certainly not be felt in the kitchen. The fire on the hearth gave plenty of warmth and a cheery reddish glow to the entire room and beyond. The cooking pots, hanging in the fireplace, wafted delicious aromas throughout the courtyard as the two women, and several strong young vassals, prepared the morning meal and packed up the victuals for the trip.

Perhaps it was a blessing that the kitchen master was never underfoot this early in the morning. Even when there was a trip to prepare for, he preferred to lie abed.

"Still thinkin' about them lads, are ye?" asked the heavy woman sympathetically, as she wiped the flour off her hands and went about her normal routine with great efficiency. Every smidgen of flour was recovered and returned to the flour bin.

"Aye," answered Sarah.

"Ye likin' the Brus or the Randolph?"

"I'll be missin' Edward," she said, staring out the window in front of her.

"Oh, Edward is it?" smiled the woman. She tended to agree with that pick.

"And Thomas."

"Both?" questioned the cook, turning toward Sarah in surprise.

"Both." answered Sarah, and she put more victuals into boxes for the trip. "I'll ne'er have either, so I can miss them both, if I fancy," replied Sarah, sadly. She handed a large box or sack of stores to each of the young men who were helping tote and fetch things for the cook wagon.

After wrapping a heavy shawl around her shoulders, she picked up the remaining large box of foodstuffs in her own strong arms and walked out the kitchen door and into the courtyard. There, all was but choreographed tumult, with preparations for the trip clamoring in every corner of the place.

Sarah wandered through the crowd of armed men and weeping women, who were making last minute preparations and good-byes, with the songs of the piper sweetly melancholy in the air. The warmth of the early spring sun on her face felt good, but the coolness of the breeze and the lingering snow on the ground was a quick reminder that winter had not yet done its last work of the season. She shivered underneath the shawl.

Sarah off-loaded the weighty box into the arms of the cook's lad and looked around to see if she could spy Edward or Thomas. Both were against a wall, competing at throwing a knife at a dry leaf a few paces away.

Unbelievable, thought Sarah, frowning at the sight. She pulled her shawl tighter around her, both for warmth and to better show her well-formed figure.

Thomas glanced up and caught sight of the alluring Sarah watching them from across the way. He smiled at her meekly and kicked Edward, who was concentrating on his next toss.

"Stop kickin' me, ye bastard!"

"Ye had best look yonder," said Thomas through clenched teeth and a broad grin.

Edward turned and saw Sarah standing in the middle of the courtyard, still with a frown on her face. He waved and smiled, sheepishly.

Sarah stared for a moment then sashayed seductively toward them.

"Ye are leavin' this mornin'," she said, stating the obvious.

"Aye," said Thomas. "Will ye miss us?"

"I see little reason," she looked askance at the two knights. "Ye never seem to miss *me* a'tall while ye're out gallivantin' about the country-side."

"Gallivantin'! Gallivantin'!" Edward acted incensed, but his smile and his flirtatious approach to her gave the lie to his words. "Ye'd think we were naught more than common layabouts, rather than knights of the realm!"

"'Knights' my foot," she mocked them.

"Aye, knights!" insisted Thomas, in earnest. "Knights owin' fealty to our laird! And right now, our laird takes us away from here..." he moved closer to the young woman and touched her hair, "and from ye, Sarah, Lass, much to our dislikin.'"

"Ach, ye're likin' it fine, ye scoundrels! But, ye needn't think I'm savin' my biscuits for ye, neither. My biscuits'll not get stale while ye're out playin' at bein' 'knights.' So, farewell to ye, 'Sir Knights,'" she curtsied ever so slightly. "Think ye of my fresh, hot biscuits when ye're out in the cold," she whispered to them seductively, "...and doin' without."

"Oh, Sarah," Edward began, "don't be like that. We... both of us, love yer ... biscuits."

"That's true, Lass," added Thomas.

"So, then, ye would like some of my biscuits before ye depart?" she smiled.

"Aye," said Thomas, quickly, "I would."

"A'right, I'll have some, too, then... if Thomas is havin' some... I might as well have some, too... aye," stammered Edward. He began feeling quite hot in spite of the nippy morning air.

"Aye, ye might have a wee bit of Sarah's biscuits, Edward, but I want first bite," said Thomas, his eyes dancing with excitement and his trews getting tighter.

"Nay, Thomas, I am the older *and* I'm yer uncle. I get the first bite," argued Edward.

"Both of ye can have the first bite, ye arguin'... jackasses!"

"How's that?" puzzled Thomas.

"Here's all the biscuits ye can have!" she said, unknotting a cloth pouch from around her waist and holding it out in front of them. "Biscuits!... Just plain ol'... *damn* biscuits!" she scowled and thrust the cloth into Edward's hands. "Talk about *them* biscuits when ye be layin' on the cold ground, late at night, and see if they warm ye!"

Thomas looked at the little twist of biscuits, his trews now suddenly back to normal as he said, "I thought jackasses brayed."

Sarah simply shook her head in exasperation. Turning on her heel, she left and returned to the kitchen door, but not without a last look back at the two young men whose attention she had held so dear but a half moment ago.

She wiped the free-flowing tears from her eyes with the back of her hand and watched the two young nobles dig into the pouch and munch on the biscuits. Men! She thought angrily. She then disappeared into the kitchen.

Across the courtyard, Robert came out of the keep door with Christopher at his elbow. He was dressed in the breastplate that still held the dent from John Comyn's blade. Bareheaded as usual, with his helmet tucked under his arm, he now sported a fuller beard, neatly trimmed.

His obedient dog shadowed Robert's every move.

"See that this gets to Bishop Lamberton," commanded Robert as he handed a sealed parchment to Christopher, "Bishop Wishart already knows of my plan."

"I have two of my best men here. Lady Christian and I will personally see that it gets there, Robert," returned Christopher.

"Aye, I was hopin' ye'd understand the importance of it," said Robert, handing his helmet to his twelve-year-old squire, Andrew Stewart, as he passed. The youth was already laden with armor that included Robert's dress breastplate for the upcoming event, and, though the boy fairly staggered beneath his load, he took the helmet and piled it atop the other clothes and armor.

"There's Alexander," said Robert, sighted his brother riding into the courtyard. "I want to get whatever information he has gathered from the south these last few days." Both men approached the large horse reining up in front of them.

Alexander's thin, muscular body dismounted and he gladly clasped Robert's hand.

"Andrew! A cup of wine for my brother!" shouted Robert to his squire.

"Aye!" was the boy's quick answer, and he threw the brightly polished armor onto the muddy ground. Robert frowned when he saw his fine breastplate laying pell-mell with the rest of the armload.

The squire, seeing his master's displeasure, started picking up the bundle, but Robert repeated his order, barking, "Wine for my brother!'

Once again, the bundle, including the breastplate and helmet, was dumped in the mud. The squire ran quickly to get the wine without the slightest glance toward Robert for fear he would again misinterpret his lord's frown.

A groom arrived and took Alexander's horse by the reins, and headed toward the stable with the tired stallion.

"I'll need a fresh mount for the ride today," said Alexander to the man.

"Aye, Milord, it will be so," answered the groom, and Alexander turned back to the two men.

"There is much talk at Cambridge about ye, Robert," spoke Alexander in low tones. "Ye are much maligned by many, and secretly praised by a few. I, of course," he teased, "remained neutral." This elicited a wry smile from his brother.

"Anything in regard to the king?" asked Christopher hastily.

"I hear he wants the return of his castles at Dumfries and Dunaverty... and Ayr, and Rothesay," he continued with an ever-broadening smile, "and Tibbers, and even John Comyn's little castle of Dalswinton. That's what ol' 'Longshanks' wants, so's the word."

"He knows how to get them," remarked Christopher, tapping the hilt of the claymore strapped to his waist.

"But no whisper of a plan afoot?" asked Robert.

"'Tis said..." Alexander wagged his head back and forth, all the while looking into the eyes of his brother, "he wants ye and all yer kin dead, which is probably true. And, I also heard he has sent for his cousin, the Earl of Pembroke, that fellow who married the sister of John Comyn."

"Aymer de Valence," said Robert, "Thomas Randolph speaks often of him."

"Aye. But that's only rumor, nothin' more," replied Alexander. He took the small utilitarian wine goblet from the hands of the squire, who had been standing dutifully in the cold wind, holding the vessel. "Thank ye, lad," he said.

"Milord," acknowledged the boy as he hurriedly attacked the chore of gathering up the master's belongings. Finding mud on one edge of the fine breastplate, he quickly wiped it off on his own tunic, hoping no one had seen, but afraid to turn and see if anyone had.

Robert shook his head and smiled as he watched the boy. "He'll make a fine squire, and even a knight, one day." The boy left with the bundle and made his way toward the arms wagon, leaving Robert's helmet on the ground where it had fallen. Robert shook his head again in disbelief, walked over, picked up the helmet and tucked it back under his arm. "One day," he commented with a smile, "one day."

"I'll be to horse now," said Christopher, motioning for his mount. He tucked the message for Bishop Lamberton into a small pouch under his cloak.

"God be with ye," said Robert as Christopher climbed upon his horse.

"God be with ye," echoed Alexander.

"And God grant ye safe journey to Scone, Lord Robert Brus," said Christopher, taking Robert's hand in farewell. Then, he wheeled around and made for the gate. In a moment, he was across the drawbridge and on the road toward Saint Andrews.

"We'll be on the road, directly," said Robert, turning to Alexander and putting his arm across the smaller man's shoulder. "We wait, now, only for yer sister-in-law."

"Aye. Where's brother Thomas?" asked Alexander, scanning the courtyard.

"He and Nigel have gone ahead to Scone, makin' necessary arrangements," answered Robert.

"That's good," replied Alexander with a yawn and a stretch, adding, "Think I'll take a wee nap in the bed of one of the wagons, soon as we're out of sight of the castle."

"Aye, ye deserve a sleep for sure, Alex," said Robert, slapping his brother's shoulder. "Spyin' is wearin' on the mind and the body."

At that moment, Elizabeth emerged through the keep doorway, followed by her two personal maids.

Her husband thought she was exquisitely beautiful in her new dress, subtly embroidered with a festooned lion rampant on the bodice, and a handsome plaid shawl around her shoulders. But, he also thought she was beautiful in her plainest garb.

Robert strode to her, took her hand, and kissed it. "Ye look as radiant as this glorious day, Lady Brus," he spoke, waving his hand across the span of the sky.

"And ye, Lord Brus," answered Elizabeth with a restrained smile, "are the most handsome man alive, dented ol' breastplate and all."

"Andrew has the good one settled on board the wagon, woman," he justified his decision to wear the old one. He leaned toward his wife and nibbled her on the cheek.

"Nay, nay," whispered Elizabeth teasingly, "'Tis not appropriate, and besides, yer beard tickles..." she continued her thought visually with a raised eyebrow and a sideways glance toward the gathered throng.

Robert looked around, "Aye," he reluctantly agreed. Their private moments would have to be later.

Taking account of the throng, she said, "Ye have yerself a bit more army than ye had when ye left with those twenty knights, a little more than a month ago."

"Aye, and we have garrisoned six castles with volunteers," answered

Robert, adding, "More will join us on our journey this week, they will."

"Ah," mused Elizabeth half aloud, "if my father could see me now."

"And, if he could?" asked Robert as he placed her arm across his and both walked toward the crowd. The two maidservants followed.

She took a deep breath and said, "Me, prancin' off to Scone to be Queen of Scots, and ye the king... and my father, one of 'Longshanks' most favored lieutenants. I think he would be rather perturbed with his rebel son-in-law... *and* daughter."

"He'll get over it," whispered Robert unconvincingly. "In a year or two... he'll come see his grandchild... or maybe, grandchildren... for sure." He grinned.

Elizabeth was quiet, wondering what the next two years would hold for her family, and for Scotland. She knew that King Edward would not accept lightly this rebellion of the only man in Scotland who could hold any kind of alliance, army or government, together. She breathed a deep sigh as she turned to look at the stone keep once more, having been so happy there. Would she ever see the keep, or such happiness, again?

Robert helped her onto her handsome white stallion. His daughter, Marjorie, was already astride her palfrey and talking to several children of about her own age, standing on the ground beside her.

The two maidservants climbed into a waiting horse-drawn cart in which two chairs had been lashed, and made themselves comfortable by piling blankets on their laps to ward off the morning chill.

"Ye'll be a'right," said Robert earnestly, while gently patting Elizabeth on the leg.

"I ne'er had a thought otherwise," she returned spiritedly.

Robert smiled at her, then turned and signaled a groom to bring his huge chestnut Belgian from where the groom held it a few paces away. Andrew held the controversial helmet while Robert effortlessly mounted, then reached to take his helmet from his squire, and fitted it on.

Edward Brus saw his brother in the saddle and shouted to the others, "To horse!"

The squire hoisted Robert's newly-painted yellow and red lion shield up to him. This'll not be long in bein' shed, Robert thought as he hefted the heavy shield.

Ten knights and seven hobelars, or horsed archers, mounted and proceeded in twos to lead the others through the gate and across the drawbridge. The women went next, then the wagons. On foot, servants followed the wagons, though some of them jumped into the wagons as the drivers urged the oxen to action with calls, whistles, and prodding with sticks and lashes. Following were seventy-two foot infantrymen, two beef cattle, a handful of sheep, a milk cow, a herder, and two dogs to tend the stock. Lastly, two dozen additional knights marked the rear of the caravan.

Robert drew his claymore, held it high above his head, and swung it in a circular motion. His huge destrier reared up; the heavy armor and leather clanged and crunched as the great weight returned to earth with a jolt. Then, with a loud whoop, Robert spurred his horse to the front and the procession was on its way.

"I can just imagine Father on the battlefield, whoopin' like that, callin' to his men to fight on and to win," said Marjorie excitedly as she held her own spirited mount to a walk.

"And a whole nation to do the same," added Elizabeth in a whisper, as she leaned toward the girl.

The rest of the procession passed the seventy-two foot soldiers, who lined the exit, cheering and shaking their pole-axes, halberds, and pikes in salute, while waiting their turn to join in the line.

Robert returned their salute by placing his claymore across his chest. The entire procession was thus fed through the gate, across the wide moat, and down the rutted, muddy road to Scone.

. .

It was miles away from the castle and early afternoon of the same day when Robert, still riding in the lead, reined up his mount and threw up his hand for the procession to halt. The knights immediately assumed defensive positions and Elizabeth spurred her stallion toward the front of the line, where Robert was assessing the danger.

"What is it, Robert?" asked Elizabeth as she rode to his side.

"A lad, yonder, on a black palfrey, blockin' the road," he answered, looking about for other possible horsemen. "He just stands there, not makin' way, nor offerin' any threat."

"Surely, ye are not afraid of a poor trifling lad, and ye with yer army, are ye, Robert?" she teased.

"What holds my interest, woman, is that he carries the blue and white shield of the Douglas," said Robert, ignoring her tease.

"'Tis curious... The Douglas is dead these many years," she agreed, and her mild fascination increased as the black horse and its rider began to approach at a walk. They quietly continued to watch, not only the rider, but the area surrounding them as well, to see if the lad was perhaps a decoy for attackers.

Robert could detect nothing that indicated there were others near. Finally, he said, "Our curiosity will be satisfied soon enough now," and he spurred his horse to meet the on-comer before the lad got too close to the women and the column.

The youth continued his easy pace.

Elizabeth, joined by three of the knights, kept an eye on the two as they met and casually stopped, facing each other.

Robert properly spoke first, asking, "Why stand ye here in the road, lad?"

"Ye be Laird Robert de Brus of Carrick and Annandale?" asked the rider, ignoring the question.

"I am. And who would ye be?" Robert immediately liked the young man's confident gaze that met his own without fear.

"James Douglas, Milord, recent squire to Bishop Lamberton." He bowed his head in respect.

"And are ye akin to Sir William Douglas," the laird asked, suspecting the answer by the boy's demeanor.

"I have the great honor to be his son, Milord," was the straightforward response. "They call me 'The Black' Douglas."

"For the black locks ye're tossin' about, or...?"

"Aye, 'tis the locks, I fear," laughed James. At that moment, he swung his leg over his mount's rump and dismounted, leaving his shield on his saddle. "Milord, I am told ye are goin' against King Edward," he paused and lowered himself to his knees, his voice strong and sure. "If that is yer intent, I ask that ye take me with ye."

Robert also dismounted, and, offering the young man his hand, pulled James to his feet.

Observing from her distance, Elizabeth said quietly, "I suppose he's not too dangerous, then." She wheeled around and went to the cart where her maids were riding.

"I would advise ye to take advantage of this break for a bit of exercise and any necessaries," she said, at which the women both jumped from the cart. Elizabeth remained in the saddle, however, and kept one eye on Robert and the stranger as they discussed the past and future.

Robert was saying, "I knew yer grandfather, and fought many times 'long side yer father, Lad. They were brave and able men, and, I trust, ye are of the same seed."

"With God's succor," replied James. The young man reverently placed his hand on the shield with its three white stars on a blue bar above a white field, "This shield was my father's. It, and the honor it represents, is everything that is my inheritance. All else went when 'Longshanks' executed my father in the Tower, and placed my ancestral lands, including Castle Douglas, in the hands of Sir Robert Clifford. The good Bishop pleaded with the king for the return of my lands and title, that I might properly care for my mother and family, but his words fell on stony ground."

"Lamberton is a fine man," Robert nodded. "'Tis regrettable that Edward would not hear his pleas and grant yer mother sustenance."

"Aye, Milord, but as the king has chosen, thus shall it be. He has made me doubly his enemy. I will avenge my father and mother, and defend Scotland, to my last breath. I will regain my family's heritage. And if, as I have heard, ye have decided upon accepting the crown of the Scots, then, for the good or the bad, my fealty shall be e'er with ye."

"We are now on our way to Scone, where I shall soon be crowned, God willing."

"Then, My Lord Robert, I do now swear before God that I shall defend ye, and Scotland, to the end of my life."

Robert was overwhelmed with the young man's pledge and expressed his great gratitude, adding, "James Douglas, son of Sir William Douglas, hero of Scotland, kneel!"

Edward Brus moved to the front of the halted caravan in time to see the young Douglas kneel before his brother as Robert's great claymore came forth from its scabbard. "I don't think he's cuttin' off the poor lad's head, so he must be creatin' Scotland a new knight."

Edward watched Robert touch the tip of the sword blade to each of the kneeling youth's shoulders, after which the two climbed atop their mounts. Edward gave a signal, and the retinue quickly reformed for travel.

"Climb aboard, quickly, ladies," ordered Elizabeth.

"That was not much of a stretch," remarked Marjorie as she reined up beside Elizabeth.

"We'll be stoppin' for the night, soon," replied Elizabeth. The knights before them moved on, and she and Marjorie proceeded at a walk behind them. "And before ye know it," she continued, smiling at the young girl, "in a day or two beyond the Sabbath, ye'll be in Scone."

"But this is only Wednesday," complained Marjorie.

"Aye, and a beautiful Wednesday at that," returned Elizabeth.

Robert Wishart
Bishop of Glasgow

MARCH 23ᴿᴰ 1306
THE ABBEY IN THE TOWN OF SCONE

The Bishop's foot came down heavily upon the oak plank floor of the ancient abbey and he looked up at his companion with a mischievous sparkle in his aging eye. He stomped two more times then said, "Sounds solid enough, doesn't it, my lad?"

"Aye, Yer Grace," answered the puzzled eleven-year-old squire. He had just rolled the heavy carpet back at the Bishop's behest, exposing the area of the floor on which the old man was now demonstrating …something. The boy knew not what.

"None would guess the secret that lies beneath my foot, for they ne'er would know there was anything of interest beyond this stout oaken board, they wouldn't," said Robert Wishart, Bishop of Glasgow, with delight.

The squire was curious but courteously silent.

"Take this," instructed the bishop as he unsheathed the razor-sharp dagger he kept deep in his clerical robes and handed it to the boy. "Now, with this wee sgian dubh, pick at that length of board, right there, aye, that's right, so that ye can raise it up a bit, lad." The board loosened easily as the boy obediently twisted the blade of the small dagger into the tightly fitted seam between the plank designated and its neighbor.

"Now, pull it out, laddie!" said the bishop with almost childish exuberance. "Pull it out!"

The boy returned the knife to the bishop, then with his long, thin fingers holding accessible the gap he had wedged open, he pulled the short board from the floor. That, in turn, released another, longer board. Quickly, for a man of his age, the Bishop got down on his knees to remove the second plank, after which a large section of the flooring was easily removed, revealing a space that, to the boy, looked and smelled like an open grave.

He knew that important people were often buried under the floors of churches, and he began to lose his curiosity about what was beneath this one.

Nevertheless, he helped the old man lift the heavy section of floor out of the way and push it on top of the rolled carpet. The bishop peered into a pitch black, man-sized hole.

"Get us two of those candles!" commanded Bishop Wishart, pointing behind himself as he put his head deeper into the hole, trying to get his eyes to adjust to the blackness before him.

Retrieving two candles from the holder on the table, the youth reluctantly drew close to the hole with a candle in each hand, then got down on his knees and elbows to see what the darkness concealed that the bishop wished to reclaim.

The old man turned and dangled his feet into the hole. The squire gasped at the perceived danger and started to his feet to fetch help, when the bishop chuckled and said, "It's a'right, Laddie! Do not fret so!"

The somewhat relieved boy slowly returned to his four-point stance with the two lighted candles flickering in his thin, nervous hands.

"I distinctly remember there being a stair in here, lo, those many years ago," he said to assure himself as much as the boy. Then he felt his foot rest upon something solid, and slid his haunches off the edge of the opening to stand firmly on one of the expected steps.

"Ah, my foot has a hold," said the old bishop, and he felt with one toe for the next step. "There 'tis," he smiled at the youth, and his bald head disappeared into the blackness, "Come, lad, hand me a candle and I will light the way ahead of ye," he said in a slightly muffled voice. "And be careful; the steps are worn smooth and a wee bit slippery."

The squire placed one of the candles in the elderly cleric's up-stretched hand and obediently climbed down the faintly visible steps cut in the rock to the floor of the small, secret room beneath the abbot's private chapel. He followed his leader to an alcove, a few steps off to one side of the subterranean room.

"'Tis cold, and it stinks down here, Yer Grace," complained the lad as he scrunched up his thin shoulders against the dark as much as the chill.

The old man ignored him and knelt before a large chest that he himself, a more youthful abbot at the time, had tucked against the wall in the corner, then closed up the chamber and left it a secret, until now.

"I was not able to save the hallowed 'Stone of Destiny,' nor the kingly crown, itself." He paused as he opened the moldy-smelling chest.

Bishop Wishart strained to lift from within the chest a large crockery jar, sealed tightly against moisture and air with beeswax. He strained his old body to set it down gently upon the stone floor and reached back into the chest to retrieve a second, almost identical jar.

He whispered reverently, "However, I did manage to hide these few things from those evil hands, praise be to God!"

The youth stood puzzled, looking at two old earthen vessels that seemed most commonplace and unattractive to him, while the Bishop gazed upon them with reverential reserve, hesitating to disturb them further.

Finally, the squire asked softly, "What's in the jars, Yer Worship?" He was holding his sleeve over his nose in an effort to lessen the smell of earth and decay, and craning his neck to see better as he watched the bishop run his aged fingers across the tops of the two cherished urns.

The old cleric imagined again the grand history their contents must have been a part of, many years before even his birth.

"These humble clay pots contain the robe and the banner of the crowned kings back unto the days before Scotland was," he said. With that, he again retrieved his sgian dubh from his robe and sliced through the beeswax on one of the jars until he felt the cover move.

He set the top gingerly onto the floor and reached inside the container to pull out a folded cloth that glittered in the flickering light, then got to his feet and let the material unfold. Reaching above his own head to prevent the robe from touching the floor, he held it up in the candlelight for the lad to see.

"'Tis beautiful," said the young squire, his eyes dancing with an excitement that now matched the old man's. "May I touch it?" he asked in a hushed whisper.

"Aye," he answered, "for ye and yer fellows are the reasons there is importance to it at all."

The boy ran his fingers across the sewn gold threads that had lost none of their luster from being hidden away.

"And, look upon this, Laddie," said the bishop as he handed the cloth to the boy and knelt again to unseal the other jar. From within this one, he partially unfolded the great banner of past kings with its red lilies and ancient lion symbols, and asked, "See how the past springs alive in yer hands, and in yer heart, when ye caress this sacred work."

The eleven-year-old squire reached out, touched the banner, and was struck with pure reverence, so that he, too, sank to his knees.

Marjorie Brus

CDARCh 25th 1306
The VILLAGE OF SCONE

Colorful flags and banners wafted gaily in the early spring sunlight, though there were still traces of winter snow lying about in the northern shadows of the buildings, and viscous mud was the main ingredient in the by-ways. The enterprising townspeople had been at work most of the night making the pastries, breads, and sweetmeats they now hawked to the gathering landed and moneyed visitors come to see the historic coronation of Robert de Brus.

Children played in, out, and between the knots of excited adults; though the young did not understand its importance, all joined in the celebration. As the sun rose higher in the sky the anticipation got all the more fervent. Then came the subdued clanging of a single bell at the cathedral, calling the notables to attendance at the event with a steady, measured rhythm. The Gothic arched wooden doors swung open and, Henry, the abbot of Scone, quietly directed that stones be placed against both to prevent their blowing shut in the gusty wind.

All who could do so put aside their normal business and hurried to the yard before the abbey, making sure to leave a broad path open to the doorway for the arriving guests to move easily through the crowd of curious onlookers. Many of the old folks, having seen the arrival of guests at the splendidly mounted coronation of King John de Balliol on St. Andrews Day, 1292, were disappointed that there were now pitifully few elegantly dressed nobles and knights and beautiful ladies.

Balliol's crowning was unlike any other in Scottish history, and was brought about by the unfortunate and closely timed deaths of King Alexander III and his only direct descendant to survive him, the infant "Maid of Norway." Succession was thus thrown open to the late king's nearest surviving relative, but none could easily declare whom that might be.

Alexander III descended from King David I through his grandson King William the Lion. John de Balliol and Robert de Brus, "the Noble," grandfather of the Robert de Brus being crowned this day, had both descended from William the Lion's brother, the earl of Huntingdon, who had no surviving sons. Robert de Brus was son of the earl's second daughter, Isabel. John de Balliol was the grandson of the earl's eldest daughter, Margaret. For the difference in generations and other reasons, many thought de Brus should be king. Others objected, because de Balliol, though a generation further from the king, descended from the earl's eldest daughter. There were a dozen others who also tried to claim the crown.

Eventually, the situation deteriorated to the point of imminent civil war.

The Guardians of Scotland requested the aid of King Edward, brother to their late king's first wife, to help adjudge who should be the next King of Scots. Unbeknownst to them, Edward had already violated Scots territorial sovereignty by occupying the Isle of Man, but outwardly he agreed to help, demanding "temporary" suzerainty over the country, which the Guardians, to their later regret, agreed.

There was a long, drawn-out court proceeding before the choice was finally made, and it was de Balliol, based, it was said, on the English law of primogeniture. All the Scottish earls and barons were required to swear allegiance to the new king, but the de Brus family did not, believing they had been cheated of a crown that was legitimately theirs. There were many who held the same belief, and further, that Edward had chosen to benefit himself and England, rather than Scotland, by choosing the most malleable of the claimants... John de Balliol.

The grandfather was forever after known as "The Competitor," in remembrance of his valid claim to the throne.

Even before de Balliol was crowned, he was called "Edward's puppet."

Thus it had been incumbent upon Edward to assure Balliol's acceptance by making much of him and his coronation. Hence, he came to Scone with hundreds of English noblemen and knights, magnificent in their ceremonial robes and armor, heralded by clarion horns, and followed by a lengthy train of attendants and courtiers of all descriptions.

There were alms aplenty to go around that day, all right.

But that was more than thirteen years ago. Alms fall more freely from fat, richly embroidered purses and fine linen or silken sleeves than from barren pouches and coarsely made or worn out tunics, of which there seemed to be an abundance, this day. There were slim pickin's to be had at the coronation of Robert de Brus, and not just among the common folk.

Inside the cold, dark nave hung the great banner of lions and lilies, on a line strung between two columns at the east end. There were so few candles within the nave that it would be fair dark as pitch were it not for the brilliant sun outside and the sanctuary's surviving tall arched windows. In the chancel stood a small choir of young men and boys who began singing as the lords and ladies and other dignitaries present took their cue and moved quietly into the church to view the momentous proceedings.

There was neither chair nor bench upon which a member of the gathering might rest, and unless they brought their own, none but the royal family had a cushion on which to kneel. The only chair in the entire building was to be used as throne for Robert, and was set squarely at center on a dais constructed for the purpose, before the altar in the sanctuary.

William Lamberton, bishop of Saint Andrews, his imposing person bedecked in his most impressive robes, approached his more humble colleague Bishop Wishart, as he stood chatting with the abbot. Hidden from the convening participants by a hanging tapestry, the clerics spoke in whispered words. "Greetings, Bishop, Abbot," Lamberton hailed his old friends.

"And a charmed and famous day to ye, Bishop Lamberton," said Wishart with a cheery smile that seemed to reflect the sentiments of many present in spite of the inherent danger. The Abbot merely nodded, a broad smile on his face, as well, but he soon excused himself to greet the Abbot of Inchafray, who was just arriving.

"I understand ye granted absolution and forgiveness to Robert de Brus for the unfortunate incident in the kirk at Dumfries," said Lamberton, leaning down to Wishart's level to insure confidence.

"Aye," the older man replied, suddenly frowning and adding without a flinch, "and I'd do it again, if need be, and I were called upon."

The large bishop drew up to his full height and looked down sternly at his feisty elder, "And, ye know what this means, Robert?"

"Aye," he replied, tears welled up in his eyes. "'Tis the very life of Scotland, it is, for sure."

"Not a gainsay have I for that, ol' friend," said Lamberton with a smile and a wee bit of mist in his own eyes. "But, Rome will have all our heads when word of these days' events reaches the ears of the Holy See."

"Be it so, then," replied Wishart, looking up at his friend, "and hope, when the ax doth threaten to fall, that we are glib of tongue and quick of foot."

"Aye, Sir," agreed Lamberton, chuckling wryly at the gallows humor.

David Murray, Bishop of Moray, joined the two as they waited for the ceremony to begin, and a quiet greeting among them ensued.

"Not many of our earls have come to behold this day," somberly observed Murray, who was nearly as tall as Lamberton, but not of his weight.

"Only Malcolm of Lennox and the Brus' ward, Donald of Mar, have I seen take their places," said Lamberton.

"There are four such brave souls here," claimed Wishart. "Lennox, Mar, John of Atholl... and Alan of Menteith, all are here to witness."

"And more to come?" asked Bishop Lamberton.

"Nay more," replied the old man shaking his head. "The rest are either of the Comyn family or hold their allegiance to Edward because they put their names to the Ragman Roll."

"Scarce a tenth full, the abbey is," again remarked Lamberton, "even including the knights, who, I see, have assumed their places along the walls."

The three fell silent as Elizabeth and Robert's daughter, Marjorie, entered with two young knights as escorts. They walked the length of the nave to the sun-filled sanctuary, and the Bruses knelt together on a long cushion below the dais in front of the altar, and remained there in prayer for several moments.

Marjorie crossed herself and stood, with the help of her knight escort, and waited for her stepmother to finish her prayers. Glancing up as she stood, Elizabeth perceived and nodded to the three figures in the shadows, who nodded piously and smiled at their soon-to-be-queen.

She joined Marjorie and walked to the opposite side of the room, as the Bishop of Moray whispered to his fellows, "Elizabeth will make Robert, and Scotland, a fine queen. A more noble or devout lady I never knew."

"Aye," both responded.

As the trio watched and commented amongst themselves at the continuing arrivals, there entered two of the sisters of Robert de Brus, Lady Mary de Brus, and Lady Christian Seton with her husband, Sir Christopher Seton. At the next figure striding into the room, Lamberton rolled his eyes upward and opined with disdain, "And here's that rogue Thomas Randolph! Surely, when he is crowned, the King will be forced to choose his companions more carefully!"

Bishop Wishart smiled. He greatly liked Thomas, though sometimes not his ways.

"Since the Earl of Fife is unable to perform his rightful duty, do ye suppose the ceremony will be regarded as legitimate?" asked Bishop Murray.

"Neither did young Duncan participate in the crownin' of King John, David," chided Wishart. "Yet, he was certainly received by the Community of the Realm as our sovereign."

"Aye, but Sir John de Saint John was 'legally' appointed to act as Duncan's surrogate. We have no such authority for anyone to act in his stead, today. Have we?" Moray persisted. "Is there even one who is *willin'* to place the crown on de Brus' head?"

"I know of none," bluntly stated Lamberton, shaking his head.

"Aye," replied Wishart sadly, "'tis not a perfect affair, but these are arduous days and desperate actions replace unachievable civilities."

The choir changed to a more joyous and uplifting hymn when Robert de Brus entered, unannounced and resplendent, with the ancient robe flowing over his highly polished, gold and polished steel ceremonial body armor. The huge claymore hung conspicuously at his side, and his left hand rested on its pommel as he walked. Robert's squire, Andrew, himself bedecked in a long robe and carrying two tall candles, followed proudly in his wake.

All but a few of the men in attendance bowed, and the ladies all curtsied, to greet the Brus as he passed.

Approaching the sun-dappled dais, Robert took notice of the "throne" chair. It was a fine chair, ornate and cushioned, but he had rather have sat upon that homely boulder called the "Stone of Destiny," on which Scottish kings, from earliest times through John de Balliol, had always been crowned before this.

That ancient relic was stolen on orders of King Edward as he plundered Scotland in 1296 to prove that his subjugation of the country was complete. Along with the Scottish crown and other royal accoutrements, religious artifacts, including Scotland's holiest relic... the Black Rood of Saint Margaret, believed to be a piece of the true cross... were removed to England. The Stone of Destiny was taken as a prize of war, and Westminster Abbey received the stone as a gift from Edward to his patron, Edward the Confessor.

Robert genuflected before the altar, crossed himself, rose, and turned to face the gathering, his square jaw set in determination. With his family by his side, he seated himself upon the throne chair to be crowned Robert, King of Scots, and to approach a most uncertain future.

The three bishops emerged from the alcove to take their places on either side of the throne. Wishart's young squire, he who had helped retrieve the royal vestments, approached the throne from the other side carrying a pillow made of exquisite silk brought from the east by Robert's father, also called Robert. While in the Holy Land on crusade the elder de Brus had purchased the rich cloth in a Jerusalem bazaar. Upon the pillow rested an unadorned circlet of gold, hastily but deftly fashioned, which would suffice as substitute for the crown that Edward had unlawfully claimed for himself.

The bishops prayed earnestly that the holy event be blessed in the names of Saint Andrew, Saint Mary, Mother Scotland, and the Scottish people, who had suffered so at the hands of the English, and now perhaps had a chance of breaking the tyrannical bonds Edward yet imposed upon them.

At Wishart's signal, his squire brought the crown closer to the bearded man seated in the chair. The boy wrinkled his nose in anticipation of encountering the well-remembered musty smell of the robe that Robert was now wearing and was pleasantly amazed when he found none. He looked at Robert and grinned. Robert returned his smile, then looked at the thin circlet on the large pillow.

It has no ancient festoonin' and no weighty tradition that must be lived up to, thought an amused Robert. So this must herald the beginnin' of new times.

He glanced at Elizabeth, who held her head higher as she looked into his eyes. Both doubted that another earl present would come forth for him, and so she gave her husband a subtle, approving nod.

He turned and beckoned the four Scottish earls to come face him and do the kingdom honor. They slowly obliged, and though Robert carefully observed their movements, not one indicated a willingness to place the crown upon the head of Robert de Brus.

The three bishops stood apparently reticent to act on Robert's behalf, for which he was just as glad

This is an awkward moment, thought Robert, as the choir sang in heightened anticipation, and no one moved to save the day. I shall have to place the crown upon my own brow, and his hand lifted but slightly from the arm of the chair.

At that point, Robert Wishart, the old bishop and patriot, suddenly began praying loudly and strode forward. At the end of his prayer, he picked up the crown from the pillow educing a slight gasp from the throng. He stretched to his full height to hold it in view of all as he placed it on the royal head, but Robert stood and looked down at his old friend.

"Nay, Bishop," he gently said as he took the crown from Wishart's trembling hands, "though I am eternally grateful for your willingness."

Robert sat on his throne again, and as the bishop said a few additional words, most of which were inaudible, Robert placed the gold circlet upon his own head. 'Twas done just that quickly. Afterwards, the bishop made the sign of the cross in the air before Robert, turned, and walked away, palms pressed together, head bowed.

For a long moment, there followed unexpected silence.

Bishop Lamberton, breath abated, nodded to the choirmaster, and the church was suddenly filled with music of joyous celebration, upon which all the Scots within the church, old and young, male and female, clerics and laymen, eventually even the dubious, applauded in a great swelling of pride and excitement.

With his close family and kinsmen crowding around him on all sides, Robert rose to greet the applause as one-by-one the earls, nobles, and knights came in turn to his place at the feet of Robert de Brus, now Robert, King of Scots, and swore fealty to him.

Robert's eyes filled with tears, knowing that their doing so showed great courage and patriotism, as all present fully understood that these actions would be considered treason by King Edward.

Above the church, bells rang out again, gaily this time and in celebratory profusion, to say the new king was crowned. The people waiting in the courtyard and nearby cheered in anticipation of seeing their new king.

Two squires in the service of the bishops were at last ordered to reopen the huge, old wooden doors that led into the courtyard. Cheers again roared from the crowd as Elizabeth placed her hand upon Robert's and they walked together, through the meager audience, out the doors into the bright sunlight, and greeted the town.

Robert's piper, who had been with the Brus family for most of his life and had known Robert's father and his grandfather "The Competitor," as well, was perhaps the proudest of them all as he arranged his drones against his shoulder, filled the bag, and began to play an old song of ancient kings and ancient victories.

He had played but one tune and a bit more before, as he stood proudly keeping time with his foot, he felt someone come alongside and touch his arm. Cutting his eyes around, but otherwise standing in place, the piper saw beside him a youth of perhaps fifteen years. Tucked under the lad's arm was a battered set of pipes.

The boy looked at the old piper and with a waggle of his head asked if he might play, too. The piper grinned broadly, affirming his approval, secretly hoping that the lad could play well enough to keep up.

The young piper blew into the blowpipe to fill the ancient bag, and the drones began their discordant song. The elder man had to concentrate hard to maintain the air he was playing, then suddenly, the lad jumped into the melody with the assurance of an experienced musician, and the two played gracefully together, as if they'd always done.

The mournful pipes sang as lonely background to the cheering crowd, but the old piper thought they were the essence of the hour as tears streamed down his craggy old face and disappeared into his gray beard.

The young men of the town and countryside crowded close to the royal couple to pledge their loyalty to the crown, and to pledge their lives in the fight against the English. Some were, no doubt, inspired by the colorful knights and wanted to be like them; others simply wanted matters to be ended with the usurpers from the south. No doubt the pageantry of the occasion brought out much patriotism that would otherwise have lain dormant indefinitely.

Robert accepted them all and thanked each one.

The four earls joined Robert and Elizabeth in saluting the people as most of the various members of the Brus family mingled in the gathering.

Nigel and Agnes stood back against the opened door facing the courtyard, for she had a disquieting fear of this talk of war that seemed to dance upon the air above the crowd. Her dismay was as far in the direction of foreboding as Nigel's was toward enthusiasm for joining the battle.

His love for her conceded to her sense of dread so that they withdrew from the joy of the day, and her love for him kept her from hiding under the bed.

The three bishops stood to the side, basking in God's glory and privately congratulating themselves at the significant part they had played in the success of the day.

"'Tis a miracle indeed," said Bishop Lamberton, beaming with pride.

The old bishop of Glasgow agreed with a nod of his head and tears flowing, for he had thought he would never live to see another independent King of Scots.

From that moment began revelry and jubilation that prevented early sleep by anyone in Scone that night. Word quickly went out to farm and town across the near countryside; there was a new-made king of Scotland, and though he had set the crown upon his own head, he had been crowned at Scone.

God save the King!

Before quiet settled upon the village again, it was early dawn, and the morning star stood low on the horizon.

. .

In the first daylight hours the next morning, as Robert and Elizabeth slept peacefully in each other's arms, there arose a sudden, loud commotion on the road in front of the large house in which much of the Brus family was temporarily staying.

"What is happenin', Robert?" asked Elizabeth as she sat bolt upright in the bed after having been shocked to consciousness.

"I know not," he answered grumpily as he got up from the bed, grabbed his claymore, and stepped quickly across the cold floor to gaze out the second story window onto the muddy road.

He wiped the window clear and squinted into the brightness of the early morning sun, then said, "'Tis a young woman on horseback, and a spirited one at that."

"Horse or woman?" asked Elizabeth as her feet touched the floor.

"Horse or woman, what?" He was too sleepy for riddles. They, especially, had enjoyed a particularly long evening before going to bed the night before, as everyone wanted to celebrate the coronation with the king on his first night. And celebrate they did, into the wee hours, which were, at present, not so long ago.

"Spirited!" said Elizabeth, a bit exasperated and groggy, herself.

"Oh," he said smiling at his tousled queen, "actually, both."

Elizabeth wrapped a blanket about her and came to the window. With a corner of the blanket she rubbed a good-sized clearing of pane for herself and viewed what transpired below.

There was the horse, just as Robert had said, and on it, a most spirited young woman who was arguing with the steward of the house. She was dressed in men's clothing, so that the long red hair that had come exposed from under her hood and the subtle ways her clothing clung to her body were the only tell-tale signs of her womanhood.

Robert hadn't mentioned that with the intruder were several squires, each having a horse to ride and one to lead, and not pack horses, either; each was as fine a destrier as Robert had seen in many years. If the attractive young woman were not enough to pique his curiosity, her magnificent horses certainly were.

"What are they saying?" asked Elizabeth. "Can ye make out their words?"

"She wants to see me, apparently," remarked Robert.

"Hm-m-m. Then, Sire, she's too pretty a young thing not to want to see me, too," teased Elizabeth as she wrapped herself more tightly in her makeshift mantle to ward off the chill in the air.

Returning his claymore to its scabbard, Robert next took the poker from the hearth and stirred up the fire, and put another good-sized log on the top.

"Ye'll be warm directly," he said, stretching and yawning as he went to his wardrobe for more presentable clothes in anticipation of the knock on the door, which came rather soon.

"Aye," he shouted through the door to answer the knock.

"Yer Lordship," spoke the Steward in a loud voice, "'I beg yer forgiveness, Sire, but there's a young woman below who claims to be the wife of Lord Buchan, and... and she wishes to have an audience with ye."

Robert remained silent for a moment, and the Steward added, "Aye, she says 'tis important for the King of Scotland, Sire."

Robert looked at Elizabeth and she at him. Robert scratched his still sleepy head and longed to crawl back under the covers with Elizabeth and put the young Countess off until a more decent hour. But instead he instructed the Steward, "Feed her and her companions their break-fasts and have her wait. The queen and I shall be along, presently." After the steward departed, he turned to Elizabeth and added with a seduc-tive grin, " ...but first, we must awaken properly! After all, this is our first full day as sovereign, and ye cannot refuse any request from yer king."

Elizabeth stepped quickly and laughingly avoided his grasp, though for but a moment. With a quick recovery, he wrapped his strong arm about her waist and pulled her close to him, whispering, "I hope the Countess is a patient woman!"

.   .

The king and queen entered the great hall within the hour and there found the bonny nineteen-year-old who claimed to be the Countess of Buchan, sitting alone at the table, picking at the remains of the food the Steward had brought. As soon as she saw the royal couple, the red-haired visitor stood and turned toward them, then bowed low, as noblewomen did at the English court.

"Arise, Lady Buchan," commanded Robert as he led Elizabeth to a chair on the hearth and seated her. "'Tis too far from London for such formalities this early in the day."

"Sire," the woman responded as she stood erect, still in her heavy cloak as it was cold in the great hall without a roaring fire.

While at the fireplace Robert stoked up the weak blaze, adding more fuel to help knock the chill out of the room.

"I welcome ye to my temporary home, Milady. I shall have a word with the Steward for not having prepared the fire to comfort ye." Then to his wife he said, "My dear, may I present the Countess of Buchan."

The young woman curtsied, less formally, to Elizabeth as Robert said, "Countess, my wife, the Queen of Scotland."

Elizabeth acknowledged the curtsy with a smile and a nod. Seeing the Queen's genuine smile, the Countess felt somewhat more at ease and began quickly to account for her presence.

"With yer permission, Sire, I will explain my intrusion at such an odd hour," she began. Robert waived his hand to indicate that he wished her to continue as he sat in a large chair near Elizabeth.

"My brother is Duncan, earl of Fife, and, as ye know, yet but a lad of sixteen. He is also, since our father's death, a ward of King Edward, and so was certainly not able to assume the traditional duty bestowed upon him as the one whose honor it is to lay the crown upon the head of the new King of Scots"

"This one is fast as lightnin' in the sky," remarked Robert, amused at the amount of information she had divulged in only half a moment.

The countess drew herself up to full height as her green eyes flashed at what she deemed was an affront, or worse, an expression of disbelief.

"Ye can't stay out of poor graces with the ladies, can ye, Robert?" said Elizabeth, gently chiding his poor manners. "Forgive yer king, Countess. He wakes badly when he has not completed his slumber."

"Indeed, Milady, I meant no insult, either to yer person or to yer words. Pray continue," Robert apologized. This was not at all what she had come to expect of a king, having grown up in the era of Edward.

"Sire, I truly am the Countess of Buchan, and the sister of the Earl of Fife, as I claim. My name is Isabel MacDuff, and I rode with my companions for two nights and a day to get here ere the coronation, which I understand, was yesterday."

"Aye, it was," Robert confirmed.

"My Lord King, I came all this way to uphold my brother's honor and do for ye that that he could not do for ye, yesterday."

"Which was what, yesterday...?" queried Robert, losing her meaning.

"Put that wee crown on yer head, Robert," said Elizabeth.

"Aye, Sire. In lieu of my brother, I have come to crown my King properly as my fathers have done before me, and my brother would do, could he but be here."

Robert looked at the woman, unsure of what he could trust about what she had said. "Countess, is it not so that yer husband's loyalties are to King Edward, and that he is also near kin to the Comyn family?"

"It is so, Sire, but..." she started to say, but was interrupted by Elizabeth.

"Which makes it all the more remarkable that she is here!" Elizabeth spoke in her stead, having been taken with the young woman's ardor and frankness.

She stood and walked to her husband. "Robert, ye are her king! And, if captured, she will pay dearly for what she is offerin' to do for ye, and for Scotland, now."

Robert said nothing but sat in his chair, looking at the two women, first one, then the other. He often wished Elizabeth would keep her own counsel, at least before outsiders, though she was most often right in her judgment of honest character and sincerity.

Again, the countess opened her mouth to say something, but Elizabeth frowned and motioned to her to be silent. The young woman stood quietly on the hearth and began to realize some warmth from the fire. Removing the heavy, mud-spattered cloak, she revealed that she carried two weapons: one a sgian dubh, was not common, but neither was it unusual for a woman to carry; the other, a short sword, certainly was. Robert and Elizabeth both noticed the armament hanging from the young woman's belt when she crossed to the table to lay her doffed cloak there. Robert came to his feet.

"By my grandfather's beard!" he exclaimed, amused. "This woman comes with more blades than half my foot soldiers!"

Crossing his arms, he strolled around the young countess, gently taunting her, "Do ye come to murder yer king for Edward, or do ye disguise yerself as a man to make safer yer journey to Scone?"

"Neither, Sire." Her freckled cheeks flushed as she responded to his teases. She turned to face him directly, and said matter-of-factly, "I have come to fight for Scotland!"

Turning his face away and pretending to clear his throat, Robert restrained an impolite guffaw, for he realized that the pretty young girl was speaking from her heart. He also knew that this snip of a girl would not last through the first wave of an attack, much less survive a battle.

He finally asked, trying to be kind, "And how, should I permit ye to join my army, might ye be of benefit to me in a fight? Could ye join the pikemen in forming a wall against Edward's horsed knights? Could ye wade into his soldiers of foot and lay waste to them with yer claymore? Could ye..."

"Perhaps not with a claymore," speaking softly she interrupted the king, her cheeks still brightly red, "but I am deft at wielding a short sword. And I have achieved an excellent skill with both cross and long bows, having hunted stag with my father and brothers."

For what seemed an eternity to the two women, and but a moment to Robert, the only sounds to be heard were the cracklings of the logs on the hearth, as the king ruminated upon the problem laid before him.

Though he greatly admired her courage and spirit, he could not in all conscience entertain a thought of taking her into battle. Neither did he want to break her zeal or diminish her boldness.

Finally he said firmly, "I cannot take ye into the field with my army." The countess dropped her eyes in great disappointment. "Yer merest presence on the field would distract my soldiers from their purpose, leading to their destruction and, perhaps, the loss of the battle."

He looked at Elizabeth, who kept a stoic countenance knowing that Robert's decision was just, if discouraging to the countess.

After giving her a moment to adjust to the setback of her desires, he took the girl by her shoulders and said, "Isabel MacDuff, Countess of Buchan, sister to the Earl of Fife, I would be honored if ye would place this crown, again, upon my head, that I might have a proper, traditional coronation."

"It would be my great honor, Sire," replied the Countess, after which she went down in another deep curtsy. Of the things she had asked, this was more than she had hoped to receive.

"Steward!" shouted Robert suddenly, as he helped her return to her feet. Isabel was startled and jumped.

"Pay the king no mind for his yellin'," explained Elizabeth to Isabel. "He takes his whoopin' too seriously for the comfort of those around him, whether indoors or out." Robert frowned, feeling put upon for being constantly chided.

The steward right away presented himself before Robert.

"Sire," said the steward in a low bow.

"Send word to Bishop Lamberton, who is conductin' mass at the abbey this morn," instructed Robert, "that in the early afternoon, today, there will be the recrownin' of the king in the proper fashion."

"Aye, Sire," answered the Steward, who started to leave thinking Robert was finished.

"Stay man, I am not done with ye, yet," continued Robert.

"Aye, Milord?"

"Tell the Bishop that there will be a representative from the House of Fife to do it proper. Then, wake my brothers and sisters and tell them. And see that the earls, if they're still here 'bouts, are proper informed. But tell no one else, for they that I've said will serve well as the witness body."

"Milord," said the Steward as he started to leave, then glanced back to Robert to see if there might have been a last-second addition to his roster of requests.

Robert realized the man's hesitation, considered an additional command, then waved him on.

The man turned to leave again.

"Wait," said Robert.

"Aye, Sire?"

"Tell the Bishop, also, that the King and Queen will be along directly for mass."

"Aye, My King."

"Seems strange to be addressed so," said Robert with a grin to the two women as several kitchen servants brought breakfast for him and Elizabeth.

"Seems strange to worry the poor steward so, it does," retorted Elizabeth.

Isabel hid her smile from the king.

. .

And so it was that King Robert de Brus of Scotland was, for the second time in as many days, crowned with a simple circlet of gold on the sunny afternoon of Palm Sunday, in the year 1306.

Prince Edward
Prince of Wales

APRIL 5ᵗʰ 1306
WESTMINSTER CASTLE

At the outset, the servants scattered as far and as quickly as their wits and feet would carry them. The king's harangue echoed through the halls and chambers of Westminster like thunder rolling across the naked fields, and none wanted to be near to where the lightning struck. And on the storm did rage.

"I've seen you caressin' his stiff little pecker and him a'lettin' you!" screamed King Edward with exceptional vehemence, even for him.

Twenty-two-year-old Edward cringed before the irate king like a seven-year-old about to be spanked. Prince Edward was spoiled, complete with pouting lip and quivering chin. Hate poured out of his teary, reddened eyes, and it was plain to all who knew him that no one was ever going to stand in his way, except, of course, his father.

The King sat on an ornately-carved and cushioned high-backed chair, topped by an elegantly detailed and gilded crown that shown above his head, much like a glowing halo. Beside him was a long table set with a fine, white linen cloth, and pewter dishes laden with a bounty of food that lay untouched.

The king's long, narrow feet were soaking up to the ankles in a pot of warm water, surrounded by towels to sop the splashed water as he thrashed about in his maniacal tirade. Nearby stood a squire tending a cauldron of hot water over the fire, to replace that which spilled or grew cooled.

The hot soak treatment was designed to increase circulation in his legs since the monarch had recently lost some use of them through the progression of his disease.

"I only want him to have an appropriate, but small earldom, Sire," whined the younger Edward, wiping his eyes on his silk-embroidered velvet sleeve.

He sat in a similarly designed, though smaller, chair opposite the king's. Above his head was carved and gilded a small crown and the emblem of the Prince of Wales.

He lolled back with one leg thrown over the chair arm in direct disrespect to his king. He sniffled, "Piers is a dear friend and..."

"And keeps you away from the company of the ladies," interrupted the king, slamming down his great, bony-fingered hand upon the table.

"He is a great knight and I admire him, Father," the son bleated, though he remained slumped in the huge chair and his foot moved back and forth in a nervous pattern on the stone floor only a yard or so from the pot of water.

"You are tryin' to give away lands to this... *Piers Gaveston,*" the king pronounced the name distastefully, "that you have not yet inherited! My kingdom is still *mine!*"

He lowered his eyes and his voice and added in a pained lamentation, "And when you do inherit all that is now mine, I fear it will waste through your fingers as your days now do." The king rubbed his bare, failing legs with his large hands.

Sensing that his father was weakening, the prince stood from his chair in a vain attempt to dominate the old man, "Father, Piers is a great knight! He has beaten *all* of your best in tourney and in..."

"Yes, he beats them!" The old dog's eyes bored holes in the whelp's courage. "He beats them! Then he struts about like the little cock that he is, bragging and abrading them! Not a man *I* would trust in *any* company," added the king firmly, and Prince Edward sank back upon his chair.

The old man's eyes roved back and forth and a sneer beset his haggard features as he queried, "Have you, or he, ever considered that, perhaps, he defeats my knights only because they know that he is your favorite? And that you will one day be their king?"

"But wait!" he said as loudly as he could in his excited, high squeak. "Just wait until he stands... presuming he yet can... up to his ankles in gore, the dead and the dying of a *real* battle laying about him. *Then* see what a dashing figure he cuts among his fellow knights! Let him... let him..." the sovereign then began to cough uncontrollably, again, his sickness exacerbated by his ire.

The prince but looked at him in his coughing fit and made no move to comfort or to help him. He smiled cunningly, knowing that the old man's last breath was the only thing that stood between himself, sitting in this scolding chair, and being seated on the throne... the attainment of the English kingdom, with all of his wants appeased.

The king grabbed the draped end of the tablecloth and coughed into it hard. Presently he regained his composure, wiped his hands on the cloth, and looked at his son, knowing full well his thoughts.

"I am not dead, yet," he said with a mixture of anger and disappointment, as he straightened his frail body to its full sitting height, topping his son in the opposing chair by almost a head.

Realizing he could not best his father even in the old man's weakened condition, the prince slumped again and, biting his lip, transfixed his stare on the king's pan of sloshing water.

The old king unsheathed a dagger that he kept on his person and purposefully laid it on the table, all the while staring at his cosseted son.

The prince worried what evil intent his father had invented for him, or perhaps for his lover. But King Edward took a withered apple from the bowl of fruit and, with one long sweep of his arm, flung the remainder of the bowl and its contents aside. He placed the apple on the table between them. With no show of emotion, he quickly took up the dagger and stabbed it through the apple, the cloth, and into the table so that the apple was pinned in place.

"There!" he said vainly, almost hoping that the man he wanted his son to be would have the strength to follow his next advice. Leaning forward and staring into his son's eyes he hissed a challenge.

"You can rid yourself of me, here and now! Merely take up this blade and pare my heart as I have pierced the apple; it is no different." He paused and waited for a response. With none coming, he leant back and went on, "Don't worry, no one will question you. History records many such overthrows and seldom are they challenged. Here, I will make it easier for you. I will shut my eyes!"

The old king closed his eyes. The prince put his hand on the table and it hesitatingly moved toward the dagger, his shaking fingers aching to snatch the blade from its place in the fruit and stab it into his father's chest, once, twice, thrice... In his mind's eye, it was done! But, alas, his courage failed, and he who would willingly commit patricide instead slumped weakly back into his seat.

The king opened his eyes. "No heart for the grabbin' of power, my prince?" he asked, again disappointed.

There was a long pause in the conversation before Edward spoke at last to his father, taking another approach. "Father, your reign has been exceedin' long, and equally as distinguished." He noticed the old king nodding, pensively, and so continued.

"But now, you are old. And sick. It might be..." he had to word this carefully "...that a sovereign in your time of life, havin' only one son to inherit the crown, would wish to spend his remainin' years in peace... without havin' to wage war on the rebellin' Scots, or watch over the tax collectin' barons in your parliament." His father's face was frozen. The prince stood and talked quietly.

"You have a young, pretty wife, Father. Why not spend your declinin' seasons with her, rather than in dealin' with court intrigues." The king moved not at all. The son decided it was time to forward his gambit. He leaned over to put his face as close to his father's as possible, and whispered, "Abdicate, Father! Abdicate your throne, that I might ascend to it and come to my full flower as king, without your having first to die."

"If you have not the character of a man, you will never come into your full flower," growled the old king without changing his expression. "And death..." he looked coldly into the face of his only son, "...comes to every man, even princes."

At that moment, Sir Fulco Ballard appeared in the doorway and bowed.

"Enter and speak," commanded the king, waving. The prince returned to his chair and sat sullenly.

"The earl of Pembroke has arrived as you have ordered, Sire," said the steward with another low bow. The prince snorted derisively.

"Hold him where he waits 'til I summon him," said the king.

"As you wish, Sire," Ballard answered, bowed, and left.

The prince giggled behind his hand, showing a distinct shift of mood.

"Pray tell me what brings that silliness forth?" asked the king with a frown.

"Just thinking," he replied through more giggles.

"What?!" demanded the king.

"Piers calls Pembroke 'the ol' Jew'!" he laughed heartily, thinking his father would share in the joke. He was mistaken.

"No one is immune from his stupid slurs! Why should the earl of Pembroke be excluded?" The king shook his head and added firmly, "Gaveston is tolerated by men of consequence *only* because he is *your lover*!"

The prince, chastised by the insult to his beloved, stopped his giggling, and suddenly sober, sat bolt upright in his chair once more.

"We have troubles," announced the king, "troubles not worthy of the soiling of our own hands, but they must be dealt with, and quickly."

"And what 'troubles' would those be, Sire?" the younger man asked, smugly.

Edward's eyes stared over his son's head at a vision of the old man's making, and he spoke, "You think you're shed of shit but it always seems to come back to you."

There was a pause as the king's physician entered the room unannounced, as was his privilege. As he neared the table, he bowed slightly and, without speaking, went to the king's chair where he stooped to swirl his finger in the pot of water, testing its temperature. Finding it barely tepid, he summoned the squire to bring some of the hot water and add it to the foot-soak. The king winced a bit as the added heat reached his tender ankles, but he continued his chain of conversation.

"Robert de Brus has set himself up to be King of Scots," he said.

"When did this news reach us?" questioned young Edward, now paying rapt attention.

"A messenger, this morn... from the north."

"But *you* are the King of Scots!" yelled the prince. "And *I* shall be when you are gone."

"And I am still, and so you shall be," said the king resolutely. "This usurper will not live out the spring. I am settin' a trap, and you must take your proper place in the unfoldin' of it."

"In what way?" the prince asked. Instead of a straightforward answer, his father seemed to speak in riddles.

"You are *my* rebirth, you are *my* four white swans, and many will swear fealty to me, and to you, just as they did with the great King Arthur those many years ago," replied the king.

"I don't understand," said the prince, again becoming suspicious of his father's intentions. "What do I need do?"

"All in fair time, my son," said the king as he sat stroking his thinning beard and looking glassy-eyed, while his plan played out in his inner vision. The prince remained seated across from his father, and during the interminable lull in the king's conversation, was close to nodding off.

It was a quarter of an hour later when the old king again came suddenly alive and yelled, "Where's Pembroke!?"

The prince came up in his chair with a start.

"The damn water's cold, again, physician!" accused the old man loudly. "I'm gettin' the shakes, too!"

The black-robed physician quickly entered from an anteroom, and brought a shoulder wrap for the king. Without a word he put the wrap over the king's shoulders and took the pot of tepid water away. A servant came in his wake and, going down on his hands and knees, wiped the monarch's feet dry and placed warmed woolen stockings on them.

"Pembroke!" again screamed the king, his once strong voice sounding more like that of a boisterous, cackling hag.

The Earl of Pembroke entered, assisted somewhat by a swift push from the tense Sir Fulco, who knew full well the consequences of the king's wroth.

The Earl bowed after regaining his balance, and greeted his lord. "My Lord King."

Aymer de Valence, Earl of Pembroke, was a large, somewhat overweight man, who presented himself in a wholly unkempt manner. His nose was coarsely shaped over his scraggly beard, and further, his clothes were disheveled, and he had an odor about his person that greatly exceeded that of the whisky on his breath.

"Sir Aymer," greeted King Edward, as graciously as he could manage. "Sit you down to the table there and we'll talk of the state of the kingdom."

Aymer sat on the opposite side of the table as he was commanded, his eyes immediately falling upon the lavish table of food, set, and spilled, before him.

"Have you invited me to dinner, Sire?" asked Aymer.

"Eat as you wish," said the king, "After all, we are cousins, are we not?"

As he began to squirm in his chair, not knowing the intended outcome of his father's actions, the prince wondered why his father played "old" Pembroke, so.

"We are," Pembroke answered the king as he picked a particularly juicy pheasant leg from the plate in front of him. "'Tis cold," he remarked as he took his first bite.

"I shall have another one cooked for you," replied the king and opened his mouth to give the order when Aymer interrupted.

"Nay, Sire, do not trouble yourself. I like it as well cold," he said, thinking he could eat it quicker that way.

"As you desire, Cousin," seduced the king in a voice thin and sweet as treacle, and, after a few more moments of pleasantries, he baited his trap. "Have you heard the news of our poor Red Comyn being so cruelly stabbed by Robert de Brus at Greyfriars?"

"I have, Sire. He bein' my own brother-in-law, I was most distressed," Aymer nodded and said through chewed food as he wiped grease from his beard with his already grimy sleeve. "Terrible killin'."

"The Scots don't like that sort of behavior, especially as the murder was in the blessed church, and so forth." The king was fair clucking at the abject shame to be heaped on de Brus.

"I agree," said Aymer, more interested in his next choice from the table than the conversation.

"Well, damn it, man! Why, then, are you not infuriated to your livin' soul?" hollered Edward, pulling the dagger from the apple in frustration and repeatedly pounding its pommel on the table to get the earl's attention. "You seem more for your own belly than revenge for your murdered kin!" He tossed the knife aside and it skittered off the table and across the floor.

Pembroke sat upright on the bench seat, eyes wide with fear, food dangling from his mouth and fingers. Somewhere in his mind, there dawned the idea that he was not there for dinner.

"Uh... Milord... I am angry... yes, certainly... revenge... that's what my mind has been fraught with for these last weeks... revenge!" He swallowed what he had in his mouth with a hearty gulp of wine and wiped his fingers on his belly.

"And how were you going to kill the Brus?" led Edward with a cruel sneer.

"Well..." suggested Aymer, grasping at straws, "it o... occurred... that he should ...um ...meet the same fate as you, yourself ordered for William Wallace ... August last?"

"Ah!" Edward was more than pleased at the thought. "Yes! That is exactly what I would do... if I could presently mount a horse," said the king assuredly. "He should be hanged, taking care not to break his neck or let him otherwise die. When he has lost all awareness, he should then be revived... to have his entrails and organs torn from him and burned before his eyes. 'Tis indeed unfortunate that he cannot survive that..." he sorrowfully began, only to end coldly, "...to know the bite of the headsman's blade, and the drawin' and quarterin' of what's left... "

Aymer replied with a single sniff from his large nose.

The king then got to the real nub of the meeting.

"The lands of Fife, over which I hold authority as the earl's guardian, makes for a goodly income in a year, at least five hundred pounds sterling. I have five more years of that guardianship and that income, before the boy attains his majority." Knowing that de Valence was hanging on his every word, and after leaving an enticing silence, the king finished his thought. "I offer those five years to you, Lord Pembroke, as reward for the capture or the killin' of the former earl of Carrick, Robert de Brus."

Sir Aymer's bushy brows rose and the eyes beneath gleamed at the possibility of such immense wealth. "That is, indeed, a handsome recompense," said Aymer, fairly drooling at the possibility.

Then he thought again, of having to face the Brus on his territory, and reconsidered somewhat. "But, alas, Sire, I cannot accept such a venture, for I am but a poor man amongst my peers, and have not the where-with-all to finance such."

Edward knew that Aymer had his price and that he had but to find it to reach agreement.

"I'll bargain you thus," offered the king, tipping the scales further, "since you have been Lieutenant of the Northeast in the past, you know the country and, I'll wager, have many friends... Scots... who would, perhaps, refuse the Brus and remain loyal to their true king..." he indicated himself.

"Never would they turn on you, Milord," interrupted Sir Aymer, ignoring the fact that many of them had done so in the past.

"I... believe that is true, Cousin. However, the Brus roams the land and tells all that *he* is the King of Scots," the king said angrily and glared across the table.

Recovering himself, and in an easy way, he continued with a grand gesture of his hand, "Eat up, man!"

Pembroke, his eyebrows now knitted, was confused as to the king's plan, but deemed it prudent to remain silent while the king went on.

"You are an able enough fighter. You have an army. Your king needs you to rid Scotland of this scourge, and restore that rebellious people unto their rightful sovereign."

The prince now understood the plot afoot, and why his father had wanted him to witness this negotiation... or, at least, he thought he did.

"But, fact remains, My Lord King," Aymer flatly explained, "I've the wit to be of service, but I hain't the money." He nibbled on small bites of food in his same careless manner.

"How many can you assemble in your force?" asked the king.

The prince sat forward in his chair with renewed interest.

"Oh... m-m-m... 'bout fifty knights, mounted... couple thousand infantry, includin' bowmen... a couple hundred squires..." enumerated Aymer, thoughtfully.

The king turned to the Prince of Wales. "Fetch me yonder box, Edward," he said, pointing to a good-sized coffer that sat on the next table over.

The prince did as he was asked and the weighty box was laid in front of King Edward. He looked at the figures of saints carved in ivory on all sides, interlaced with gold embellishments around the panels.

Pembroke's attention was now fully riveted on the fingers of the king, drumming atop the box.

"What say... I make you Lieutenant of the Northeast once again... or, perhaps... Warden of all Scotland... that you might be in catchin' distance of Robert de Brus and his gang of renegades. Hm? What say you, Cousin?" The king added bait to his trap.

"I would have mutiny within the fortnight for lack of coin to pay and supply my troops," confessed Aymer, shaking his head.

Edward opened the elegant chest with the lid toward Sir Aymer so that he could not see the contents. The prince, overcome with avarice, looked over the old king's shoulder and into the strongbox with inner excitement.

Tantalizingly, the king slowly turned the coffer toward Pembroke. The earl quickly stood and grabbed a candle from the table and held it close above the box, the better to view the suspected precious contents. He was not disappointed.

"One thousand pounds sterlin' should alleviate your distress," said the king as the earl's mouth fell open. To further advance the seduction, he added, "Two years' income from the lands of Fife. Of course, this is but a small portion. The rest will come... later."

"What would you have me do, Sire?" asked Pembroke from within his obvious trance.

"Repair with your army to the town of Perth. From there, have as you will in town and countryside, without mercy, against all who would oppose you. Word has come from Rome; Brus is excommunicated... and thus denied the church's protection... as is anyone aligned with him. He has had himself crowned king, but Rome recognizes it not. You are thus certain of gatherin' a greater army as you travel, assurin' the failure and capture... or death... of Brus, and all his kin and all his seed," gloated the king.

"Aye, Sire," answered Sir Aymer, gulping a great swig of wine to control his dizziness.

"Further, you are to carry before you the dragon banner," continued Edward, adding, "All who are taking part with Brus, and are captured alive, will suffer the execution of Wallace. Exclude none!"

"Yes, Sire," he replied, though the mere thought nauseated him.

"And, one more bit of business in this bargain," Edward added.

"Yes, My Lord King."

"You are to take Sir Phillip Mowbray and Sir Ingram Umfraville as your closest consultants, and place them second in the chain of command of your army. They are both with wit and courage, and are close Comyn kin, same as you."

"And who will pay these gentlemen... my seconds in command?"

asked Sir Aymer, attempting to up the wages for his services.

"If they demand compensation, then pay them from the box," said the old king, offhandedly. "But, they'll not ask, for they are proud and chivalrous."

Pembroke was puzzled by the remark.

"Do not ponder too much, Cousin, it will make your head ache," said the king with subtle sarcasm.

Pembroke was quickly satisfied as Edward carefully closed the lid to the beautiful box and tried, however unsuccessfully, to heave the heavy chest across the table. The earl was greatly pleased at what he presumed was the added gift of the costly chest.

"I may have the box, too?" asked Aymer, placing it in front of him on the table.

"Bring me the head of the Brus in it, and it is yours."

Isabel McDuff

APRIL 9ᵗʰ 1306
KILDRUMMY CASTLE

Fifteen miles, more or less, west-southwest of Aberdeen, Kildrummy Castle had lain for nearly a century atop a broad, green rise in a wide valley between gently rolling hills. Erected near the River Don using the gray and roseate-hued native stone quarried from the den to its north, the original fortress had been constructed for King Alexander II by Gilbert de Moray, then Bishop of Caithness.

In the beginning a simple polygon in the aptly named "rubble" style, the citadel was less than well-designed by later standards. And when in the middle-thirteenth century a chapel was added, it had been built through the eastern curtain, permitting a certain loss of protective strength in order for the chapel to lie upon the required east-to-west axis.

Its faults became abundantly clear when, in 1296, Edward of England conquered the stronghold. However, his occupation of fortress Kildrummy had turned out to be a boon to its eventual military viability.

King Edward was among the era's most erudite castle builders, and while he had Kildrummy under his control, English stonemasons had cut, shaped, and polished ashlars for an exterior plinth, adding strength and support to the north wall.

At opposite ends of the north curtain were built two large towers, the western one being the principal keep, or donjon, which was called the Snow Tower, or Snowdon. Its eastern counterpart was the Warden's Tower, which was adjoined by the small postern gate and its portcullis.

Near the center of the north curtain was the great hall, the largest room in the castle, with its huge fireplaces and arched windows. To its east was the massive kitchen, abutting also the chapel and the Warden's Tower.

Upon the south entry Edward added a gatehouse consisting of two "D" shaped towers, which required anyone entering the main gate to pass through a long tunnel in order to reach the portcullis. The tunnel was lined on all sides with narrow archer's slits, often called "murder holes," behind which archers could stand in relative safety while firing on invaders.

A drawbridge spanned the moat outside the main gate, its mechanism lodged in the gatehouse's second story. On the south bank of the moat rose the barbican, a smaller gatehouse with its own oaken gate and sturdy portcullis, the first line of defense for the main entrance to the castle.

Two additional towers were constructed along the east and west curtains, making a total of six, all connected by parapets, or wall walks. Each tower could be sealed off on both sides, forbidding entry to any who might breach the wall or attain the parapets.

Within the courtyard were numerous small buildings, mostly of wood, and having thatched roofs. It was in those humble quarters that the necessary trades and shops were housed, foodstuffs stored, troops billeted, and animals sheltered. When the fields outside the castle walls were unavailable, as in times of siege, animals grazed on the courtyard grass and were fed from the castle's stores of silage and grain.

With a steep and difficult ascent to reach the top of the natural rise along the north wall, and wide, deep ditches filled with water on the other three sides, the castle stood now, better able than any other in Robert's possession to withstand direct attack or siege.

It was here that Robert felt secure and comfortable, and it was here that he brought his family.

. .

The warm hues of the setting sun played across the stone of the castle parapet wall, making its naturally rose-hued coloring even ruddier. Elizabeth's fingers ran along the wall as if she were unconsciously thinking of escape, then drummed restlessly as she gazed at the beautiful patterns of the clouds. It was Sunday, a day of rest, yet it was scarcely restful, being a day of preparations.

Robert joined her there, putting his arm around her and holding her close to his side as both of them faced the sinking sun in quiet reverence.

At length she took a deep breath and asked, "How long will ye be gone?"

"Three, perhaps four weeks."

"I'll miss ye."

"Aye, and I ye," he said softly, then added, "but we need an army, and I am the one who must raise it."

She turned toward him and held him even closer, and laid her head on his chest. He returned her embrace and nestled his cheek in her silky dark hair.

"I've always loved the view from here," she said as she turned back to the glorious colors of the last light, "but now it gives me a queer feelin' I don't understand. Perhaps it's that, when the fightin' begins, and it will directly, yonder placid field may well be heavy laden with English and Comyn, layin' siege."

"Save Sterlin,' 'tis the strongest castle in all Scotland, and passin' well-provisioned... and comfortable, woman," Robert defended his choice thinking she was fearful of staying there.

"That has little to do with the overall," she returned sternly, staring up at him directly into his blue-gray eyes.

"Are ye havin' a vision, woman?" he asked, trying to understand.

"Nay," answered Elizabeth, "but I don't like bein' without ye, and I'm fearful for the others within these walls... I have dreams that are not within my grasp, and I want to know that they finish differently than they play out in my head."

"What do ye mean?" asked Robert frowning, completely mystified, "We are well garrisoned here, ye will be safe! Nigel will be here with ye, too."

"Would ye have me wringin' my hands and cryin' constantly in yer absence instead of thinkin' of how best to change what I see?"

Robert considered her thoughts then smiled and said, "Do what ye will, woman," for he knew full well that if the castle *were* to be taken, all within the walls would most probably be slaughtered. At this his heart sank, and he held her all the more closely, though he thought Kildrummy would surely hold.

Later that night, as Robert entered the solar in the donjon, he laid a sheathed short sword on the bed near Elizabeth's bare feet, poking from under the cover.

"What's that, man?" she asked as she propped herself up on her elbows and looked down at the weapon at her feet.

"A little protection," he said with a smile as he sat on the bed and removed his shoes and stockings.

"Afraid to come to bed with me without that wee bit of a blade, are ye?" She smiled.

He smiled at her joke as he stood to remove his clothes. He loved her way of illustrating her opinions with a simple tease. "I thought ye'd need it to ward me off, tonight, woman," he returned with a grin and a playful leer, adding, "I'm that lustful for ye."

Elizabeth watched him disrobe and tried to memorize the beauty of his broad shoulders and deep chest, the way the light played upon him as he dropped his shirt and kilt on the floor and went to the washing stand.

He had always been muscular and fit, but in recent weeks, since he had begun training the young knights, his physical beauty had taken on near perfection in her eyes. She watched unabashedly as he went about his evening ablutions and her heart ached at his loveliness, so soon to be removed from her.

She sat a bit higher up in the bed, and the cover slipped to her waist exposing her bare breasts. Robert turned to see her gazing at him and, always stunned by her beauty, found this time to be no exception as he simply stood at the foot of the bed and admired her.

Though she loved it, this amorous attention disconcerted her, so that she soon flushed and turned over, pulling the cover over her head as she did. This left only a few locks of hair teasingly kissing the top of the cover as she said from under, "Come to bed, dear king."

"Aye, my queen," he answered with a smile... and he did.

. .

As the sun made its next morning's appearance, it was partially overshadowed by refreshing spring rains that came and went, as did the knights, villeins, and squires in the courtyard. Finally, all was made ready for the king's departure.

Robert was dressed in his coronation armor as he led the procession out the gate, across the drawbridge, and away from the castle, with trumpets blaring and colorful banners and flags flying.

Edward, Alexander, and Thomas Brus, Thomas Randolph, and Christopher Seton followed; then came the standard bearer and the knights. Mounted on magnificent destriers, armor glistening as the rain plinked on it musically, all were slogging through the mud.

Each man was proudly uniformed with a tabard showing a red lion rampant on a yellow field, thus signifying they were of the army of the king of Scotland.

The Queen, with Robert's daughter Marjorie, and his siblings Nigel, Christian, and Mary, all stood by the gate, along with the entire host of the castle, cheering their legion on to success.

Elizabeth bolted from the others and ran to the nearest tower, quickly making her way to the wall walk where she and Robert had stood in each other's embrace only yesterday. At this moment, it seemed a lifetime ago.

She waved, knowing Robert would not look back. Her heart ached and tears came streaming freely down her cheeks to mingle with the spring rain as it gently splashed upon her face and breast.

Then, as if because she wished it so, he did turn in his saddle to look back, and caught sight of her head and arm above the wall; having answered her wave, he again faced forward and rode on, to look back no more.

As the entourage made its way up the valley northward, the sun appeared between the clouds enough to form a rainbow, perfectly arched over the armed array.

"Thank ye, God," whispered Elizabeth as she, like Noah, took the heavenly bend to be a favorable sign. God would answer her prayers and return him safely home to her, she was now sure. She had to be patient, that was all.

As she stood watching them, the last of Robert's men rode through a stand of trees and disappeared into the forest beyond.

Aymer de Valence
Earl of Pembroke

MAY 18th 1306
CUPAR CASTLE, FIFE

"Up the bell tower, Laddie! Quickly, now!" commanded Bishop Wishart to his young squire. The boy nimbly climbed the metal rods inside the tower to reach the uppermost opening, overlooking the countryside.

The morning sun was rapidly giving way to dreary overcast as low rain clouds and patchy fog moved in from the west. The old bishop, having led the attack that sent the English scurrying from Cupar, knew that his success could be short-lived.

"What ye seein,' Laddie?" the old man's voice echoed up the narrow tower interior.

"As ye thought, Sir, 'tis a great army comin' this way," answered the scrawny boy.

"What be their number, Lad?" asked the bishop. "Ach," he remembered that the youth could not count above ten and instead directed, "call down to me the length and the breadth of them."

"They are four riding abreast, and the length... well, they stretch from t'other side of the last house on the road out of the village to... beyond the far wood along the river, how far I cannot tell. But, still they come," hollered the boy down the shaft as he leaned over the edge of the opening to balance himself for a better look.

That is thousands, for sure, thought the old man, rubbing the top of his almost totally bald head. Then he asked the squire, "Do ye see any banners, my boy?"

"If ye be askin' if they be English and Comyn, my thought is they are, Milord," said the squire, agilely descending the rods to where the bishop was waiting. The youth had seen enough of the English in his short time to recognize their dress and their manner, so that the Bishop had no doubt of his word.

"Quickly, my lad, fetch my horse from the stable, saddle her, and return to me in my study," the bishop ordered as both of them walked swiftly down the hall of the small abbey.

"Aye, Yer Grace," the squire replied as he trotted away to open the door nearest the stables.

The old bishop watched the boy as he ran outside with such ease. Oh, to be young again would certainly be a blessing... at this time, especially, he thought, hastening as best he could, turning the corner, and opening the door to his study.

He went straightaway to his desk and began scribbling as fast as his gnarled old fingers would, and still form legible characters. The note, when completed, contained as much information as he could definitely state or reasonably estimate, on the approaching English-Comyn army, and news of events and occurrences of recent days. He was just heating the sealing wax when the squire knocked on the study door.

"Enter," said the preoccupied voice from the inside.

The squire entered as he was told, saying, "Yer horse is ready to ride, Bishop."

"I'll not be the one ridin', lad," said the bishop as he held the folded parchment and dripped hot wax on it to seal it closed. He then removed a gold signet ring from his finger and applied it to the puddle of hot wax, thus affixing his personal seal.

"But, I've yer horse all saddled..." protested the young man.

"*Ye* will repair in all haste to Kildrummy with this message for King Robert, and none other. Ye know him by sight, do ye not, for ye were at his crownin'?" queried the bishop, handing the young man the letter.

"Aye, but ye, Yer Grace? What will become of *ye*?" asked the concerned lad.

"Ach, they will not dare harm the cloth," he answered, sounding assured for benefit of the boy, "but neither will they let me leave to warn others, as ye can do...if ye hurry, lad!" With that he waved his hands as if to shoo the squire out to be on his way.

The squire had been with the bishop for most of his eleven years and so looked upon the kindly old cleric as his father, or grandfather. He suddenly hugged the bishop, for he feared he would see him no more.

"What's this?" said the surprised bishop. The lad answered not, but his eyes welled up with tears, and the bishop then knew the meaning and returned the hug. "Be off with ye Lad; I'll be fit and joinin' ye at

Kildrummy in a day or two," prattled the bishop trying to take the edge of worry from the boy.

"And, if ye don't come?"

Without another word, the old man gently pushed the boy out the door, and walked with him down the hall and out to the courtyard where the saddled mare stood waiting. The squire tucked the letter deep into his doublet and mounted the horse. "But, what if ye don't come?"

The bishop looked up at the young man and smiled, "Then, Laddie, the horse will be yers."

The squire looked down at the old man from beneath knitted brows, "Ye *will* be followin'?"

"Aye, for sure," he said in a comforting voice, and changed the subject. "Now, ye walk out of here easy and head in that direction. When once ye are over yon rise, whip this horse like the devil's at yer heels, for surely, he is. Don't look back... and don't come back. God ride with ye, lad." The bishop then made the sign of the cross before the youth.

The squire held tight to the saddlebow and the old man slapped his horse's rump. As he watched, the youthful messenger and the stout little mare made their way through the postern gate and disappeared to the north behind the castle, just moments before the advance guard of Edward's vast army, winding inexorably along the loch road from the south, approached.

Simply the noise of that many feet moving along the ground at the same time, and the clamor of equipment jostling against horses, soldiers, and wagons, sounded in the stillness like a distant and closing storm, well suiting the castle denizens' mood, as well as the weather.

The bishop walked to the center of the courtyard, a lone figure in a sudden shower of pouring rain, as the captain of the garrison guard came to him and said, "We cannot hold longer than a virgin's kiss against these many, Yer Grace." Realizing to whom he spoke, the man flushed, but the Bishop nodded in agreement.

After a moment's contemplation, Robert Wishart surmised, "Captain, this castle has so recently been declared free by us that yon army no doubt believes it still in English hands." Thinking quickly he added, "Take our banner down and send it to me immediately, and greet these invaders as fellow men-in-arms. Once in the cover of dark, ye and yer men slip the guards and hie for Kildrummy to join King Robert."

"Aye," the man answered and immediately trotted away to do as he was bade. He first ordered the Scots' banner to be lowered and taken to the bishop, then called his men into a tight knot and told them of the plan.

"But what of the people who live here at the castle?" asked one of the men.

"We hope they will go along with the ruse... and if not, we'll be fightin' our way out," said the captain with a smile, knowing such was impossible.

As the soldiers dispersed into the castle population, there came the blast of trumpets announcing that the advancing army was at the gate.

To give the appearance that nothing was amiss, the guard captain and the gentle bishop stood together just inside the gate to greet the leaders as they rode in.

Each man's blood ran cold as he saw the dragon banner fluttering so elegantly among others on the increasing late day wind. "No quarter!" whispered the captain.

Sir Aymer de Valence, Earl of Pembroke, led the procession. Despite the rain, his pompous person sat astride his destrier in all his armored glory, topped with a bright red plume of feather, and grinning so that it occurred to the bishop that his fat lips appeared as upturned serpents, that had taken up residence in that scraggly mass of beard.

Behind him rode the standard bearer with the leopard banner of King Edward. Many knights pushed into the small courtyard, among them, Sir Phillip de Mowbray and Sir Ingram de Umfraville. The English soldiery lined up in great force before the two figures waiting to greet them.

"I heard the rebels took this castle of late," said Sir Aymer, looking down on the bishop and the captain.

"The Brus was here," stated the bishop coolly and truthfully, "but is no longer. We could no more have prevented his entry than we could have yers, Milord."

The leather saddle scrunched as Aymer leaned forward in it and asked, "And what be your name, cleric?"

"I, Sir, am Robert Wishart, Bishop of Glasgow, and this is Captain Alexander, of the castle guard." The captain touched his helmet.

Sir Aymer looked at the pair suspiciously, then turned to address his companions. "Ne'er trust a damned Scot," he sneered, remembering too late that he was in the company of many Scots, and he regretted the statement as soon as it left his mouth. But, having command granted privileges, and Aymer merely turned and pretended he had said nothing offensive.

Sir Phillip and Sir Ingram, both being Scots, looked at each other and said nothing. They knew he needed them and their followers to quash the Brus rebellion, and that was also their desire.

"The great hall awaits yonder, Milord. If ye and yer lieutenants would care to replenish yerselves, victuals will be made ready at once," offered the bishop.

Aymer climbed down from his huge steed and to a young squire handed his oversized shield, adorned with alternating white and blue bars and red birds. As the squire struggled with the heavy shield, Pembroke stared at the bishop, whose gaze was steady and open, but whose robes were as humble and poor as were the clothes of the people he served.

The earl removed his helmet and handed it to the squire, then walked a few paces, still staring at the old man. "Wishart!" He scratched at his beard and after a short interlude asked, "Are you not the one who attended the so-called 'crownin'' of the rebel Robert de Brus?"

The bishop was honored to have been in attendance and would not be squeezed for a lie. He thus admitted the same with a calm, "Aye."

Aymer came so close that the old man could smell his ripe breath and turned his head a bit to avoid it. The corpulent earl at first believed the frail bishop to be fearful of him and moved even closer, but the old man would not be intimidated and held his ground. Failing to cow the much smaller and more aged man, the warrior first thought to strike the impudent cleric down in the courtyard dirt, but decided such a fit of pique would not be wise in his present company.

Then an expression of cruelty crossed the earl's face; "Set him in irons!" he commanded, before passing the captain by and striding into the great hall without another thought to the bishop.

The other nobles and Aymer's advance guard followed, as the knights and their squires dismounted and began to attend to their duties. The massive army already had prepared to encamp on the grounds beyond the castle gate, completely surrounding the little village and trampling the just-sprouted fields of corn.

The little bishop was roughly taken by two knights to the blacksmith's, where heavy iron bands were hammered into circlets, which were closed and riveted upon each of his wrists and ankles. They were then joined to iron chains so weighty that the poor bishop could barely lift them. The feisty old man was chained to a post in the courtyard for all to witness King Edward's displeasure. Among the Scots of Cupar, however, it was a mark of honor.

That night, the Scotsmen who had comprised the small garrison individually walked near to the bishop, but did not stop or attract attention.

One-by-one, he quietly blessed them before they found their way out of the castle and made their escape.

He would let none try to break him free, knowing it would

jeopardize the safety of all.

So brazen was their escape from within a completely surrounded castle that, upon discovering their absence, Lord Aymer accused his Scottish troops of having aided them.

In fact, the garrison soldiers had merely mingled in with the other Scots in the great, sleeping army and waited for it to be on the move again. From there, each eventually "deserted" without even being missed.

. .

In the early evening hours two days later, the exhausted young squire from Cupar rode through the gate of Kildrummy. His journey completed, the squire finally allowed himself to relax, and slid help-lessly from the saddle. Two guards grabbed him as he fell.

Edward Brus saw the boy ride in and came quickly to his side.

"The king!" whispered the boy through parched lips. "The king," was all he could say. Edward picked him up and carried him to the great hall, where the recently returned king and his captains were planning their next moves.

"What!?" barked Robert at the interruption, as Edward carried the boy through the door. Robert left the table, followed by his dog, and came to assess the condition of the boy.

"He obviously came a long distance at great effort, and he but said, 'the king,'" related Edward. "I thought it important."

"I know this youth," said Robert as he took the boy's face in his large strong hands, "He is Wishart's squire. Give him water and a bit of brandy and see if he recollects his tongue."

A short time later there was sputtering and cursing coming from where Edward and the young squire were sitting on the floor.

"The king!" cried the lad along with a string of obscenities. He was still somewhat delirious. "I must see the king!"

Robert again arose and went to the side of the boy, "Powerful curses from a *bishop's* squire, young lad!" admonished Robert, seeing that the boy was not too much the worse for wear.

"Too many times within earshot of uncivil knights, Milord," answered the eleven-year-old. Robert laughed heartily, as did they all around the table.

The squire quickly remembered that he sat before his king, whom he had recognized immediately, and swung around to kneel on one knee.

Robert bade him rise, which he did, if unsteadily. "I bring a letter for ye, King Robert," he said, reaching into his doublet to retrieve the missive he had put there two days past.

As he drew it out, he realized it was sweat-stained and crumpled, and was shyly embarrassed, but had no choice other than to present it.

Robert and Edward both saw the seal of the Bishop of Glasgow affixed to the letter and realized its implications.

"And what of the bishop?" asked Robert of the young squire.

"He was well when I left him, but I greatly fear for him, Sire," lamented the squire. "A great army from the south approached Cupar when Bishop Wishart sent me away. I alone got out ere they arrived." The youth lowered his head to hide his tears. Edward put his arm around the boy and hugged him.

"Andrew!" shouted Robert, loudly and suddenly, startling the bishop's squire and making him jump.

Robert's own squire, Andrew Stewart, showed himself from an alcove where he had observed the events unfolding.

"Aye, Sire," answered the twelve-year-old.

"See that he... What is yer name, lad?"

"David, Sire."

"See that David is fed and bedded down," ordered Robert, indicating the bishop's lad.

"Aye, Sire," responded the obedient squire, scrambling to do so.

Robert then looked at the skinny sprite of a boy, dwarfed by the great knights who surrounded him, and said, "Ye have done great service for yer country, this day, David. I'll not forget it."

"Thank ye, Sire," said the boy, grinning proudly and wiping away his tears.

Robert and Edward returned to the table, and the dog to his self-imposed sentry duty at the fireplace, where the negligible fire barely dispelled the chill of the night air.

The other men pushed in tight to hear the contents of Wishart's letter as Robert began to read it aloud.

"'To Robert de Brus, King of Scotland. My Lord King.'" Robert cleared his throat to hide his humility at being so addressed.

"'Yer spies may have reported this to ye prior to yer receivin' this letter, but as I know little of yer information resources, I will say all that I know, and hope that it reaches ye safe.'"

"'There foments troubles in the south lands recently, I am sad to report.'"

"'Only two days from this writing, the primate of our church, Bishop Lamberton, yer kindred spirit in freedom, and that good man, Henry, abbot of Scone, were taken in chains to London by the command of Lord Pembroke, who marches north with a great army under direct orders from King Edward.'"

Robert frowned deeply as he continued with the letter, "'Lord Pembroke has been charged with extinguishin' the rebellion, and all who follow ye and yers will suffer, if caught, the death of William Wallace. Also, none who does the murder of them that follow ye will stand charged for the same.'"

"'I am informed further, that Dumfries Castle has fallen, and poor Roger Kirkpatrick suffered a most terrible agony when the English stabbed out his one good eye with an arrow tip, and threw him without to wander blind.'"

"'Another length of sad news is that yer home of...'" Robert stopped reading aloud for a moment and looked up, fighting back the emotions and praying he could change the words on the page if he just would not read on.

He left the table and leaned against the mantle stone over the fireplace, staring into the consuming flames. The dog sat up at his feet and licked his hand; Robert scratched him behind his long ears.

Alexander Brus quietly picked up the letter from where Robert dropped it on the table and resumed the reading in a subdued tone, "'...yer home of Lochmaben... has been sacked... and all yer kin and servants within its walls were... brutally murdered. Neither were they allowed to be shrove.'"

Edward looked at Thomas Randolph. Both thought of pretty little Sarah from the kitchen.

Edward brought both his fists down hard on the table and slumped onto the bench. Thomas left the hall for the fresh air of the courtyard. As he stepped into the coolness of the outdoors, the tears that had welled up at the news of Sarah's death broke over the rims of his eyes and flowed hot down his cheeks. He stood in the shadows to hide his weeping, and sobbed as he could not remember ever having done, before. "Sarah," he wept. "Oh, Sarah."

In the Great Hall, Alexander Brus continued to speak of the letter to the others. "The rest is in a quickly scrawled hand, and 'tis some smeared, but I think I can read it, 'The English are at the gate. There are...'" he tried to make out the word, "'...thousands, well armed, and they march with the dragon before them. All is lost here, but I hope to save the... garrison to fight for ye another time.' 'Tis signed, 'Yer subject and friend, Robert Wishart, Bishop of Glasgow.'"

There was quiet around the hall for long moments as each of the men absorbed the bad news.

"Where is Aymer likely to hole up and operate from?" asked the king, his low voice finally breaking the silence.

"Bring a map," said Sir Neil Campbell, a newcomer to the group, and already smitten with Lady Mary Brus, the King's unmarried sister. Others in the group of councilors were Sir David Inchmartin, Sir Simon Fraser, Sir Hugh de la Haye, Sir John Somerville, and the royal standard barrier, Sir Alexander Scrymgeour. All had thrown their lives and fortunes behind the Brus, and now stood to lose as much as he.

They gathered in various states of sorrow, anger, and disbelief, around the large table.

"Ye need no map, man. There are but two places suitable for such an army, without exposure to surprise attack," offered Sir Christopher coldly from the far end, "Perth and Berwick."

"Aye, for sure. Both large, walled towns and newly reinforced by Edward," added Thomas Brus.

"Perth is more central to the lands he wants," said Robert. "That be his destination."

"Let's go for him!" exclaimed Nigel, eager for his first taste of battle and to avenge Lochmaben.

"Patience, little brother," counseled Robert, "Lennox, Atholl, and that young Black Douglas will arrive tomorrow, and we'll want their notions ere we act, half-witted."

They all nodded or otherwise agreed.

"Ne'ertheless," continued Robert as he paced the length of the table, "we'll send to the highlands for our supporters and conscripts. Have them muster here on the tenth day of June, and each must have with him twelve days' rations, and armor, weapons, and mounts as each has, or that his immediate lord can provide for him."

"What size army do ye think we'll have for goin' against Pembroke's thousands?" asked Sir Neil calculating the odds.

"We'll have thousands of our own," bragged Edward, rising to his feet. "And aside of that, the spirit and skill of each true son of Scotland is always greater than that of a son of England, by at least *tenfold*!"

The subdued table cheered briefly at his rhetoric, but none there believed in his heart that each of them could slay ten of the enemy, and live to tell of it.

Robert, assuming the head of the table, again, said pragmatically, "We'll have between four and five thousand, accordin' to my tally. We'll fight them where we find them, and we *must* win, for 'tis not just our own lives, but those of all our families, in dire jeopardy. Let no man think otherwise, 'less he be counted a swaggerin' fool."

After a moment of solemn contemplation by his fellows, Christopher stood resolutely to raise his goblet of wine high above his head and offered a toast, "To The Brus, our true king, and to free Scotland."

All stood and drank.

PENTECOST, MAY 22ND 1306
LONDON

"Father bought me a great dappled Belgian in honor of my knighthood," bragged John Airth, the nineteen-year-old squire son of a minor, but fairly well to do, baron in a remote western earldom of England.

"Well, my father took the finest and bravest from our herd. He is black as midnight, a spirited stallion," retorted his friend James Dunbar, also from a wealthy baron's brood. Both young men were about to become knights by order of Edward, King of England.

It was still in the early morning hours when the two young men turned the corner of the busy, narrow streets near Westminster Palace in London.

"If our robes are not ready, I will cut out the heart of that ol' bastard tailor," teased John as he grabbed the handle of his dagger.

James laughed just as they entered the tailor shop.

"Happy young men, that's what I like to see!" exclaimed the tailor, not realizing that the merry conversation involved his heart being cut out. However, he did know why they were there, and proudly fetched the ceremonial robes from their place in the workroom, holding them high in either hand.

"Are they to your pleasure, gentlemen?"

"You would know better than to foul the goods given us by the king, would you not?" asked James, haughtily.

"Indeed, sirs," the old tailor's reply was accompanied by a low bow. He knew just how to handle his clientele from many years of service to all manner of powerful and near powerful individuals close to the seat of royalty. "They are to the exact specifications of your family colors, and the rest we will see as soon as you try the fit."

James and John belied their pretended maturity and their noble breeding as they eagerly scrabbled into the beautiful, long, flowing robes that would surround them in the ceremonies that evening.

They both paraded in front of one another, and the tailor's mirror, for longer than most maidens their age would take to beautify themselves, but they found little to fault. They both were more interested in the pretense and flights of fantasy than in finding flaws, anyway.

"We shall take them as they are, tailor," announced James, who spoke for both, "for we need them this day. Tomorrow they will be worthless."

"Our fathers will arrive directly to pay you for your work," said John, thinking to cheat the tailor.

"Gentlemen," started the old tailor who had dealt with such ruses numerous times, "men of your obvious stature in life surely would not expect their fathers to pay for the tailoring of robes for their knighthood ceremonies!" He shook his head slightly and pursed his lips in disapproval, but not enough to cause resentment and, thus, rebellion.

James looked at John, neither knowing quite how to respond to the old man. At last James asked, "How much for your work, tailor?"

"Merely one shilling, three pence... each," replied the tailor, doubling his due because he could.

"We hadn't realized it was that small an amount," said James arrogantly, reaching into his pouch for the required coins, as did John.

The old man took his pay, and the robes of his making, which he folded neatly and tied in paper, before proudly handing them back to the two young men.

"May God always go with you, gentlemen," said the tailor obsequiously, holding the door open for the two encumbered squires, who took no notice of the blessing.

The old man closed the door behind them, and turned back to his shop as he waited to repeat the same, or a similar scene, over and over, during the course of the day.

• •

It was late in the warm afternoon as James and John dressed in one of the tents set up in the yard of the Temple before the royal palace of Westminster. The crowds of curious onlookers had become an ever-increasing mass, causing the king to order most of the apple trees and a garden wall near the Temple removed, that visitors could better view the grand spectacle.

James and John were but two of almost three hundred sons of earls, barons and knights, the flower of England, who were assembled for their induction into a special knighthood created by King Edward.

As gifts from their monarch, each squire had been given a helmet, spurs, a sword, a lance, a suit of armor and, of course, satin and linen cloth, and gold threads for their ceremonial robes, and material for a mattress and a quilt. For all this, Edward had paid a small fortune, but he knew he had purchased absolute fealty from the new crop of knights, and their fathers and kinsmen as well.

"Another draught?" asked James as he poured wine into a goblet for himself then pointed it toward John, whose young squire was just finishing the last buckle on his perfectly polished new armor.

"None more for me," answered John, now fully armored, complete with sword and robe, and admiring himself in a small mirror held by his squire. "I want my head about me on this solemn occasion."

"Solemn?" questioned James with a snicker. "We're here to raise the fires of hell, don't you know?" He gestured wildly.

His companion shook his head. "Not I. I am here on a holy quest," he countered, adding as he passed by James and out of the tent, "you raise hell-fire with the others."

"So I shall," mumbled James to himself, for John was now far beyond earshot and basking in the enthusiasm of the cheering, pressing throng, and the fluttering admiration of the eligible young ladies in the crowd.

The evening was spent in revelry and feasting, the likes of which no one there could remember. There were delicacies prepared to exotic recipes from France, the Holy Land, and the northern countries, as well as the most extraordinarily luxurious food of the evening, the swans, roasted and served in an exquisite sauce.

Near the midnight hour the bizarre ceremony began. King Edward sat upon a huge gilt throne in the Temple of Westminster Palace. His bejeweled fingers held an equally gem-encrusted goblet, filled with wine, and he was dressed in the finest royal vestments. His throne occupied the middle of the dais, with long tables placed to either side of him. Edward gloried in the knighting ceremony.

The three hundred prospective knights, pressed tight by their families and other onlookers into the Temple, were stifled and crushed as the proceedings began with a two-hundred-voice choir singing hymns, and unheard blessings by the regional bishop, who was not a fit speaker for such a large and noisy throng.

Certainly, the king heard neither the singing nor the blessings, as his senile mind had seeped back into something he had read of an ancient history, and he beheld a vision of himself, embodied as King Arthur, knighting members of the Round Table.

"I strike thee, Sir Lancelot," he whispered in his age-and-wine-induced vision, in which a heavenly host sang and praised God for the rightful things to be accomplished by these daring and bold men of the Round Table. He reached across four live ceremonial swans, each with a tiny golden crown upon its graceful head, and touched the sword blade to the shoulders of the warrior kneeling before him. This is my rebirth, my new body of new knights, he thought in his reverie.

His mind went swirling as the vision of famous knight after knight came before him to be struck into knighthood by himself as the great King Arthur de Pendragon, creator of Camelot, ruler of the entire kingdom.

Edward reveled in his daydreams, where he found great pleasure in mental fancies, having little strength left to enjoy a physical life.

The delusional king was suddenly shocked back into the present moment as he realized the singing had stopped, the prayers had ceased, and there was only the mumbling multitude, wondering why the king sat dumb on his throne.

"Bring on the swans!" ordered King Edward without further hesitation.

Trumpets sounded and a gold-embroidered-satin covered table was carried out to the dais and placed before him.

The attendants were dressed in colorful splendor, and had such exactly choreographed movements that this was the only moment of complete quiet. The throng stood in awe before the two living swans on the table, one black, the other white, facing each other in front of the king.

They were held fast in place by golden netting and were surrounded by green laurel leaves and gilded reeds. Affixed upon their heads with wax were tiny golden crowns.

Pendragon had four, but two will do for my reach, thought King Edward as his ceremonial sword, heavily gilt and jewel encrusted, was brought forth and placed into his excitedly trembling hands.

The Prince of Wales was dripping perspiration from the oppressive heat of so many bodies gathered in relatively close quarters, full armor, and a heavy ceremonial robe, as he walked up and stood before his father.

The king sat as high on the throne as he could manage; his legs would not support him to stand for more than moments at a time. He did not want to give the appearance of weakness, or that he was not in control at this knighting of his own son and his new rising army.

John Airth and James Dunbar stood in the midst of the hall as the ever-pressing crowd packed everyone even tighter together.

"Will we ever get knighted this evening?" grunted James, crushed in beside his friend.

"Bless God, we will," answered John, mopping his face with a linen cloth.

Somewhere in the middle of the crowd, one of the soon-to-be-knighted squires fainted from the heat and the crush of the multitude, and for a while was carried upright, to and fro, by the movement of the crowd. No one noticed his condition until there opened a space large enough for him to fall to the floor. Soldiers pushed their way through the throng to rescue the poor man, but they were too late to save his life.

"Kneel, my son," commanded King Edward, oblivious to the death in the crowd. Edward obeyed his father, kneeling before him and the captive swans.

"I strike thee knight in the service of the crown of England," spoke the king, reaching across the table between the two swans and touching each shoulder with the tip of his sword. He then commanded, "Arise, Sir Edward!" The prince stood, to hear his father say, "To Edward Plantagenet, Knight, in celebration of this day, I, Edward, King of England, grant unto you the dukedom of Aquitaine, and all the lands, dwellings, and privileges pertaining thereto. From this day, you shall be called Sir Edward of Caernarvon, Prince of Wales, and Duke of Aquitaine."

Young Edward looked up with surprise into his father's eyes. He had not expected such a title and lands. He smiled to show the king his pleasure. But the king returned not the smile, instead sitting stoically on his throne to show his son the way of a king.

"You are the first Swan Knight of the modern era," said King Edward. "You, Sir Edward, shall bring forth all others present, who have been called to swear before God, and be received into the Swan Knights for the glory of England."

The newly knighted prince, truly resplendent in his royal ceremonial armor, turned to the crowd, raising his sword high above his head.

All in the assemblage cheered loudly, and the waiting squires and young warriors standing closest to the dais were suddenly forced forward, into the line of regular soldiers protecting the front of the platform.

Several of the guards fell backward, and the youthful squires, losing their footing, sprawled upon the downed soldiers with the full weight of themselves and their armor. Though there was a great comic scramble by the soon-to-be knights to extricate themselves and regain their composure, only the few in immediate proximity were aware of, and took delight in, the young men's embarrassment.

As young men knelt before him, one after another, the king's enthusiasm grew strong, but his body weakened rapidly. He eventually beckoned two servants to hold him up as he stood, at which the throng cheered. But Edward knew he could not persevere.

At that point, with great effort, the king started to speak in a quavering voice. "I swear, by God in heaven and before the swans…" as he spoke his voice grew all the stronger, and, holding his sword hilt side up so that it resembled a crucifix, he avowed, "…that I shall hence set forth to Scotland, and whether I live or die, avenge the murder of our poor, slain kinsman and servant, John 'The Red' Comyn, and the desecration of the Holy Church!"

All cheered again, led by the Prince of Wales, who swung his sword in a circle over his head.

The king motioned quiet, at which the crowd grew hushed as suddenly as it had cheered, so that the king could be heard to finish.

"And... and when we are shed of this traitorous rebellion, I shall ne'er levy war on Christians again, but shall journey to the Holy Land and there kill only the heathens and their kind."

King Edward then sat, totally spent, amidst enthusiastic cheering. Shortly, the younger Edward called for quiet, again.

The crowd gradually hushed as he began to speak, "I swear, before the swans and the King of England, and *rightful King of Scotland...*" the crowd loudly cheered and applauded until the prince continued, "... that I shall march at the head of this grand army, and I shall not sleep two nights in the same place, 'til we breach the borders of Scotland!"

All cheered wildly once again, and King Edward closed his eyes and smiled, for he was well pleased with the behavior of his son this night.

The Swan Knights pushed through, one-by-one, to swear fealty before the king and the swans, then knelt before the Prince, who, at his father's direction, struck each of them upon the shoulders into knight-hood.

When the three hundred or so knights were all struck, their fathers and the other nobles, through the weight of sheer enthusiasm, came forth to swear fealty and to extinguish the evil rebellion in the north.

. .

Thus, on the thirtieth day of May 1306, all of the newly-made knights, led by the Prince of Wales and accompanied by a contingent of one hundred foot soldiers, saluted the king and set forth to Scotland, as they had sworn to do.

The remaining army, commanded by King Edward, himself, would follow in slower fashion, as the king had to be borne about on a litter. They were to rejoin in Carlisle within a fortnight.

Fergus

JUNE 16th 1306
A SMALL VILLAGE SEVERAL MILES FROM LOCHMABEN

Six or so hens and a small, multi-colored rooster scratched in the dirt for bugs and bits of grain in front of the stick and stone hovel where two old men, Seamus and Argyle, were sitting on a low bench arguing the folk politics of the day.

"Ye think, me friend, that the Laird of Annandale will protect us from the English, now that he's got himself to be king?" questioned Seamus.

"Send them English whelps whinin' back home with tucked tails, he will," returned Argyle.

Both elders sat nodding in agreement and watching the women down by the stream, beating the laundry on broad flat rocks worn smooth by generations of their mothers doing the same.

A slight misty drizzle had begun to fall, but not heavily enough to drive the men indoors or the women from their chore. The mist came and went, alternating with periods when the sun burned through the overcast and gave the sky a milky luminescence.

"Bad omen though, him killin' that Comyn in the kirk," said Seamus, finally, shaking his head in fear of heavenly retribution.

"The bishop said it was blessed, 'cause he was only protectin' hisself," defended Argyle. He grimaced as he poked around in his ear with a small stick, and brought it out carrying a bit of earwax, which he rubbed off on the edge of the bench.

"Well, ye know, the English have already taken Lochmaben, again. 'Tis the third time in me own memory," said Seamus pointing his old, gnarled cane down the hill in the general direction of Castle Lochmaben. "Murdered all there, they did. And I recollect his grandda' livin' there peaceful, only a few year ago."

"Aye," was the return, "but ye forget, there were few there to fight them off."

"I'd say... that weren't too witty on the laird's part," gainsaid Seamus.

"Ye'll see, soon 'nough," argued Argyle, though he wished Robert had left Lochmaben better manned.

"Best do, 'cause I heard tell of a'plenty of English, with many knights, holin' up in Carlisle, and they're mad as devils about the doin's of the Brus," said Seamus, then added, "'Course, hain't no mind of common folk, 'cept we get in the way of their sword work."

Argyle stood. "We just might all be drug into this fracas," he remarked at about the same moment he noticed a glimmer emerging from the wood on the edge of the horizon. "See there? Soldiers come."

"No doubt to garrison Lochmaben. Nary a body's been there since they took it over. Folks been too scared." Seamus squinted to bring the distant glimmering into focus.

"All the same, I'm hidin' on the hill," announced Argyle, and he hobbled his old body around the house and up the hill toward the wood.

"Who comes, grandda?" asked Betsey as she emerged from the shelter.

The women brought their meager belongings up from the stream and came to ask the same question.

"Soldiers, I reckon," said Seamus, who was senior in the small gathering, "Soldiers to the king of England, I reckon."

"Why say ye, 'English'!?" loudly queried a panicked neighbor.

"'Cause the Brus' hain't nowhere around these parts, and he's lettin' folk wander in and out like the breeze while he gallivants around the countryside 'savin'' us all," expounded Seamus philosophically, but no ears heard, for the women hurriedly scattered to collect their babies and cattle and hide them in safe places.

Argyle made it to the edge of the wood on the hill and stopped there to catch his breath and survey the countryside.

He expected to see his friends and neighbors following him, but instead he saw about forty brilliantly armored knights, riding fast beneath two banners: one, the three leopards banner of King Edward, and the other bearing two swans facing each other, one black and one white.

Their armor glinted and flashed, even in the dullness of the hazy late spring sun, as they fanned out to take in the whole village in one swath, blocking all escape.

The knights had given their shields to be carried by trailing squires on ponies, for they knew the village was most probably without weapons. Only a few villagers had the courage to fight back with sharpened sticks, but it was to no avail.

As Argyle watched from his sanctuary, steel sword blades wielded by cowardly knights slashed through men, women, children, and livestock. No living creatures that were seen, not even the chickens scratching in the yard, were saved, except for several of the young women.

"God in heaven, they're killin' them all," yelled Argyle, sinking to his ancient knees as, before his eyes, the horror unfolded on the ground he had stood upon only moments earlier.

"Poor Seamus, me last friend on all this earth," he lamented with tears streaming freely down his wrinkled, weathered face. "And the babies, too! Oh, God in heaven... God in heaven..." The old man bent down and buried his face in his hands and tried not to hear the faint screams and agonizing cries coming from his village.

Some of the knights split up and searched the surrounding area for more satisfaction for their bloody blades while others put a merciful end to the wounded.

It was all over within minutes.

Argyle recovered himself enough to know that the soldiers would soon sweep in a wider arc to see if they could turn up anyone who might have escaped from the village, and he knew he could be of no help below.

He stood with the aid of his walking stick and started to move away through the misty wood, when he saw three knights, working their way up the hill in his direction.

Shrinking deeper into the shadows as the large destriers came closer, the old man, who, as a youth, had traveled with The Contender on his crusade to the Holy Land, hid behind a large tree and began to pray silently, his tears of grief mingling with the gathering fog to streak his face.

He could hear the hooves moving through the underbrush and the clank of armor plates, and he smelled the sweat of hard-run horses close on to him, but remained as still as a frightened rabbit.

Argyle heard one of the knights say, "They had no time to get this far."

"'Tain't easy gettin' rid of vermin," remarked another, swinging his sword through the underbrush.

The random chopping and mangling of the bushes by the three continued, though half-heartedly, for a few more minutes, and when they had satisfied themselves that there was nobody hiding in the wood, they turned and headed lazily down the hill to join their comrades.

"Vermin?" whispered Argyle to himself as they moved away. "The likes of us are vermin, to 'em?"

Suddenly struck with pure anger that welled up within him and overcame his fear, the ancient Scot hobbled, cane in hand, to the edge of the wood and began shouting epithets at the retreating knights.

One turned in his saddle to see the old man shaking his cane and his fist in the air, and heard the vague sounds of his voice. "Damn him! We missed one cursin' ol' prick," he said to his companions.

The second knight turned in his saddle as all three continued to ride down the hill. "Who wants the honor of killing such a worthy foe?" he laughed. "You, Paxton?"

"I'm too damned hot and tired for riding that far back up the hill. Besides, there's some wenches in the village," said the third, "I want to get there before they're all used up..." He cut his eyes around to his compatriots and grinned, licking his lips lasciviously. All three laughed and whooped. "And, besides," he added, "what's one more crippled ol' Scot worth in this war, anyhow?" He kicked his horse and trotted down the hill, followed by the second knight.

The first turned again in his saddle to look at Argyle, standing alone against them without a chance of survival.

"Today is your lucky day, you ol' bastard," he said under his breath, then urged his horse faster and charged down the hill until he caught up to the other two.

Argyle sank to the ground in a complete fit of tears and anger when he realized they had abandoned the chase.

"No!" he challenged as loud as he could. "Come back, ye sons of whores! Ye cannot leave me here, alone!" But the three were beyond the hearing of his anguished words, and continued down the hill to the village and their carnal pleasures with the hapless women and girls.

The Scotsman sat there, snuffling and whining until he could see them no more. "Why hain't they a'comin' to kill me, too?... Why!?" he whimpered. "Why were my prayers to save myself answered...? Where is this 'King Robert' who promises to protect us and keep us from the defilements and slavery of the English?"

Exhausted, he collapsed in a heap and lay as he fell, cursing the English who had destroyed his village, and the Scottish king who allowed it to happen, until he slipped into a cold, wet, fitful sleep.

· ·

Early the next morning he was awakened by the splatter of rain on his tear-streaked face. He shook his head to relieve it from the excesses of the rainwater, and the throbbing, brutal imagery passing through his brain.

Then it all came tumbling forth in vivid pictures.

"The village!" he shouted as he sat bolt upright, and a searing pain stabbed through his back and shoulders like molten iron.

Every muscle in his old man's body resisted movement.

Through the misty landscape he could see the charred remains of the hamlet in which he had lived since boyhood. He shivered in the cold, gray light.

Finally he struggled to his feet and walked down the slope with much effort, his soaked old body no longer a priority to his wit as he began his painful descent.

The villagers he knew so well lay hither and thither in pools and rivulets of bloody, muddy water. Argyle had never seen anything of this magnitude, even in the earlier wars with the English. This was truly a new level of evil brought to helpless folk, he mourned.

His friends... all... dead around him. His world crushed in total defeat. What more in life was there for him?

His head began to spin and his heart to pound heavily in his chest as his fingers and arms tingled. His vision grew black at the edges and his legs crumpled from under him, dropping the old man again to his knees. There he sobbed pitifully among the carnage.

At last a merciful trance overcame him and he grew silent as stone. The rains increased to torrents, and the rains lessened to mist, and through it all, the old man remained quietly in the mire.

He would die there with his friends and neighbors, he decided. It would be appropriate, since he had lived all his life among them and their kin.

In his deathwatch, he thought he heard something. The wind? A wolf or the like, coming out of the wilderness to feed on those, now but carrion, around him?

For a moment, he gripped tightly his walking stick, thinking he would defend his lost neighbors from the beast. But, he would soon be one of the dead, and what was the use of it?

Whatever was coming for them sought but to live.

He dropped the stick.

Then, he heard the sound again, and realized that it was close. There was, within the space of three or four rods, he estimated, a low moan that sounded more human than beast-like.

His eyes involuntarily scanned about the direction of the sound.

"Life?" asked Argyle of the gods in a gravelly, unearthly rumble deep in his throat.

He regained his stick and stumbled to his feet, and made his way in the direction of the moan. Rain spattered his eyes and he wiped them frantically as he examined the dead along his path.

There was a child, eyes frozen in a heavenward gaze, its mother face down in the ruddy mire, her arm surrounding the bairn, even in death.

With his walking stick he poked at several corpses, including that of his friend Seamus, and knowing them to be dead, moved on.

Working his walking stick under the chest of one large-framed man, he pushed with all his might, lifting the fellow up from his belly and onto his side, after which a pitiable complaint emanated from him.

He had found the source of the moan.

"Fergus!" shouted Argyle. "Be ye dead, or do ye yet live?"

"Livin' for now," said Fergus. "See what burns and aches my back so."

"Ye've been slashed w' a sword, man," answered Argyle, quietly. It was probable that Fergus would soon die, he knew.

Fergus fainted once again, and Argyle shook his head in dismay.

"Why him... of all I knew... why did he survive and none other? I ne'er knew this lad for much."

With the help of his stick the old man stood and turned away. He would leave the younger man to his dying. There was nothing to be done for him, anyhow.

Argyle shambled off.

A few steps away he stopped and looked back at the muddy figure. "But, I cannot!" he argued loudly to the atmosphere. "He is far too heavy and long for me to manage, and I'll do naught but prolong his suff'rin'."

With one gnarled and callused hand, he wiped the rain and mud from his own face, and after a moment found himself staring down into the rain-filled hoof prints left by the steeds of the marauding knights.

"A-a-r-r-gh!" a low rumble erupted from his throat.

He spat at the knights in absentia, turning to face the direction from which they had come.

"Ye'll not... have this victory without a fight!" he exclaimed with great hatred, pointing his walking stick at the prostrate form of Fergus.

"Argyle of Lochmaben Glen will not surrender another soul to ye... ye dog-tailed hounds of Edward Plantagenet! D'ye hear me?!!" he yelled with all his might.

The gray clouds had given little break from the wetness. Argyle quickly made a poor shelter from the charred ruins of the villagers' huts and the remains of the retainer fences around the butchered animals.

That done, he slung his woolen sash beneath the larger man's arms and, with straining, short pulls, eventually dragged the dying man under it. At least he was affording poor Fergus a temporary respite from the rain.

Once inside, he stripped the slashed kirtle and shirt from the man's back and tended his gaping wound as best he could with what little he had. Though there was caked blood on Fergus' clothing and back, not much oozed from the gash, for which Argyle was grateful.

He splintered an old bone from the trash pit and, taking a long, slender piece of it, bored a hole in one end to make a sewing needle. Then, with a long, thin piece of sinew, he set about sewing up the gash across Fergus' back, which took hours. He finished by light from a pitifully small, smoky fire, well after dark.

Mixing handfuls of mud with some herbs and leaves he had just last week selected from the hillside and stored in a small pouch, he prepared a poultice and packed it in a thick layer across the sewn wound, hoping to draw out the poisons and evil within it.

With that done, he lay back and rested.

"Dear God, if ye let just this one but live," prayed the exhausted Argyle, "I'll know the purpose of my own survival... I will."

Christopher Seton

JUNE 18th 1306
THE TOWN OF PERTH

"Send forth the Earl of Pembroke!" shouted Robert de Brus from the back of his armored horse, his red and yellow shield at the ready, his sword not yet drawn. He sat astride his pawing horse on the road before the entrance to the walled town of Perth. With him were Edward Brus, Christopher Seton, and Thomas Randolph.

Several guards hastily appeared from within the tower keeps on either side above the city's western gate.

"From whence did they appear?" asked one aghast guard to the other as they recognized the party.

"I know not! They're just calmly standin' there as if to take the afternoon air," said another as he looked over the fields and woods, searching for an army of Scots and finding none.

"Somebody best run for Lord Pembroke!" said another, who was approaching the throes of panic. "Close the city gates!" he hollered repeatedly, and in good order the city's heavy gates were closed and barred.

The first guard hied himself down the tower steps to find the sentry captain.

"Captain! Captain! The Brus is at the gate!" yelled the guard within his last ten or so paces before actually coming into his commander's presence.

The captain, his heart suddenly having leapt into his throat, said not a word but grabbed his helmet and ran the height of the stairs as fast as he could.

Robert saw the small, feathered plume atop the captain's helmet and recognized that he had reached the next level in the chain of command, at least, and so renewed his demand.

"Send forth the Earl of Pembroke!"

"Who demands so about the earl?" asked the captain, winded.

"I am Robert de Brus, King of Scots, and I'll not wait long for Lord de Valence! I suggest ye fetch him with naught more ado!" shouted Robert in a strong, clear voice.

The captain's head disappeared beneath the wall as the trumpets sounded within the town calling the garrison to battle alert.

"I'd say we got their attention," said Edward, sitting on his own heavily armored mount next to Robert's.

"We're sittin' here like slow-witted cattle, waitin' for the slaughter," complained Thomas, uneasily. He straddled his armored beast on Robert's other side.

Christopher Seton held his position behind the trio and said nothing. Robert's dog stood faithful vigil among the horses' enormous hooves.

They were facing down a town of several thousand citizens and some six thousand combat-hardened soldiers, the latter of whom would most willingly cut them down on sight for a mere percentage of the reward on their collective heads.

"I'm commencin' to worry about this plan of yers, Robert," fretted Edward.

Gesturing toward Thomas Randolph, Robert said, "He says Pembroke is an honorable man, and has befriended him on various occasions."

"Actually, I said I never *knew* him to renege on his word as an honorable man," clarified Thomas.

"They're comin' alive, Robert," remarked Christopher as his wary eye scanned the top of the increasingly busy wall walk of the town.

The head of Aymer de Valence, Earl of Pembroke, suddenly appeared from behind the wall, some forty feet above the four standing alone on the road. He took a full minute to study and understand the situation, then said to the man at his side, "These are the Scots about whom you are so concerned, Captain? Four of them?"

"But, Milord," the captain returned, chagrined, "he announced himself as 'Robert de Brus, King of Scots' And I..."

"Edward Plantagenet is the 'King of Scots,' as he is King of England. I suggest you remember that, Captain, if you like wearing your head upon your shoulders," Pembroke ruthlessly rebuked him. The captain sullenly clenched his teeth and said no more, while the earl looked down upon the four Scots below.

"That you, Randolph?" Pembroke suddenly spouted loudly, spying the young Scot.

Thomas grinned at his old friend and said, " Aye, 'tis," and no more.

"Mixin' in evil company, you reckon?" shouted Pembroke, goading his young friend.

"Reckon not," returned Thomas, twisting uncomfortably in his saddle.

"Milord Carrick!" Pembroke refused to call him else. "I reckon you have saved me the trouble of huntin' down you and your bunch of ruffians," yelled Pembroke, directing his say to King Robert.

"We are here, Milord Pembroke." At that, he signaled Sir Christopher, who raised his shield high above his head. Before the eyes of those on the wall of the town, the woods and wheat fields behind the Brus grew suddenly black with the heads of the camouflaged Scottish horde. Now it was the turn of the English to be discomfited.

"We have no intention of runnin' from a fight, should ye want one," returned Brus. "To the contrary, I challenge ye to come out and face me in honorable combat."

"These walls are for the taking, Sir, if you think you can," bellowed de Valence, smacking his crude heavy hand on the stout stone wall behind which he stood. "Come as you may please."

"I have no siege engines to invest these walls that ye cower behind, Pembroke," taunted Robert.

"It is of no interest to me, Sir, that you came ill-prepared to conduct a proper siege," sneered the disheveled earl as he wiped his nose on his sleeve and laughed at the Scots' shortcomings. All on the wall laughed with him except Phillip Mowbray and Ingram de Umfraville, who were flanking Pembroke and observing a highly different set of circumstances than was he.

"I desire no siege, My Lord Pembroke. My challenge is to ye, as a knight of the English court, to meet me in personal combat." Then, in deference to the physical condition of the older man, he added, "If ye are indisposed, ye may select any champion ye wish to fight in yer stead. Or, ye may bring yer army forth and meet mine in fixed combat. 'Tis yer choice."

"And why," chortled the confident Pembroke, "would I want to leave these stout confines?" Turning to the group of sycophants aligned along the wall with him, he commented, "This is the would be 'King' of the Scots... A dolt, with dolts a'followin'!"

They all laughed loudly.

Robert ignored the insult and continued with his purpose. "Chivalric tradition holds... and I have word from yer honorable friend, Sir Thomas Randolph, here, that ye *do* adhere to the chivalric code... that if ye will not come out to fight me one-on-one in a joust, or yer army against mine on open ground, then ye are to forfeit the town and all of its holdin's, forthwith," stated Robert matter-of-factly.

This brought on another round of boisterous laughter from the wall, as a servant handed Sir Aymer another flagon of wine, which he heartily gulped between laughs.

The Scot waited until the laughter died and all could hear before asking, "Then ye are not an honorable knight, Sir?"

The derisive mirth on the wall quickly died.

Pembroke, enraged at the obviously intended insult, grabbed a crossbow from a soldier standing a few paces away and aimed it unsteadily at the four mounted Scots.

"Take *this* to your graves, you damned whelps of Scottish whores!" he spat uncontrollably as he too quickly loosed the bolt. It pierced naught but the ground between Robert and Thomas. The horses nearest the bolt flinched as if a fly had bitten, and the dog moved away from the missile's landing point, but the four men neither flinched nor moved.

"Yer friends have stingers," said Christopher to Thomas as he looked down at the bolt protruding from the earth. Thomas did not respond, but sat looking toward the wall.

"Thinkin' on killin' my dog, are ye?" yelled Robert to the big choleric man leaning over the top of the wall.

"Are we not goin' to pull back?" asked Edward, concerned about their being within such easy arrow range.

"Ye have a shield. If a flight comes, use it. We'll not move 'til we get the answer due us," determined Robert, not looking at his brother but keeping his eyes fixed on the progressions on the wall walk above.

Out of sight of his fellow Scots, Sir Ingram grabbed the earl by the arm and turned him to get his attention, "Sir Aymer, if ye will but listen to my thought, I will have vengeance for my Comyn family, and ye too will have yer way!"

"To hell with your vengeance! Comyn was my kin too, but I hain't carin' shit for vengeance. I'm here at the pleasure of King Edward, and I will do as he has charged me to do... eradicate this Scottish rabble!" shouted Pembroke as he waved the crossbow in the air.

Umfraville spoke, "They are many, Milord, but they are mostly untried knights and villeins and farmers armed with their hoes and scythes. There is no better-trained army in the world than ours! We can beat them on open ground and be done with it! No scourin' the countryside seekin' them out of their holes, and them with the ability to attack us almost at will as we wander."

"I agree," said Sir Phillip decisively, moving closer to the side of Sir Ingram.

"You two must have gone daft," said Pembroke in angry disgust. "Brus himself admitted he has no siege engines. We are well stored and can hold, right here, until King Edward and his army join with us. But *you* two... *you* want to march out with your flags a'flyin' and relinquish our stronghold, to meet the Brus at *his* convenience!"

"What's it to be, Pembroke?" yelled Robert from the roadway as the discussion on the wall continued.

"Daft is it? Daft to think that ye, the Earl of Pembroke, will share the reward given for the destruction of this..." he waved his arm in the general direction of the Scots, "ragged army that our sovereign, King Edward wants so badly to be rid of?" questioned Sir Ingram.

"Why don't I simply have all these men shoot the son-of-a-bitchin' 'king' where he now stands, eh?" asked Aymer, his eyes protruding from their sockets in his ire, as he waved the uncocked crossbow, up and down the walk, taking mock aim.

Umfraville dropped his voice to a dramatic whisper, "Because then, Milord, ye would have a martyr, like Wallace." The earl snorted, but Umfraville continued. "Only this time, 'twon't be the common rabble who worship his memory, nay! 'Twill be the earls and the barons, and the bishops, aye. The 'community of the realm,' have enough power to keep the rebellion goin' for years, even without the Brus, and that is sure to displease King Edward."

Now, Pembroke was listening. Phillip picked up the tapestry and continued to work on the weave. "Many of those who now stand with ye will switch allegiance soon enough if one of their own be murdered in cold blood." He gestured toward the Scottish army, gathered in the fields and woods and said, "But, were he killed in *battle...*" he paused to let the thought settle on Pembroke, "...*there* be the end of the rebellion, and none to mourn it. Edward then has Scotland, and we shall have our reward and the satisfaction that our Comyn kin have been avenged."

"And yonder are the army ye need to destroy," Ingram hissed. "'The Scottish horde' are now ripe and for the reapin', just outside these walls."

Below them waited the four Scots, their patience growing thin.

"This hain't workin'," lamented Thomas as the moments passed.

"I think Aymer's takin' a piss," remarked Edward in a vain attempt at levity.

"It will work," insisted Robert, ignoring Edward's remark. "It must."

Pembroke, meanwhile, was studying the faces of the two Scotsmen who stood before him. He was thinking on whether or not they were trying to trick him, for he never trusted anyone who spoke in Scottish tongue.

Then, just as quickly as his temper flared, his greed played in through his alcohol-deadened senses as he thought of the reward. "Fife's wealth will be mine with the head of Brus," he said, almost to himself, forgetting his agreement to share with Umfraville and Mowbray.

"*Ours*," reminded Phillip. "Fife's wealth will be *ours*."

Pembroke nodded his head in feigned agreement, thinking that, if they or one of them survived the coming battle, he could break such agreement later, somehow, and the monies of Fife would all be his. He never truly considered it otherwise.

Sir Ingram was suddenly inspired with a second plan and said to Pembroke, "Wait, Milord, God has just given me a way to rid the land of this evil."

"And what might that be, Scotsman?" asked Sir Aymer, suspicions again ruling his instincts. But, as he listened to the plan that Umfraville laid out for the destruction of the army that stretched before the castle, Lord Pembroke's pallor changed from near purple to the excited flush of anticipation.

His eyebrows raised with glee as he realized that the Scot at his side had just given him the gift of victory and the end of Scotland's fighting force.

Sir Aymer turned to look over the wall. "I agree," he yelled down to King Robert.

"Agree to what?" returned Robert, demanding that Aymer spell it out.

Pembroke took another swig of wine and leaned out over the wall as far as he could manage to assure his being heard, then loudly announced, "To engage our armies in battle, with the town and castle falling to the winner, man! However, I'm sure you will agree that, the day being late, we've not enough sun remaining to fight a proper battle."

Pembroke paused, then proposed, "So, Lord Brus, what say that you and yours journey to Methven Park, a few miles in yonder direction, and we'll meet there for battle on the morn?"

"I have yer word?"

"Indeed, Milord. I now affirm in front of all here that I shall be at Methven Park on the morrow. I swear before God." Aymer grinned broadly.

"Agreed!" shouted Robert loudly as he wheeled his horse, then added to his cohorts, "Now, we're high-tailin'... ye comin'?" His three companions turned and followed.

"'Tis God's will," said Sir Phillip, thinking on the newly hatched plan. The three nobles watched the four Scotsmen ride down the road toward Methven with Robert's army following.

. .

"Yonder's the park," said Christopher as the four leading horsemen turned a bend in the road that revealed a wide expanse of lush meadowland before them.

"Appears to be a reasonable battle area," said Edward as he rode to Robert's side.

"Aye," remarked Robert, hesitating, "but why would Pembroke give us the choice of first position on the field?"

"He knows he has us outnumbered, Robert," Thomas said with a shrug, "and if he kills us all he accomplishes his mission. To his way of thinkin', it matters not if he loses a thousand more men than need be in the doin'... he just hain't got to pay them when they're dead."

Robert rode to the center of the park, in fact a game preserve for the town of Perth. There were other, similar fields around, but as far as Robert's battle-trained eye could see, this one was ideal for the purpose of waging war.

The chosen field was about a furlong by somewhat less than that, a patch of semi-flat land, bordered on two sides by trees. On the third flowed a burn from which he had access to ample fresh running water for now, and it was wide enough that his army could not get out-flanked from that side as a full battle progressed. His archers would cut them to pieces.

Edward rode up to Robert and asked, "Where do ye want yer command tent pitched, Robert?"

"On the far side, among yonder stand of trees," commanded Robert pointing to the corner of the field to his right. "It's a wee bit uphill and allows a better view of the field. And the sun will catch it first in the mornin.'"

Sir Simon Fraser, a large, battle-hardened highlander and old friend, who had been in the ranks of knights and barons standing before Perth, came to Robert for instructions. "What do ye have for me, Bobby?" he asked.

Robert turned in his saddle and smiled at his old comrade who had traveled far to be at his side this day and said, "Send the archers to the hunt; there should be plenty of game nearby. I want all to have full bellies when they face battle on the morrow. Then, return here with yer captains and we'll lay a plan for meeting the English."

"Aye, Sire," answered Fraser as he turned and rode back into the ranks beyond the arriving knights to the archers, who were traveling on foot farther back. "Archers to the hunt!" he commanded several times as he rode through the lines. They obeyed without further explanation, for their deadly talents were also put to use gathering meat for the force.

Once past the archers, Fraser rode to the captain of the infantry and ordered him to send at least one thousand men to the surrounding area to gather what other edibles were at hand for the soldiers, in case there was insufficient game to fill all the hungry bellies. He also instructed that others set the horses and other livestock to pasture. When it was done, he returned to the park where Edward was overseeing the erection of the command tent, and several other tents for the earls and barons.

Alexander Scrymgeour, the royal standard bearer, arrived in full exuberance, virtually prancing his mount across the field, holding high the pennant of red lion rampant on a bright yellow background, and waving it proudly all the way.

"Aye, war *is* glorious," Nigel Brus smilingly remarked to his brother Alexander. They sat mounted, overlooking the imminent battlefield.

Alexander's Scottish pride swelled, also, as he saw the red and yellow banner and the flag bearing the Cross of Saint Andrew that followed, but he saw no glory and adventure. Instead, he said, "I cannot agree with ye, little brother. I see this fight only as a means to attain Scotland's freedom from that English despot, nothin' more." He paused and looked at the handsome young knight, his baby brother who had never seen a battle, and asked, "Look over this brae and tell me what see ye here tomorrow at this time, Nigel."

"My heart pounds all the quicker when ye add such a noble purpose to the fight," returned Nigel. "I feel the greatness of our forefathers coursin' through my body. I see a great victory at hand, here, on this grass before us. Do ye not?"

"I see a bloody mass of brave men who will be no more, no matter who is the victor," answered Alexander. "And I pray that ye and the rest of my brothers be not among them."

The two sat in silence until Alexander turned his horse toward Robert's tent and rode away. Nigel watched him and struggled with conflicted emotions. He still wanted to experience the exhilaration and daring of a great struggle, and would willingly give his life if necessary, in his country's service. But Alexander's words had altered his concept of what battle must be like. He had not considered that his brothers, or any of them, might be killed, and the lightness had left from his youthful expectations of adventure.

Thomas Brus and Thomas Randolph were managing preparations on the field of battle, while others busied themselves with building campfires and cooking for the hungry crew, still spreading into the park. Many of the men had a remainder of the twelve days' rations, required by King Robert when he ordered them to muster, and so went straightaway to fixing their meals.

Robert, wearing his simple circlet of gold for a crown, sat astride his great destrier and played out a plan in his mind from the highest ground.

Sir John Somerville and Sir Hugh de la Haye, both brave and noble barons having many skirmishes with the English under their belts, stood their mounts just behind the king, and played a second scenario between them. They would propose it at the plans meeting later in the evening.

"What rim guard did ye want, Robert?" asked Edward Brus, shattering Robert's thought with his sudden appearance and question.

"As ye have done will be sufficient this night, Edward," returned Robert, "for we know at what hour the enemy comes."

"Aye, then 'tis done," replied Edward as he dismounted, stretched, and walked to the command area to relax and have a bite to eat. He removed his heavy body armor and laid it aside, then put on a white linen shirt and strapped his sword around his waist. Without the fifty pounds of metal weighing him down, he felt more relaxed already.

Most of the other nobles and many of the knights had done the same, and the camp was filled with men looking forward to a good meal and a night's rest after the hard march that had brought them to this place.

Nigel and Alexander joined the gathering officers in the small clump of old, large trees, close to the burn. The squires took the horses from the men as they came into camp to rest. After unsaddling and feeding them, the hostlers penned them inside a barricade.

Viewed at the length of a man's arm, the setting sun was two fingers above the horizon in the park at Methven when Robert noticed a changing pattern of colors on the mane of his horse. He turned and watched the clouds, dramatically engaged in a war of darks and lights, soon to be won by the dark.

He thought of Elizabeth on the wall walk at Kildrummy and wondered if she were there now, witnessing the same terrible and beautiful drama as he.

Robert looked back across the peaceful field. Men were scattered everywhere, sleeping, telling stories, or lies, depending on their point of view. Some were gigging for fish and turtles in the creek, and yet others were fixing their suppers around the campfires that stretched the width and breadth of the field, the hundreds of dots of fire growing smaller toward the distance.

In the middle of the field was a huge bonfire being set to serve as a rallying fire in the early evening hours.

Some of the foragers were now drifting back into the camp, as some twenty-five or thirty returning archers placed their small quarry of rabbits and various birds in the hands of the cooks. Before long, those with larger kills came dragging them in, and it began to look as if everyone would have fresh meat for supper.

The game was promptly dressed out and put to roast or boil on the fire, and before long, more arrived, and more, until the whole camp was deliciously aromatic with the smell of cooking meats.

As the sun lay one finger above the horizon, Robert was leading his horse by the reins around the perimeter of the field, checking for sink holes or other dangers to his battle plan.

He greeted all the men and women that he encountered and called many by name, wishing them well in the battle on the morrow. Robert was personally proud of each and every patriot gathered at his side.

Once he felt confident that he knew the lay of the land, Robert mounted and headed his horse toward the command area, where he dismounted and handed the reins to Andrew. The boy took his horse to the enclosure where all of the hundred and twenty-three horses were being readied for the night.

Robert shed his armor. "Hope Pembroke comes in the early part of the day," he said to all around while taking his claymore from his waist and hanging it around his neck in the usual manner.

"Aye, armor on a summer day can be hot as the hinges of hell, and that's the truth," said Alexander Brus as he leaned deeper into the curved trunk of one of the large trees and closed his eyes for a well-earned rest.

The earls of Lennox and Atholl sat across the fire from Robert. Lennox asked, "What plan have ye for the battle?"

"When Hugh and John join us we will discuss my plans and theirs, and choose rightly from the mix," said Robert, pulling a piece of rabbit from the spit, "and what ye men have to throw into the stew will be for consideration also." Lennox and Atholl nodded and continued their eating.

The king's piper was playing a few paces away from the tent and Robert listened for a moment, taking in the mournfully beautiful strains.

"Walk among the men so that they may enjoy yer playin'..." commanded Robert as he took off his crown and laid it beside him on the log, then added, "and, for God's sake, play somethin' more light hearted."

The old piper did as he was told and some of the men, as always when they heard the pipes, were inspired and followed him to hear more. The dog raised his head with a melancholy howl in sympathy with the droning.

Andrew, the king's squire, and Robert Wishart's squire, David, set about to bright polish Robert's breastplate near where the horses were tied for the night.

"One day I will have a horse of this magnificence," bragged Andrew, patting Robert's great Belgian, "and I will be the king's own champion."

"I already have the bishop's horse," bragged David as he, too, admired the king's great steed.

"The bishop may not be kilt," said Andrew, "and the mare's not yers 'til he is."

David was quiet and suddenly dispirited as he realized the weightiness of the other boy's careless remark. "Aye," he said as he threw fodder at his small horse's front feet and left to attend his other chores.

Andrew felt badly and wished that he could take back what he had said, but he knew there was nothing to do now but let his counterpart go.

Sir David Inchmartin rode into the camp and reined up near the now-blazing bonfire. His packhorse carried concealed armor and weapons while he was dressed in ordinary clothing to be able to move inconspicuously among the populace.

"Catch Sir David, there," ordered Robert to a squire standing nearby.

"Sir David, Sire?" asked the squire, who did not know the man.

"Sir David Inchmartin, the one who just rode in near the fire and cannot see us in the shadows of these trees," Robert pointed in the fire's direction.

The young man saw the newcomer and said, "Aye, Milord," and did as he was bade.

"Ye et, David?" asked Robert as the young knight came into the command area.

"Nay, Sire. I took no time to sup for fear I would come too late and miss the fray."

"We're set for the morn," said Robert, and Inchmartin frowned.

"Morn it may be, but, while on the road here, I saw many men with weapons gatherin' around Perth," replied Inchmartin.

"No doubt settin' for an early beginnin' on the morn," said Robert, confident in Lord Pembroke's word. "We'll be set by the crow o' the cock ourselves."

John Somerville came to the command area and sat on one of the large logs brought into place by several of the squires. He helped himself, as did David Inchmartin, to small chickens just brought in by a plump camp woman who obviously knew how to cook them to perfection under the most primitive conditions.

"Where's Hugh?" asked Robert.

"He'll be along directly," said John.

"Let's get this meet goin'," suggested Lennox, wiping his greasy hands on the soft spring grass.

Christopher Seton strolled up to sit beside John Somerville, and Thomas Brus sat on the other end of the log. Sir David Barclay came into the group and leaned against a tree, picking the meat from between his teeth with his sgian dubh.

Robert pulled more meat off the hot rabbit on the spit and ate it heartily.

Pouring wine for his lord, Andrew noticed how the only light now came from the fires, the sun having sunk completely below the horizon, and thought that it certainly didn't seem like a great battle could break this tranquil scene as quickly as the morrow.

The bishop's squire, David, his heart weighted greatly with missing the old fellow, now heard that that the poor cleric had been arrested and sent to an English dungeon. He went to rub down the bishop's little mare, more to comfort himself than the horse, but found it of no value to him. Deciding that a short ride might keep his mind off his sorrows, he saddled and mounted the horse and rode out a ways on the road toward Perth.

Beneath the trees, Robert was eating and talking to his gathered council. "I'm thinkin' that we put our pikemen in phalanxes like those Wallace used at Falkirk," he said between bites of steaming rabbit. He wiped his hand on his shirt and, with a convenient stick, quickly drew the perimeter of the field and the beginning of a battle plan in the dirt and ash at his feet, ""We'll place the phalanxes thus... that will draw their mounted forces into our pikes, thus... " he scraped another line into the dirt, "and break them into smaller groups. Our horsemen, here... we'll release at that point to sweep down and ..."

"Why Wallace's trick?" interrupted Lennox, frowning angrily. "He lost at Falkirk, and damned bad, too!"

"Aye," explained Robert, throwing away his rabbit bone and flashing a look of displeasure at Lennox. "But usin' phalanxes is not the reason he lost Falkirk. It's why he held as well as he did, havin' precious little else to oppose the English cavalry with after John Comyn and his horsemen fled the field. It had all to do with cowardice and poor arms, and naught to do with phalanxes. Havin' no mounted troops, Wallace's defeat at Falkirk was but the simple result of bein' o'erwhelmed by more than his poor lads could withstand."

"What makes ye think this be not the same as what we shall face on the morn, Sire?" asked Lord Atholl.

"We have forty-five hundred to Pembroke's six thousand. We have far more mounted knights, more trained men than had Wallace at Falkirk," said Robert. "And the most precious asset we have, is that they can do one thing that we cannot."

"Which would be?" asked Atholl curiously.

"Go home," stated Robert simply. Most of the assembled men nodded somberly, knowing they must win, or die.

"Our archers," continued Robert with the plan, "we will place here," he stuck the small branch into the map near the forest at the crest of the long rise, "until they commit their infantry. Unlike Wallace, we have long bows... and can rain arrows down on them as we will. Once we have their number reduced sufficient, we can form a semi-circle and close in from the sides..." he closed his fingers slowly until he made a tightly clenched fist, "for the final victory."

The nobles and officers had little more to say.

Hugh de la Haye joined the meeting as Robert turned to John Somerville and asked, "What say ye of the plan, Sir John?"

Somerville looked up at Hugh, then back at King Robert and shook his head, "I know not, Sire. Your plan may work and it may not, but I have nothin' to best it."

"Any suggestions, Lennox?" he asked. Lennox shook his head. "Athol?" He, too, gave a negative reply. "Anyone?" The grim-faced Scots looked from man to man, but no man spoke.

"Then we'll talk of command positions ere first light. Go get some rest, and God be with ye."

• •

About a mile and a half down the road toward Perth, Wishart's unhappy squire was absorbed in musing about the destiny of the old bishop, for he knew he had been taken to London and there he would probably be executed. Little heed was paid to his surroundings until he was suddenly shocked to attention by a shout...

"GET HIM!" yelled a voice.

In the pale evening light the squire saw, just ahead of him, the army he had seen at Cupar castle less than a month earlier.

They were in full battle dress and traveling at a good pace for Methven.

"They're not waitin' for the morrow!" said the squire half aloud.

An Irish hobelar from the English army broke ranks and urged his small horse straight for the boy.

The lad turned his mount quickly and kicked her flanks as hard as he could.

She was not a fast horse but sensed her master's distress and gave all she had to the flight. Still, she was no equal to the hard-charging mount of the Irishman.

The hobelar notched an arrow as he rode and loosed it at the youth.

The arrow was so close that the feather cut his ear.

He could hear the hobelar behind and three more arrows come close by.

David was sweating heavily from fear and action as he whipped the little mare all the more.

He saw the glow of the bonfire just ahead and took comfort in being so close, when he felt the sharp pain of the next arrow pierce his back and exit his chest. His lifeblood flowed through both openings, soaking his shirt.

Again, as when he had ridden from Cupar, all he could think of was warning King Robert.

The hobelar reined in and discontinued the pursuit when he saw his arrow had hit its mark, believing that his mission was accomplished. But, he didn't realize the tenacity of a young lad who dreamed of being a knight in the army of a free Scotland.

"The English are upon us!" shouted the wounded lad. "The English!" His high-pitched voice carried across the park, but not the clarity of his words.

Robert stood at the first shout. His dog came to his side.

"What's that lad whoopin' about, Robert?" asked Edward as he approached the king from behind. The king listened acutely as he tried to make out what the youth was shouting.

"English," said Robert, "He said English."

Some of the men lying about got to their feet, shook their companions awake and grabbed their weapons as they could.

The wounded youth, struggling to hang on to his saddlebow, headed for Robert's command tent, but it was plain he was losing control of the mare.

"Somethin's sure amiss," said Thomas Randolph, strapping his sword around his waist.

"Aye, but what?" said Lennox, arming himself.

The old bishop's squire reined up in front of Robert, the nobles, and his officers. The men could see that the boy was near collapse as he strove to sit as high in the saddle as he could manage.

The body of his white shirt was now fully blood red except for around his collar.

With his last breath on earth he repeated his warning, "My Lord King... English... 'pon us!"

Robert caught the boy as he fell dead from the saddle and laid him easily on the ground, as Edward and Thomas set off to warn the rest of the camp.

"A brave lad," Robert said, closing the boy's lifeless eyes. "Twice he gave all the courage he had to warn us, and this time his very life. We must see that his warning came not in vain." He stood and drew his claymore, throwing the sheath on the ground.

"Amen," prayed Lennox as Robert ordered the drums sounded for battle. All the camp was alive, but many were addled from the quick awakening and knew not if the wan light was dawn or dusk.

Andrew knelt at the side of his dead friend and touched his cheek. He had difficulty realizing that his fellow squire, younger than he, was so easily gone.

Robert grabbed Andrew by the arm and pulled him to his feet. "No time for grievin' now, Lad, lest it be for us all! Saddle my horse, quickly!" he ordered, then turned to his officers and said in a calm but decisive voice, "Prepare for the battle, for they come now, expectin' to catch us by complete surprise."

"What *now* is the plan?" asked Lennox as Edward and Thomas Randolph reined up their mounts in the campsite, their horse's feet kicking fire and ashes about as the heat singed their hooves.

"There is the enemy!" shouted Robert pointing down the road, then added sarcastically with anger, "See? They are led by Sir Aymer, so bold, so brave, so chivalrous!"

Randolph sighed deeply and dropped his chin to his chest, feeling badly that he had inadvertently misled the king.

"The plan, King Robert!" insisted Lennox, hoping there was one.

Robert looked Lennox in the eye and said, "The plan, good friend, is to kill English, in any way we can! What they hope to accomplish with trickery this night, they dared not try with might on the morrow!"

Andrew came forth in haste with Robert's horse, on which he had brought the king's hauberk and coif of mail, his helmet, and his chest armor. Robert handed his great sword to the squire, and as he reached for his hauberk, the whole load slipped off the saddle and landed in a heap on the ground.

"Damn!" fussed Robert in frustration, but just as quickly put the heavy coat of mail over his white linen shirt and strapped his claymore around his waist.

He grabbed up the upper body armor and slipped his head through the straps at the neck, then raised his arm in front of the squire and pointed to the buckle straps. "Quickly!"

The nervous squire buckled the armor as fast as he could.

"Done, Sire."

Robert turned to study the battlefield once again.

"Yer tabard, Sire!" called the young squire.

"Tabard be damned!" shouted Robert angrily. "They'll not know king from knight 'til they feel the slash of my blade."

With that, Robert mounted his unarmored horse. He was bareheaded, whooping his loudest, and swinging his huge claymore in a circle to rally his knights and infantry.

The squires ran hither and thither with various pieces of weaponry and armament for the knights, who were falling into each other in trying to arm both horse and man.

"Look, they're up and about!" shouted Umfraville as the English forces drew near to Methven Park.

"It matters not," grunted Pembroke in his coarse way. The rigors of riding in all the weight of full armor caused his breath to come in rhythmic bursts. "See, they are still... in sordid array and... most of them prayin'... they have another hour... to live. They will... not be the foe they... could have been!"

"We must pounce at once," urged Mowbray.

"Patience, Scots! Your... doomed countrymen not squirmin'... enough for you?" goaded Pembroke, watching two-and-a-half-thousand men, camp-women, and a few children, scurrying for their lives across the open field.

"They're the Brus' countrymen, not ours," insisted Umfraville, sullenly.

"No matter," replied Pembroke as he signaled the bowmen and hobelars into action, "This should thin... their mass effectively."

He laughed, and motioned for another flagon of wine.

While most of Brus' infantry was simply trying to flee the rain of arrows that they knew would be coming, the braver ones grabbed their halberds, pole-axes, knives, and sharpened sticks, and moved toward the approaching enemy.

Lennox and Atholl, who had also managed to dress in their mail coats and some armor, mounted horses that their squires had brought them and rallied the forty or so knights under their commands.

Robert signaled with his claymore that Lennox and Atholl were to take the right flank in the line.

"Sir Christopher, align our knights to the left," barked Robert as he wheeled his horse and saw the hundred brave men who were alone and attacking the leading wave of the English army.

"Shield!" commanded Robert, and it was in his hands immediately.

Edward and Nigel saw what their brother was about and called for their shields also.

The forty-seven Irish hobelars poured onto the battlefield; their small swift, saddleless horses were as extensions of their own bodies, for man and beast worked as one. The arrows the hobelars shot from their powerful short bows were quick and deadly, and the unprepared Scots' ranks were all but decimated by the first flight.

Robert, Nigel, Edward, and six more of Robert's knights made straightaway for the hobelars and pushed themselves and their great horses between the rapidly shooting Irishmen and the embattled soldiers.

The remaining ninety-five Scottish knights were held back by Lennox and Atholl in the more traditional battle order.

The great mass of English archers, having marched into position behind the hobelars, began to launch flight after lethal flight of arrows at the fleeing crowd as it ran for cover or escape. Scores of shafts found the exposed backs of unwilling takers who began to fall all about, only to be trampled by their comrades.

The Scots knights urged the panicked and defenseless throng to outrun the arrows' range as they mounted their destriers in preparation for their own part in the battle.

Robert and his small band were hardly noticed by Pembroke as he gleefully cheered his bowmen forward to the unchivalrous slaughter. Led by their king, the nine mounted Scots were on top of Pembroke's Irishmen before they realized it. The hobelars' small mounts were no match for the massively larger destriers of the knights, and their otherwise murderous weapons were left ineffective in such close quarters against the towering mounted enemy, who chopped and slashed a wide path of destruction through their ranks.

Robert, first into the fray, killed four in quick succession as his knights caught into the battle and quickly cut down more.

"Sound the trumpets, withdraw the hobelars," shrieked Sir Aymer in alarm as he suddenly realized the rapid decline of his crack force of mounted bowmen. The trumpets immediately sounded, and those hobelars who could still withdraw did so thankfully. They wanted no more of the trap in which they had suddenly found themselves.

Some of them, unable to turn their ponies to flee, jumped off their mounts and slipped away by scurrying around and through the legs of the Scots' large horses. One such fellow was quick-witted enough to pull an arrow from his belt quiver as he slid from the haunches of his dying mount, and shove it deep into the belly of one of the Scots' horses. The poor creature reared and cried in pain, throwing his rider to the ground with a loud thud and a clang of armor.

From the back of his mount, Nigel helped the stunned knight to his feet, grabbed a hobelar's loose horse, and pulled the rescued man across the small beast, then both retreated across the field. "Hold on to the belly hair!" commanded Nigel to the knight, who was bouncing so badly that he was near falling to the ground again.

Robert and the others were still taking their toll on those hobelars who could not escape.

"That one's the Brus!" shouted Sir Phillip above the clamor of battle when he suddenly recognized the Scottish king. Pembroke looked at the knot of battling men toward which Mowbray was pointing and, not recognizing any of the usual symbols of a king, dismissed the identification as false.

Brus' small band of rescuers and rescued retreated back across the field. Robert realized that the difficulty the horses were having traversing the less than quarter mile, were the dead and nearly dead of his countrymen, lying everywhere about him.

The English had caught them ill-arrayed and without protection, and had wreaked terrible damage upon them, while they, the Scots, had killed less than thirty of the enemy.

"Withdraw the archers!" commanded Pembroke. He then turned to his two Scottish seconds and remarking with a sweaty grin, "Now, this will be generous to my passions."

"What plan have ye, now?" said Sir Ingram, "Look at them runnin'! As badly as we have beaten them, they'll surely flee into the night. The best they can wish for is revenge another day!"

"You know not your prey," returned Pembroke, angrily swigging another gulp of wine. "Brus will not give up 'til he is dead, and so traps himself into not leaving the field. As he remains, so do his worthless underlings, and we are free to complete his downfall."

Brus' Scots, hearing the screams and moans of agony of their fellows all about, stiffened their own resolve to fight on. Two men, killed during the first flights of arrows, had fallen into the fires and their corpses laid a sickening stench of burning flesh across the field. Men and animals lay with their entrails about them, lending more of battle's foul smells to the formerly peaceful park.

Amid the horror, Robert reached his line of mounted knights and wheeled his horse around to assess the damage and how to strike the next blow.

The moon, full and large, arose in the east and lent a silvery edge to the grotesque scene.

"Lances!" ordered Robert.

"My lord, before we throw away our lads in a hopeless show of courage we must consider that we can now escape a far superior force," suggested the Earl of Atholl. "They've lain waste to more than a third of our army, by my reckonin'."

Robert turned and glared at him with such vehemence that Atholl realized he had made an unwise suggestion and returned to his position at the head of his knights without further word.

The squires bundled the long, steel-tipped battle lances so that several boys could cooperatively carry a large number, and quickly brought them to the line of knights. One-by-one, the king, his brothers, Christopher Seton, Thomas Randolph, the Earls of Lennox and Atholl, and knights Simon Fraser, David Inchmartin, David Barclay, Hugh de la Haye, John Somerville, and ninety-seven other battle hardened warriors, took up the knightly weapons and joined in a battle line.

"Sound trumpets for lances," commanded Pembroke, as he and Sir Phillip Mowbray and Sir Ingram Umfraville calmly led the English and Comyn knights to the field in a single column, as if parading to a friendly joust. All were fully armed and armored, and numbered one hundred and five.

The Scottish royal standard bearer, Alexander Scrymgeour, splendidly ran the length of the Scottish battle line, waving the red lion left to right.

In his words and deeds, Robert rallied the knights and the infantry, mustered behind the line of horse by Thomas Brus.

"The good Bishop of Moray has promised ye that those who die here for Scotland will have their places in heaven awaitin'," shouted Robert as he paced his mount in front of them. "I pray that he is right, and that, if ye fall, it is into God's arms."

Though still bareheaded and armored minimally, the king gave no thought to his own mortality, saying instead, "Yonder, our foe displays the dragon banner. That is a declaration that ye will get no quarter from them... and that ye will, if defeated, be murdered to the last. Therefore, if any man be not willin' to die for Scotland... ye must leave, now... for to remain here is certain death, if we fail!"

He looked up and down the ranks of his remaining force. Not a man stirred. After a moment, Robert shouted, "Then we fight!"

The Scots voices roared as one, as Robert shouted, "For free Scotland!" and the roar doubled so that, across the field, Pembroke could barely hear his nearest companions.

The Brus pulled his horse around and moved through the line of mounted knights to the forefront, where he stood calmly, facing his enemy amidst the uproar of his army.

"What lies you reckon Brus told that beleaguered rabble to solicit such a din as that?" Pembroke sarcastically asked Sir Ingram, once the Scots' rousing cheer diminished to the point he could be heard.

The two sat for a moment before Pembroke rose in his stirrups and turned left and then right shouting, "Show them what a commotion English soldiery can make!"

Umfraville unsheathed his sword and swished it around in the air, letting out a war whoop, after which the English soldiery all dutifully cheered.

"Ready!" commanded Robert, leveling his lance toward the English line.

Visor shields dropped on Scottish helmets and, more or less in unison, their lances leveled forward. The horses began to paw the ground excitedly as they anticipated the coming charge. Robert started toward the English at a walk and was quickly joined by his line, which drew up alongside him, left and right.

"Ready!" commanded Pembroke to his troops.

The English knights dropped their visors and lowered their lances.

Robert's knights spurred their mounts.

Pembroke's knights spurred their mounts.

The two lines of knights gained speed until they galloped toward each other at full tilt, paying no heed to the dead and wounded that lay scattered on the field between them.

Robert led at the center of his line and Pembroke, his. Destiny decreed that they should meet in personal engagement.

In what seemed like an eternity, the ground between them melted away until their lance points passed each other. Instantly there was an abrupt, deafening clash, as armor and shields crumpled, lance shafts splintered, and brave men's lives suddenly ended, at lance-point or by fearful trampling steeds.

Barely half the knights on either side withstood the heavy blow, and the bonfire, now the primary light on the battleground, showed the ground around the center of the field heavy with horse and human slaughter. The grass became slick with blood and trampled flesh so that the men fighting on it could barely hold their footing.

Robert's lance blow had unhorsed Pembroke, who lay sprawled and dazed on his back among the dead and dying. The infantry from both sides rushed into the melee and began tearing at each other with all the malice and violence their individual weapons would allow.

Robert wheeled his horse and, drawing his great claymore, set to working it expertly against those English knights and infantry nearby.

Philip Mowbray had been unhorsed and, though otherwise unhurt, he'd had the breath knocked out of him. He lay writhing upon the ground, gasping for air, until gradually, the English knight gathered his senses and struggled to stand. As the blackness filling his eyes cleared and he was again able to see, he soon recognized the nearby familiar figure of Robert Brus, wielding a deadly sword to great effect.

Mowbray now knew that God had deliberately placed him at the strategic spot to end the Scottish rebellion! So inspired, he staggered across the carrion between them and boldly grabbed the reins of Robert's horse. He then began bellowing his loudest, "Here! Help! I have the new-made king!"

Robert's dog growled and nipped at Mowbray's painfully unprotected hindquarters until the lord, cursing and out of patience that no one came to his aid though he held the Brus, kicked the dog with his armored leg and rendered the cur senseless among the battle's other casualties.

Pembroke was lifting his visor and getting to his feet when he heard Mowbray yelling above the noise of battle. In the firelight he could see that Mowbray did, indeed, hold fast the reins of King Robert's horse. He drew his sword and headed toward the embattled king.

Robert, under attack by an armed pack, could not get unencumbered to give Mowbray a blow and knock him loose from the reins.

Christopher Seton, seeing his brother-in-law's predicament, rushed to his aid. His mount, trotting across the uneven field, lost his footing at such close proximity that he crashed into Robert's horse, pushing him forward. The horse's great neck swung in the direction of the one holding the reins and knocked Mowbray under the trampling hooves.

The gore-splattered horse reared and the suddenly unbalanced king was flung backward to the ground. Pembroke, already closing on him, managed to lay a blow hard upon Robert before he had gained his footing, and the king struggled to stay upright. Reeling and slipping over the carnage, with Pembroke pressing his advantage and flailing him at every opportunity, the king was unable to do more than block the gasping earl's frantic strikes.

Randolph drove his armored charger between the two men and with his claymore swung a hard blow at Pembroke. Though Pembroke successfully deflected the assault with his shield, it put him on the ground once again.

"Ye'll suffer the sting of my blade for this, Randolph!" swore Pembroke from the ground. Looking at his bygone friend lying so ignobly among the dead, Thomas laughed, then kicked his horse and rode on to fight more.

Robert retrieved his horse and, remounted, was soon again in the midst of the fray, defending his homeland.

A small band of Scottish hunters, hearing the noise of the battle, hastily returned from the foraging task to which they had been assigned. When they came to the ridge of a low hill overlooking the battlefield, all they could see from the light of the moon and the bonfire was that there was a massive battle in progress.

"They jumped us ere we were ready!" said the first bowman.

"'Twas to be on the morrow!" lamented another, his eyes round in surprise.

The third man threw his string of rabbits to the ground and started for the field.

"Wait!" said the first, grabbing him by the shirt, "Ye cannot go in there, now. Ye cannot even tell who is on our side! There is nothing to be done!"

"My da is there! Let me be!" he cried and tore the hand of his friend from him. He ran headlong through the darkness toward the battle, stumbling all the way.

"Stay here, we should, 'til we know the outcome, I say," said the first bowman. The second agreed, and so they watched what they could from where they were, though they squatted with their arrows nocked and ready to loose.

Sir Alexander Scrymgeour, the standard bearer, held ground in the midst of the fray. He kept his sword along the staff from which he whipped the red lion back and forth, and when an enemy approached his perimeter, he brought up the sword and defended the banner.

His high profile on the field made the flag bearer a particularly enticing target for any knight who wanted to win attention for himself, and because of that, Scrymgeour was repeatedly attacked, by seasoned warriors and by those seeking their first bloodying.

Sir Ingram Umfraville saw his opportunity to capture the red lion, a great blow to Scottish zeal, and came upon Sir Alexander's back as he was engaged from the front. Awaiting his moment, Umfraville foined his sword deep into the Scot's underarm, where the raised arm created a brief opening to the chest between arm and chest armor.

Shocked at the attack from behind, the valiant Sir Alexander tried vainly to remain in the saddle. Losing blood rapidly, he was finally unable to maintain his seat.

As he fell, the lion standard went before him, and the flagstaff snapped beneath his weight as he smashed against the ground.

Nigel saw what happened and, holding tight to his saddlebow with one hand, swooped down nearly to the ground with the other, rescuing the royal standard. He then wheeled his mount and cursed in fury at Sir Ingram, demanding single combat between them.

"Come as ye will, ye petty whelp!" yelled Umfraville. "I'd as soon kill ye *and* yer traitorous brother for Comyn's revenge!"

Umfraville held his sword high and kicking his mount started for Nigel, who suddenly realized that he had dropped his claymore alongside the dying Scrymgeour. He was left with no weapon with which to face Umfraville's determined onslaught, but found himself holding only the shattered staff entwined with the red and yellow ensign.

Having no choice and no time to lose, he gave forth his war whoop and charged at Umfraville, using the broken staff as a lance. Umfraville was somewhat taken aback, and failed to dodge the young Scot's assault.

With a loud crash, the two men collided. Umfraville raised his shield at the last moment but was dislodged from his saddle and struck the ground with a heavy thud.

Nigel rode beyond and, realizing what he had done, unfurled the standard and waved it wildly about. Those Scots who saw what happened were greatly cheered by the spectacle, and fought all the harder.

The battle was shifting away from the bonfire, which burned brightly midway on the field, as Robert's claymore continued to taste fresh blood at every swing. His devastated army, by sheer will, gained the center ground once again.

"Onward, Scotland!" shouted Robert. "The battle is all but won... and victory will be ours!"

The brave Scots fought on, but soon were again pushed deep into the battlefield. The gallant Sir Hugh de la Haye and Sir David Barclay had both fallen, as had another twenty or so Scottish knights, and hundreds of infantrymen, who had fought fiercely for their homeland, some with no more than sharpened sticks and bare hands.

The English fought with equal zeal, and hundreds fell to Scottish blades. Once fallen, the dead and dying no longer cared that they had been English or Scots, for the battle raged only for the living.

For those thousands, during the span of an hour, the hopes of

Scottish freedom sloughed off like mud from a barren hillside in a rainstorm, but still Robert thought only to fight on.

"We launch a final assault!" ordered Pembroke when he saw the battle advantage going to the English. The trumpets sounded and all of the English reserves readied themselves for their part in the battle.

Aymer de Valence, the Earl of Pembroke, whose horse had been slain from under him, mounted a horse he found wandering aimlessly through the field and rallied his reserve troops. With a wild, drunken shout, he then struck straight for the knot of the battle.

Thomas and Alexander Brus saw the coming onslaught and knew the fresh English troops would overrun the Scots, now fighting only with valiant hearts, for they neared absolute exhaustion.

To preserve any hope of a free Scotland, they recognized that they must rescue their king before the English reserves reached him.

"We've got to get Robert to withdraw!" shouted Thomas Brus to Alexander over the battle noise.

"He will not!" returned Alexander. "I fear we may have to extricate him against his will."

"Aye, there be the rub," Thomas shouted, and turned to meet the onslaught of two English knights, their swords raised and near.

Nigel, with high enthusiasm and thinking the battle would belong to the Scots, was yet swinging the royal standard as he ran his horse to and fro for the length of the battlefield, inspiriting those freedom fighters still embroiled in the bloodletting.

His first experience at war was everything he had imagined it would be, exciting, valiant, and enormously fun.

Nigel's ebullience was to be short-lived. Out of the corner of his eye he sighted Robert as the king's horse gave way beneath him and he fell to the ground amidst numerous enemies. Nigel's heart jolted in his chest, and he quickly jerked the reins to turn his own steed in his brother's direction, fearing the worst.

Forcing his way through the turmoil, he at last saw the great claymore rise above the heads of the enemy and carve its way through them, felling several and causing the rest to back away. At that, Nigel laughed aloud, and quickly rode to Robert's side.

He pulled his foot from his stirrup and offered his hand to his brother. The king quickly pulled himself up behind his rescuer on the destrier's broad back, and away they rode, Robert's claymore discouraging all from approaching too closely.

"Thank ye, little brother!" the king shouted as he glanced about the field.

"That was too close, Rob," Nigel seriously returned, having realized the panic he felt when his brother fell. "We need ye alive, Sire!"

"Ach, ye fret too much, brother," the blood-spattered king said, and with his claymore, pointed to an unmanned stallion skittishly paralleling their course. "That big fellow, yonder, Nigel. See him?"

"Aye," answered Nigel and turned to intercept the great horse. In a moment Nigel was able to reach out and grab the reins, and Robert quickly swung himself directly from behind Nigel to the captured stallion, and with a quick glance and salute at Nigel, returned to battle.

Watching the king ride away, Nigel was approached by Thomas. "Did ye see him go down?" Nigel asked.

"Aye, he could be gone just that quick, and then it's all over," Thomas answered. When he looked at his brother, tears were streaming down his face, so he looked away in an effort not to embarrass him. "The battle goes against us, Nigel. Do ye think we can talk him into withdrawin' from here?"

"Nay. He'll not hear of it," Nigel said, wiping the tears off with his sleeve.

"Aye, so we thought," Thomas said. "But he must, or Scotland dies here with all these brave lads."

"Then 'tis over," Nigel whispered through constricted throat.

"Aye, for this day, in this place. But there will be other days, and other places... as long as Robbie lives."

"Then he must leave the field."

"Aye."

The two rode to Edward, and were joined by Alexander and Thomas Randolph. All had received the news and, agreeing that the battle was truly lost, their faces grew dark and set in resolve as they determined to extricate Robert and remove him from the field at all cost.

"I'll get some others and we'll press a wedge through the fray," said Randolph. "Ye four get Robbie out and we'll meet in the mountains to the west!"

"Agree," said Thomas Brus, wheeling his mount. He immediately set out toward King Robert who, though still in the thick of the fight, was visibly wearing down.

"Robbie!" yelled Thomas Brus when he neared the king. "Ye must retreat!"

Robert heard the words but ignored them. He refused to believe that the day could not be won, even when such word came from his own brother. With Thomas at his side, he felt renewed, somewhat, and carried the fight harder into the English throng. But even with Thomas' help, his energies were dissipating rapidly, and more and more English tried to close in on the two.

Thomas Randolph, Christopher Seton, and Sir John Somerville, along with eight other Brus knights, moved in tight to surround Robert, and fought to clear a hollow so that he had no more enemy close around to fight.

Pembroke, Mowbray and Umfraville, who were in an excited and elated mood and could fairly taste the blood of the Brus, had already commanded their knights and reserves to force the surrender or take the life of every rebel Scot who walked the terrain.

As they moved in for the kill, Robert yet argued with his brothers and friends against retreat. His Scot's temper was turning to fury at the suggestion.

Lords Lennox and Atholl heard the English trumpet sound, again, and saw Pembroke and his fresh reserves coming across the red-running ground. Knowing that the Bruses were taking Robert from the field, they rounded up their remaining knights and left.

"I'll not leave 'til I've done what I set my foot here to do!" insisted Robert, livid that such was suggested to him, and irate that he could not force his defenders out of his way.

"God damn it, Robert! Open yer eyes, man! Look about ye! We are lost, and that's a fact," Thomas insisted. "Ye are leadin' a dead army now!"

"I will not leave! Now, get the hell out of my way! I will go down fightin' if that is God's will!" insisted Robert rabidly.

"Nay, Robert! Ye cannot throw down yer life for naught! If ye do, Scotland goes down for naught, too! Can ye not see that?" Alexander argued at his other elbow.

All the while his family pushed him toward the woods, containing him tightly within the wedge formed with their own horses, and protected with their own bodies and weapons. He struggled to free himself of them until, seeing there was no reasoning with his king and knowing no other recourse, Thomas balled his huge hand into a fist and knocked Robert hard on the jaw, saying, "Forgive us, Robbie. Ye leave us no other way."

The unconscious king slumped forward in the saddle and slipped toward the ground, only being prevented from doing so by Alexander's close proximity.

His great claymore, blood-drenched so completely that it was fully red and sticky from one end to the other, slid from the king's hand and stuck upright in the ground beside him. As the group prepared to make their escape, Thomas retrieved the fallen sword and used it to good advantage in the ensuing retreat.

Edward had grabbed the reins of Robert's horse, and as the others opened the wedge to re-form and escape, he pulled the reluctant mount away from Methven Park. They savagely worked their way through those unfortunate English who happened to find themselves between the king and escape, and finally made it off the field and into the woods. The Scots' trumpeter sounded retreat but Robert heard it not.

Pembroke, triumphant and vengeful, shouted, "Take all prisoners to the center of the field!" as his horde reached the knot of severest fighting, where he assumed he would capture the Scots' leaders.

Some few rebels, having given their best for their cause, fought to reach the edge of the fighting and left hastily through the trees behind them. Others died in those last moments, having fought with such valor all through the battle until, at last, there was no more fight left. And then it was over.

Pembroke casually walked his horse back and forth and looked at the prisoners in the light of the bonfire's dying embers. "Kill all wounded of Brus' band," he ordered, "and the rest, put over there!" He pointed to the bonfire.

'Twas there he recognized Thomas Randolph.

Pembroke grinned broadly at him, feeling great pleasure at seeing him sitting with the other vanquished Scots. Next to him were Simon Fraser, John Somerville, Christopher Seton, seven knights Pembroke did not recognize, and less than a hundred of the proud infantry who had marched to the field a few hours before.

The others were all dead, or being put to death at that moment, save those few score who had managed to disappear into the woods and across the river when the trumpet sounded the end of the battle.

"Where are those cowardly Bruses?" asked Pembroke, deriding their leaders before the defeated Scots. "Are they among the dead?"

"I have not seen them, Milord, neither here among the prisoners, nor among the dead," replied Sir Phillip Mowbray.

"Not one?" Pembroke scowled. "Not one Brus laid down his life for his 'king'?" he ranted.

"Nay, Milord," Mowbray responded.

"Then find them!" screamed Pembroke uncontrollably, "'Tis *their* heads that our king prizes most highly!"

. .

That night, Pembroke's army, triumphant, but failed in that they had none of the Bruses in custody, marched the pitiful captives of the Scottish army back to Perth, either in shackles, or bound with stout ropes. 'Twas a useless indignity, for the men were all so spent they had nothing left with which they might cause a disturbance.

Ironic, thought Thomas Randolph as he passed through the gates of Perth, how we stood defiant before these walls only this afternoon, and now most all are dead. "And this small band will soon join them on the shores of the River Styx," he said half aloud.

Yet, for all of their sense of glory and honor in winning the battle, not one in Pembroke's army dared sleep outside the walls of the city that night, for they knew that King Robert and his small band of followers yet roamed free.

John de Strathbogie
Earl of Atholl

JUNE 27th 1306
THE MOUNTAINS NEAR LOCH TAY
TWELVE MILES NORTHWEST OF METHVEN

A deluge poured continually upon the small, hidden encampment of King Robert and his Methven survivors. In and around the rocky caves where they dwelt was naught but water and mud. They had built some crude shelters, but were forced to endure the punishing elements for fear that too large a construction would betray their presence to the wandering bands of English soldiers out looking for them.

Pembroke had upped the prices on their heads in his frustration after Methven.

The remains of Robert's army, including many traveling wounded, consisted of no more than five hundred men. All were bivouacked in small random clusters down the hill from the caves.

"Riders comin'!" shouted Edward Brus.

King Robert raised his rain soaked head from its depths of thought to see the incoming men.

Nigel Brus shouted, "'Tis the Black Douglas, and ten more."

Robert rose to greet Douglas and his men, who could not have been more soaked had they swum to Robert's cave.

"What brings ye to these wilds, young Douglas?" he called above the splattering rain.

"Ach, 'tis yer needs, Sire, and yer needs alone, for sure. I wander in the wilderness in a rainstorm ne'er for myself, for fear that the rain may give me a badly needful bath!"

Edward frowned.

But Robert enjoyed a well-needed, robust laugh and shouted, "Ye'll have to be clean, young Douglas, for we have no shelter here... 'cept our shields that we've tied in the tree branches, and if we are set upon by the English as ye have come upon us, we will be right sorry for the riggin' of them."

"Ye would have known, Sire, for ye have men all about these hills to recognize yer enemy!" shouted James Douglas as he maneuvered his horse into the main camp, followed by his men.

"Aye," remarked Robert, "that we do."

Douglas dismounted and came to greet the king. The rain came down even harder on them, so they had to talk all the louder to be heard above the downpour.

"'Tis surely comin' down like a cow pissin' on a flat rock!" yelled Douglas as the rain whipped into his face, and streamed into his mouth every time he opened it.

"I've ne'er seen it worse," agreed the king before asking, "Ye have word of English in the area?"

"Not run into any since two days back, before the rains started," said Douglas. "They're surely lookin' the countryside over for ye with hearts full of vengeance and fear."

"Fear?" asked Robert, surprised. After all, it was he and his army who had taken the drubbing at Methven, and he had lost three thousand men. Why should the English fear him now?

"Fear of 'Longshanks' and his wrath against them, for sure," was the reply, but not from Douglas. Instead, it came from one who had ridden in with Douglas and now dismounted to stand a few paces behind him.

"And who might ye be?" called Robert.

"Sir Gilbert de la Haye, at yer service, My Lord King." He bowed his head, showing respect. However, it caused his cowl to fall off his head and rain poured down his back, and he brought his head up quickly and covered it again with his cloak.

Robert looked at Sir Gilbert for a long moment, for he took to strangers slowly in these days. He then asked, "Ye kin to Sir Hugh de la Haye?"

"Aye, he is my nephew, and I am looking for him as I have news from his mother," said Sir Gilbert, smiling.

Robert's face grew somber and he turned and walked a few steps into the cave, then motioned Sir Gilbert to follow.

"I am painfully sorry to have to tell you, Sir Gilbert, but Hugh was lost at Methven," spoke Robert quietly when Gilbert reached his side.

"My God!" lamented Sir Gilbert in great sorrow. "His poor widowed mother will ne'er get beyond this."

"Hugh was right bold and was regular in takin' down the enemy.

He was cut through his mail-coat with a pole-ax. I saw him fall, for he was fightin' near my side. But, alas, they came too many, too quick... He fought valiantly to the last breath."

The Douglas came to Haye's side and patted him on the back, standing with him to share his great grief that he might bear it. After a few moments, Douglas said softly, but through gritted teeth, "I swear to ye Gilbert, that if I live, I will wreak revenge upon the English for what they did to Hugh at Methven Park."

"Its not just English, but the Comyns and their lot, too, that we fight," interjected Edward Brus as he came up to join the three men inside the cave.

Robert introduced his brother Edward to Sir Gilbert, who had by then recovered himself somewhat, and said, "There are many of yer army scattered here 'bouts in hidin.' Some, so I've heard, have been captured in castles as far north as Aberdeen."

Elizabeth! thought Robert with a jolt. 'Twas as severe a blow as if he had been struck in the heart, and without hesitation he ordered Edward, "Elizabeth and Marjorie! Bring Nigel to me! And John Strathbogie!"

"'Tis done," answered Edward as he returned to the downpour.

"Damned rain! It's makin' despondents of us all," said Robert, angrily.

"And keeps the English from searchin' ye out," added Douglas, matter-of-factly.

Robert mused for a moment on the statement, then said to Douglas, "Jemmy, I want ye to undertake a task for me."

"Aye, Sire?" the young knight replied.

"I would have ye go among our lads who suffer least from wounds at Methven, and gather up as many of them as ye need to form several small bands of rovers. Direct them as ye will to go do to the English, and their Comyn bunch, what they are tryin' to do to us."

"Search them out and attack them in their small bands?" asked Douglas.

"Aye. Find them that are out lookin' for us and turn the victory to ours. And when the fields around Perth are dry enough, burn them, and every hovel, cottage, or pig sty where the enemy might seek refuge," continued Robert, adding, "This will keep them poorly fed, poorly arrayed, and poorly rested. They'll become fearful of their every move, and soon they will give up this way of doin' things."

Nigel came into the cave, dripping rainwater from every part of his clothes. He was still somewhat cheerful, but much of his enthusiasm for the fight had worn to cautious maturity that showed immediately in the demeanor of his young and beautiful face.

"Ye sent for me, Sire?" he reported to the king as ordered.

"I want ye to take a score of horsed men and repair to Kildrummy to fetch Elizabeth and the other womenfolk. Bring them here to us that we might protect our own," ordered Robert.

"I will bring all that want to come," returned Nigel as he slung more water from himself. He couldn't imagine any woman wanting to live like this.

"Meet us near Tyndrum," said Robert as he took his claymore from around his neck and strapped it on his waist. "And take Neil with ye. He'll want to see the Lady Mary."

"'Twill be done, brother," said Nigel with a slight smile. He turned to leave, as did James Douglas, but both stood aside as John de Strathbogie, earl of Atholl, entered the cave.

Strathbogie was the last remaining earl in the company of the king since the Earl of Lennox disappeared while leading a band of English pursuers astray toward the south, the morning after Methven. No one yet knew of his fate after that day.

"My Lord?" said Atholl, bowing slightly and trying to maintain a sense of dignity in the wilds of wood and rain. Atholl was a large heavy man with little fat, and nearly covered the aperture to the cave in which he stood. His ample, woolly hair, which made him look rather untamed under the best conditions, often rubbed against the overhead near the front of the cave as he passed through.

"John," said Robert, reaching to a rock ledge on which stood a small flask. In it was his own dwindling supply of whisky, and he poured the earl a meager cup, "...ye look as if ye might could use a bit of Scottish spirit, old friend."

"Aye, for sure! My whole skin, and I swear, even my bones, are wrinkled from the wet," remarked John Atholl with a broad grin, gratefully taking the cup past his dripping beard and feeling the warming fluid burn his tongue and tingle his lips. Though it was a pitifully small dram, he appreciated the king's generosity in such times of want.

"Good thing it's but a summer rain, otherwise we would all be wet, *and doubly cold*," laughed Robert as he put his arm around John and drew him closer.

"Johnny, I need for ye to go to the south and find us shelter, in castle or town, that we can use to recruit more men to our cause. We must be leavin' this place soon, for Pembroke's spies will locate us if we long remain."

Scratching a sudden bite on his back, he added, "Besides, if we remain longer in the rain, these damnable lice, to which I have furnished shelter and sustenance all these days, will drown, and I wouldn't want to be an inhospitable host!" The earl laughed understandingly as Robert produced the culprit and squashed it between his fingers.

"If ye are not here, Sire, where can I find ye?" the earl asked.

"When ye have arranged a place, send a messenger to the Tyndrum, where we will await ye as we can."

"I shall do as ye ask," answered Atholl, sipping the last drop from the cup. "But ye know it will be only temporary at best, for English are pourin' into Scotland like this infernal rain pours on our heads."

"The rains will cease to pour, and so will our enemies," returned Robert with a smile.

"Always the optimist, ye are, Bobbie," remarked Atholl as he handed the cup back to his friend and king.

"I've brought ye another we found wanderin' about, Sire," said the Douglas from the mouth of the cave.

"Aye? And who would that be?" asked Robert, looking beyond Douglas and outside the cave, where he saw his squire, Andrew Stewart.

Robert was well pleased and greatly thankful, but asked the boy in a gruff voice, "Did ye bring my dog with ye?"

"Nay, Sire. I alone have been hidin' in the bush for these many days, and livin' off berries and roots and none else," explained the youth, adding, "and had I the dog, I might have eaten it, tail to ears, instead of the berries."

Robert laughed at the statement, and was right glad to see his young charge unharmed, for he had feared the boy had been killed or taken prisoner at Methven.

Andrew drew closer, stood in front of the king and, from inside his tattered, sodden tunic, withdrew the simple crown that the king had casually set on a log in Methven moments before the battle.

Robert was greatly moved, to the point of tears welling up in his eyes, but he remained otherwise stoic as he said, "So, ye saved my crown, ye did."

"Aye, Sire," replied the squire, his thin body shivering in his wet clothes.

"Ye could have traded this for a meal or two, lad," Robert gibed as he took the crown and placed it atop his wet, mud-stained head.

"Nay, Sire. Not in peril of my life would I have parted with it," returned the boy.

Robert drew the brave young man to him and hugged him tightly with true affection. With tears streaming down his face, the squire returned the king's embrace.

The king sent someone to fetch food for the boy as a ray of sunlight pierced the gloom of the cave, and shortly, the sound of the rains began to subside while the child ate his fill of the best the camp had to offer.

"Now's our chance to git," said Edward quietly, looking out the mouth of the cave into the sun dappled wood, where near and distant echoes of men praising God for the end of the rain could be heard.

Fulco Ballard

JUNE 28ᵗʰ 1306
THE CASTLE AT CARLISLE

King Edward decided that Carlisle, being recently re-fortified and positioned just south of the Scottish border on Solway Firth, was the perfect place for him to reside while directing the war against the rebel Robert de Brus.

"Methven is ours!" the despondent king mused aloud as he twisted agitatedly in his huge chair. "We have rightly and thoroughly crushed this rebellious rabble, yet we have not one... *not one...* of the Brus family dead or in irons."

The Prince of Wales stood across the table from his father, dressed in chest armor and mail coat. He asked plaintively, "What would you have me do, now?"

"It is obvious that your indiscriminate pillagin' won't work!" screamed the monarch.

"I know of no such, Father," returned the young knight.

"One thing you must know of me, Edward; I have ears and eyes everywhere!" the old king hissed in disgust. "I know your falsehoods ere they leave your maw."

"But Father, we are just following your order!"

"My *order* was to make it so Robert Brus could not survive among the common riffraff, who would think him their savior!" fussed the king as he coughed deeply from his chest.

The prince stared at his father and wished this wracking, bone-jarring cough would turn into the old man's death rattle. But, with much effort the king returned upright, much to the prince's disappointment, and looked at his son defiantly, wheezing, "I am... *not*... dead... yet!"

"Pity," said the prince sarcastically, but well under his breath.

"You have killed every living creature and destroyed everything you have come upon!" the king, having regained his vocal powers, continued to excoriate his son. He stared at the younger man with hate and revulsion in his gaze. After a few moments he shouted, building to a crescendo, "You have killed and burned in the lands of our enemies! You have killed and burned in the lands of our allies! Do you not know the difference?"

"I have killed in your service, Father," said the prince, again sarcastically.

"You and your swan knights have killed as it pleased *you!*" screamed Edward.

They glared at each other another moment longer, until Edward, pointing his long bony finger at a chair, ordered his son, "Sit!"

The prince hesitated, then thought better of it and, like a child remanded to the corner, sat in the heavy wooden chair across from the king. His sword dangled across the chair arm as he looked aimlessly around the room and asked, "What would you have me do, if you sat on my saddlebow always, and directed my every move?"

"I would have you act as if you were an honorable man," replied the seething king.

"As you would act, Father? You, who are known as the 'Hammer of the Scots?' I merely follow your example," mocked the prince.

"I have always followed the Code of Chivalry," the king insisted.

"And what of your disallowing the captured knights of Brus' army to ransom their lives, as is customary in the 'Chivalric Code,' My Liege? Were they not all put to death?" asked the prince unemotionally.

"Rein in your knights or I will!" shouted the king, slamming his palm hard upon the table and ignoring the prince's question.

There was silence in the small room for a full minute as both men absorbed the other's say.

Then the king picked up and unrolled a map of Scotland, and set candlesticks on the four corners to weight them down.

"Here, see what I have plotted," ordered the king as he leaned over the map for a better view of its entirety.

The prince reluctantly pulled his chair to a position where he could see the map, as the old man's gnarled index finger pointed to the east, about half way up the coast. "Perth. 'Cousin' Aymer de Valence holds the town and commands the areas around, at least passin' well. That will drive Brus to the southwest, here," he traced his finger across the lands of Atholl, Lennox, and Galloway.

"And what of Kildrummy? Is the castle there not still in the hands of the Scots?" asked the Prince.

"It is, but Brus would not go there for fear of being trapped," replied the king with assurance. "He must go south where he can escape to the sea." The prince started to wax interested as he saw the old man's plan unfold.

"Ah," the elderly warrior-king continued, "but we shall put our galleys on the west coast, while our swan knights push him ever westward!"

"A brilliant plan, Father!" For once, the compliment was genuine and, as such, was savored by the king.

"I have long been known as an exceptional general," replied the king with a wrinkled smile. "Now, will you kill as it benefits England?"

The prince stood and looked down at his aged father, thinking, just for the prideful moment, that he was glad to be the son of Edward Plantagenet. Then he recovered his haughtiness and said, "The heavy rains have stopped for now. We shall resume our pursuit in the morn," said the Prince. "Meanwhile, I take my leave, Sire," he said with a respectful bow, adding as an afterthought, "I have a young wench I've kept waiting much too long."

Would that it were a wench, thought King Edward as his son turned on his heel and left the room.

SUNDAY, JULY 5th 1306
PERTH

The Scots, so despised by King Edward, had almost all been taken to Berwick for transport by sea to London for prison and execution. There some were hanged, others drawn, depending on their rank and offense.

The more treasonously the king thought they had acted, the more horrible the death sentence handed down, without benefit of trial. The ones he wanted to come to his side were simply thrown into prison until they begged for mercy. Many died there from wounds or disease. But not all.

"Have ye turned Randolph, yet, Milord?" asked Ingram de Umfraville.

"He is hard as stone," answered Pembroke, shaking his head. "It is that stubbornness that makes him worth the trouble. Besides, it occupies my wit."

"He and Sir Christopher will have to be dealt with soon. King Edward is now in Carlisle and sends queries about them almost daily," said Sir Ingram, applying not very subtle pressure to the rotund earl.

"I know... I know," returned Pembroke with an aggravated edge to his tongue. "For Christ in heaven's sake! I am assured they have information that may be important to the squelchin' of this insurrection, and you can't squeeze words out of the mouths of dead men!"

"It is yer head in the noose, English, if ye fail," reminded Umfraville, threateningly. He smiled wryly as he turned quickly and left the room.

Aymer sat at the solar window and stared over the high wall toward the field where Robert's army had lined up the afternoon of the battle. He thought of the sneak attack he had led on Umfraville's advice, and came to the unbearable thought that he had acted unchivalrously at Methven. But as quickly as that idea occurred, it was dismissed.

"Whisky!" screamed Pembroke. Two servants brought him a bottle of whisky and poured a goblet half-full, then set the bottle on the table and left.

Aymer drank as deep as his deepest thought, and the more he drank the shallower the thoughts became. He wanted desperately to save that damned Thomas, yet found no way to save his own life from the king's wrath in the doing of it. After all, the king had ordered that all captured while in the service of the Brus would be killed, with no exceptions. "Did we not fly the dragon banner a'front of us as we attacked at Methven?" he pondered aloud. "Was that not fair warnin'? If Thomas would only cooperate, both of us might retain our heads. That cantankerous young fool would see us both in hell!"

Methven was a far distant fortnight ago to Thomas Randolph and Christopher Seton, imprisoned in the dungeon at Perth. Kept continually shackled, hand and foot, they were every day tormented for information about the Brus and his plans.

The pair had refused to accept their own releases in exchange for closely held secrets, but fed Pembroke's inquisitors information that revealed nothing of consequence. They knew Robert had been badly beaten at Methven and would change his strategy from the core out.

"It's me, ye, and the dog. We're all that's left," remarked Christopher, looking wistfully through the bars of their cell, his chin resting on the shackles around his wrists. His stomach churned every time he thought of what awaited them: not a battle, in which they might well be killed, but execution, of which there was no uncertainty.

"Well, they hain't a'goin'a kill us on a Sunday, sure," returned Thomas, who lay, eyes closed, on the straw in the corner. His wont was to delay thinking about the probable consequences of his circumstance.

"And why reason ye in that manner?" asked Christopher, turning away from the window and facing his cellmate, who had been dozing.

"Too damned lazy to tie the rope, they are," smiled Thomas as he squinted one eye toward Christopher, who stood in a shaft of light coming in from the small window.

Christopher chuckled, briefly, but soon turned solemn and added quietly after a long pause, "Well... if they kill us, they can't eat us."

Thomas now laughed at Christopher's statement. "If they do, I hope they choke!" he retorted.

Christopher then sat at Thomas' feet, his knees doubled up to his chin. "It would be unholy to kill us on a Sunday," he mused aloud. "On the other hand, if they should, we may go directly to heaven, and not have to wait around for Sunday to come, again."

Thomas didn't know whether to laugh or remain mute. Christopher was getting beyond his level of conversation. He felt awkward and turned his face toward the wall.

Christopher continued, not aware of his friends awkwardness, "I wish I was with Christian in the green hills, overlookin' a peaceful loch somewhere... listenin' to the pipes... and talkin' to her quietly... about how many children we'd have, or some such... that would have no meanin' to another body... but it would be the world to us."

"God A'mighty! Ye're worse than the inquisitors!" said Thomas, who could take no more and jumped suddenly to his feet.

Christopher broke out from his reverie and realized the effect his words were having on his friend. "Ye're right, ol' friend," he said with a forced smile. "Like me to hum ye a tune?"

"Well notioned," said Thomas, who could wade through a crowd of soldiers, meting out death without pity for their suffering, but could not bear such impassioned talk of a simple man for his home and wife, and a future with her he would almost certainly be denied.

Christopher began to hum. It was Thomas' turn at the window as he took Christopher's place there and completely absorbed his melancholy.

. . .

As the Sunday evening shadows fell, Lord Pembroke summoned his friend to a small room in one of the many towers overlooking the court-yard.

"What method are ye to entertain me with this night?" asked Thomas sarcastically as he was thrown at Sir Aymer's feet with the heavy sound of chain.

"We should let you out for a bath once in a while, Thomas," sported Pembroke as he looked down on him. "You smell worse than piggery shit on a hot day."

Thomas grunted, nothing more.

"Whisky?" Aymer nudged him with his foot. "Made up in the glen by good Scots 'stillers." With one foot, the earl nudged the taciturn Randolph.

Thomas grunted once again, but took the cup Sir Aymer handed him.

"You reckon, Thomas, that you and Sir Christopher are the most stubborn men in all Scotland?" asked Pembroke, shifting his weight as he sat in a low chair next to Thomas. He gave the shackled knight a moment with his cup, which brought the captive a brief respite from the putrid swill he had been served in the dungeon.

Then Pembroke subverted Thomas' thoughts, saying, "You must be real heartbroke 'bout your kin, the Bruses." Thomas looked up at him with suspicion, but said nothing. "I mean... the way they ran from the field, yonder," the earl waved his hand in the general direction of Methven, and then quietly sipped from his own cup. "Yes, yes, yes. Run off, they did, like the cowards they are... and left you, and a'plenty of other good men, too, to get caught shieldin' their arses for them."

Thomas didn't answer, but drank deeper from the cup of whisky.

He'd had no spirits since before Methven and this tasted especially good.

Pembroke silently refilled Thomas' cup and set the flask down beside him. Staring into his own cup, he finally said, "This must end tonight, ol' friend," adding almost wistfully after quaffing all in his goblet, "there be nothing I can do to alter that." The excess liquid had poured out the corners of his mouth, disappeared into his scraggly beard, and wet his shirt farther down.

"What do ye want of me?" asked Thomas dully, feeling that, somehow his friend meant to save him, but he knew not how.

"Turn," said Pembroke almost casually, then his mood changed to an angry tone and he leaned suddenly forward, shouting at Sir Thomas, "Swear allegiance to King Edward and *live*, man!"

"Robert Brus is my uncle, ye know," answered Thomas in a low, calm manner, adding softly, "A man don't turn on family."

"Men do, right regular," contradicted Pembroke, quaffing another draught from his goblet. It was a good while before one of them spoke again, as both of them grew progressively more intoxicated and less talkative. The earl continued to refill their cups.

As the sun went below the horizon, and it grew darker in the small chamber, Thomas suddenly became aware of the flicker of flames from the courtyard.

"The fire's for me?" asked Thomas, knowing Pembroke was up to something. "I'll not fear the fire!" His tone didn't alter.

"Turn, Thomas! Turn to the English! I can then save you," said Pembroke, now almost begging.

"It's not information ye want?" asked Thomas.

"It was never information," said Pembroke, smiling. "You and I both know that all plans changed after Methven. I saved you and Seton for conversion. I must admit, you have refused long," he nodded, his eyebrows lifted. It was a moment before he added, "I admire that. Even so, now it is at an end. Turn now or die tonight by the noose and draw."

Suddenly Thomas heard a commotion in the courtyard. He dropped his cup and dragged his heavy chains to the small window and gazed down on the happenings below.

Sir Aymer moved in tight behind his captive and, being about equal in height and weight, held him fast to the window as he whispered in his ear, "We are much alike, you and I, and I would trust you, Thomas, more than I trust Umfraville or Mowbray, if only I'd have your word."

"Never!" shouted Thomas as loud as he was able since he was being squeezed.

"We'll see," smiled Pembroke as he put his hand out the window above Thomas' head as a signal, "Witness your own demise within the quarter hour, if you do not agree."

There was a sudden commotion below, and Thomas watched as Christopher was dragged to the gallows by six brawny English soldiers. Thomas couldn't believe his young eyes and choked out, "Why Christopher? I thought ye wanted both of us to turn?"

"Spoil one, save t'other," said Pembroke as he struggled to hold Thomas into position. "That is, if you do want to save yourself."

Thomas watched as they placed the rope around Christopher's neck.

Thomas shouted through the window, "God save you, Sir Christopher Seton!"

Christopher looked for the voice's location and saw Thomas' face in the window. He shouted back, "Tell Christian I love her! Long live free Scotland!"

Tears filled Thomas' eyes and blurred the gruesome scene before him as he shouted to his old friend, "I'll be seein' ye in heaven this night, Christopher, for I am next to die!"

The rope tightened on Christopher's neck and Thomas could feel it closing around his own as his great hulk of a body sank to the floor despite Pembroke's efforts to keep him hoisted to the window and watching.

"A'right." mumbled Thomas as tears streaked down his contorted face.

"A'right, what?" Pembroke pressed for a definitive answer.

"I'll swear. Just stop the execution," urged the defeated Thomas.

"'Twill be done," said Pembroke, but as he looked out the window to speak the order, he said nothing for seconds.

"Say the order, man!" begged Thomas.

Pembroke paused, then said, "Sir Christopher Seton lives no more... thanks to the clumsiness of my hangman and the way Sir Christopher jerked himself at the height of his hang, and broke his neck. He made sure that he would escape the quartering."

"Thank God in heaven for that blessing," whispered Thomas, "I would not have wanted him to see what I've been whipped to."

"What say you?" asked Pembroke.

"Ye have my fealty," said Thomas reluctantly, "such as it is."

"Don't feel badly," returned Pembroke, "the highest minded nobles, includin' the high and mighty Robert de Brus, switch sides right regular, and are thought none the worse for it."

"More whisky," said Thomas as he ignored Pembroke's patronizing and sarcastic prattle.

Sir Aymer set the bottle on the floor beside him and left the room.

"See that the smith gets the shackles removed on this one, tonight" commanded Pembroke as he came into the passageway where the guards awaited their prisoner. Knowing Randolph's despair, he added, "See also that he does not harm himself."

"Yes, Milord," returned the chief guard.

"And for the sake of the good people of Perth, see that he is bathed before the morn, and with rose petals," chuckled Pembroke. He then followed the circular stairs of the tower to ground level and disappeared into the castle innards.

"Don't know about you, but I beg God that ol' Pembroke jumps in the bath with that one," remarked the one guard to the other. They both laughed at their little joke.

Thomas sat inside the room and drank all the more, to the sound of Christopher Seton's removal from the gallows and courtyard. He heard the lumbering roll of the cart across cobblestones and the dull noise his friend's body made when it was indifferently dropped into the wagon like so much peat for the hearth.

Unable to listen more, and mewling like an infant, he beat the heavy chains on the cold stone floor to drown out the echoing sounds, and worked at forcing the fiery liquid from the bottle down his constricted throat.

He thought, Where is Robert? Where is Christopher? Where have they all gone?

Thomas Brus

JULY 17th 1306
IN THE MOUNTAINS ON THE SOUTH END OF LOCH TAY

The men of King Robert de Brus' army were getting grumpier and leaner by the day. As they moved from heather-laden glen, to wooded mountain, to craggy pinnacle, and back again, they were barely managing to keep beyond the ken of Pembroke's spies. Occasionally, fights broke out over the smallest incident. That required punishments be meted out to the instigators, which made everyone even more irritable. Even the king was often in a foul mood.

The core of five hundred survivors from Methven was dwindling in number, as desertions were not uncommon and food was scarce at hand. The camp makers that were left did what they could with the meagerness of the hunt, most of the bowmen having been lost at Methven.

Almost every member in the camp cheered when one of the horses fell dead from exhaustion or hunger. On such a night, there was good eating enjoyed by everyone. Only the knight who had owned the horse was sorrowful, but he, too, ate the horse stew.

They were bivouacked on a hill in a wooded area where they had visual command of the surrounding valley. Loch Tay glistened in the valley on the far side of the hill.

"Today, we hunt," announced Robert as he kicked Edward's boots to awaken him.

Edward opened one bleary eye and mumbled, "'S'not full sun yet."

"'Tis only a wee bit of fog in the air, young brother," teased Robert. "It'll leave us as the morn wears on. Besides, deer like to be killed early, so that their meat is not tough from walkin' 'round all day." Again, he kicked his brother's foot.

"A'right," Edward surrendered as he stretched and yawned, loudly enough that half the camp knew he had risen. "Ye'll not give me peace 'til I'm awake, no how."

"Aye," agreed Robert as he picked up his longbow and quiver, and with great, long strides, set out up the hill.

"Wait!" shouted Edward, kicking off his dirty blanket. "I hain't even pissed yet!"

"Piss and walk, piss and walk..." said Robert as he got farther away, "when we reach the top ye'll be all pissed out."

"Be damned if that be so," muttered Edward as he grabbed a bow and quiver and struck off behind his brother.

"May I go, too, My Lord King?" asked Andrew as he ran apace and caught up to Robert.

Robert stopped and said, "I have no crown and no armor on today, Andrew." Seeing in the boy's eyes waiting disappointment in expectation of being refused, Robert said, "Aye, if ye'll simply call me 'Sire' for the day."

Andrew observed, "Ye have yer claymore about yer neck, My Lor... Sire."

Robert laughed, a good, hearty laugh. It felt good.

Andrew smiled back at him, then turned to fetch his bow and quiver.

·   ·

As the sun neared the zenith of its arc for the day, Robert's bow-string twanged and the arrow ran true into the shoulder of a large buck. The animal bolted lithely across a log and into a thicket, though able to use only three legs.

"Ye got him, sire!" yelled Andrew. "Ye got him square!"

"Ye ne'er truly have a thing 'til it's in yer fist, young Andrew," reminded Robert. He nocked a second arrow and set off walking cautiously into the thicket, Andrew following respectfully behind, an arrow in his own bow.

"There, Andrew. There we have him, truly," said Robert, pointing to the buck. The great creature lay in the underbrush in his dying throes, Robert's deadly arrow heaving in unison with the buck's last labored breaths.

The youth whistled softly. "I ne'er saw an arrow pierce so deep at that range," remarked Andrew in wonderment.

Robert returned not a word but took the buck by one huge antler and dragged its limp form out of the brush, to where he could affix it to a pole for Edward and Andrew to carry back to the camp. He had deftly tied the forefeet together, and was in the process of binding the others when Edward came over the ridge to admire the large buck at his brother's feet.

"Kilt us supper, I see," said Edward, handing Andrew a handful of berries he had picked on the way and carried in his pouch. They had found precious little to breakfast on while they hunted.

"Aye," said Robert with a squelched sense of hunter's pride, and asked, "Have ye brought anything for the pot?"

Edward, with a weak smile, held up a brace of fat hares.

"Ach!" growled Robert, casting a furtive wink in Andrew's direction, "I'm weary of hares," he said. "Ye can eat those."

"I don't get venison?" asked Edward with wrinkled brow.

Robert smiled and winked again at Andrew. "Maybe, if ye'll cut a good, stout staff to carry him back to camp on."

While the two men completed preparations for carrying the heavy buck, Andrew wandered down the hill a ways and climbed out onto the edge of a cliff having a particularly good view of the valley below. It was not long before his sharp eyes caught sight of something that clutched him in fear.

"Sire!" the boy loudly whispered, crouching close to the rock and waving for the two men to join him.

Robert and Edward walked to the edge of the crag near where Andrew lay overlooking the valley.

"Scots, and in arms!" whispered Andrew.

Robert and Edward, having slid up to the rim on their bellies as had Andrew, looked at the plodding figures below.

"It's a contingent of about twenty, and only trouble to us if they're spies," remarked Robert.

"Blow yer horn and wave," suggested Edward. "See what they do."

Robert thought about the danger of giving away their location to spies for the English, but since Robert's band was far more numerous, twenty men were no direct threat. And, since he was preparing to relocate the camp in the morning anyway, it seemed a worthwhile risk, so he blew a blast on his horn.

After a few seconds, the band of men stopped and looked around to find the source of the trumpeted ado.

Robert repeated the blast, at which one of the Scots pointed in their direction and the contingent turned to climb up the hill toward the camp. It was deemed that they were friendly, but Andrew continued to watch their progress yet a while.

Out of the brush from over the crest of the tor, several of Robert's men showed themselves and hailed as they came upon the three hunters. "We heard yer horn, Lord Robert," said one of the men. "We been lookin' for the camp all mornin.' Ye changed it since last we were here."

"There's venison in yon clearin'," said Edward, pointing, "and a pair of rabbits layin' on the ground yonder, too. Give a hand gettin' them back to camp."

Robert looked at the men as they turned. "That man with the red plaid sash, haven't seen him for a spell," said Robert, "Bring him to me."

Edward pulled the man away from the other two and brought him before Robert, who spoke to the man with some suspicion. "What be yer name, man?"

"Cuthbert, Sir," said the familiar, bearded face.

"Not seen ye in camp of late, Cuthbert."

"Been gone," was the abrupt reply.

"Ye know that's desertion, do ye?" asked Robert.

"Came back," protested the man with raised bushy eyebrows, as if to say, "it's not desertion if ye come back."

"Why'd ye leave us?" asked Robert trying to get to the nub of his leaving for fear the man was a Pembroke spy.

"Me wife was a'birthin' another son… number six," was the proud reply, and he continued, "E'er'thin' is good with them, so… I came back." The man spoke openly, and Robert believed his demeanor as much as his words.

Robert smiled, "Congratulations, Cuthbert. I pray the boy grows strong and healthy and brings pride to his father by his actions."

"Thank ye, Milord," said the man with a smile and a hesitant bow. Unaccustomed to being around royalty, many of his countrymen felt awkward when addressing their king.

"Go with the others to fetch the carcasses down the hill," Robert said.

"Aye," he turned immediately to obey.

"And Cuthbert…" The man stopped and looked back.

"Aye?"

"Let me know before ye or yer cronies take a notion to leave camp again." The man nodded and went to help with the kill, leaving Robert smiling.

"What are they up to, now, young Andrew?" asked the king, returning to where Andrew lay, watching the armed Scots across the valley.

"Movin' on toward us, Sire," was the reply, "Looks like the earl."

"Earl? What earl wanders about, save Pembroke?" queried Robert, thinking the lad had erred.

"The one from Atholl, Sire," explained Andrew.

"Strathbogie! John Strathbogie lives and has found us, praise God!" whispered Robert. As he turned to tell Edward the good news, the three newcomers lugged the deer, suspended beneath the pole, with the two rabbits dangling from the end, and went past them down the hill toward the camp

Good dippin' stew and good company tonight, the king thought. "Come, Andrew," He said, "Let's see what else we can scare up for the pot."

Later that afternoon, the party Andrew had spotted from the cliff arrived in the camp, dressed in a wide array of skins and clothes, and such armor as they'd had with them when they escaped Methven. Though some showed scars from the battle, all were now fit and robust.

"Any of that Scots belly wash have ye left?" asked John Strathbogie as he was warmly greeted into the primitive camp by Robert and Edward.

"We may have a wee drop left for yer gullet," said Robert, smiling at his friend.

Edward retrieved a bottle and a ram's horn cup from under his blanket, poured a cupful and handed it to John, who, still mounted astride his destrier, drank the dram down and heaved a satisfied, "Ah-h-h!" as he wiped his mouth with the back of his hand.

"Another?" asked Edward.

"Nay, lad. We'll save a bit for what looks like a mighty tasty supper," he replied, seeing the two freshly killed deer hanging gutted on a tree near by.

"Aye," piped in Andrew, "and the big one kilt by the king himself!"

"What's the matter, Eddie? Have ye lost yer bow, that yer brother must do all the huntin'?" the Earl of Atholl laughed. He and his four knights and eighteen mounted soldiers got down from their horses and began to stretch their legs.

Edward dismissed the tease with a disgruntled, "Humph!"

"Did ye find us a place to rest 'til we gather with the others?" asked Robert.

"Only place the English hain't grabbed up is Dunaverty Castle."

"Thought that might be the case," returned Robert, casting his eyes downward in disappointment, and realizing his choices were being squeezed out of existence.

"Ye know, Robbie, Nigel is here 'bouts lookin' for ye, same as I was," said John.

Robert's eyes widened, "Ye saw them?"

"Two days over yonder," he said, nodding and pointing to the east. "We split so's we could find ye the better."

"Women with him?" asked Edward.

"Aye, 'bout twelve, includin' the queen," returned the earl.

"Andrew!"

"Aye, Sire?"

"Saddle my horse, quickly," commanded Robert.

"What's the jawin'?" asked 'The Black' Douglas as he came to greet the recent arrivals.

"Nigel and the queen are here 'bouts and I aim to find them," said Robert with an excited heart but a worried mind. He didn't know whether to be overjoyed that his Elizabeth and the others were so near, or to be fearful that they might fall into the hands of Pembroke's minions.

"Make two large tents from branches for the women," he ordered.

"The women need but one tent," protested Edward in confusion.

"I know," said Robert, preparing to ride.

"I'll jaunt along with ye," said James Douglas, and he trotted off to get his own horse.

"And I," said Edward as he picked up two fat rabbits from among others and pushed them into his pouch. A camp woman frowned at him, for she had just cleaned them and was readying them for the stew pot.

"We hain't goin' to get none of the venison," explained Edward as he threw his saddle on a mount.

"May I go, sire?" asked Andrew as he brought the king's horse forward, "I have squire David's horse, and I know she's small, but I'll keep up, I promise."

"Saddle up, then," said Robert as he mounted. Several others scattered to saddle their steeds as Robert made his way down the hill toward the valley.

"Ye leavin' just as I get here?" asked Atholl in his booming voice.

"Leavin', we are!" shouted Robert without looking back. "Enjoy the supper."

"What say ye 'bout this leftover whisky?" shouted Atholl.

Robert raised his hand, as if to say, "have it" as the four knights and the squire rode past the earl and down the hill after him.

. .

The riders went east, keeping to the higher regions so they could seek out Nigel and his precious company. That night was spent on the highest point in the area, looking for any sign of campfires. They built a lean-to shelter and cooked the meat before pitch dark would more likely expose their position.

"Must be beyond one or 'nother of these ridges," said Edward as he looked into the blackness.

"Reckon," said Robert, beginning to worry that the entourage had been detained by a band of Pembroke's men. But on the other hand, he had not seen any of them in his travels, either.

"Andrew and Douglas are sleepin' hard," remarked Edward as he sat beside his brother. Then he asked suddenly, "Reckon we're goin' to survive this fracas we started?"

Robert turned to look at his brother in the paleness of the moonlight. "Why ask ye that?"

"Don't seem like events are fallin' much in our favor," he returned, gouging at the dirt between his feet with a stick.

"The English commenced it, and even if we don't live to see it through to the end, others will."

They sat quietly pondering what had been said for a short while before the king stated thoughtfully, "Scotland must get shed of the likes of 'Longshanks'! He gives not a haet for the Scots. Less even than he does the Welsh. As long as he treats us like his personal chattel, there will be Scots who will fight, for their children's freedom, if not their own, whether ye and I live or die."

Edward nodded his head in understanding. Then, after a moment he stood and said, "Goin' to look about on the other side of the rise."

"Aye," agreed Robert as he and one of the knights stood guard over their sleeping companions. Mid-point in the night, Robert aroused James Douglas, Andrew, and the other two knights, to stand lookout while the first watch slept.

. .

It was just as the dawn light struck the sky with a deep purple and peeled back the black of the night that Andrew's young eyes glimpsed the barest flicker of a flame on the edge of a wood across the valley.

"We must wake the king, Sir James," whispered Andrew.

"We know not who lit that fire, lad. Let him sleep," said Douglas.

As the sun peeked over a far mountain and its light formed the valley anew for the day, Douglas saw a band of over twenty riders emerging from the wood and heading across the valley toward them.

"Now, wake the king!" ordered Douglas, "and saddle his horse, right away."

Once Robert and Edward were awakened, the six men and the king's squire peered into the valley at the train.

"I think it's them, Rob," said Edward. "Nigel always prefers a black horse, and it looks like him a'leadin' the pack."

Suddenly, halfway down the mountain on which they stood watching the train, a glint from the early sun reflecting off a helmet caught The

Douglas' eye. He touched the king's shoulder and pointed below them, whispering, "See, there, Sire."

"Damn!" exclaimed Robert as he saw the colors they carried. It was a party of Lord Pembroke's searchers, looking for the Brus. They had already seen Nigel and his command, Robert could tell by the way the leaders were behaving.

"We've only seven, Rob, with few weapons and no armor," said Edward trying to gauge the odds.

"And we have the greater fear of loss," said Robert, thinking of the women. "But," he sighed, "could be they're only spies and have no notion to strike."

"Even if they are spies, we must keep them from their report," said Edward. "Looks like there's about twelve or fifteen of them."

"Agree," said Robert. "We can walk the horses down the grade 'til we reach their level, then attack across on them. We have surprise and wildness as allies."

They set off down hill as fast as they could without signaling their presence, for they had to destroy the contingent of Pembroke's men and catch up to Nigel, all in a short amount of time.

Arriving at the level they deemed to be that of the English soldiers, they mounted and started to ride across the face of the summit. From farther below they heard voices speaking in an English dialect.

Robert pointed toward the English and motioned for the others to follow. Then he brazenly descended the hill and started talking loudly in the dialect spoken by the invaders. Having no visual contact, the English took them to be riders from their own party.

The Scotsmen fell in behind the column, and they no wiser.

After a short ride, Robert confirmed that the English were heading to intercept Nigel's company, and he was not in a mood to give quarter when his queen was in jeopardy.

He quietly drew his claymore and held it above his head to show those behind him, suddenly let out a hellish war whoop, and rushed down upon the last Englishman in the queue. Before the unfortunate fellow knew he was under attack, Robert's blade cleaved him clear from his breast to his pelvis.

Panicking at the sudden ado behind them, the other Englishmen started to scatter, some trying to wheel their great horses to face what was befalling them, others trying to reach a clearer spot in which to engage their attackers.

Edward and Douglas set to yelling war whoops to pound English nerves, and each picked the closest man to him and dispatched him as he saw best.

Andrew, trailing the others on his little mare, jumped from the saddle and quickly took the sword and bloodied sheath belt from the first slain. He was wrapping the belt around himself when he suddenly was faced with what seemed to him at that moment, the largest horse and fully armored knight he had ever seen. Through the knight's open visor, the frightened boy watched a soulless grin come across the man's face and the knight drew his sword and urged his horse forward.

The sheath and belt slid to the ground as Andrew held fast to the broadsword with both hands and, in desperation, swung at what he could reach, striking the great horse square on the soft muzzle.

Though it was a slight injury, the pained animal immediately reared, preventing the knight from holding his view of the boy.

By the time the horse's hooves were again on the ground, the agile boy had run beneath the raised horse and come up on the awkward side of the knight, where he could not easily reach the quick sprite with his sword. At his rider's command, the horse spun around to give the knight a better aim at Andrew, but again, the boy was not where he was expected to be!

Cursing loudly, the knight spun again, but only glimpsed the boy.

The knight became agitated at the restrictive helmet, and so pulled it from his head and flung it on the ground. Even so, about the time the invader again caught sight of the lad, Andrew desperately flung the sword at the knight's head.

It was a freak accident. The point of the missile pierced the man's skull through his eye socket, and he fell backward off the horse and lay writhing on the ground. Andrew could not move his feet and stood spellbound by the sight of the dying knight.

Mercifully for both, the knight expired quickly.

Robert and the others had gained a sufficient advantage by their ruse and surprise and had killed all the enemy party save one, who had run away at the start of the ruckus.

"He's too far ahead," said Robert. "Pembroke will know where we are inside of this day."

Glancing around, he asked, "Where is young Andrew?" Alarmed for the safety of his squire, Robert kicked his horse and hied back along the trail to search for him. When he reached the site of his own first strike of the skirmish, he saw Andrew still rooted there, looking at the knight he had slain.

"What's the story here, lad?" asked Robert, relieved that Andrew yet lived.

"I... I killed him... Sire!" Andrew answered in trembling voice, and promptly threw up.

Robert dismounted and stood beside the brave young man. It was plain the knight was dead, and that Andrew was the only one standing, albeit without weapons.

The boy being greatly shaken, Robert did not want to distress him further by asking how he had managed such a feat. Instead, he quietly said, "His horse is now yers, my lad; ye've earned it this day." The king then put his arm across the boy's shoulders to comfort him as he yet trembled at the sight.

"I didn't know it felt this way to see a man die that ye, yerself, have killed," the young victor lamented as hot tears flowed down his little boy's face.

"Aye. Life is a precious thing, the most precious thing a man will ever have," said Robert.

Andrew's heartbreak still not being assuaged, Robert added, "Lad, if ye had not killed him, he would certainly have killed ye, and I would have found ye lying yonder in his place. Then, I would have had to kill him anyway. So, it would seem, he was just fated to die here."

With that, he gently guided Andrew toward the horse, and hoisted his squire onto the magnificent, fought-for mount.

Robert retrieved the dead knight's sword and sheath, and his fine leather belt, and handed them to the boy. "These are yers, by right of conquest," he said. "But, ye'll have to tend to yer horse's bloody nose, though it seems he's in no danger from the wound."

He also bent down and picked up the knight's helmet and breast armor and fastened them to the boy's saddle.

"Now, we hasten, Lad, before Sir Nigel gets too far along," urged Robert, and he swung himself into his own saddle.

When they reached Edward and James, they and the others had about finished rounding up the remaining horses and armor of the slain soldiers. The Scots had suffered hardly a scratch in the short engagement.

It was not long before Robert and the others reached the clearing and could see far across the valley. Robert saw Nigel and his train well ahead of them and gave them a blast on his horn. The progression of riders continued on without hesitation.

"Wind's blowin' in the wrong direction. They can't hear," observed Edward.

"We'll have to ride them down," said Robert, and kicked his horse to a much faster pace. At full gallop, it was but a short time before they were seen by the rear guard of the entourage.

"Riders!" shouted one, and he turned toward them, weapons at the ready.

Nigel turned immediately and rode to the rear of the column to face the incoming band. He quickly set up his defenses and formed a loose phalanx around the women, then waited for the charging horsemen to strike. With great relief, he recognized his two brothers at the head of the small company bearing down on them.

"'Tis Robert!" he shouted.

Elizabeth, on hearing his name, immediately dismounted and stood awaiting his arrival with great anticipation. She had not seen him in such a great while, and she ached to see that he was whole and well after the escape from Methven.

Robert rode up and dismounted in the midst of the party, having eyes only for Elizabeth.

He took her in his arms and kissed her as if no one else stood in that grassy plain but the two of them, though loud cheers arose from those around them.

"Da! Oh, Da!" screamed Marjorie as she grabbed her father's arm. He turned and gave her a big hug and swung her around. "I'm too old for that any more," she protested in good humor as he set her lightly again on her feet.

"Oh?" said Robert proudly. And taking a better look at the young woman who was his child, he had to agree that she was too old for girlish games.

"Good deeds ye did, Nigel," praised Robert.

"As ordered, Sire," returned Nigel with a smile as he slapped his brother on the back.

Christian Seton dismounted and hugged her newly arrived brothers. "Have ye any word of Christopher?" she then asked, hopefully.

The mood of the little reunion changed to dour with the question.

Robert looked at her tenderly and said, "I fear that Christopher has been lost, but I have no confirmation. He was last reported as bein' imprisoned at Perth with Thomas Randolph, and since then... I've had no word. I'm sorry."

Christian's eyes welled up with tears and she said nothing as she stood looking up at Robert, not wanting to believe what she was hearing. How could her brother say so calmly that her Christopher had been lost? What did that mean, 'lost'?

Finally, she fell against Robert's broad chest and wept, bitterly. Robert held her tightly until her sobs lessened and she stood on her own again.

Elizabeth then put her arm around her sister-in-law's shoulder and walked away from the others with her to help her deal with the fact that her husband was probably dead. The queen knew that it could just as easily have been her own husband cut down, and she said a special prayer at vespers that evening in thanks that he yet survived.

Standing beside her father and her uncles, Marjorie wiped tears from her own eyes. Her Aunt Christian was so distraught, the young girl thought her own heart would break, but as the men stood talking among themselves, the king's daughter shyly noticed young Andrew, still astride his new destrier. As she stood looking at him, he carefully ignored her gaze. She was not brazen enough to speak to him.

Tugging at the royal sleeve, she asked, "Who sits that great horse, Father?"

"Ye recollect not Andrew? My squire from Lochmaben?"

"Nay, Father," she returned, quietly.

"Young Andrew yonder, havin' no arms of his own, mind ye, killed his first full-armed English this morn, and now rides his mount," bragged the king, as much to the other men as to Marjorie. As he went on with more detail, Marjorie smiled at Andrew, who timidly smiled back, his faced flushed bright red.

"Must have been a fierce warrior to have an armored horse that size," remarked Marjorie, still eyeing Andrew. "Somehow, Father, I don't recollect him as bein' one of yer squires."

"Ye recollect me, My Lord?" asked Isabel, the Countess of Buchan.

"The lady who ran off with her husband's horses? Who wanted to fight for freedom, and the one who, as a member from the House of MacDuff, proper crowned me King of Scotland? That be ye?" asked Robert smiling all the while.

"Aye," she said with a return smile, "and ne'er a moment sorry for the doin' of it, neither." She held her head high and proud, as was her wont, Robert remembered as well.

"Her husband, to save his own worthless hide, has placed a bounty upon her head," said Elizabeth, a tone of anger in her voice as she rejoined the group and slipped her arm around Robert's waist.

"And *good* King Edward," she continued sarcastically, "has placed us all in dire jeopardy, by proclaimin' that all who follow ye, and their families, are outlaws... and no punishment will befall those who abuse us, no matter in what manner."

"The bastard!" Robert spat. "'Tis one thing to make war and fight men, but who else but Edward would deliberately war upon women and children by turning every foul sort loose on them with impunity! Damn him!"

He held Elizabeth tight to him as their conversation was interrupted by Neil Campbell and Mary Brus, at last coming to greet her brother, the king.

After Mary hugged Robert, she returned to stand close by Sir Neil. Robert looked at her with one eyebrow cocked as if to ask what sort of business was between the two of them.

"Sire," Neil began, somewhat flushed at his own impudence, "Mary and I were married in a simple and quick ceremony in Kildrummy's abbey while the women were being fetched, though in so doing, we risked yer displeasure."

Robert said nothing, but his mind's eye flashed on remembrances of his little sister, now a woman... and married! He didn't realize their discomfort at his silence until Neil spoke, again.

"We ask yer blessin' on us... and our marriage," said Neil, and he and Mary knelt before the king.

Robert smiled at their humbleness as he put his hands upon their bowed heads and said, "Ye have my blessin', and may God provide ye with all the bounty of this glorious land fore'er more. Amen."

All around said, "Amen."

The couple then stood and Robert affectionately hugged them both together. "Welcome to the family de Brus, Neil Campbell. Ye must love my sister greatly to put yerself in our camp during these times. And, I trust ye will defend her from all harm, no matter from what quarter," he looked grimly at his new family member.

"Aye, Sire, I swear," answered the young Campbell soberly.

"We've got to get!" reminded James Douglas, who had stayed astride and alert.

"Aye," said Robert. "That coward who got away will have English swarmin' around Loch Tay, soon. To horse, all." With that he led Elizabeth to her mount and lifted her into her saddle, then did the same with Marjorie before putting foot in his own stirrup.

"Our camp's not far from here," said James, reassuring the women that this leg of their journey was near an end.

Thomas Randolph

JULY 22ND 1306
ABERDEEN

Two weeks had passed since Pembroke's army took Aberdeen from the Brus' supporters, who had taken it from the English in May. King Robert was a prudent and powerful leader, but once he was gone from them, his leaderless men seemed to lose the ability to hold their ground. Pembroke was running rampant through the countryside.

Within the confines of Aberdeen there was a tavern, housing the keeper and his family in the upper chambers, and the public eating and drinking quarters below.

Pembroke soon found, more or less simultaneously, the fearfulness of the tavern keeper and his wife, and his own lustful fondness for their two winsome young daughters. The parents wanted to live, and their daughters were insurance of their continuing to do so, at least as long as Pembroke's interest was piqued by the girls' here-to-fore virginal charms.

Aymer de Valence, Earl of Pembroke, had taken for his own, not only the family's living quarters, but their very lives, as well.

"You know, Thomas, I'm willin' to share... one... of these young, voluptuous things with you," said Aymer, who was lying nude in the large bed in the keeper's bedroom with the two equally naked daughters, one pressed closely against each of his ample sides. He was as content as he could imagine being, and for a practiced hedonist like himself, that was quite an accomplishment.

Thomas Randolph was also naked, and sat on a chair a few paces from the bed. He seemed fixated on his hairy blonde body, but was actually caught up in his own thoughts of the great price he had paid for his life.

He realized the young women were no different than he. All three had prostituted themselves in order to cling to life, such as it was.

"They are most comely," admitted Thomas, looking up and gulping more wine from his bottle.

"Aye," returned Aymer, "their hair is the color of fire, their eyes the color of new spring grass, and both with a willing passion for pleasing their lord. No matter what you ask, they acquiesce to, and most charmingly, too." With a chuckle, he grinned at one of the daughters as he caressed her sister's breast.

"When you wed," he opined, "you'll be able to please your husband from your wedding night. Most wenches as young as you have no knowledge of what I have taught you here, in your father's bed."

"How is it, Aymer, that they are so willin' to take up with the likes of an old fart blossom such as ye?" asked Thomas.

Aymer, insulted at being referred to so, suddenly swung his legs around and sat his fleshy, naked body on the edge of the bed. The two sexual slaves hastily rose to their knees and pressed their nubile bodies against Pembroke's pimply back.

"What in hell's bloody name are you sayin'!?"

"I'm drunk," Thomas averred, truthfully.

"You bloody well better be *somethin'* lest you forget 'twas *I* saved you from the noose and the ax! I mean *not* to have a damned *priest* hangin' around my neck," screamed Pembroke as he shrugged off the two women and went to the small open window to relieve himself.

"What!? Who in hell pisses on our heads?" yelled one of the irate guards from below.

"You have the noble piss of the Earl of Pembroke splattered on you," announced Pembroke angrily, "and I can piss anywhere I damned well take a notion."

The guards said not a word, but thereafter stood clear from beneath the window.

"They hain't always stupid," remarked Aymer, chuckling at the predicament of the poor guards as he sat back on the bed. Immediately, the women were again at work trying to please the earl, who was himself wondering if Thomas was going to honor the promise of fealty that he had hard wrung from him.

Thomas swigged from his bottle again and, realizing Aymer was staring straight at him, offered his bottle to share.

Aymer took it and drank. Rivulets of red wine fell upon his rotund belly from his beard and left streaks down into his pubic hair.

"I don't know why ye wanted two women when ye've but one pecker," observed Thomas, looking at Pembroke's dangling organ.

There was a full moment of silence as Pembroke's eyebrows knitted tight and his piercing eyes stared directly into Thomas.' The women, sensing that Pembroke had tensed, withdrew in fear and sat back from him.

Suddenly, Aymer laughed raucously.

Thomas laughed with him.

"I knew you'd come about!" said Pembroke, "Now climb in and be with us."

"A'right, which one's mine?" asked Thomas, succumbing to drunkenness.

"Makes no difference to me, have as your passion wills," said Aymer, pulling the two roughly by the hair of their heads to the edge of the bed in order to give Thomas his free choice, and feeling that he was a generous man in the doing of it.

Neither noticed that the younger sister's eyes were full of tears.

．　．

The late afternoon air was unusually hot, and as it grew into evening, Thomas and Aymer became weary of sexual folly and their appetites turned to food. Aymer sent the two women to the tavern kitchen to fetch them a meal. The earl had made sure the larder was well stocked for him, his guests, and even the hostage hosts.

"Thomas!" insisted Pembroke as he sat in the chair and kicked the bed where Thomas was sleeping. "Wake up, Randolph!"

Thomas' eyes opened to thin red slits as Aymer pushed and shook him with his foot.

"Victuals come yet?" he asked, still half asleep.

"Hain't come, but I've a mission for you."

"Naught victuals, naught mission," returned Randolph.

"The mission's on the morrow, you stupid son-of-a-bitch."

"Then let me sleep 'til the morrow," begged Thomas.

"I want you to take Brus' dog a ways to the southeast," said Pembroke.

"What's Robert's dog got to do with me sleepin'?" asked Thomas, who slowly forced himself to come alive, though he was feeling awful.

"A spy has come from near the head of Loch Tay. The traitor Brus and his family appear to be headin' toward the lands of Lorne," explained Pembroke.

"Too much wine. I don't understand," said Thomas as he sat on the edge of the bed and held his throbbing head in his upturned palms.

"Heed this, Thomas! We're waitin' here to lay siege to Kildrummy, as soon as the Prince of Wales gets here. He's comin' with his three hundred knights, and siege engines brought up from the south," said Aymer, and he finished a second decanter of whisky for the afternoon.

"Can ye not let poor Robert have at least one damn castle in all of Scotland?" asked Thomas, wishing the day would end so he could sleep his hangover away.

Aymer threw the empty bottle into the cold fireplace with the crash of glass on stone. "You *are* goin' to Lorne to stir hellfire against the Brus, or your arse will be back on the gallows!"

"As ye will, Milord," answered Randolph at last and in resignation.

"You have no need for formalities in private, man," returned Pembroke, suddenly mellowed, having gotten his way. "We are the best of friends... so much alike... are we not?"

"Aye," said Thomas quietly, "the best."

"Then you'll leave with the dawn?" asked Aymer.

Thomas nodded his head with no expectation of escape from the duty assigned. After all, he was just another of the whores of the Earl of Pembroke.

John Macdougall

july 30th 1306
the land of argyll

Since his forces were poorly arrayed to carry the fight further to the enemy, Robert needed desperately to rest them in the castle at Dunaverty. To this end, he sent his newly acquired brother-in-law, Neil Campbell, who held sway in the land of Kintyre, where dwelt the Campbell clan. The Campbell chieftains hated Edward Plantagenet with a passion near to Robert's own, and were sympathetic to the cause of Scottish freedom.

Thomas Randolph, meanwhile, was sent by Pembroke to Argyll, which lay more than a hundred miles southwest of Aberdeen, and close to where Robert and his dwindling army secluded themselves in the mountains.

He arrived at the ancient castle, built in the old fashioned "motte and bailey" style: the motte was a huge, steep earthen mound, the bailey, a large area of fairly level ground at the base of the motte, protected by a stout log palisade. It, in turn, was ringed by a moat, the water filling it being diverted from a nearby stream. Atop the motte stood a sturdy, two-story keep.

Hounds inside the bailey howled and barked loudly seeing Robert's dog, being led on a long leash up the pathway to the crude drawbridge across the moat.

Randolph, dressed in light armor, stopped his horse just short of arrow distance. His six men-in-arms came on either side of him as the dog rested its bleeding paws by lying at the horse's hooves. One of the men carried the leopard banner of King Edward.

Within moments, the drawbridge dropped and there stood John

Macdougall, the twenty-two-year-old son of the earl of Argyll. He was dressed in a chest plate of armor, a long shirt almost entirely covered by his chain mail, and boots. He had a youthfully thin, yellowish, beard that matched the color of the hair on his head.

He seemed in full command of his garrison, barking orders for the defense of the castle as he himself stood boldly on the bridge in front of his gathering men.

"Why have ye come to the land of Argyll?" asked the defiant Scotsman.

"I pray, Lord of Lorne," spoke Thomas unconvincingly, "to seek yer help in the name of King Edward of England, whose banner we come under this day."

"And who are ye, that asks this thing?" interrogated John Macdougall.

"Sir Thomas Randolph, in the service of the Earl of Pembroke, and he in the service of King Edward."

A moment of dead silence lay between them as the young lord puzzled out his options.

Then he abruptly shouted, "Come!" and walked back into the bailey, up the hill, and into the keep. Thomas and his men followed into the bailey, where Thomas left his men and the dog, and he alone mounted the hill and entered the blockhouse to talk to the young leader.

After the usual terse and meaningless greetings were exchanged, Thomas was offered a chair at a large wooden table. The smell of the cook pit, close at hand, caused Thomas to remember the primitive home cooking from his childhood. Suddenly, he realized how much he had missed it.

"We will sup presently," stated John gruffly.

"I would be honored to break bread with ye," lied Thomas, for he liked the young noble not at all.

"Pray, Sir Thomas, what brings ye here, to me?" he asked, fully aware that his domain was well off even the slightly beaten byways.

"The large dog I brought and tethered in yer bailey belongs to Robert de Brus, who calls himself..." he took a deep breath, "'King of Scotland,'" explained Thomas, playing the part of Pembroke's ambassador.

"Damn ye! Ye brought the cur of Robert de Brus to *my* door?" asked John Macdougall in anger and no small amount of fear.

Randolph flinched not, but sat in his chair and quietly said, "I have a purpose that I bring him to ye."

The lord controlled himself enough to hear Thomas out.

"The Earl of Pembroke asks that ye seek out Robert de Brus, who lurks about in these mountains close at hand, and destroy him, along with all his family, and thus the rebellion against the crown of England." Thomas' voice was flat and emotionless, as if reciting something learned by rote.

"I will savor the moment that I personally snuff the life from Brus with my bare hands for what he did to my uncle in the Dumfries kirk last winter," said John through clenched teeth, his bluster accentuated with the pounding of his fist on the table before him.

Thomas was unimpressed, continuing, "The dog in the bailey loves his master to the degree that he would follow him to the fires of hell," he said, "and as he is no doubt with his brothers and most of his supporters, ye can track the bunch of them with that dog set on his trail."

"I see yer plot," answered Macdougall, as trenchers of wild boar and hot bread were laid before the two men. "Come, eat and drink, and we'll make a toast to the downfall and destruction of Clan Brus and their ilk."

Thomas enjoyed and praised the food, but in his heart he hated the thing he was doing. He thought of himself saying to John Macdougall, Ye young prick! Ye don't have one-tenth the courage it would take for ye to look upon Robert de Brus, much less challenge him! But, he didn't say it, having sold his allegiance to Pembroke for the past few weeks and whatever life he might have left before him.

. . .

Three days later, as Thomas Randolph started his return to Aberdeen and Pembroke, he and his small band crossed the ridge near Tyndrum, above an ancient Druid shrine that had been rededicated to Saint Fillan of Glendochart, the venerated sixth century monk. He intended to stop and pay homage to the most revered holy man in Scottish history, but, looking down upon the scene, he saw Robert's army gathering at the site.

Randolph remained astride his horse and waved the other men on over the hill, away from the Scots. The dejected knight stayed a short while and looked longingly at the four hundred or so as they grouped around the shrine and knelt there with Robert. With all his heart he wished he could join them, no matter what their fate, for he was sure they would not last out the next month.

"God and the saints be with ye, dear friends," prayed Thomas quietly to himself, then, kicking his horse, he rode after the leopard banner toward Aberdeen.

As were many places and customs that were originally Druid or pagan, this shrine was rededicated by the Christians to their own purposes, it being easier to establish new meanings to old habits than to establish totally new habits. Thus it was that the sweet spring that had once been designated as holy by the Druids, had become a Christian holy site as well.

Unaware they had been observed, Robert was deliberate and meticulous in showing proper homage to St. Fillan. He had become increasingly aware of the people's superstitious fear that he was doomed for the killing of Red Comyn in the church at Dumfries. In their eyes, absolution by the Scottish bishops had not removed the stain on Robert's soul, as proven by the fact that he had been without success in battling the English and the far-flung Comyn family.

Whether by chance or by fateful design, an old Druid priest was at the shrine as Robert knelt, begging forgiveness from God for the killing. Aware of who Robert was and the people's feelings about him, the old priest guessed the king's purpose and came to Robert straightaway, put his hands on Robert's head, and absolved him of all the sins he would endure in the name of freedom for his people.

With Robert's thanks the old priest left, and afterward, none could swear for certain whether he was apparition or real. But they accepted the blessing all the same, and praised God as they stood in the field and on the hillside surrounding the shrine.

"Perhaps now I can get beyond this curse or whatever obstacle it is that keeps me from attaining my kingdom," whispered Robert to Elizabeth, who came and quietly knelt alongside of him at the humble shrine.

"Take it as a good omen, Robert, for ye are deservin' of a good omen 'bout now," she replied as she laid a necklace of silver, in a Celtic cross design, at the base of the spring.

After their prayers and their leaving, the ragtag army of Robert de Brus turned south toward Dail Righ as the next leg in their journey. To a man, they were looking forward to the long awaited and much needed rest they were promised upon their arrival at Castle Dunaverty, on the southern tip of the land of Kintyre.

Warrior from Argyle

AUGUST 14th 1306
LOCH LOMOND, NEAR DAIL RIGH

Robert was leading his small band through a wilderness around Loch Lomond, near the village of Dail Righ, when Andrew rode pell-mell toward him.

Robert pulled up and waited for his squire to reach him.

The king knew something untoward had happened by the manner in which the boy rode, galloping the huge horse and whipping him all the way.

"What's the reason for yer panic?" he asked when the boy reached his side and pulled up.

"Sire! I... was over on... yonder ridge... and..." said Andrew between desperate gulps for air.

Robert immediately surveyed the landscape but saw nothing out of place as James Douglas and Edward Brus came to join the knot.

"Men, lots of them... yonder hollow..." gasped Andrew as he regained more control on his breathing.

Robert, Douglas, Edward, and the Earl of Atholl rode up to the rise overlooking the hollow to speculate the odds.

"There they are, comin' through the trees," observed Atholl pointing below.

From Argyll, John Macdougall had gathered his forces, primarily consisting of the Macdougall family and many hundreds of blue-painted infantry, in the war of revenge against King Robert for the murder of John 'The Red' Comyn.

"Great many more than we have," remarked Robert coldly, "but most are on foot."

"Don't slight the worth of those woad-blue devils," warned Atholl, "I've seen them fight before, and was beholdin' to the Lord God that they and I fought on the same side."

"Our best defense is with the mounts," insisted Edward.

"Hain't that yer ol' yellow-gray huntin' hound, Robert?" asked Atholl, again pointing.

Robert looked at the dogs leading the trackers, and exclaimed, "Damned if it isn't! They're trackin' me with my own dog!" The four men dismounted and watched a moment longer, hidden in the trees.

"We'll be set for them," said James Douglas.

"We need to find out their plans before they reach our main body," said Robert.

"How so will that work?" asked James.

"I'll lead ten mounted knights and fifty men on foot to right here, behind this rise, and when they come closer we will attack and scatter their forces. We will then retreat to where the rest of ye will be waitin', behind that stand of trees, yonder," he pointed. "As they come after us, set what bowmen we have to thinnin' their ranks, so that ye can then charge out with our mounted troops and do away with them," explained Robert.

"Not a proper form," commented Atholl, disapprovingly.

"Doin' what's proper has done naught but get us killed, up 'til now," philosophized Robert, turning for another look at the terrain. The four men remounted and rode back to the waiting army of anxious warriors.

"Nigel, take the women far down that trail and we'll protect this entrance from here," ordered Robert. "None will get to them except over our dead carcasses." The trail he chose was such that it fell off to the water's edge on the loch side and was protected by a cliff on the other. There was no room for two to pass each other for most of its length.

"What's wrong?" asked Elizabeth, who had partially overheard the orders given to Nigel as she rode up.

"There's Comyns over yon ridge, fixin' to strike us," barked Robert. He really resented the use of his dog by his enemies.

"And ye want us to hide down that trail! Is that what ye've got Nigel set to do?" said Elizabeth testily, matching his gruffness with her own.

"Aye, woman," returned Robert, "'tis the prudent thing to do!"

"Prudent or not, aren't our lives in danger here, too?"

"Aye," said Robert reluctantly.

"Then, we'll fight along side ye!" said Elizabeth with an iron resolve. He had seen the same flash in her eyes before, and knew there was no time to argue her down, even if he wanted to. But he also saw that she was right; that they all, at this moment, had their lives in jeopardy's path and must prepare to defend them.

"Very well, Elizabeth," he stroked her face lovingly, and kissed her lightly on the lips. "You and the other women will stay back and be part of the third wave," Robert brought his thin ringlet of gold crown from his pouch and affixed it to his helmet, then pulled up the hood of his chain mail and set the royal helmet firmly on his head and raised the visor. "When they fall 'neath my claymore this time, they will know they have been slain by the king," he said to Elizabeth with a smile.

She smiled back, drawing her short sword from the sheath strapped to her back, where she had taken the habit of carrying it, and motioned for the other women to fall in with her.

Agnes began to weep, but did as she was ordered.

At the suggestion of the Countess of Buchan, all of the women had dressed in men's clothing to disguise their sex, and carried short swords and daggers.

James Douglas and Edward Brus formed up the advance team to be led by Robert, followed by as many bowmen and armored and mounted knights as they had, and then by footmen with halberds, axes and sharpened sticks.

Alexander and Thomas Brus, along with Gilbert de la Haye, led the second, main part of the force. Nigel and others mixed in with the third force, including the women.

Tears streamed down Agnes' face. The tension for anticipated combat had all of the Scots' nerves on a bare edge, but like the men, the women set their jaws and readied themselves for battle.

It was only a moment before Robert's trap was ready for the springing. He was just below the rise, where he could hear the hounds bawling as they came up the hill on the other side.

At the precise time he adjudged to be the moment to strike, he gave his loudest and fiercest war whoop and, with drawn claymore, urged his horse over the little hill, his knights and men following upon his heels with much calamitous noise and yelling.

"My God in heaven, what is that?" screamed John Macdougall as the sudden sound and action sent lightning bolts of fear up his spine.

The Macdougalls, except John, were in the front lines but not mounted, and scattered through the wooded landscape like small fish attacked by a bigger one. Robert's men rode behind them as best they could and cut them down. John Macdougall and several Argyll chieftains, all on horseback, emerged on the edge of the wood in time to see the carnage.

Robert reined up his horse short of the trees, with the remainder of his force. Both sides stared at each other for a long moment, then Robert suddenly wheeled his horse and high-tailed it back across the ridge top, followed by his cadre.

A great cheer went up from the Argyllsmen to see the backs of their enemies fleeing the field.

"Let's run them down," said one of the chieftains.

"Could be a trap. He gave in too easily," cautioned another.

"We are here for revenge!" shrieked John Macdougall, half his face painted blue, his thin beard tied in a red ribbon. He was by then shivering mad with rage and the excitement of anticipated combat.

"They attacked us, and like scythes at the harvest, cut us down, and ye two sit on yer arses and jabber 'bout what it might be like on yonder side?" At that, Macdougall rode into the clearing and screamed his high-pitched war whoop so that all the men came forth from the trees and followed him up the hill toward the track of Robert's army, now out of sight over the rise.

The two chieftains looked at each other, shrugged and followed, but they had no enthusiasm for it.

Robert wheeled again and took a position halfway between the crest and his main body. The remainder of his forward guard did likewise.

"Steady men," cautioned Robert, as it sounded like hundreds of screaming wildmen were coming over the rise, straight for them.

John Macdougall was the first to breach the top of the hill and there saw Robert's little band standing stone still. Some thought, they waited stoically for the onslaught of Armageddon.

But Armageddon was the farthest notion from Robert's mind.

All of the men that charged behind Macdougall were on foot, mostly naked, and smeared with bright blue paint, as was their warrior custom from ancient days. Their weapons were sharpened sticks and long-handled axes. Thinking they were against a much smaller force than they had been expecting made them all the bolder, and they rushed forward, down the low rise.

Robert watched as they expended their energies crossing the wash, and let them get within fifty paces before he, himself, whooped, reared his horse, and charged into the swarm of blue, wild warriors.

James Douglas and Edward Brus were directly behind him as he led the attack, the other knights and men fiercely joining the mix.

Many of the blue-painted bodies flowed red with their own blood as the broad swords of the knights put forth their damage.

Robert's foot soldiers fought hand-to-hand combat with their axes, sticks, and even fists, and dispatched as many of the blue ones as they lost themselves, keeping the knights from being run over by sheer numbers.

Robert boldly led by example, remaining in the forefront of the battle, the great claymore arcing high above his head and swinging nearly to the ground, clearing a great swath through his enemies with every pass.

John Macdougall, driven by pure rage, and in close proximity to the Scottish king, was fighting desperately to gain one-to-one access to him, but was consistently driven back by the wanton enthusiasm of his own blue army.

The Argyllsmen were quick in proving to be more than was expected as they attacked low, thrusting their long sticks into the unprotected bellies, and chopping at the legs, of the otherwise armored horses.

"Should we now attack?" asked an anxious Sir Gilbert, who was stationed with the main body.

"Robert said to remain here," reminded Alexander Brus sternly.

'The Black' Douglas was the first Scot to be unhorsed, due to five lengthy ax wounds on his horse's legs and belly. He stood on the top of his dead horse and persistently took the lives of his enemy as his tall, young, muscular body continually swung its deadly sword.

It was only moments before two other knights lost their horses to those terrible axes.

Still mounted, Robert and Edward smote great numbers of the enemy as their claymores swung first to one side, then to the other.

"Retreat!" ordered Robert. Those who still had able mounts lifted some of the ones who didn't onto their own, and fled to the rear.

'The Black' Douglas was among those who had to fight while withdrawing on foot.

Edward and Robert, leading the front, backed their horses into a narrow part of the wash and held the wild men at bay long enough for their comrades to pull back to the main body. Then, they quickly abandoned their own positions.

"After them! After them!" commanded John Macdougall when he saw Robert and his men in apparent flight. The Macdougall chieftains this time joined in the war whooping, as did the entire body chasing Brus' troops.

Waiting in their assigned places, the women heard the dreadful roar of the battle and the shrieking of the attackers. "That's the most horrible sound ever," said young Marjorie, her eyes wide with raw fear.

"'Tis that," said the queen, "but draw yer blade and fight, and if fate demands yer life, go down fightin' like the daughter of the Scottish king that ye are."

Marjorie gritted her teeth as the sound of hundreds of whooping, wild voices got louder by the second. "Why do we but stand as they come to us?" she complained, impatient at the waiting.

"Yer father knows warfare. It is his decision," responded Elizabeth.

Just then, Robert and Edward joined the main body and Robert's claymore was seen above the heads of his army, as he wheeled his horse and poised himself to give anew the signal to attack.

The Argyllsmen came roaring down the hollow and around the stand of trees where the Brus army, three hundred and fifty strong, awaited them atop a slight rise. Seeing the formidable foe standing before them when they had thought theirs was going to be an easy rout of less than twenty men, the Macdougalls in the forefront stopped their attack.

Robert gave the signal and his eleven bowmen loosed as many arrows as they had in their quivers. Each archer was capable of having as many as five shafts in the air at once.

The arrows exacted their toll on the stalled enemy, as Robert and his knights led the main body of men rushing forward in a screaming, deadly mass.

Many from both sides were slain within minutes.

This is Methven revisited, thought Robert, as blue Macdougalls came at him from all sides and he slashed with his claymore on either flank of his destrier.

James Douglas lost his second mount of the fight, but fought on like a fiery demon with his two-handed claymore, until he was stabbed in the back by a blue warrior wielding a sharpened stick. He fell onto the rapidly burgeoning pile of dead and dying men. As he lay moaning and bloody, his attackers turned their attention to others.

After sailing their last flight into the enemy, the Scots archers abandoned their bows for battle-axes and ran screaming into the fray, swinging wildly. Nigel still held back his force of approximately fifty men and the women.

Some of the Macdougalls saw an opportunity to get behind the main clutch of the fighting, and came attacking swiftly upon Nigel's reserves.

Agnes screamed when she saw them coming toward her, and Nigel, who had been preoccupied with the main battle, was instantly and acutely charged to attack.

"Ladies, yer time is now at hand!" shouted Elizabeth, and she twisted in the saddle to backslash a blue attacker, who fell immediately, holding his bloody throat.

Young Marjorie's horse jumped as a Macdougall ax did its worst to its belly and legs. She screamed as her beast died and collapsed under her, and she fell to the ground with the wind knocked out of her.

Overcome and unable to breathe, she passed out.

They tried to get to the queen's horse in the same manner, but she reared her mount and spurred it on to attack them boldly.

Christian, bitterly angry over the presumed loss of her husband Christopher, and being a strong, large boned woman, was a force to be reckoned with as she charged her mount into the enemy, hanging on to the side of the saddle as her sword did its work.

Mary was no laggard as she grabbed one Macdougall by the hair and slit his throat with her dirk.

Nigel and his men mixed in tight with the women, as all were fighting for their very lives.

Isabel, the Countess of Buchan, got her chance to fight when she saw a chieftain break through Robert's knot of battle. Spurring her horse toward him, she attacked with a vengeance. He dodged her first swing and prepared to deal the deathblow as she passed. But, realizing that she was a woman, he hesitated. That was all the edge Isabel needed. Her blade swung back across his face, slashing his eye and nose and drenching him in blood. He dropped his weapon and brought his hands up to cover the wound. Isabel wheeled and brought her sword around toward his neck. The chieftain fell from his horse, headless.

Rather than let the dead man's horse wander back to the enemy, she grabbed the reins and led it away.

Andrew saw a Macdougall prodding the unconscious Marjorie with a stick as she lay on the ground. The boy spurred his horse to get 'round behind the man, then jumped from the saddle onto his back, flailing him as hard as he could.

Seeing the boy clinging tenaciously and beating the devilment out of the naked man, who was dancing around wildly trying to get the lad off him, a foot soldier ran up and killed the man with a single dagger blow to the belly.

The boy and the soldier then pulled Marjorie up onto Andrew's saddle, and after mounting behind her, the boy rode off down the trail toward safety.

Sir Gilbert was fighting at the side of King Robert when the long axes of the Macdougalls cost him his horse. He was pinned under the horse by one foot when the animal fell with him, but shirked not from the killing. He struck at any enemy who passed near, but knew it would be but a moment ere his predicament would be his death.

Edward Brus, recalling being in the same dilemma at Dumfries Castle and Thomas Randolph's coming to his rescue, dismounted to repeat the exploit for Gilbert's benefit. Though he struggled considerably in trying to roll the horse's dead weight enough for Sir Gilbert to extricate his foot, he finally managed.

The freed knight stood and signaled his thanks, and both men threw themselves back into the fray. Neither lost an opportunity for taking the lives of the enemy.

John Macdougall finally positioned himself to sate his raging desire for combat with King Robert. Robert, recognizing who the knight was, moved forward through the melee to engage him, when Macdougall suddenly went down into the crush and disappeared from sight. His horse had been accidentally stabbed through the neck with a pike by one of his own men. He fell to the ground, dazed. Robert moved away.

As the battle boiled on, the field of standing men became thinner and the bodies of the dead and wounded grew in number. Many of the mounted knights were now on the ground fighting, as they too had lost their greatest advantage, their horses.

Robert was one of only four who still rode, and as he wheeled about to assess the battle, he saw James Douglas, seriously wounded, on the ground near where Gilbert de la Haye and Edward Brus were surrounded by the enemy, bravely fighting in hand-to-hand combat.

Thomas Brus was in much the same predicament on the other side of the small wash that was the battlefield.

Alexander retreated to Nigel's position to start the women and the the army down the trail where they would be inaccessible to the horde.

Robert realized the dire peril the remaining body of fighters were in and ordered a general retreat.

"Get those two out of there!" commanded Robert to five soldiers who were backing away from the fight.

"Aye, Sire," said one, and they ran to help James Douglas and Gilbert de la Haye to a rear position and down the trail. The fierce Macdougalls were tiring from the fight, the same as Robert's men, and the retreat was with minimum conflict.

The wash was a mass of crimson bodies. Robert's brave four hundred now numbered less than half that. Those who could manage to walk away from the field went with him, and those who could not were fated to a death by an Argyllsman's ax. There were no prisoners taken on either side.

John Macdougall, still lying on the ground across several bloody bodies, slowly came to his senses as the surviving chieftain poured drops of homemade spirits into his mouth. The lord sputtered and opened his eyes, "What in hell's name happened?" he asked, looking over the terrible slaughter all about him.

"Ye were knocked out," said the chieftain.

"The battle, man," screamed Macdougall. "How went the battle!?"

"Hain't over, as yet," stated the chieftain as he handed the skin flask to John, and withdrew, having recognized as kin a man who was lying dead near the lord.

"Damn! Son-of-a-bitch!" he exclaimed. "That's my cousin's husband, it is, lyin' there in that bloody mess! Ach, poor bastard."

"There's a lot of cousin's husbands lyin' here 'bouts," snapped John, trying to stand.

The chieftain caught him as his knees buckled and he started to spiral to the ground, once again. The lord's temper flaired at this own weakness.

"I'm fit! Turn me loose!" insisted John Macdougall, writhing from the man's grasp and staggering about over the gore around him. "I want to see the corpse of Robert de Brus... Show it to me!"

"Ye'd be havin' to follow that loch trail down a ways, to find the livin' Brus, Milord," related the chieftain, "but, ye'll not find him among the dead."

"Then why in God's name are we just layin' about, as if on a picnic!?" growled John, whose pride consumed his judgment.

"Tired," was the answer. The man sat on the slimy, red ground and conserved what energy he had left.

John's wits left him altogether, and he went about the field, stumbling over bodies, rallying the living, and taking revenge on the wounded, and even the dead, enemy. "Get up!" he screamed incessantly to his men, "Get yer blue arses up and after the Brus!"

"Ye'll not get him down that trail along the edge of the loch, and that's where ev'ry last one of them went," commented the chieftain.

Seventy-some men rallied to John's call for continued pursuit, as the others laid out from disgust at his obsessed behavior. "A horse!" he demanded as he saw his dead horse on the ground. "Bring me a horse!"

The chieftain untied his own horse from a tree branch and walked it over to John. "'Tis the last one that's not gone with Brus, or layin' about dead," he remarked without passion. John took the reins with an angry stare, for he knew the chieftain would go with him no farther, but would walk home and take the remainder of his men with him.

"We've lost a plenty today," scowled the chieftain. "We'll not lose another just for the sake of your vengeance."

John mounted and went down the wash through more scattered carnage. The seventy loyalists followed.

"Get to 'em!" ordered John as he pointed his sword down the trail.

The seventy jogged as John rode his horse in their wake. A short run down the trail they sighted the rear guard of the escaping army.

"On 'em, ye fools!" shouted John Macdougall. "They're gettin' away!" In his frenzy, he started kicking at the nearest of his troops with his unstirruped boot.

The shouting alerted Robert in the rear guard. He turned his horse to face the pursuers, who, in turn, cowered back at the sight of him, well bloodied, with scarlet claymore drawn and waiting for them on the narrow trail.

"After him!" fanatically screamed Macdougall as he swung his own sword about, "After him, or I'll whack yer damned heads off, myself!"

The group worked their courage to a renewed frenzy and attacked lone Robert for he had ordered the remainder of his troops to continue along the trail to safety.

The wild men charged him, but only one or two at a time could get within striking distance because of the limited width of the trail. Robert took them as they came, and was able to hold the entire contingent to a standstill. It seemed to him the brave soldiers were casting their lives away to the wind.

Macdougall was now beyond livid with rage at the failure of his troops.

Then he spotted several men, two of them brothers, whom he knew well as being among the most treacherous fighters in his army. He went to them and set out a plan, which, once laid, sent the three off in another direction. After giving them a head start, he called off the remainder of his men, all the while cursing Robert, and swearing undying vindictiveness against him by the Macdougall clan.

Seeing the enemy withdraw, Robert stood until he could see they had truly left, then wheeled his beast and slowly followed the trail after his army, by now quite a ways gone. He kept stopping to look over his shoulder, now and then, having no reason to trust Macdougall.

He reached a place in the trail where there was no room to turn a horse around and the cliff wall was fairly low. Atop the wall Macdougall's three men waited for him to ride the trail beneath them. When he did, they acted as instructed by John Macdougall.

The first jumped down in front of him and grabbed the reins of his horse. Grinning, he screamed, "I've got ye now!"

"Other men have spoke those words," returned Robert as his blood-red blade took the man's arm and shoulder completely from his body in a single stroke.

Seeing his compatriot's arm severed so effortlessly by the great claymore, the next marauder stumbled and fell to the ground beside

Robert. The third jumped directly onto the horse's rear and grabbed Robert by the throat with a full arm, but was too small to break his captive's neck. He could, however, close off his wind.

The would-be strangler's clumsy companion reached his hand through Robert's stirrup to pull himself up. Feeling the hand in the stirrup, the king quickly placed his boot atop it and clamped the hand tight in the stirrup. He then kicked his horse and drove him forward so that the man was dragged along the rocky trail.

For a moment, Robert could get to the agile man on his back with neither sword nor fist. At length, the choking grip of the man on his back was effecting its purpose, and Robert was unable to get sufficient breath to long remain in the saddle. In desperation, the king reversed his sword direction and struck over his shoulder with the pommel of the sword, hitting the man squarely on the head and breaking his skull.

The man slipped from the horse like a rag doll. Dead before he hit the ground, he rolled down the slope and splashed into the shallows of the loch.

The last assassin was still being dragged alongside the galloping horse, unable to pull his hand free of Robert's snare. Able to breathe, again, Robert quickly dispatched him with a single blow to the ribs, then lifted his foot and released the hand, and the body fell aside the trail.

When the Lord of Macdougall cantered down the trail to view the corpse of Robert Brus and found instead his bloody, dead assassins, he cursed and swore all the louder, but by then, Robert was well beyond earshot.

. .

It was near sundown when the first of Robert's devastated army struggled to the far end of the trail, which ran for miles along the edge of the loch. They were, one and all, near death from wounds and exertion, and as they reached the clearing between the loch and the wood, some two hundred paces away, they fell on the ground, exhausted.

Only Elizabeth remained standing. She was one of the first to get through and when most of the soldiery had arrived, she still had not seen Robert. In growing desperation, she asked every group that entered the clearing if they had word of the king. All said they had none.

Soon, the last man she could see came in from the trail, and he was not Robert.

Elizabeth stood stoically staring back down the trail. The other women were too tired to stand vigil with her, and lay about on the late summer grass, thankful for their own continued life.

Many of the army fell soundly asleep immediately upon sitting or lying on the ground. The walking wounded, including 'The Black' Douglas and Gilbert de la Haye, were at the edge of the loch, cleaning their wounds as best they could.

Then, suddenly there came the thunder of hooves from the trail.

Elizabeth drew up taut as her eyes fixed on the fast dimming ingress.

"Robert!" she exclaimed as he came into the clearing on his great Friesian horse.

Robert smiled as he rode to her side and dismounted, to be clutched in a thankful, warm embrace.

"Ye thought me dead, did ye, woman?"

She held onto him as he pulled the chain-mail coif from his head, and he kissed her for a long moment. She trembled in his arms and would not release him from her tight embrace. He could not easily push her away, and so, with a wag of his head, motioned Alexander to his side.

"Set pickets!" he quietly ordered.

"Aye," said Alexander, "and thank God ye're whole, Rob."

"Change those pickets out, right regular," continued Robert, "lest they drop asleep at their posts and we have Macdougalls swarmin' over us all, again."

"Ye think they'll be comin' at us again tonight?" asked Elizabeth, looking into his eyes. He shook his head.

"They've got to be as worn out as we are, and lickin' their wounds same as we're doin', too," replied Robert. "But, we have to prepare in case. Ye ne'er can tell what the Macdougall might do."

. .

That night was spent in sound sleep laced, for many, with nightmare images of the battle with the Macdougalls. Even the bravest and boldest of the warriors slept with their hands on their weapons.

. .

Early the next morning, Robert and his brothers rode along cliff trail to see if the Macdougalls were in mind of pursuing, but found no sign that they were.

"See here, Robert," said Alexander as he spied a particularly large boulder seated close to the cliff and overlooking the trail. "If we can drop that stone down here, it'll block their passage, should they come this way," said Nigel. "They'll have a terrible time unseatin' a stone of that size, especially since they can't get behind it, once it's in place."

"Agreed," said Robert, and the five men dismounted and climbed the face of the cliff. In relatively short order, they had chopped down a stout tree and, with all of them putting their shoulders into it, they finally levered the boulder over the edge of the cliff. As Nigel had expected, and prayed, the great stone swapped end-over-end, and pounded deep into the trail below.

"That will afford us a day, perhaps, but no more," observed Robert as they inspected their handiwork.

The brothers remounted and rode back to the clearing to a meager breakfast of yesterday's biscuits and not much more. Most of their sparse supplies were lost with the horses that went down in the battle, but Robert's main concern was for the lost warriors.

"By my reckonin', we lost 'bout half our four hundred yesterday," said Robert as he finished his biscuit and washed it down with water.

"We have only nineteen horses, 'cordin' to my count," added Edward. "This hain't goin' to work, to go back for that Macdougall bunch anytime soon." The men continued their banter, with all joining in except Thomas, who was always quiet, and Douglas, who sat dour and unsmiling, keeping his thoughts to himself. He set down his biscuit before peeling his shirt back from his shoulder wound for an inspection of the damage.

Finally, Robert asked, "Jemmy, are yer wounds painin' ye much?"

The brooding knight glanced up at his friends and seemed about to speak, but instead, just shook his head.

"Then what bothers ye, Lad?"

James Douglas washed down the last of his breakfast before saying plainly, "We've got to get the women back to Kildrummy, where it's safe."

Robert frowned at the thought of sending Elizabeth away so soon, but waited to hear the young knight out.

"We worry more for the safety of the women," continued Douglas, "than for ourselves, and are more likely to get killed because of it."

"They fought their own," argued Nigel who had been up half the night consoling Agnes' tears. " They killed their attackers."

"James is right," Alexander interjected, "but not for the reasons he gives."

"And the reasons ye think?" asked Robert.

"We cannot protect the women, and they, in the long of it, cannot protect themselves, not out here," answered Alexander. "Two months ago we were four thousand, five hundred... now we are a worn out two hundred, with most everybody in Scotland runnin' us purely to death."

The gathering fell totally silent as the warriors contemplated Alexander's truth.

"It will be hell tryin' to get to Dunaverty," opined Edward, "and if we make it not there... 'tis dead we are, for sure."

"Why don't ye send the womenfolk to the Orkneys?" said Thomas, breaking his silence. "England's Edward won't dare touch the lands of Norway, even though their queen be our sister."

"Good thought, Thomas," said Robert, "I will seek council with Elizabeth, for it is her life and the lives of the others, includin' my daughter, if we err."

Within the half-hour the women returned from morning ablutions and Robert drew Elizabeth aside to talk to her about his plan.

"I hate the idea of wintering in the Orkneys apart from ye," protested Elizabeth. "I want to continue with ye, to whate'er end we may reach."

"And I desire to be always with ye," he held her close to him. "But, it is not just ye I worry about. What about Marjorie and our sisters? Should I also place their lives in Edward's hands if I fail?"

"Then have them retire to the Orkney's until we can send for them, but pray, keep me with ye, Robert! Both of Edward's wives traveled with him... and no doubt brought him great comfort and solace! Even when he was capturin' Nazareth, Eleanor was by his side...and his young French queen accompanies him still."

She clung to him tightly, trying to make him want her to stay.

"Edward rides as he always has, at the head of perhaps the world's greatest army... while I have naught but the lads ye see here. I cannot further endanger ye and the other women for my own pleasure and comfort... though I would ne'er part from ye if I knew the future would still find ye preserved."

He turned her face to his and kissed her tenderly.

Elizabeth closed her eyes and turned away from him, knowing his mind was shut against her further pleas. "Ye know that I would rather die than be separated from ye, again. But, I shall not grind ye to a jot to have my will. I would not wish to be as a shrew in yer rememberin's of me."

"Never," he said. "Though distant, ye and I shall always be together. I shall ne'er stop loving ye." He drew her close and kissed her again holding her tightly after.

"I shall have John Strathbogie escort ye and the other women there," said Robert quietly, finally taking her arms from around him but holding both her hands. "He has been there before."

The Queen sighed and nodded, sadly concurring in his choice of escorts. "He knows also the Earl of Ross... and Ross can be a most treacherous man."

Robert drew Elizabeth against him and hugged her again for a long moment. She knew he hated parting from her as much as she did, and her tears were for them both.

"We will be together again soon, I promise," he tried to console her.

"Promise not those things o'er which ye have no control, my love," cautioned Elizabeth. "Yer fate as king must precede all else."

Robert's gaze rested upon her face, her eyes, her dark hair, her kiss-moistened lips, trying to imprint her entire being into his memory, knowing that, in the best circumstances, it would be the spring before they met anew. Finally, he pushed her gently away and said, "Gather yer women, then. Macdougall cannot be far behind."

She went as she was bade and looked back not at all. With leaden heart he watched her walk away, finally turning his person and his attention toward instructing Nigel and Atholl on carrying out their parts of his plan.

"The two of ye," started Robert, having called the two lieutenants to council with him, "are to escort the women to Kildrummy. There they can rest awhile, and there I want ye, Nigel, to fortify and hold our only remainin' castle. 'Tis strong enough, and with proper provisions will hold for months against a siege."

"Aye, Robert," replied Nigel. "We can hold out 'til next summer if need serves."

"I will raise more troops and relieve ye ere spring," said Robert with a smile of confidence.

"And my part in this strategy, Sire?" asked John Atholl.

"Ye, Milord," said Robert, "will take the ladies, after they are recovered enough to make the trip, to the Bishop of Moray, who has exiled himself on the main isle in the Orkneys."

"Aye, Robbie," returned Atholl, "'Twill be done else the blood will flow no more in my body."

"I know," replied Robert.

"Yer confidence is not misplaced," said Atholl, sincerely.

"Tell no others of this plan," reminded Robert. "Be they tortured for information, I want them to know nothin' to say."

The Earl of Atholl took Robert's horse, Nigel had his own mount, and the eight women had theirs, so the remaining nine horses were assigned to two knights in armor and seven squires.

Andrew refused the invitation to go north, since he felt duty bound to remain with his king. Thus he turned his fine horse over to a fellow squire, though with assurance of reclamation, soon. His friend smiled and gladly agreed.

Andrew then walked to where Marjorie was mounted on her horse and told her goodbye. She said not a word, but removed a gold ring from her index finger and pressed it into his palm. Then she leaned down and kissed him on the cheek.

He smiled broadly as she rode off with the other women. Looking at the gift she had given him, he tried to put it on his finger, but it would not fit. He took a fine thong of leather and put it through the ring, and tied it around his throat. Opening his shirt, he dropped the ring inside.

No one liked the parting since they had been so recently reunited, but death lurked disguised behind every tree, and Robert's rebellion seemed to be another quickly passing bid for liberty that few of his countrymen saw of worth.

King Robert, The Black Douglas, Gilbert de la Haye, Edward Brus, Alexander Brus, Thomas Brus, seventeen other knights, and one hundred sixty-two warriors of various rankings and skills, were left.

Robert called Andrew to his side. Lifting his arm, he commanded, "Unbuckle the breastplate!"

Andrew frowned, for he didn't quite understand the reason, but did as he was ordered. Robert pulled the heavy chest armor from himself. "God, it feels good to be shed of such a burden," he said, throwing the armor on the ground. The boy remembered when he was scolded for doing the same.

Now, the king had the attention of everyone in his immediate company. "Do likewise," said the king gesturing all around. "We have no further need of these encumbrances."

"Of mind are ye, Robert?" asked Edward as he unbuckled Thomas' armor.

"We have no horses and have a long and dangerous journey ahead. We will need to move swiftly and quietly through the wood 'til we meet up with Neil, and hopefully, ships, to take us to Dunaverty," explained the king.

"Weapons?" asked James Douglas.

"What ye can carry," replied Robert as he looked down at his own pile of armor and weaponry that Andrew was stripping from his body. He noticed the scar in his chest armor from the blow he received from John Comyn in Greyfriars Church.

"Ye follow like an evil ghost, ye do, Red Comyn," whispered Robert into the air. "Ye'll hang about my neck no longer."

With that, he kicked the breastplate, picked up his hand weapons, and strapped his great sword around his waist. "Let us be gone from this place, for it smells of death," said Robert with a stern resolve.

They, every one, abandoned their armor there in the clearing, took only their swords, daggers, bows and arrows, and set off on a twelve-day hike south to Cardross, near where Robert had agreed to meet Neil Campbell.

. .

As Robert and his men were leaving the clearing, John Macdougall was leading his remaining blue army fast down the trail with renewed vigor for the fight. When he came upon the enormous boulder blocking his way, he went into a furious fit and screamed curses on the house of de Brus and swore that he would follow Robert to the ends of the known world. But he was unwilling to climb the cliff and leave his horse behind in his pursuit of his nemesis.

Instead, he dismounted, cut a switch, and beat Robert's dog unmercifully. The dog yelped and growled at the young Macdougall, but could do little else, being held fast by two strong minions of the Lord of Lorne.

Reluctantly, and emotionally spent, Macdougall withdrew his forces back down the trail to find another way to the south, where he instinctively knew Robert had to be headed.

Agnes

ΛUGUSC 21ˢᵗ 1306
KILÐRUOOY CASCLE

After a grueling six days' ride, Nigel and his small contingent of men, boys, and women at last arrived in mid-afternoon at Kildrummy Castle, having left there only weeks earlier. The women were particularly stressed and tired, not only from their long journey over highland and lowland, but also from their great fear for their loved ones still in the company of King Robert.

The guards immediately recognized Sir Nigel and lowered the drawbridge with some hastily mustered fanfare of trumpets and a personal greeting by Sir Robert Boyd, left in command in Nigel's absence. Sir Robert was over six feet tall and muscular, and though certainly not beautiful of face, he had pleasantly rugged features, with thinning black hair and beard. He was completely devoted to the rebellion and to Robert as king.

"Welcome back, Milord Nigel," said Sir Robert, approaching the travelers as they entered the courtyard.

"Good afternoon to ye, Sir Robert," was the reply from Nigel as the party dismounted.

"We thought the lot of ye were done in by Pembroke's gang," said Boyd.

"Nay, but I see ye still have a tabard to wear about, Robert," teased Nigel.

"Must have been some bad business," said Robert Boyd, ignoring the tease.

The queen strode forward to where the two men were standing and asked sternly, "What word of Pembroke?"

Sir Robert bowed deeply at the sudden appearance of Elizabeth and then reached to kiss her hand.

"Enough of the formalities! Pembroke, man! Pembroke!?" she demanded.

"He stands in Aberdeen, My Queen," said Sir Robert, standing tall to present himself as best he could in the presence of Elizabeth, not only his queen, but a beautiful and admirable woman in whose service he would willingly give his life.

"And for what or whom does he wait?" asked the queen.

"For siege equipment, being brought from the south, accordin' to our spies," returned Sir Robert.

"To be used against Kildrummy?"

"I'm fearful so, Ma'am," was the answer.

"We saw English spies lurkin' in the trees nearby, but thought little of it," remarked Sir Nigel as Agnes came to him and held his arm possessively.

"They've been here, tallyin' the odds of a siege... but none can puzzle an entry 'cept to wait us out, I'm sure," explained Sir Robert.

At that point, poor, exhausted Marjorie came to Elizabeth's side and leaned her head on the queen's shoulder. "Sir Robert," asked the queen, "could you show us to our quarters?"

"The solar in Snowdon, of course, Ma'am," answered Sir Robert, "and Snowdon for the other ladies, as well."

"Thank ye, Sir," said the queen, "and be prepared for our departure early on the morrow."

He bowed low. "As ye wish, My Queen."

"Nigel, I would have Lord John meet me in the great hall as soon as he is settled into his quarters," she requested.

Nigel smiled and bowed in agreement, and all dispersed to their beds for a long evening's rest before setting out on the second leg of their arduous trek.

．　．

The next morning, under the command of his sovereign, John, Earl of Atholl, protector of the queen, Princess Marjorie, and Lady Mary Campbell, led them and their entourage forth on a journey, the destination of which was known only to them. The women dressed as squires to skew the spies' reports to the Earl of Pembroke.

Lady Christian Seton, Nigel's Lady Agnes, and Countess Isabel MacDuff remained in Kildrummy with Nigel. It was he who had the task of holding the castle until Robert could get re-supplied from Ireland or the north islands, where he had family support.

Nigel Brus

AUGUST 25th 1306
KILDRUMMY CASTLE

Pembroke's siege machinery had arrived and was being set up on the grounds before and to the sides of the fortress. The earl, too, was there, dressed in his most gaudily festooned clothes, and silver armor outlined in gold. Sir Thomas Randolph accompanied him by command, and Sir Ingram de Umfraville and Sir Phillip Mowbray, by choice of vengeance.

Fresh from his father's side in Carlisle, the Prince of Wales was in attendance with his swan knights, renewed in his resolve to take the last fortified resting place yet remaining in the possession of the dwindling rebellion.

The besiegers were convinced that all whom King Robert held near and dear dwelt within Kildrummy, and to have them as hostages would make the prize all the sweeter. The capture of his family would soon bring Robert de Brus out of hiding and easily into their grasp, or so they reasoned.

"They mean to have us routed before the end of the month, I think," said Sir Robert Boyd from the wall walk. He and Nigel were watching the procession of workmen and their constructions.

"We have stores enough to last 'til spring," said Sir Nigel confidently, "We need only to hold them from the walls 'til then."

"They look as if they're 'bout set for the attack," remarked Sir Robert, pointing to the belfry tower, being assembled piecemeal as the various parts arrived by hay wagons commandeered from the regional farmers.

"They'll be rollin' it up to the wall 'fore long, for sure," returned Nigel. "That may be the most worrisome piece in their arsenal."

"Meanwhile," smiled Robert, "I'm havin' long fire arrows made."

"Plannin' on burnin' some of it down, are ye?" asked Nigel, grinning.

"Aye, with a long enough arrow and a strong enough bow... and a hot enough fire," replied Boyd with a smile and a wink.

. .

A hot enough fire. Boyd had a small amount of a substance that would make a hot enough fire, if he could just place it where he wanted it. That's what the long arrows were for.

After leaving Nigel he went directly to the armory and, from within a protected corner away in the back, he retrieved a squat, sturdy, tightly sealed jar having faded Arabic writing down its side. He carried it to a table in the middle of the room, and there set the jar down, carefully.

From a cloth pouch he wore slung under his shoulder, he took a number of small, thinly blown glass bottles, setting them on the table beside the Arabian jar.

He looked at the assorted items before him and wondered if his idea would succeed. At long last, he heaved a great sigh and set to work.

From its quiver, he pulled one of the long, headless arrow shafts he'd had made. He turned it this way and that, examining it carefully. It had been perfectly fletched, was straight and true. Rather than affix a point to the arrow, he hardened the end of the shaft, placing it, repetitively, in and out of the coals on the armorer's hearth until it was like iron.

Finally satisfied, he slid the headless end of the arrow into the mouth of one of the glass bottles. It was a perfect fit, he decided, and he smiled to himself. He completed the hardening process on the other arrows, and took them to the table. He then dragged a tall stool to the table and, sitting, stretched out his legs underneath it.

Very carefully, having made sure that everything around him on the worktable was bone dry, he removed the seal and opened the Arab pot, and gagged as the foul odor of its contents reached his nostrils. He heaved several times, producing nothing.

His mistake was that he had refused to believe that the awful stench of the Middle Eastern mixture was as bad as he remembered. Once again, he was convinced.

Boyd gradually recovered from the nausea and, in spite of recurrent episodes, proceeded with his task. First, he picked up a small spoon and reached into the blackness of the jar to scoop out some of the inky contents. Slowly, he drained the unctuous mess into one of the glass bottles.

When all the bottles were over half full, he laid the spoon across the top of the pot. A single drop of his sweat fell onto the side of the jar and ran slowly down to the table. He froze. He held his breath and moved slowly away from the table lest he drip sweat into the mixture.

He removed his kirtle and used it to wipe the sweat from his face and arms. His plot would certainly go awry, and perhaps take a good portion of the building with it, if one drop of moisture mixed into the Arab concoction. He quickly closed the nearly empty jar and set the bottles to one side, safely away from the work area.

The rest of the job went faster, requiring only that he put the bottles on the ends of the arrows and seal them, somehow. He settled on string, wrapped around each arrow and pushed painstakingly into the mouth of its bottle until the opening was tightly filled and the bottle and arrow were one. He then wrapped tallow soaked cloth around each shaft to make it a fire arrow, when the time came. Then, all he had to do was wait.

· ·

Later that night, as the moon played hide-and-seek with the dark amongst swiftly moving clouds, Nigel Brus ordered his strongest archer to come to the wall walk, where they met with Sir Robert. It was he who brought the special, long arrows, tipped with the bottles, and their fearsome contents.

"Think ye can hit the belfry yonder?" asked Nigel of the bowman, pointing to the structure. All three men knew it was well beyond ordinary range.

The bowman pulled on the heavy, long bow to test its strength, then wet his index finger in his mouth and held it above his head to read the wind's direction. "Maybe, Milord," he answered, "but, 'twill be a good trick with those heavy bottles on 'em."

"Well, ye have six such as this one. Do the best ye can, and see if ye can make them English right mad at us," said Robert Boyd. He lit the cloth on the first arrow with a faggot he had brought from the hearth, and handed it to the archer.

The archer nocked the arrow onto the string and pulled the bow full strength. He could feel the heat from the fire at the tip of the arrow draw close to his bow hand as he aimed the missile at the four-story, wooden belfry.

He loosed the flaming shaft and watched its trajectory, cursing under his breath as the wind carried it too far downwind to the left. Nevertheless, when it landed within the enemy campsite, it did cause quite a stir. As Boyd expected, the glass bottle broke open on impact and from where they stood on the castle wall, it looked as if fire spontaneously erupted for ten or more paces around. Nigel and the archer stood with their mouths open.

"Looks like the arrow's riggin' works," remarked Boyd with a broad smile.

"What in the world?" asked Nigel.

"Greek Fire," Boyd answered.

"Greek Fire? From where?" Nigel persisted.

"We captured a small amount on one of Edward's supply trains. Been savin' it for the right purpose," Boyd grinned. The trio watched as English soldiers tried to stamp out the fire, only to set their footwear ablaze. Then, they went to put out the fire with water, but instead watched it rise atop the water and float to a nearby tent. It, too, was soon burning. The Scots slapped each other on the back and whooped and hollered.

"Ready for yer next shot?" asked Nigel. He now believed they might eliminate the threat from the belfry, which was designed to roll up to the castle walls with numerous armed soldiers inside. Dropping a draw-bridge onto the battlements, it would thus provide the soldiers direct access to the top of the castle's walls.

"Aye, Milord," said the bowman, heartened, "I'll hit it for sure on this go."

Robert Boyd blew gently on the fire wick as he crouched low and close to the wall. The arrow burst into flame and the bowman took careful aim before loosing it to make its graceful arc in the black night sky.

"Damn good!" Nigel shouted when he saw the arrow slam high against the side of the belfry and burst into flames. The fire oozed with the thick oil, down the structure. "Damn good shot!" The alarm that spread among the soldiers in the camp alerted all to the fire, and they soon created a great commotion while attempting to extinguish the roaring blaze, as the third arrow hit its mark.

"Plenty busy, they are, now," remarked Nigel a few minutes later as the wall walk became crowded with cheering and shouting Scotsmen.

"Where they gettin' the water to fight the fire?" asked Boyd.

"From our moat," explained Nigel with a smile. "They've got a bucket brigade set up, protected by mantlets," he explained. Another bowman, standing to his right, leaned over the wall and loosed an arrow. A scream of agony and a splash was heard below. "Some we get, some we miss," Nigel shrugged.

"That gambit workin' for 'em, I wonder?" asked Boyd, seeing several bodies floating in the moat, already.

"They're puttin' every man to the quenchin' of it," returned Nigel, "but since nobody can safely get on top, they can't reach the upper floors of the belfry with the water. The funny part is, if they could, they'd be worse off!" He laughed.

Meanwhile, in the camp below, the Earl of Pembroke was not nearly so calm, nor was he nearly so sober, as he stumbled from his tent in the barest of clothing, dragging his beautiful chest armor in one hand and his sword belt in the other.

"What in the Goddamn hell goes on, here?" he bellowed loudly.

"The Scots are attackin', Milord!" yelled Umfraville excitedly from a position closer to the burning belfry than was Pembroke's.

Pembroke stopped and drew his sword for fear that Sir Ingram was correct in his assumption, then walked in haste to the side of his Scottish aide.

"They've fired my belfry!" observed Pembroke, in disbelief and anger, "Damn bastard Scots fired my belfry... I hain't got off the first missile and they've fired my belfry!" He stood agape, staring into the conflagration a few moments before he really started swearing.

From the wall walk Nigel saw the rotund figure silhouetted in front of the fire, shaking his sword menacingly in the air, and dragging his armor behind him, while everyone else rushed about in disorder.

"Is there no way to put it out?" questioned the archer. Boyd laughed aloud at the thought.

"Aye, there is," Nigel joined in the laughter. The archer looked perplexed from one nobleman to the other. They seemed to be enjoying a private joke.

Boyd finally said, "Piss on it!"

"Milord?" the archer frowned, his eyes wide in disbelief.

"That's the way ye extinguish Greek fire," Nigel nodded, laughing still.

"Naw," the archer shook his head, thinking the two knights were mocking him.

"'Tis true, man," Nigel assured him. "That will work." The three of them then enjoyed a roaring laugh together.

The belfry was a huge bonfire, lighting up the night sky and casting burning embers into the gentle wind for distribution upon the heads and chattels of the hapless English.

"They comin' for us tonight?" asked Boyd, still somewhat amused.

"Reckon not," replied Nigel, "but, that is one mad bastard, standin' on yonder lawn."

"I *can* hear faint curses echoin' through the hills," mocked Boyd, who could, in fact, hardly hear himself talk for all the cheering around him. He looked out over the chaos and said, "If three fire arrows will do that, why not let them have the others?"

Nigel and the archer smiled.

As the arrow tips were lit, the strong bowman loosed each toward the command tents the English had thought were erected beyond arrow range. Two arrows hit their intended targets, and the other set the trees above them afire. Their effect was brilliant as a momentary diversion and, perhaps, at least to Nigel, more valuable as a prideful spirit booster for the Scots.

Soon the unquenchable flames threatened Pembroke's catapults, and most of the camp was put to moving the lumbering siege machines farther out of range. The frantic activity in the English camp lent great mirth and entertainment to the Scots, and it would be late in the night before the smoldering remnants held less appeal than a straw bed and a blanket.

With the Scots' jeers and taunts as a background, Pembroke screamed in his fury to one of the English soldiers close by, "You! Get me Thomas Randolph!" The soldier ran off and returned, followed by Randolph, who walked up to Pembroke in no particular hurry.

"What be yer need?" he asked, half asleep and scratching.

"Bring me that damned cow!" spat Pembroke with a deep scowl.

"Cow?"

"That dead, bloated, stinkin' cow we passed on the river edge 'tother day, man!" insisted Pembroke. "Remember?"

"I recollect the stink, for certain, I do," returned Thomas.

"Then get it, man! Bring it here!"

"Aye, Milord, first light."

"First light be damned! Ye'll take a litter and have it *back here* by first light!" shouted Pembroke, and left to claim the largest remaining tent.

Thomas watched Pembroke storm away. The turncoat Scot could not believe the earl's insane behavior, but, as ordered, he commandeered six strong soldiers and a litter pulled by a draft horse, and set off by torchlight toward a spot on the nearby river, where he thought he remembered the dead cow having been.

"I'm gettin' some sleep, 'cause they hain't likely to let us rest in the morn," remarked Boyd as he left the ramparts and went to bed. Nigel nodded in agreement, set the pickets on the wall and went to bed.

. .

The next morning, fog lay thick over the area at first light, when Nigel arose and climbed to the wall walk. He had wanted to get an early glimpse at the English camp to assess the damage, but could see nothing of it through the impenetrable haze.

Robert Boyd soon joined him. "Peaceful, hain't it?" he remarked.

"So far," remarked Nigel, "but they're stirrin' about more than usual for this time of day." He sniffed the air and peered into the misty curtain, adding, "There's a strange stench..." he sniffed and frowned, "...like the smell of rottin' flesh... waftin' about this mornin', too. Do ye not smell it?"

"English cookin'?" smiled Robert impishly.

"No doubt," returned Nigel with a chuckle.

Soon, as the two men stood quietly talking, the fog began to burn off, somewhat, and the top area of the belfry exposed its charred skeleton.

Nigel and Robert congratulated each other with smiles and handshakes on having eliminated at least one of the machines that their enemy had brought work against them.

The cocks in the courtyard crowed as the castle came alive with activity, preparing food for breakfast and readying materials for use when the attackers mounted their assault. Those who had been through a siege before knew the English would come as soon as it was clear enough and make an attempt to scale or breach the walls. Their expectations were well founded, for as the fog disappeared about mid-morning, the entire English contingents of both armies, the earl of Pembroke's and the Prince of Wales,' stood at the ready for the first onslaught of the siege.

The prince was in his full armor, prancing about on his great black stallion and directing his three hundred swan knights on how best to show their might to those within the castle. He had lost not one of his elite knights in his lightning attacks that had so far assured his domination of the common folk of the southeastern portion of Scotland. On the other hand, he had only brave men with sticks and rocks to stand against him.

Thomas Randolph had managed to retrieve the bloated, rotting carcass of the cow, though his men had grown greatly nauseated and several nearly fainted from the task. Once it was in camp, Pembroke ordered it strung to the largest catapult in the arsenal. The men charged with doing so retched and heaved the entire time, hardly able to stand the foul odor emanating from the poor beast. The stench grew even worse as the sun grew hotter.

Pembroke, seemingly unaware of the malodorous carrion's presence, sat astride his mount and glared at the top of the castle wall in pure hatred of the Scots. Not only had they burned his belfry, they had joked and laughed at him as he stood in front of them in his near nakedness and made a drunken fool of himself.

When the moment suited him, he took out his broad sword and bisected the taught rope that released the catapult's pent-up arm, and flung the carcass.

The cow was so thoroughly rotted that the sudden motion caused pieces of its flesh to scatter across all who were near. Being the closest, Pembroke received a greater portion.

The stunned earl sat amidst the fetid mess until suddenly, he began screaming and ranting, uttering the foulest curses he could think of as he picked large and small stinking pieces of flesh from his beautiful war suit and armor.

Randolph, who had realized the potential for such splatter, had prudently stood behind a nearby tree from where he witnessed the entire fiasco. He but poorly contained his laughter as Pembroke retired to his tent in a cursing fit of rage.

Adding insult to injury, the bulk of the carcass did not make it over the wall, as Pembroke had intended, but hit the wall squarely at only three-fourths of its height, then fell unceremoniously into the moat.

"They'll be sorry about that," laughed Nigel. "The moat stinks bad enough without Bossy floatin' in it."

Robert Boyd agreed as he bent nearly double at the spectacle.

Edward, Prince of Wales, found nothing humorous in the event and ordered the first wave of missiles to be launched.

The Scots on the wall saw them coming and instinctively stooped as the spear bolts passed over their heads and landed in the courtyard. The flying spears wounded several hapless souls and killed one.

"Clear the courtyard!" commanded Nigel to those exposed in the enclosure. "There'll be plenty more a'comin'!"

Fireballs were next to be catapulted over the wall and land inside the castle yard, but the people were ready with buckets of water and shovels full of dirt, and the fire found little time to spread to the wooden buildings within the castle walls.

Agnes saw the flames from her apartment in the donjon and tearfully repaired to the abbey only two buildings over, to pray.

Isabel MacDuff and Christian Brus, who had dressed in men's clothing and were armored with breastplates and helmets, rushed to the courtyard with their two young squires, carrying crossbows and a large quiver of bolts.

Isabel danced aside as she was barely missed by one of the large spears that had been hurled over the wall.

"Are ye hit?" asked Christian.

"Nay," said Isabel, "but I'll not walk so boldly about in the courtyard, anymore." Both women laughed nervously and made their way to one of the towers that led to the wall walk.

Pembroke, in the meantime, was in his large tent being undressed by his two red-haired slaves. They had no choice and knew not to laugh or refuse to help as they peeled the putrid, hanging flesh from his person and removed his armor and threw it out of the tent.

"Perhaps, Milord," said the elder sister, "it would be best if ye took leave of yer tent for the more breezy outside."

"Get this decayed filth from me, woman!" he demanded of them both. They both complied as best they could while trying not to vomit from the stench. The earl being in such a black mood, they did not know what he might do to them if they became too sick to minister to him.

And thus, as the attack continued, Pembroke was being stripped of his clothes and his dignity as the young women followed the naked man out behind the tent to scrub him down with his perfumed soap, and pour buckets of drinking water over his body.

"Bring me clothes!" he ordered his valet, as he stood in the bush, dripping wet, the two women toweling him. The old valet returned in a moment with a suit of clothing that was slightly too small for him, and certainly not nearly of the fine quality as was that he had just ruined.

"A gift from Sir Phillip," said the valet.

Pembroke reluctantly donned the clothes and rejoined the attack after having commanded the two sisters to clean up the mess of his tent.

The Scots fired not an arrow as the incessant pounding by the English continued. For over an hour the air assault kept up a constant deluge of deadly projectiles before the sudden quiet. It was then that the English dispatched men with scaling ladders to all accessible sides of the castle.

"Here they come, Scotland! Let them not breach the walls!" yelled Nigel Brus as he saw ladders capable of reaching the level of the parapet. The Scots were ready to repel the advancing foot soldiers with cauldrons of hot oil and heavy stones to rain onto the attackers' heads.

Defending bowmen shot those carrying ladders across the long field surrounding the castle, as the English longbowmen moved their log mantlets ever closer to the castle.

"Breach, yonder! A breach!" screamed a soldier to Nigel's right.

"Robert, the other side of yon tower," ordered Nigel, pointing.

"Aye," said Robert Boyd, and he ran toward the opening gap, motioning to several of his men to follow.

The English poured across the battlements and onto the wall walk.

There was little room to maneuver on the narrow wall walk, but the

Scots were holding their own. Newly arriving English, having climbed their ladders to the top of the wall, were hesitating there, afraid of jumping on top of their embattled comrades.

Wounded English fell or were pushed off the wall into the courtyard, and if the fall didn't kill them, the townspeople beat them to death with whatever came to hand. Prisoners were not a luxury the castle residents could afford, since the besieging English assured them of no resupply. The same people, so vicious to the enemy, tried to save Scots who fell from the wall walk, but few survived the fall.

Isabel, standing inside a tower at the parapet level, saw the invaders hesitating at the top of the wall and took aim with her crossbow. As she released her bolt, the closest one fell backward from the wall, screaming all the way to the moat below.

That felt strangely satisfying, she thought, handed the crossbow back to her squire for reloading, and took up a second bow for the next shot.

Christian was inspired by Isabel's success and, drawing her sword, rushed the closest enemy and ripped him between the joints in his light armor. He screamed and fell into the courtyard.

Isabel continued to fell soldiers as they attained the top of the wall. Seeing their comrades fall upon clearing the top, those behind were in no rush to take their places, and within the span of a half-hour the Scots had repelled the attack and pushed the ladders to the ground, some carrying soldiers with them.

"Makin' ladders with our own trees, don't seem right, somehow, does it?" questioned Christian rhetorically as the English retreated back across the open field toward their camp.

"Better that than facin' those horsed knights on open ground," replied Isabel with a smile as she wiped sweat from her brow with her sleeve.

"Ye ne'er killed a man in battle ere this, did ye, Isabel?" asked Christian.

"I've just passed my twentieth birthday..." she said reflectively, then added, "Nay, I've not done many things... that I'll be doin', now."

Christian smiled approvingly. "Christopher and I fought many skirmishes side-by-side," she said in an almost wistful way as Isabel took her older friend's arm, affectionately.

"I was married before, did ye know that?" said Christian as tears welled in her eyes. "Dear Christopher, if he is dead, is the second husband I've lost to these English bastards."

"Freedom comes but dearly to some, others have it not at all, and many sadly let it escape their grasp. But perhaps sadder are those unwillin' to pay the cost of bein' free," returned Isabel, and the two women retired from the wall walk and sought drink and food and rest.

"We must have more than a hundred English dead floatin' in the moat and thereabouts," said Nigel looking over the wall.

"They'll be back this afternoon," assured Robert Boyd as he sheathed his claymore.

"Aye, for sure," replied Nigel as he felt the first few rain drops hitting his face, "and we'll be ready for them, rain or not."

. .

For three rainy days thence, Aymer de Valence and the Prince of Wales fought through the muddy, rain soaked landscape, attempting to scale the walls of Kildrummy castle. To no avail.

Sir Nigel Brus and his men and women fought valiantly and held the walls. Many more of the English died than did Scots, but there were three thousand more English troops bivouacked in the wood, and opposing them, only one thousand Scots garrisoned in Kildrummy Castle.

AUGUST 26th 1306
SANCTUARY OF SAINT DUTHAC IN EASTER ROSS

John Strathbogie, Earl of Atholl, had successfully completed his orders from King Robert to see Queen Elizabeth, Princess Marjorie, and Lady Mary Campbell safely to the northern shore of Scotland, some hundred miles from Kildrummy. There, the Brus women were secretly lodged in the sanctuary of Saint Duthac in Tain, waiting for a galley to take them to Orkney Island. Their plan was to winter out of harm's way with David Murray, Bishop of Moray, who, since bishops Lamberton and Wishart were imprisoned in London, was the last active bishop left in Scotland who had spoken out on behalf of the rebellion.

Tain, in Easter Ross, fell under the sway of the Earl of Ross. No sooner had the queen and her party arrived within the boundaries of his domain than spies, placed by the earl along his border, alerted him to their presence. With the notion of capturing the fugitives for his sworn liege, King Edward, the earl immediately set out in search of them, leading a contingent of forty knights.

Unaware, the royal fugitives awaited their transport.

"Ye reckon it'll be here this night?" asked Elizabeth of John, who had parked his large, burly body in an open window of the sanctuary. From there, with the moon as his only light, he searched the blackness of the sea for the first glimmer of a sail from the north.

"Don't rightly know," returned John continuing to scan the undulating sea. "The others asleep?" he asked.

"Aye," spoke Elizabeth, "but, ready to go at a moment's notice."

"We'll not have one to spare when we see the sail."

"Makes me nervous to be in Ross," admitted Elizabeth.

"Ah, don't worry. The earl here 'bouts hain't a bad sort," said Atholl trying to put an easier edge on the situation.

"I'll still feel better when we are on the galley and..." Elizabeth was suddenly interrupted by a loud knocking on the main door of the apartment.

Atholl drew his claymore and went down the hall to the entrance as the pounding continued and demands to open in the name of the Earl of Ross were heard.

A priest and several monks rushed to open the door, but Atholl waved his large claymore and they shrunk back into the shadows of the large columns. John Strathbogie then returned to where he had left the queen.

"They have found us, Ma'am!" he said.

"Just when the galley has arrived," said Elizabeth quietly, pointing toward the sea.

"Damn!" whispered Atholl as he heard the voice of the Earl of Ross commanding his men to search every alcove.

"We'll ne'er make it," said Elizabeth as she first analyzed the situation.

"They must get beyond me to touch ye, Milady," said Atholl roughly and with determination as he turned to face the entrance.

Elizabeth drew her short sword in the darkness, but as she held it out toward the many voices of the searchers, she perceived the fruitlessness of the action.

"'Tis of no worth, Sir John," she said quietly. "They have us."

Atholl shushed her as the voices came closer. He was not about to give up his responsibility so easily.

"John!" whispered the queen emphatically. "We are women, and they dare not harm us," she said, more hopeful than sure, "but ye will be killed on this very ground."

"Yer point, My Queen?" he whispered loudly, somewhat puzzled.

"The galley awaits," she said quietly. "Take to the window. Ye and yer men waitin' by the dock will make it! We women are lost, no matter."

"But my promise to King Rob..."

"As queen, I command ye to go," she interrupted through gritted teeth. "Get out that window, now!" The earl of Atholl was torn and hesitated until his queen reiterated, "Now, man!"

The bolted door shaking stirred him finally to action, and turned to go out the window, vowing, "I will return to save ye all as they take ye from this place."

"Open in the name of Ross!" demanded the captain of the contingent as he pounded all the louder.

"Go!" commanded the queen as Marjorie and Mary, awakened by the noise, rushed to her side from an anteroom to where she stood, still with drawn sword.

The door began to give way, splintering against the hammers of Ross' knights.

Atholl, seeing no better choice, reluctantly jumped from the window.

There followed curses and low moans from below the window, which was intermingled with the continued fierce pounding on the barred door.

Elizabeth quickly went to the window. Faint movement in the shadows revealed Atholl limping into the tree line toward the dock and his awaiting men. "Godspeed, dear friend," she whispered.

The broken door finally collapsed to the flagstone floor with a loud crash, startling Elizabeth, Marjorie, and Mary. The Ross knights at once moved into the room with torches high and weapons drawn. Elizabeth held her sword unnoticed in the folds of her dress.

The Earl of Ross entered the small suite of rooms. "Search these premises throughout for more rebels!" he demanded before he noticed Elizabeth standing at the window. He strode across the room toward her to see the importance of her position, and she walked away, hoping to divert his attention from the window.

"It is a beautiful late summer evening, Milady," he said mockingly as he looked toward the sea.

"'Tis, Milord," agreed the queen in an equally mocking tone of voice. The earl started to step away from the window, but spun suddenly around and all but leaned out, straining to see toward the harbor.

"By God in heaven!" he screamed in shock as he saw the galley sail in the harbor. As he turned and crossed by the queen to give orders to his men, Elizabeth, without hesitation, struck out with her sword toward his unprotected throat.

Lord Ross was not a young man, but his reflexes were still quick. He saw the queen's arm move in his direction, and a glint of light beyond it, and he fell immediately to the floor.

A large knight in light armor moved between the Earl of Ross and Elizabeth the Queen and deflected her next blow, catching her wrist and, twisting it roughly, wrenching the short sword from her.

Marjorie dropped to her knees and screamed, "God save my mother, God save my mother!" as the queen's sword clanged harmlessly to the floor.

The Earl of Ross, having regained his nerve and his feet beneath him, turned to face Elizabeth, sweat beaded heavily on his scowling face as he looked into her eyes with genuine hatred.

"Whatever happened to receiving sanctuary in God's church?" she asked in a quiet voice, raising one eyebrow.

The earl knew not how to answer, but shouted in his rage, "Get them all from here!... Take them to the King! He'll know how to treat that shrew's glib tongue!"

Marjorie began to cry.

"Hush child," said Elizabeth, "ye are out of character."

Marjorie sniffed softly, but soon got her courage back and held her peace as her aunt Mary was pushed roughly toward them. She glared at the crude knight but knew it was of no use to say a word.

"Captain," commanded Ross, "take half your men and stop that galley in the harbor! Arrest all who are attached, sailors and passengers alike, understand?"

"Aye, Milord," answered the captain, and he turned to obey.

. .

The men in the small galley furled their sail as they neared the shore where Atholl's men were anxiously awaiting its arrival. John Atholl limped painfully down the pathway toward them.

"Get in the boat!" he shouted to his men.

The little rowboat, which the two soldiers and a squire had commandeered in the name of the queen, rocked side to side in the shallow water as they deftly climbed in. The limping earl splashed into the water after the boat and pulled himself on board over the stern.

Before they had pulled out into deep water, the earl of Ross' men appeared along the shoreline with many torches.

"Ye in the boat!" shouted the captain from the shore as five of his men nocked arrows into their bowstrings and aimed them at those in the little boat.

Atholl stood defiant in the rocking boat, though his leg was throbbing relentlessly.

The captain pointed toward the sea where the galley had turned out of the cove and was heading back north. "Ye had best surrender, Lord Strathbogie, lest ye be killed by my bowmen. Yer comrades have left ye to my kind mercies!" yelled the captain in a calm, sarcastic, but loud voice.

Atholl looked toward the retreating galley and weighed the odds. "Take us ashore," he ordered reluctantly, adding under his breath, "I've ne'er had such a time of poor fate."

The cruel men of Ross handled him roughly and he was bloodied and bruised by the time they returned him to the sanctuary where his abbreviated journey had begun.

. .

The next morning, the Scottish queen and the other women, along with their entourage, and the Earl of Atholl, by then barely able to sit his horse, were assembled for their long trek south and the will of King Edward. It was not a happy prospect.

"I am truly sorry, My Queen," said Atholl through painfully swollen and bloodied lips.

"'Tis not yer doin', dear John," returned Elizabeth as she affectionately reached out with shackled hands to brush back his hair, matted with dried blood.

The earl smiled as well as he could manage, for he knew by her touch that she blamed him not for the capture. But he himself was passing remorseful for the happening.

The horses' reins were pulled ahead of them by their captors, and all the prisoners could do was hang on to their saddlebows. The only hope among the lot of them was that King Robert would hear of their apprehension and come to their rescue.

Andrew Stewart

SEPTEMBER 6th 1306
THE MOUNTAINS NEAR CARDROSS

After the rout at Dail Righ, Robert de Brus and his remaining small band carefully picked their way through the mountainous terrain around Loch Lomond to a place near the small town of Cardross. Not far from the there, in a small cove on the Firth of Clyde, they were to meet with Sir Neil Campbell.

Having arrived only a day before the appointed time and taken up residence in the safety of nearby caves, they subsisted mainly on those things that could be retrieved from bushes and trees, and small animals they managed to snare. All were eaten without benefit of cooking, for they feared to strike a fire.

Robert dispatched James Douglas the several miles to the designated cove, to keep watch for Neil Campbell's arrival. Into the village of Cardross he sent his squire, Andrew, whom he deemed beneath English notice, to gather information on the activity of the soldiers and there.

As Andrew returned from his spying expedition and drew near the camp, he whistled. One of the well-hidden pickets stood to show himself and to wave the lad in. He threw off his filthy kirtle, and the last of the camp cooks thrust a fistful of berries into his hand. Andrew gobbled them down appreciatively, for he had not taken the time to forage anything on his long walk. He was still munching the berries when Robert sat beside him and handed him a small piece of dried meat he had been saving. The lad smiled and ate it, chewing each small bite thoroughly to savor it more.

"Ye find anything of importance?" Robert asked his young scout. Edward came to sit near them so he could also hear the report.

"Them we fought t'other day?" started Andrew, chewing the last of the jerky, "...they're there... 'spectin' us to show along these parts somewhere, but they know not where."

"What makes ye say so?" asked Edward. Thomas and Alexander came closer and squatted in the circle to listen.

"Wanderin' soldiers askin' questions, some with blue still left on their skin," relayed Andrew, adding, "but now they've got on clothes."

"Must have figured our destination," said Alexander.

"Or had good spy work," said Thomas.

"Could be they just guessed passin' well," remarked Robert. Then he asked, "What more?"

"The Earl of Lennox has lost his lands to Sir John Menteith," replied Andrew. "I don't understand all about it, but the villagers are sore worried about bein' under a new earl. Seem to like him not at all."

"John is a scourge on the house of Menteith, to my way of thinkin'," commented Robert, "'Twas his lackeys turned in Wallace to 'Long-shanks' last year."

"Oh... so that's the why of folk's fear," returned Andrew.

The brothers smiled at the lad's revelation.

"Andrew, ye've quit droppin' my armor now, for I've none to drop," teased Robert, then added proudly, "but ye are makin' great progress in the realm of politics."

They all had a good laugh save Edward, whose aspect remained sober.

"Ye recollect," he prodded, "that the earl of Menteith stood with us at yer crownin', Robert," prodded Edward.

"Aye," returned Robert soberly. "Alexander Menteith was great man indeed, and sorry for the loss of him at Methven, I was... Saw him go down... five or more draggin' him from his horse... a great warrior, a great man... a great friend."

"Aye, he was all of that. But John be of a different sort. Joined up with James Macdougall, he could be a terrible enemy," said Alexander.

"How come all the people in the whole world are against us?" interrupted Andrew, concerned.

"'Cause they are afraid of the price they must pay to be with us," explained Robert, a far off tone in his voice as he reached down and picked up a handful of the soil at his feet. "They realize not the value of their own freedom," he said as he watched the soil slip slowly between his fingers and scatter on the ground.

Suddenly his reverie was broken by a strong deep voice he recognized.

"Ye the ones seekin' galleys?" asked Neil Campbell loudly as he and

James Douglas strolled leisurely into camp.

Robert jumped to his feet as he heard the familiar voice from behind him. "Thank God ye're returned, and safe!" he said with heart-felt pleasure and relief as he grabbed the shoulders of his brother-in-law in a great bear hug. The others, too, all rushed to welcome the men and learn their news.

"We have galleys enough and more than plenty victuals for all, about three hours west of here," said James Douglas, alluding to the direction from which they had just come.

A great cheer erupted from the small band. This was better news than they had dare hoped to receive. In short order, the mostly ragtag group had gathered their wits and their weapons, and proceeded to organize themselves for the trail.

Robert moved easily through the crowd to assume command of the column as it milled about. In moments, it was an army on the move.

Down the hill, two young local men, gathering late fall grapes from the wild vines there, heard the cheer from the woods. Frightened, they hid themselves deep in the bush and lay quiet, all the while watching for movement up the hill, and it was not long before the small band of Scots warriors made their way along the inside edge of the wood and disappeared over the hill toward the west. The two gatherers held themselves as still as they could manage until they heard no more sound from the soldiers.

Finally, the lad who was shaking the least whispered to the other, "Let's get outta here 'fore they catch us and cut our ears off, or worse!" His companion nervously nodded, so they scrambled to their feet and ran headlong down the hill to the village to tell everyone what they knew of the events that just occurred in the wood.

Within the hour, news of the happening was presented to John Menteith and James Macdougall in the village of Dumbarton, a few miles up the coast. There they had twelve galleys moored in the harbor.

"Take horses and go see what they're about!" shouted James Macdougall to a Chieftain and his next in command.

"We don't know that these are Brus' men, or, if they are, whether or not he is with them," said the less-energized, newly made Earl of Lennox. Stout, neither short nor tall, with long black hair and matching beard, John had a talent for taking advantage of others' more noble aspirations to aid his own grasping reach for power and wealth.

"They stink!" said Macdougall, snarling and sniffing the air as if he smelled something foul. "They stink and I smell 'em!"

"Ye smell the piggery," teased Menteith with a smirk.

"I smell Brus!" insisted Macdougall.

"Let's wait 'til the spy returns," said Menteith, finishing his flagon of wine and motioning to his steward for another. "I'm as anxious as ye to get my hands on the Brus, but why run about rampaging for naught?"

Macdougall growled and flopped himself into a nearby chair to sulk. The steward returned with wine for both men.

They drank and they waited.

. .

Near sundown, Robert and his band reached the little cove where, as Neil Campbell had said, the galleys lay offshore, bobbing on the water like so many toys.

Edward had never had the experience of galley travel at sea, and viewed the small craft with all but dismay. "We're to risk our lives in those little things?" he asked.

"Aye, my brother," replied Robert with a momentary grin, adding more somberly, "at this point, save Nigel at Kildrummy, almost the entire kingdom rests in the hands of the captains of those 'little things.'"

"Though we have enough galleys for our purpose, we have but a few wee vessels to transport us all out to them," said Neil Campbell. "'Twill take many trips to get us all aboard."

"Then the sooner we start, the quicker we'll be shed of these hostile Menteith lands," Robert said and directed the men at the head of the column to embark directly onto the boats. He set Alexander in command of the loading.

Shortly after the Bruses started loading the Scots army into the wee boats near Cardross, the heavy oak door opened to the great hall where Menteith and Macdougall sat and drank. Dispatched earlier, the chieftain was readmitted to the presence of the two lords. Though expected and anxiously awaited, his piercing, excitedly high voice startled the two men when he cackled, simply, "'Tis the Bruses, a'right!"

John's eyes grew suddenly large with greed, imagining the wealth and lands he would be given by King Edward when he captured Robert de Brus. Perhaps, he thought, I will be given Brus' own ancestral lands of Carrick!

James Macdougall had an entirely different agenda as he screamed a war cry that echoed around the great hall and down the passageways in the huge manor house as well.

He sought bloody revenge!

. .

It was well into darkness by the time the entire contingent of Robert's soldiers was aboard the galleys. At the last, it was only Robert and 'The Black' Douglas, with six men rowing toward the last galley. The other craft had already slipped away, one by one, down the firth toward Dunaverty and safety.

Douglas was first to spot the approaching fleet.

"Look!" he shouted, pointing to the galleys of Menteith and Macdougall as they turned into the cove. "They'll block us, for sure, lest we can outrun 'em!"

"Row, ye Scots, or forfeit yer heads!" encouraged Robert as he took an oar and pulled at it mightily.

"Ye'll have us runnin' in a circle, Robert," said Douglas, and he took an oar opposite the king and began to row.

In the darkness of a waning moon, the pursuers did not realize what a prize they had nearly in hand until Robert and his men had boarded the galley and started for open water.

"There they are!" screamed Macdougall as he pointed into the near dark to show Menteith.

"We have too many torches lit aboard to see well into the night," said Menteith, who then ordered them extinguished.

"Get those damned torches doused!" yelled Macdougall to the other galleys. They quickly did as they were ordered.

"At last, Milord! A stout wind!" shouted the galley captain to Robert in great relief. "Unfurl the sail!" he commanded his men.

Two sailors stood and loosed the ties that freed the sail, and then tied down the loose ends. The captain quickly turned the craft to catch the breeze and it leapt forward, but the wind quickly proved fickle.

"Keep rowin'!" ordered the king to the oarsmen.

"There 'tis!" shouted Macdougall, smiling when he first saw the Scots' sail unfurl in the faint light. "If we catch the one, we'll catch the lot."

"Count not what ye have not in your hand," cautioned the other earl, then turned to his men and demanded they row harder, even with the sail set.

Before long, Douglas remarked, "They are gainin' on us, Sire. We cannot outrun them, for their sail is much larger, and when the wind is with them they close fast upon us."

"We'll meet them when they come," said Robert, calmly, still pulling on his oar. As he leaned forward and pulled back several times more, he looked down at the aft end and made out the shapes of the bundles of supplies and victuals stored there. There were more in the bow.

"Let's feed the enemy, young Jemmy," the king said with a smile.

A moment later, those in pursuit heard loud splashes coming from the direction of the king's galley.

"Listen!" said James Macdougall. "They're goin' overboard to keep us from catchin' them! They'd rather drown than face our swords!"

"It's splashes a'right," John Menteith agreed, "but what the hell are they..." A loud thump interrupted his thought as the galley hit something in the water. "What is that we hit?" He leaned over the side to see what was drifting by, but could not make out more than an odd shape in the black water.

"Bring that aboard," Menteith barked at one of the oarsmen. The man shipped his oar and reached for the grappling hook. The rowing stopped as the curious men pulled the box on board.

"'Nother one!" shouted a second sailor, taking the grappling hook from the first sailor and thrusting it into the water to retrieve the next object. By the time it was aboard, the box had been opened.

"Apples!" cursed Macdougall, "plain, damned apples!" The second box turned out to contain parsnips.

John Menteith hurriedly scanned the blackness across the bow of his galley for the pursued boat. We've lost them, he thought, for in the light of the finely etched crescent, he could see naught ahead of them but the twinkling stars and several more boxes on the rippling water.

John Macdougall screamed and ranted and fell to the deck in disgust.

"Another day, Sir Robert," said John under his breath in Robert's direction. "Another day, ye'll be in my grasp, and then ye'll have no space to wriggle."

Robert Boyd

SEPTEMBER 8th 1306
KILDRUMMY CASTLE

It was just after sundown on the dark of the moon, and the weary attackers had failed in yet another try at taking the castle. Only the barbican was in their control. For thirteen days the garrison at Kildrummy had held against the forces of the Earl of Pembroke, with his mix of English and Scottish soldiers, and the Prince of Wales and his army, crowned by his three hundred elite Swan Knights. Every day the old earl and the young prince had attempted an offensive, only to be repelled by the defending Scots within the well-supplied and fortified castle.

The number of English dead mounted with each day's attempt, while the Scots suffered but few casualties and were no nearer to surrendering or abandoning their stronghold than they had been a fortnight earlier. The English had tried every conventional and unusual mode of attack they could advance, and yet there was no progress. Kildrummy was, so far, impenetrable.

Prince Edward, due to his social rank, was the titular commanding officer in the field, much to the annoyance of the far more experienced Aymer de Valence. Thus Edward called the nightly war council in the command tent, with the usual exclusion of Thomas Randolph, for they lately distrusted him in direct proportion to their losses.

"Give it up! There's a chill in the night air and I say it's time to give it up and come back in the spring," said the frustrated and chafing prince to Pembroke, Ingram de Umfraville, and Phillip Mowbray.

No one spoke for several minutes.

"We could leave a force equal to theirs so they could neither escape nor be re-supplied," suggested Umfraville, finally.

"And who of us would command it?" growled Pembroke, looking around the table. No one volunteered for such lengthy and drear wintertime duty before the walls of Kildrummy.

"We dare not return to the king without Kildrummy and the Brus kin in our hands," worried Mowbray, to which they all agreed in silence.

"Back to the start," trumped Pembroke as he spat upon the floor of the tent and wiped his mouth with a white linen kerchief.

At that moment a guard appeared at the entrance to the tent and slipped around the edge of the camp table to approach the prince. Leaning low to whisper in the prince's ear, he conveyed his message, and left.

The prince frowned as he looked up at his compatriots, but relayed the news to the others. "It seems, gentlemen, that we have captured a commoner from the castle. He says he came to speak with the earl," the young prince said coldly to Pembroke, obviously resenting the fact that the earl had been sought and not he.

The commanders suddenly became curious as they looked at each other, then at Pembroke, who indicated puzzlement.

"Perhaps these Scots have sent a commoner to negotiate their peace!" chuckled Sir Phillip. They all laughed, except the prince.

"Bring him forth!" he demanded.

The man was led into the tent to stand awkwardly before the table of officers. He was short with a stocky, muscular frame, and wore a leather apron. Both he and his apron were black with grime and heavy with the smell of smoke and sweat. His eyes were extraordinarily large and he rolled them around taking in all there was to see, while the others examined him equally thoroughly.

"How is it that you are of the castle, and now walk about beyond the castle wall?" asked Pembroke with full curiosity.

"Aw, I can come and go at will, I can. Through a secret way... a tunnel... you might say, that's known to just me and a few other lads who grew up here, Milord," answered the man, suddenly remembering to doff his hat in the presence of such nobility. He wanted to do or say nothing to queer the proposal he was about to make.

"And yer name?" asked Umfraville.

"Osborne, Milord," he replied, grinning most amiably and showing sizeable gaps between many of his teeth.

"Yer position in the castle?" pushed Umfraville, coldly.

"I'm the smithy, Yer Worship."

"The *smith?*" Umfraville glared, wondering why they had bothered to talk with such a half-witted fellow this long. "Tell me, smith, why should I not slit yer filthy gullet where ye stand?"

"Because I can give ye what ye want, Milords!" hastily replied the man, now standing on shaky legs, his sense of bravado vanished. The tired prince snickered at the thought that this serf could provide them anything that they might want.

"And what service might we want of ye, varlet... perhaps the knowledge of this 'secret' passageway?" asked Mowbray, suspecting that such a passageway might lead them into a Scottish trap. The others, too, were losing interest, for the prospect was strong of the man being a schemer and a fraud, at best, and probably far worse.

"N-n-nay, Sire!" said Osborne nervously, for he feared his plot was unraveling. "That would serve ye poorly, for it is a tight fit and winds so within the wall. Ye would ne'er get soldiers in armor into the fortress that way."

"Well then, what?" demanded Pembroke, urgently.

With all the courage he could muster, the frightened blacksmith blurted, "First, Milord, ye must agree to pay me for my service, once ye are inside the castle..."

The Prince of Wales jumped to his feet and grabbed the haft of his sword. "You filthy, sniveling little jot! You are of less significance than yon louse on your person, and you presume to demand of me?! Do you not know who I am?!"

He started to draw his sword and the ironmonger sank to his knees in despair, thinking all was lost, his gamble failed, his life forfeited.

But it was the brazenness of the gamble that piqued the curiosity of the Earl of Pembroke, who rose to his feet abruptly and asked Edward to delay his intended assassination.

"Sire, if you would grant me a moment?" he wheezed. The young prince paused in lifting his long sword, but the flash of his eyes let the earl know there was danger where he was treading. In return, the earl bowed graciously, hoping to allay the future king's anger against himself. He then turned to the blubbering smith.

"What is it that you would have in return, 'once we are inside the castle,' knave?!" Pembroke barked sarcastically.

"Gold, M-m-milord... as much as I can carry," blurted Osborne in tearful response.

Prince Edward snickered and dropped himself upon his chair. He now thought he was in the presence of a simple madman. He would waste no effort on slaying such himself, but would send him out of the tent and to a quick death at the hands of his frustrated soldiers, who would relish cutting the throat of a begging Scot.

"As much gold as *you* can carry?! Ha! I should think, by the brawn of you, that 'twould be right far in excess of your own weight! And what makes your treachery worth your weight in gold to us?" sneered Pembroke, standing over the kneeling rustic.

"This man is wasting our time!" interrupted Umfraville testily, and the smithy cringed; his large eyes looked about for a way to flee.

"Let him speak his notion, then we'll kill him," counseled Pembroke, who was fast becoming the only table member still thinking that the man possibly had a use. More than that, he wondered what the man had in mind that he could have considered to be worth such weal to the English.

"Speak then..." cried Umfraville, "if ye have any wit about ye at all."

Osborne's words of treachery spilled forth to the men of the table. And now, they paid mind to the smithy as he had hoped.

. .

In the wee hours of the next morning, within the castle walls, the bellows of the smithy's fire were fast building a hot fire.

All the gold I can carry, they agreed... I agreed, thought Osborne greedily as the fires grew hotter with each breath of the bellows. It was all he could do to suppress himself enough not to give away the plan. For the first time in his life, he was deliriously happy.

Only the pickets were awake and they thought nothing of the smithy being early at his work. Before long Osborne was satisfied with the temperature of his white-hot coals and threw a plowshare into the hot pit. He then walked about outside the shop where it was cooler, as he often did, all the while marking the locations and vigilance of the sentries.

Within the half-hour, as the early light was at its barest, the plowshare was at its hottest and glowed as white as the heart of the fire. The smithy returned, after having made sure that there were no others up and about in the courtyard, and carefully pulled out the plowshare with his tongs and quietly walked it out of the smith's shed and toward the corncrib. The glowing plowshare furnished enough light that he could have found his way all the way across the yard in this darkest night, but the familiar corncrib was only the next building over.

Once there, he wasted no time, and with all the strength he could muster, tossed the weighty hunk of glowing metal to the apex of the heap of grain, the winter's stores. The dust in the crib caught fire with a whoosh as the blacksmith sneaked back to his hovel behind the shop and greeted his unsuspecting wife, just rousing for the day.

"Up early, are ye?" she asked, unconcerned.

"Aye," he said, grinning to himself as he sat in his rough-made chair and thought of all he was going to do with his gold. It was all but in his hand; he had carried out his end of the bargain.

It was not long before the grain was roaring aflame, and soon the fire reached the roof of the wooden corncrib and began to consume it. At first, a guard saw just a bright glow and dashed around the wall walk to investigate.

"Fire!" he screamed as loudly as he could, and more of the roof burned brightly.

Osborne smiled.

"It's a fire, in the granary!" screamed his wife in panic after looking outside.

Osborne could think of nothing except the gold. He could almost feel it, cool and smooth in his hands, and he fantasized on how much he could carry with his strong arms, built of hefting heavy iron and swinging a hammer against it for so many years.

How fittin', he thought, workin' all me life for them bastards and gainin' little for it but me great strength, and now... I'll be carryin' off as much of their gold as these arms can raise up. He laughed out loud.

"Ye crazy ol' loon," screamed his wife as she gathered her cookware and her ragged bedclothes. "I smell smoke close at hand and ye sit and cackle! Help me save these things!"

"Let 'em burn!" said the smithy, entranced.

"Get this chair to the outside!" commanded the wife who pulled at Osborne's clothing, trying to get him to move.

Osborne frowned and went into a rage as his dream was interrupted. Never again would that shrew be free to scream at him and order him around! He would soon be a king!

He had not, until then, thought to do other than take her with him when he got his gold. But now, with her shrill, frightened voice still ringing in his ears, he could not stand her to be in his presence, and he swung his great, stone-hard fist at her, hitting his wife heavily on the side of the face.

The old woman fell to the dirt floor, her prized pots and pans flung tempest-tossed about her.

"Buy 'nother one of ye, I can, only younger, and prettier," he said aloud to his stunned spouse with a satisfied grin.

As he stood looking down at her, the fire broke through from the corncrib wall and ate its way toward the blacksmith shop and the hovel behind.

He removed his heavy, well-worn leather apron from around his middle, laid it on the chair about which his wife had been so concerned, and walked out the door and into the courtyard to watch the progress of the fire.

"Bring buckets and make a line from the cistern! Men on this side, women and boys over here!" shouted Robert Boyd as he arrived only half dressed to the calamitous burning of the corncrib.

"What be the reason for this?" asked Nigel Brus, who was only a few paces behind Robert as the courtyard came alive with scurrying people beginning to form a bucket brigade to the fire, now raging through and consuming the blacksmith shop and the bakery beyond.

"I know not!" answered Robert, "but it's catchin' up to the wall walk."

Robert and Nigel threw the buckets of water on to the fire as quickly as they arrived but it did not slow the mounting flames.

The fire reflected wildly in Osborne's large eyes as he stood before his morning's devilment and but thought of his gold. He wondered when the English would see the fire and realize he had earned his reward.

Indeed, those who had bought the disaster were anxiously awaiting some sign that the plan was truly afoot, when the first signal was given. "Smoke, Sire!" yelled the first guard to spot the plume. He was reporting to Pembroke, who was then still in his tent.

The rotund earl smiled as his valet casually finished dressing him. While holding his arms out to enable his armor to be buckled, he looked casually toward his bed at his two redheaded companions, lying tightly tucked to each other in their sleep and thought, What am I to do with them after this day's success?

It was but a momentary thought, and though he had thoroughly enjoyed having them with him the weeks past, they meant no more to him than that.

Once attired, he walked out of the tent to the hurrying of troops preparing for another siege attempt against the castle walls, this time with a distinct advantage.

"My Lord Pembroke, seems the ol' fool did as he said he would," remarked Prince Edward jovially as he came to Pembroke's side.

"Aye," smiled de Valence. Then, seeing Thomas Randolph, he shouted, "Run the scaling ladders up yonder, Thomas, where the smoke is the thickest, and see if we can yet get a breach."

Doing as he was bade, Thomas soon found that the ladders would not reach the top of the wall at that point, and so set the soldiers to the task of tying the ladders together to extend their length.

"More delay to our conquest," lamented Edward, watching the men working diligently, while he stood with Pembroke alongside his tent.

"Look!" shouted James Dunbar as he and his friend John Airth were helping each other on with their armor. "Fire! Inside the castle wall!"

Many of the Swan Knights standing nearby, their hearts pounding all the faster at the prospect of gaining an advantage and possibly an end to the siege, cheered to see the destruction from within.

"Perhaps today we will do more than dress in our armor and parade about *looking* menacin'," remarked John with an excited laugh.

"Well, I, for one, am ready for the battle to begin," said James confidently as he fitted John's last buckle.

The extended ladders went up on the wall with no resistance from the Scots within.

"Up the ladders," ordered Thomas, shouting from behind a nearby mantlet, and the soldiers hied to climb the three ladders to the top of the wall. There was no resistance to their climb from the castle defenders, for the Scots had been driven from that part of the wall walk by the smoke and intense heat from the fire below.

"Can't go no farther," yelled the soldier at the top of the ladder, trying to shield himself from the heat and the blinding black smoke that stung and burned eyes, noses, and throats beyond endurance.

"Order them over the wall!" commanded Pembroke to Thomas.

"Fire's too bad," returned Randolph, "What's keepin' them from defendin' the wall is the same as what's keepin' us from breachin' it."

"Try a spot farther left, man!" directed Pembroke, and Thomas waved the men down from the ladders to change their positions.

Inside, the Scots were fighting the fire with all their strength but it was perfidious in its unceasing demand for fuel, and consumed everything wherever the wind carried it. In places, even the stones in the curtain wall burned, turning to dust. The animals not already dead in the flames and smoke were released from their stalls and pens to run madly about the courtyard in utter fear and panic, and none to stop them.

"We'll soon be losin' the gates," informed Robert Boyd.

"If the gates go, so goes the castle," returned Nigel.

"We can't even get in there close enough to piss on it," said Robert in pure frustration.

Nigel frowned and gritted his teeth, thinking of what to do next, when a frantic Agnes came to his side. "We're doomed! Oh, Nigel, we're doomed!" she wailed in panic.

Nigel grabbed her and pressed her tightly against his smoke blackened and water-soaked nightshirt. Though as fearful as she was, the young knight looked at her lovingly and said, "Ye must do yer part to help save us, my love. Ye must repair to the abbey and pray for us, ye must pray as ye have ne'er prayed before. Can ye do that for us, dear Agnes?"

Her face was twisted in anguish and fear, but she looked into his beautiful eyes and, succumbing to his request, so signified by a nod of her blonde head.

"Go now," her beloved said, "for our enemy will be upon us soon, and we must have every power at our hand and every prudent wit workin' in our favor." He smiled, the sweet, lovely smile she so cherished, then reached down and kissed her tear wet lips.

My last sweet kiss, fore'er, she thought as she looked at him. He had turned away and was already looking at the damage the fire was causing and figuring a way to survive beyond it.

As he had requested, she made her way to the chapel and went straightaway to the high altar and knelt to pray. The tall, arched window above her in the apse filtered the early morning light down upon her head, creating a glow in her fair hair so that she looked as if a halo graced her countenance.

One observing her as she kissed the cross that hung from her rosary and began her recitations might have been awestruck by her holy beauty. But, the one who watched her every move with his two large, round eyes, and more than casual interest, held no awe for the scene he viewed. Still, he stayed quiet and enjoyed the beauty he beheld.

Outside and against the castle wall, Thomas Randolph had the ladders raised again, this time to the left of the first attempt, and there he ordered his men to the top.

"Enemy comin' up!" screamed a guard through breaths choked with the smoke as he saw English soldiers crawling up the ladders and onto the wall walk.

His shouts drew more Scots to his position on the wall walk, and there the two forces clashed as the timbers below were burning out from under them.

The heroic defenders hacked at the invading English as they came over the wall, but still, numbers of the enemy attained the wall walk.

Soon there were more than twenty armed combatants jostling and fighting in the unbearable heat and smoke upon that weakened part of the wall walk, which suddenly gave way and spilled the lot of them. There were anguished screams from many as they fell; then, as abruptly as they hit with force in the fires of the buildings below, most were silenced. Those who yet screamed had survived the fall only to burn alive.

The Scots retreated to and barred themselves in the tower keep, isolating that portion of the collapsed wall walk. The English soldiers who had been fortunate enough not to have attained the hellish platform saw immediately the worthlessness of the situation and backed down the ladders.

They returned to Sir Thomas and, gagging and choking from inhaled smoke, told him of the collapse of the wall walk and the hopelessness of continuing to scale that portion of the wall. He was obviously not all that disappointed in their failure when he sent them to rest.

Pembroke, on the other hand, went into a rage, screaming and cursing scurrilously and kicking at trees with his armor-covered leather boots. Thomas merely watched and listened to Pembroke's tirade, having nothing to say to him except such that might make things worse, and so kept his own counsel.

He thought to himself, the poor bastards might survive, yet, but his heart sank when he heard the next report.

"Smoke! Smoke from the drawbridge!" yelled Sir Ingram Umfraville waving his arms and pointing with glee at the possibility of the massive gate burning.

"Ah?" Pembroke said, moving to see in the direction of the drawbridge. "'Tis passin' so!" He exclaimed, his mood running instantly from anger to cunning interest. "We'll help it along, perhaps." Then he ordered a squire to fetch a half-depleted bottle of whisky from his tent.

"Ye drinkin' to the fire so early in the morn?" asked Umfraville, knowing Pembroke's love of the bottle.

"Umfraville, you *are* an idiot," snarled Pembroke. His regard for Sir Ingram had diminished by the day since the siege had begun, though most of the time he said nothing untoward.

Umfraville took affront and departed Pembroke's presence to sulk in private. He could have challenged Pembroke for having uttered such a slur, but chose to walk away red-faced, and Pembroke liked him even less.

"Thomas!" shouted Pembroke, which brought Thomas Randolph to his side. "Got a little chore for you, I do," he smiled.

"What's yer mind?" asked Thomas. At that moment, the squire brought the half-empty bottle to Pembroke as he had been instructed.

Thomas watched Aymer uncork the bottle and take a great swig.

"What's the job, Aymer?" he asked impatiently.

Pembroke swallowed the fiery mouthful and breathed deeply to cool his burning throat before he spoke.

"The rest of these bastards don't trust you, Thomas," Pembroke began, waving his great arm in an arc to indicate his cohorts, "but, for all that, you may be the only man here I *do* trust." With that, he thrust the bottle toward Thomas.

"That my job?" asked Thomas wryly.

"Yer job is... first... to drink the rest of that whisky," said Pembroke.

"Pleasure," said Randolph as he took the bottle, put it to his lips, and drained it without a pause.

"Ye got any more such wee tasks for me?" he asked with a drink-induced growl.

"Just one," the earl replied, indicating the bottle, "Fill that, and them two we emptied last night with naphtha and cork 'em up tight." And he tossed the cork to Thomas.

"Goin' to be a hell of a drink," said Thomas, his voice still not back to normal.

"When you've done that, meet me at yonder barbican," he instructed, pointing to the area before the drawbridge, "and be quick about it!"

Thomas went to the barrel where the naphtha was kept and did as he was ordered, but with a sense of dread rather than urgency, knowing its purpose. He then strode the distance to the barbican unmolested by those in the castle, and met Pembroke who had arrived at the barbican first and brought two bowmen with him. The earl extended his hand and Thomas placed a bottle in it.

"Ready with the fire arrows?" asked Pembroke who, having a great draft of whisky in his belly, was now feeling even braver than usual.

"When you are, Sire," said the archer.

Pembroke smiled at Thomas and suddenly bolted from the safety of the barbican and ran full tilt toward the edge of the moat before the vital drawbridge. He was immediately spotted by several bowmen inside the tortured castle. Through the narrow, vertical arrow slits in the stone wall, they drew back their bowstrings and aimed their arrows toward the single desperate attacker as he hurled the bottle at the drawbridge with all his might.

The bottle arced end-over-end and smashed against the hard oaken timbers, splashing its contents in a wide pattern over the tightly sealed drawbridge.

Pembroke, having managed to halt his forward movement at the very edge of the polluted moat, could not resist taking a moment to watch the liquid flow down the sturdy barricade.

He had succeeded!

Just then the bowmen loosed their arrows at Pembroke and, startled, he lost his footing and slid down the embankment, partially into the moat. The arrows narrowly missed him as he fell, giving him time to scramble up the bank and into the safety of the barbican.

"Match that throw, Thomas," Pembroke dared, flushed with adolescent excitement.

Thomas looked at the wall where the bowmen now waited. "They're ready for the next poor bastard to poke his head out. Hardly seems fair," he grumbled.

Pembroke laughed raucously, then prodded his Scottish coadjutor, saying, "What's the matter, Thomas? Where's your sense of swash? Have you lost your ballocks in all the easy livin' I've provided you?"

Randolph knew Pembroke was pushing him into danger for his own amusement, but could not allow such a challenge to stand against his courage. With both remaining bottles of flammables in hand, he darted from the safety of the barbican and hurled them together at the upended bridge.

He spun immediately around and dived headlong for the barbican opening, even before he heard the bottles break against the timbers. As he plumped to the ground, he heard an arrow slice the air but inches from his cropped ear.

Laughing appreciatively, Pembroke shouted, "Thomas! You son-of-a-Scottish-bitch! You did it! Both well placed and spreading down its face! Well done!"

The Scot laughed in great relief as Pembroke offered a hand to help him stand. Pembroke slapped him on the back several times in a congratulatory manner, then both looked at the liquid inching down the bridge. Suddenly, Pembroke turned to his archers, waiting for his signal and bellowed, "Now, you dolts!"

Atop the wall, another flight of Scottish arrows was aimed at the open barbican gate, when the English archers loosed their fire-tipped arrows at the drawbridge and, immediately upon their impact, the naphtha whooshed into a wall of flame. The heat and smoke blowing back into their faces, the castle archers were unable to find their targets, and retreated from the gate tower.

Pembroke whooped in delight.

"Such heat comin' from both inside and outside will surely give us entry by midday," he said gleefully, well satisfied with his coup.

Thomas forced a smile, and the two of them left their archers within the barbican and retreated to the tree line, where the rest of the English army was cheering them. Thomas walked on into the trees and left Pembroke to enjoy the acknowledgments of the celebratory throng.

Having been told of the daring escapade by Aymer de Valence, Nigel ran to see what destruction had been wrought upon the main entrance. What he saw was that the drawbridge was almost fully engulfed in the naphtha-fueled blaze, and that there was no way to extinguish it.

"We can't save the gate," agonized Nigel, staring at the flames in horror. "'Tis hopeless."

"Then let's prepare for the best defense we can muster," returned Robert Boyd.

"We managed to pen up the animals away from the fire," said Isabel, pointing to the makeshift enclosure as she came to Nigel's side. "Poor beasts, some of them horribly burned."

"I think the fire will not get that far since there's a space in the buildings along the curtain," said Nigel, "but it's possible that it can leap across."

"We'll pour water on those buildings to keep that from happenin'," said Robert.

"When the gate is collapsed and the fires cool," said Nigel, "the English will come in there *and* o'er the walls. I don't see how we can defend against them."

• •

By the early afternoon, the fires had burned themselves to the extent of their fuel supply, and the stench of wood smoke and burned flesh filled the courtyard and every room within the castle.

All that blocked the English from walking into the castle now were the moat, which at this point was more of a sewer than anything else, and the ironbound portcullis gate, a great lattice of oak and iron that, once lowered, was nearly impossible to raise from outside the walls. But it had been damaged severely by the fire, and neither side knew how well it might stand against the attacking English.

The garrison and helpers took time to replenish themselves as best they could, knowing that for many it would be their last meal. Yet most within the castle feigned joyfulness to buffer their own courage and spirit, and others', too.

"I just viewed the damage," reported Boyd as he came into the great hall, where Nigel and Agnes, among many others, were eating hastily prepared food. "The portcullis is still intact. We have a chance if we can keep the English from raisin' it."

"Get our bowmen to man the murder holes in the gatehouse as soon as the smoke clears," commanded Nigel.

"That'll be but a wee bit," returned Robert as he left the great hall for the courtyard, carrying with him a large chunk of meat on the point of his dirk and half a loaf of bread.

"Do ye think we'll win?" asked Agnes in an almost childishly innocent voice.

"They've but had their streak of luck," replied Nigel with a reassuring smile. "It's our turn, now."

Agnes snuggled as close to Nigel as she could get, though he now had donned his armor in preparation for battle in the courtyard. "No matter. No matter what happens, I'll always love ye," she said.

"And I will always love ye," replied Nigel, running his fingers through the long curls that fell with such grace from the crown of her head.

"I am purely sorry that I haven't the fortitude to fight at yer side as Isabel and Christian do," she sniffed as tears welled up in her eyes.

"Ye need not be sorrowful for that," whispered Nigel. "Ye are doin' a great service in bringin' the Lord God and the saints to our side with yer prayers."

Agnes looked at him lovingly and kissed him. With haunting fears of total disaster, she withdrew from Nigel when his lieutenants joined him to plan their defense. She quietly returned to resume her prayers in the abbey.

. .

Outside the castle, the minions of King Edward also made plans. "Got the bridge fixed to go?" asked Pembroke when Thomas found him sitting in the shade of the trees, his armor scattered about upon the ground, and him staring at the last smoldering ruins of the gate. He had watched the last timber collapse, and the last flame die, with the satisfaction that it was his personal fait accompli. The redheads had brought him food and drink, and this he offered to share with Thomas by a wave of his hand.

"Aye," returned Thomas, sitting on ·the ground and partaking absently of the spread. He was not hungry, and in fact felt somewhat nauseated at the thoughts of what lay ahead in the afternoon. As he nibbled at the repast, Pembroke ate with his usual relish.

"I want you to lay back when we attack," said Pembroke, washing down a mouthful of meat with wine.

Thomas scowled. "Ye think me a coward, or what?"

"Nay, Thomas. I think nothing of the kind," replied Pembroke, continuing his voracious eating, eventually explaining himself, "But, I think you would better serve King Edward if you went not against those beside whom you have fought so closely before."

So, Thomas thought, the fat bastard thinks that, after a fortnight of doing his bidding against even my own kin, I'll not fight when the battle commences. Well, that suits me well, too. I've not the stomach for such.

He continued to scowl and, in disgust, threw down the morsels he held in his great hand before wordlessly standing to leave the company of Sir Aymer. So doing, he returned to his men, who were then finishing the pieces to the log bridge they expected to use in spanning the moat from the barbican to the now gaping black hole that had been the castle gate. Once all was ready, Thomas stood to one side, somberly watching events unfold.

The English bowmen stood behind their mantlets and poured flights of arrows through the portcullis and over the walls into the courtyard as cover for those who maneuvered the bridge into place.

Moving it at all was no easy task since it was made of newly felled trees and carried enormous weight. With ropes and the help of the great horses, the bridge was being pulled through the barbican and nearer and nearer to the cleft in the castle wall. Soon it would be close enough to be set in place, in spite of the fact that the Scots archers were putting an arrow into any man exposed to the gatehouse or the barbican.

Watching the English, Nigel realized he would soon see hundreds of soldiers pouring through the open gate if he could not stop them. "Place more men above the gatehouse!" he ordered.

Isabel waved her hand and set about accomplishing the task. Within moments, the bridge builders were having a far more difficult time holding their ground as Isabel and her bowmen set to work on them. Those shielded by the bridge survived; the others were soon floating dead in the vile moat.

A cheer went up from the Scots, but the English were not to be discouraged, quickly bringing in overhead shields and putting more workers to positioning the bridge. All too soon it was in place, and the enemy were poised for the assault. Only the weakened portcullis stood between the castle's courtyard and thousands of English warriors, now.

The English long bows were replaced by crossbowmen, rushed to the portcullis to keep the Scots from interfering with workers using pry-bars and blocks to lift the heavy gate. Only the Scots manning the murder holes, and crafty enough to aim between the shields held over English heads, were still able to fire on and kill the attacking soldiery.

The cooks and their helpers had had plenty of time to haul great vessels of hot oil and boiling water to the space above the English in the gate tunnel. As the dark tunnel below them grew crowded with their enemy, the Scots spilled the hot liquids onto the floor and they ran in scalding torrents through the murder holes, drenching the wretched English with agony and protracted, painful death.

And still, the English pressed forward.

Though the air was thick with deadly missiles between the two factions, the English made progress. The Scots could no longer prevent the portcullis from rising into the gatehouse, and soon the English had forced a large enough space beneath the damaged grating to allow the attacking troops to roll under it and gain access to the castle.

The Scots, having erected mantlets of their own within the courtyard, set crossbowmen to loose bolts into the blackened mass of the gate tunnel. At first they were somewhat effective, but once the English knights were inside in sufficient numbers to organize their shields into a Roman-style phalanx defense, most bolts struck without serious injury.

In the gatehouse tower, Isabel was joined by Christian and wreaked havoc upon those failing to make use of their shields effectively as they approached the moat bridge. Seeing the results of their comrades' slackness, the following bands soon minded the proper attitude and were all but unreachable.

Nigel commanded Robert Boyd to take charge of the wall walks and the gate defenders, while he had more mantlets rigged in front of the gatehouse tunnel. There, he and his knights stood at the ready as the long-bowmen kept pouring shafts into the tunnel.

The afternoon sun broke through the overcast producing an atypical warmth for an early September day, and warriors on both sides were rapidly becoming dehydrated. The water bucket was well appreciated as it made the rounds to the waiting Scots, and the youth carrying it became a primary target for English bowmen. More than one Scottish lad was cut down while trying to quench the awful thirsts of their fathers and uncles and brothers.

The English numbers on the inside of the portcullis kept growing as they crouched behind their shields, waiting for enough of them to gather to launch an attack. Suddenly, they burst forth into the courtyard, yelling and screaming like madmen and charging across as much of the yard as they could traverse.

The defenders immediately ceased shooting from behind their mantlets and drew swords as the English charged out of the gate tunnel into the courtyard.

Nigel yelled, "Follow me, lads!" and ran at the interlopers with all his strength, the Scots knights following on his heels. There, on the cobbles and grass of the Kildrummy courtyard, the bloodletting was appalling.

The desperate Scots cut down wave after wave of the enemy dashing from the tunnel.

Some of the archers, having mounted the wall walk to gain advantageous position and a broader field of fire, were met head-on by already bloodied swords.

The shouts and screams and clamor of man-on-man struggles were repeated hundreds of times in Kildrummy that afternoon, and echoed as well into the early evening hours, until exhaustion felled nearly as many as did weapons.

The portcullis was completely destroyed by then, giving the English as much access to the castle as they could squeeze through the gate tunnel with the Scots manning the murder holes and defending the courtyard ingress. The castle defenders also had repelled every attack as the English attempted, time and again, to scale the damaged walls.

It was then that Pembroke, tired and well satisfied with the day's progress, suddenly suggested, "Let's retire for the night! They'll be an easy rout on the morn."

The prince, also wearied from pacing to and fro in his hot armor, quickly agreed and gave orders for the trumpeter to call back those English already engaged. He then called for those not yet within the blackened hulk of Castle Kildrummy to stand down.

Most were greatly relieved that they did not have to enter the dark castle and fight an enemy that couldn't be seen, but some of the younger and less experienced were crestfallen.

"We had not our chance at glory," James Dunbar complained, disappointed that he had not been one of the first knights sent to enter the castle and display his well-honed prowess with the martial skills. He held within his mind, that he would not, nay, *could* not, be one of those unhappy souls who would taste the hot, bloody steel of the Scots' blades.

"On the morrow, we shall, for sure," replied John Airth. He was not nearly as anxious to throw himself into the horror as was his friend.

. .

Inside the castle, the Scots, weary beyond endurance, could not believe that the enemy was withdrawing from combat, and it gave them some buoyancy to their spirits that they could lie down at last. And there in the middle of the awful carnage, some laid down where they had stood, and fell instantly into deep slumber. But there was yet a gaping hole that needed to be filled, and scores of casualties to deal with before the garrison could rest.

"Throw the English wounded and dead into the moat!" commanded Sir Nigel to two knights standing nearby. "Take as many able-bodied as ye need to get it done, then see if ye can make use of what's left of the portcullis winch to pull down that damned bridge!"

"Thought we were captured, I did," said a blood-spattered Robert Boyd, stepping over many dead, unconscious, or sleeping bodies as he came into the courtyard.

"Tend our wounded," ordered Nigel to a lieutenant, then turned to Robert with the reply, "Thought so, too."

"What would be the plan now?" asked Robert, dropping wearily onto a doorstep.

"They may have made a tactical error by withdrawing when they did. They had us on the rim of capitulation," confessed Nigel.

"We hain't dead yet!" Robert smiled.

Amen, thought Nigel, and the image of poor Agnes in the abbey in her most ardent prayers came to him. He knew that she had been as faithful in her efforts as had he in his. "Must have worked," he said aloud to himself before turning his attentions to considering what materials he had at hand to patch the hole. Aching and exhausted, every man who could be roused was put to one task or another in the hopeless attempt to make the castle whole again.

There was but one gleeful man in the whole of the castle, and he had remained in the cool darkness of the abbey while nearly everyone he had ever known in his life was fighting and dying in the battle of his making.

Once the battle noises ceased, Osborne emerged from his hiding place in the abbey to review the damage that he alone had wrought, and, if indeed the English were in charge, he could collect his agreed upon recompense and begin his new life with wealth equal to that of a baron, or perhaps even an earl. In his trance, he even imagined that the king, out of gratitude, would so name him.

Touring the courtyard, he was greatly disappointed to hear the voices of the young Brus and Sir Robert Boyd still giving orders, but by the condition of the defenses, he estimated that it would not be long before he carried off his gold. He was content.

During the night, while the English slept, the Scots barricaded the gate tunnel with beams from the buildings, furniture, dead animals and other debris, and prepared for another hard fight on the morrow.

• •

As the dawn broke on the tenth day of September, the Prince of Wales exited his tent into an early morning fog. He was relieving himself at the base of a nearby tree when he noticed several of his men standing in the clearing and talking in excited tones.

"What has you so animated at this hour?" asked the prince as he strode, still in his trews and shirt, into their presence.

The men were surprised to see their leader so early in the morning and stammered awkwardly until one of them mumbled, "Your Grace... you... we... we... uh..."

"The bridge, Sire!" interrupted another, pointing to the gatehouse, "Our bridge dangles by a rope!"

The Scots had used the portcullis winch from the gatehouse

entrance and used it to partially block the entrance with the bridge, itself.

The Prince walked toward the castle to get a better view in the fog, "Those damned, sneakin' Scottish bastards!"

The men to whom he had been talking scattered like dandelion seeds in the wind, and the whole camp seemed suddenly to come alive.

The prince returned to the tent area and grabbed the shirt of the first man he came to. "Take men and set that bridge back into place, or I shall have you drawn by noon!"

"Yes, Sire," replied the suddenly nervous man, who knew not what the prince was commanding but agreed to accomplish the task all the same.

The English soldiers worked diligently to reestablish the bridge that had been put there by them only the morning before at a great cost in the lives of their comrades. However, on this morning they were better shielded from the outset, and the fog was also on their side. Thus the Scots' worrisome arrows often missed.

Pembroke arose late, particularly for a day that was to be such a glorious day of triumph. He ate and dressed casually, as a man sure to fulfill his destiny; no matter what effort he applied, success would be his. The king would lavishly reward him, perhaps with another thousand pounds sterling, or, he thought, smiling, perhaps with another earldom. Fife would be an excellent choice.

By midmorning, the bridge was back in place and battering rams were brought to bear on the mass of debris, which proved to serve the Scots none too well as a gate.

"It'll not last long," observed Robert to Nigel as the English hammered away at the makeshift barrier. "They'll be on us soon, my friend."

"Aye," replied Nigel, "but we will run it to the end."

"Aye," agreed Boyd soberly. He turned and made his way to the wall walk to repel what was sure to be the most vigorous scaling of the walls yet.

Isabel and Christian took their places beside Nigel and the other knights in front of the gate tunnel as the debris began to fall away. It didn't take long, with the English probing and pounding from the other side.

They stood and awaited the enemy's entry.

From the walls the archers randomly killed English soldiers as they approached the castle. Other bowmen, manning the murder holes above the gate tunnel and in the gatehouse, were having some success as their arrows found their way between shields and into the bodies of the amassing knights and workers inside the gate tunnel.

Then suddenly, the English bowmen started shooting at the top of the wall to cover the scaling ladders being brought from the tree line.

"Here they come!" shouted Robert Boyd, adding through clenched teeth and set jaw, "and here we stand!"

Some of the knights started toward the wall walk to help repel the attackers there, but Nigel ordered emphatically, "Nay! With me! They want our defenses at the gate weakened!"

Moments later, as the English were trying to find a weak point in the defense of the wall, the Swan Knights broke through the debris.

Nigel's men rushed and fell upon the knights as they entered.

Hand-to-hand and one-on-one broadsword combat soon repeated the previous day's bloody and agonizing mess, neither side achieving superiority.

Inside the chapel, the traitorous Osborne grew weary of the long wait for his gold. Once again, he could hear the tumult of battle, and he could almost feel the weight of his gold upon his strong shoulders. It was only a matter of time, he knew, until the earl's forces would be in control of Kildrummy, and he, the lowly smithy, could then do anything he desired. With that thought in his mind, his attentions turned to Agnes, who continued her unceasing prayer vigil.

Like to have that pretty one, I would, he mused, and he stealthily maneuvered closer to her. He began to sweat in the cool morning air as he stared at her for a long moment with his bulging eyes and fantasized the taking of the fair and youthful body.

It had been years since he had felt the flesh of one so young, and he had never had a woman so beautiful. The warmth of her, and the smell of her, were palpable to him, his fantasy was so real. She would, of course, be surprised and object at the outset. But then, after he had completed the act, she would be so overcome with his masculinity and prowess that she would like him!

Indeed, once she found that he was rich, richer than that young Brus cub she was so enamored of, why, she would love him!

Lurking in the shadows, feeding his want of her with his fantasizing, he could stand by no longer without acting on his desire! Once the lust in him surpassed his fear of possible punishment, he could stay still no longer.

As he silently approached her, he was trembling with anticipation and telling himself, "Those who would care to defend her are all but dead, anyway … and King Edward himself already said… there is no punishment …for ill treatment of the Bruses and theirs. Why, I can have her, right now… and maybe fore'er, if I want! We'll see how I like her!"

Agnes was on her knees with her rosary before the altar when he suddenly reached from behind and grabbed at her breasts.

Terrified, Agnes tried to fend him off and screamed repeatedly in her dismay, but there was no one to hear or come to her rescue.

Throwing her onto the dark stone floor, her attacker tore violently at her dress and was in just seconds pawing her bare body and slavering upon her pale breasts.

Osborne's great strength held her fast beneath him. Agnes screamed all the louder, writhing with all her might to be free, and he became that much more excited.

He now felt as if he would burst.

Running his hand up under her dress, he tore away her sensual, smooth silks and opened his trews to free his genitals.

As he forced penetration beneath her riven dress and bit with his snaggled teeth deep into her bare breasts, he was rhapsodic.

Osborne's lechery poured forth into her and onto the cold floor.

Though tears continued to roll from their corners, Agnes' eyes lost their fear. Instead, they became transfixed on the ceiling of the abbey, and Agnes made no more resistance or sound as he clumsily rolled from her torpid body.

The smith lay beside her, giggling in his great satisfaction. After a moment, he noticed that she was not moving and in his arrogance mistook it for a blissful state.

"Like that, did ye?" he asked through a slight, twisted smile.

The woman neither moved nor made to answer. Poking at her bloodied breast, he said, "Speak!!"

Nothing.

He raised up on one elbow and poked her again. "Damn ye, woman, are ye daft?"

He waited, looking her over until he grew uncomfortable being near her. He then rose to his feet and looked down on the pale, slender figure, its finery in shreds laying about her, her rosary beads scattered to all directions, and only the silver crucifix clenched in her hand.

A shaft of morning sunlight from the narrow gothic window above the altar fell across her and formed a cross upon the floor with her as its arms, its pointed end aimed at the little smith like a heavenly dagger.

Osborne, the defiler, hurriedly tied up his trews and glanced around the empty sanctuary. He grew anxious just being in the same room with the object he had so dreadfully desired only moments before. With the back of his hand, he wiped his unshaven mouth and left a streak of blood, her blood, from his wrist to his fingers.

He kicked at her leg for any response, but there was none. Uneasy, he removed himself from the abbey and sought shelter in the great hall.

The Scots on the parapet pushed the English ladders back at every attempt but the gate defense was less successful. James Dunbar, followed closely by his friend John Airth, came through the congested tunnel and into the melee of the battle for the gate.

James, well rested and mightily enthused, engaged the closest Scottish knight and was successful in dispatching the weary Scot without great effort. The notion of attaining the glory he so anxiously sought overwhelmed him and he searched the courtyard for a more worthy opponent.

"There!" he shouted aloud, as he descried Nigel Brus defending himself against two other Swan Knights, and winning.

"A shilling wager that I can take that fancy one there," said James as he pointed toward Sir Nigel.

John watched the way Nigel was fighting and said, "And should I wager against you and win, who will pay me my winnings?"

James, insulted that his friend thought he might lose in a contest with any Scot, went straightaway to the three men in combat and pushed his two comrades-in-arms aside, claiming, "He is mine!"

John kept an eye on his friend's fight as he, too, was engaged by the defending Scots. He held his own, felling two hostiles, until he saw James succumb to Nigel's blade. Then, shocked and angered, he pushed forward into the battling crowd to avenge the death of his friend.

Nigel's strength was wearing thin, and many of the men who had surrounded and fought to protect him lay dead and dying.

I cannot give in as long as there is breath in my body, he thought, still swinging his claymore at any English who approached.

There before him, with determination in his eye and revenge in his heart, stood John Airth. Circling carefully, the young Swan Knight looked for his best opportunity to strike and do damage.

Suddenly, he brought his long sword up in an arc over Nigel's head and brought it down with all his might, but Nigel blocked the blow with his shield and countered with a strike at the arm of his opponent.

The swing was at too great an angle, and the claymore glanced off the brightly polished armor, leaving nothing more than a bruise that would cause John Airth to remember the blow in coming days.

The two young knights repeatedly exchanged ringing blows, and no others dared interfere.

Forwarding a strong attack, Sir Nigel suddenly lost his footing in the carnage in the courtyard, but with great effort as he struggled to stay on his feet, swung his huge claymore one more time in an awkward blow that fell harmlessly against the Swan Knight's shield.

Sir John deftly counter-swung and struck Nigel across the belly.

Nigel froze.

But a half-second of carelessness and he knew he was done as he fell, though he yet made effort to rise. John stood over him and, raising his sword high, was ready to strike a final blow, but he looked into Nigel's eyes and could not deliver his death.

Nigel had been the stalwart leader, unbeatable, and now lay helplessly alone. All of the warriors nearby stopped at the sight of him on the ground. Many threw down their weapons and yielded to the English at the sight.

Even Isabel and Christian, who had fought alongside him with crossbows and short swords, could not believe Sir Nigel Brus was down, and ran to his side to comfort him.

• •

"They are submitting in great numbers to the will of our king, Sire," reported a runner from within the castle to the Prince of Wales.

The prince smiled approvingly at Pembroke.

Pembroke raised his head in a haughty fashion, "I thought the Scottish bastards would give a better account of themselves," he bragged.

The two leaders, along with Sir Ingram Umfraville and Sir Philip Mowbray, followed by the triple leopards banner of the victor, rode grandly through the gate tunnel where so many had died to allow their entrance.

Umfraville and Mowbray immediately started organizing the taking and dispersing of prisoners. No indignity was spared the surviving rebels as they were prodded by sword point and set upon by dogs.

The English smiths were placing irons on the crimson covered wrists of Robert Boyd near where Nigel lay wounded in the blood and gore of the courtyard ground. Christian and Isabel knelt beside him, when the unstained Prince of Wales and Earl of Pembroke came to them.

"My personal physician!" ordered Prince Edward as he looked down at Nigel, suffering from both the defeat and the grievous wound.

"Thank God, Prince Edward thought to bring forth his personal physician for my dear brother," whispered Lady Christian, looking on helplessly.

Pembroke, with a victorious sneer on his face, sat astride his resplendently armored horse behind the even more elaborately armored mount of Prince Edward. After gazing down upon the brother of Robert de Brus as he writhed in agony, the prince and the earl dismounted and stood over him with great satisfaction. Then the prince got down on one knee beside the wounded Scot.

Leaning close into Nigel's face, he whispered to him through gritted teeth, "You... will *not* die... by this wound, but by my executioner's ax... when *I* say you may die! Think not that you expire so easily."

Close enough to have heard those words, Christian's prayer of gratitude for the prince's act of mercy was shattered and her heart ached for all those who were captured, for she knew there would be no mercy from the prideful English and Comyn Scots.

Nigel, with all his strength, raised to one elbow, and a rousing cheer went up from the captured Scots. Pembroke placed one silver covered foot upon Nigel's chest and pressed him firmly back to the ground. Sir Nigel winced but made not a sound of pain.

The English victors went about the business of rousting any hiding Scots, and found Agnes where she lay in the abbey. She was made to stand and walk into the courtyard by an English soldier. Her eyes were still riveted in a constant stare and her own blood was caked upon her bare person and the remains of her garments, which trailed out behind her like a train.

Seeing her in such a state, Nigel screamed her name, but was answered not, with neither the blink of an eye nor the hint of a sweet smile, for him or anyone. She was completely within herself, perhaps forever.

Isabel quietly stood and, taking a well-worn but whole cloak proffered by a townswoman nearby, moved toward Agnes. A soldier hastily blocked her path, leaving Agnes standing all but nude before the crowd of soldiers and townspeople. Isabel calmly turned and stared at Pembroke, who finally nodded to the soldier to let her pass.

She crossed the remaining few steps to Agnes and draped the cloth around her shoulders to cover the poor, ravished noblewoman who had been her friend. "My God, Agnes," she whispered. "Who could have done this... to ye... of all people!" And she wept bitterly, and tenderly hugged the unmoving Agnes.

Also discovered in the English search, the traitor Osborne was driven from the great hall and, like an excited child, made such a clatter that he soon caught Pembroke's attention. The earl soon came to recognize him as the blacksmith with whom they had struck their bargain two nights past, and ordered that the man be brought forth.

"My gold, Milord... my gold as ye have promised!" screamed Osborne as he came to Pembroke and bowed low, then went to his knees.

Robert Boyd turned to look at the groveling smithy. What manner of insanity has he been touched with, he wondered to himself.

Pembroke looked not at the begging man, but noticed the attention he was garnering from many others in the courtyard, especially among the Scots.

"Ye promised me gold, all the gold I could carry... lead me to yer pile so that I might have my share," he whined.

"Gold! For what?" Pembroke feigned ignorance.

"For yer fire!" said Osborne, bewildered. "D'ye not remember yer bargain, Milord? I'm to get all the gold I can carry ... for givin' ye yer fire in the corncrib, night afore last," he reminded.

Sir Robert Boyd and the others then knew of the treachery with which they had been overcome, and they looked at Pembroke and the Prince of Wales with a mixture of surprise and disdain.

Pembroke lost not a second to embarrassment and said philosophically, "Aye, blacksmith. I remember you. I remember you well. And I remember that there was one named Judas who demanded thirty pieces of silver to betray our Lord. You bargained for much more, but then, you betrayed... everyone you ever knew... and so you shall have your gold."

Osborne cackled with renewed excitement as his huge eyes widened and rolled in their peculiar way.

Then Pembroke continued, "We shall melt it in your own crucible," Osborne became silent with renewed puzzlement as Pembroke gave a brisk motion to the officer standing nearest to the blacksmith and calmly finished his thought, "and pour it down your throat!"

Osborne's eyes rolled and he quaked with fear.

He scrambled to his feet and tried to run, but the English soldiers had him surrounded.

There was no escape.

As the soldiers took hold of him, his legs gave way and they had to drag him, screaming, all the way to what was left of the blacksmith shop, where the idea of treachery had been born in his mind.

Angus Og Macdonald

SEPTEMBER 11ᵗʰ 1306
DUNAVERTY CASTLE

King Robert Brus and his small company of two hundred, with the aid of the Clan Campbell, successfully escaped the Lord of Argyll and Sir John Menteith, Lord of Lennox, and reached Dunaverty Castle without further incident. There, they were greeted by the protector of the castle, Angus Og Macdonald of the Isles. King Robert had sent numerous supplies there after capturing Dumfries in February, and Angus was much beholden to him.

Dunaverty Castle pushed up on a great rock that jutted southward into the sea, and the approach on the land side was rough and relentlessly hostile. It was the perfect location to hide out and reorganize a lagging rebellion.

"How heals yer shoulder?" asked Robert when he and James Douglas sat down at a long table filled with ample, but simply prepared, food in the great hall.

"Passin' well," replied Douglas, flexing the shoulder in question. "Gilbert caught the brunt of the worst blows at Dail Righ."

"Will he live?"

"Aye, he will," returned Douglas, "but we'll probably lose two of our knights and several squires and regulars to lingerin' wounds."

"See that they have every care, will ye?" said the king.

"Aye, Sire," replied Douglas, and he reached for a piece of meat.

"I'll visit the wounded this afternoon. Perhaps 'twould be of some cheer to them," said Robert, sampling a stew with his fingers.

"They would be well pleased with that, Sire," Douglas replied as Angus Og Macdonald came into the great hall. Angus was a man of average height and the top of his head, if the two men stood side-by-side, would reach just below Robert's shoulder. He enjoyed dressing well in his environment and had the luxury of fancy brooches, jeweled rings, and other such trappings with which he decorated his equally elegant clothing.

"Brother Donald has returned from Ayr," announced Angus as he sat beside James and across the table from the king.

"Any news?" asked Robert continuing to eat. Angus plucked a grape from the bowl of fruit on the table and popped it into his mouth. His moment of hesitation gave Robert to know it must be poor news. "What?" he said, frowning.

Angus turned his head and spat the grape seeds upon the floor before he answered with, "Menteith has guessed ye are here…"

"And…?"

"And… he and Lord Botetourt now gather a fleet in Ayr to come pin ye in this place and take ye as they can," replied Angus.

"And what of the Macdougalls?" he asked.

Angus shrugged. "Back to Argyll, I would guess, Sire."

"Three days!" scowled James, "We've been here but three days and they're comin' for us!"

"We are the last kink in the noose that Edward Plantagenet has designed for Scotland. His pride fills his every thought, and his vengeance is harsh," said Robert wistfully. "There are others who see him as no danger, so… we have no choice but to fight on."

"What'll ye have us to do?" asked Angus, a strong ally to the Brus cause.

"Still run mercenaries to the Irish chieftains, do ye?" asked Robert.

The question caught the Macdonald by surprise. He was unaware that the king knew of such as the brothers' smuggling trade. "It makes for a full purse," he finally answered, if somewhat exculpatorily.

"Then ye still have strong domain over the seas here 'bouts?" said Robert.

"We do, to some limits," returned Angus, not wishing to brag.

"Then muster as many galleys and supplies as ye can for a journey tonight," spoke Robert.

"We're not makin' a stand here?" asked Douglas, quizzically.

"Nay, James, there is too much to be done to be holed up here for the winter," explained Robert, then he said to Angus, "Gather my brothers and send them to me."

"Aye," said Angus as he made a courteous bow and left the great hall to seek out the Bruses.

"Found us already!" exclaimed the Douglas in disbelief.

"They seem to know all our moves," replied Robert, "and I wonder how."

. .

Within the hour, Robert's three brothers, and James Douglas and Gilbert de la Haye were gathered around the table in the great hall. Angus and his brother, Donald, stood at the far end to get a better view of the map that Robert had laid out in front of him.

"Our first order must be survival of the cause," began Robert gravely. "Those of us who survive must carry on the fight. Swear it,!" he demanded, and looked at each of the men around the table to let them know he meant for them to swear to this principle. Each in his turn swore the oath to continue the resistance for as long as breath ebbed and flowed in his body.

Donald then told what he had heard and seen in Ayr so the lieutenants knew the dangers at hand for themselves. The situation was indeed dire for the Scottish cause, but none lost faith, and after a moment's contemplation, the men returned to the map to puzzle a secret plan of which no others would have knowledge.

In late afternoon, while Robert visited the wounded soldiers, a darkened line of clouds appeared on the horizon and the winds mounted, whipping the tops of the waves into white caps and dashing the heightened breakers against the jagged rocks at the base of the cliff on which the castle stood. With growing concern about their planned escape, the company watched the developments carefully.

"Sails!" shouted a guard from the parapet of the castle. Alexander Brus, closest to the guard, hastened to his side, soon followed by Donald Macdonald, and the three men peered eastward toward the sea. There, against the gathering storm could be seen a clutch of light-colored sails.

"'Tis the English out of Ayr," lamented Donald. "I know the sails."

"They've come ere we escaped!" whispered Alexander, surprised.

"Aye, but we are not trapped yet, good prince," replied Donald, "and with this comin' storm, the sea can be a terrible mix of troubles... for anyone ridin' on it."

"We must inform Robert and see his decision on our plan to leave tonight," said Alexander, and he and Donald ran to descend the spiral steps of the tower to the courtyard below.

"Menteith's fleet arrives already from Ayr," reported Alexander as soon as he neared his brother. Robert was somewhat taken aback, but not as dismayed as Alexander had expected.

"Well, they cannot come ashore tonight," said the king. "They will have to lay off 'til this storm blows over."

"Ye still plannin' to leave in this buildin' storm?" asked Alexander in disbelief.

"Aye," replied Robert smiling and, looking at Donald said, "Sir Donald, good smuggler that he is, has assured me that he has run mercenaries in worse seas than this, and obviously lived for the tellin' of it, so do not worry, little brother."

Alexander found it difficult believing that Robert would risk all of Scotland on the say of a mercenary runner, successful though he appeared. He gazed at the gathering clouds in the sky and shook his head. "Ye are my brother and my king, and I will go and do as ye say, but I like it not," said Alexander with a worried frown.

Robert laughed and slapped him on the back, saying, "Ye'll like it better than an English ax on yer neck, little brother."

Alexander smiled, even though he yet held misgivings as he left to complete the chores required for the night's journey.

After darkness covered land, sea, and sky, the howling, biting wind whipped about at a steady pace as Robert led about a hundred of his army and rappelled the cliff below the castle, where the rugged precipice made it unnecessary to have a castle curtain.

Once on the beach they quickly climbed into the small, bobbing boats waiting to carry them to the Macdonalds' galleys, not far out at sea. In the flash of the lightning strikes they could see the tossing English ships of Menteith, obviously anchored to wait out the tempest.

After rowing against the surging waves for a goodly time, the boats neared the larger galleys, and Robert silently hoped that the English had failed to post lookouts in such foul weather.

"Here's where we separate and leave for different destinations," said Robert to his brothers as he and Donald prepared to get into the first galley they came to. "God grant good fortune and good hunting for us all!"

"Aye, good fortune to us, brother king!" shouted Edward over the stormy sea as he hugged his eldest brother. Within a moment or two, with the help of the stout arms of the galley crew, Robert and Donald were aboard, and the galley put out its oars and pulled away into the gale.

"I hope we're not on a fool's errand," mumbled Alexander quietly as he held tight to the small boat's gunnels for the ride to the next galley in the line. Thomas Brus grabbed Alexander around the neck and jokingly tugged at him. "A'right, a'right," Alexander smiled grudgingly and shouted, "I'm not slidin' overboard, am I?"

"Ye damn well better not, 'cause I'm not jumpin' in this cold water to see to yer rescue," replied Thomas, pulling his cloak cowl tighter about his face. "No sir, not in this weather." It was not long before they reached the next galley.

"Any among ye likely to puke?" asked the captain of the galley as Thomas, Alexander, and James Douglas came aboard.

"None so far, as we're too fond of food to be throwin' it away on such," reported Thomas with a smile as another of the small boats came alongside and divested itself of more of Scotland's fighting men.

"This the lot for my galley?" shouted the captain when all were aboard.

"Aye!" answered Thomas, "we're the lot."

The captain nodded, weighed anchor and said, "Grab them oars, for ye are seamen tonight!"

"As we understood," returned James Douglas. "We are willin' and able."

"Row on then," said the captain, holding the tiller steady by bracing it against his wiry body with one deceptively scrawny arm, and pointed toward the west with the other.

The English masts, showing in the lightning strikes like sharp needles rising from the black water, grew smaller as the men labored with the oars in the rough seas. In spite of the fact that the small vessels rose upon the crest of a wave only to slide into a trough and rise again, the captain expertly steered a steady course for Rathlin Island, some thirteen miles away in a more-or-less westerly direction. The other galleys of the escaping armada followed in fair order, keeping in sight of one another by the irregular light of the storm.

Robert's galley, however, had turned off to the northwest toward Islay, which Donald Macdonald called home.

Remaining at Dunaverty, his brother Angus Og stood on the castle parapet overlooking the English ships tossing on the angry sea and left orders with the captain of the guard before retiring.

"Keep the banner of the Brus flying above these ramparts 'til ye personally get the order to do otherwise!" shouted Angus to the captain of the guard as they wrapped themselves tightly against the harsh wind and pelting rain. "And if any ask, tell them not that the Brus dwells here no more!"

"Aye, My Lord," returned the captain with a slight bow.

"Secrets are too easily lost with a loose tongue," said Angus, and he left the wall walk for a comfortable bed within the castle keep, as the last hope of Scotland was being tossed about on the blustery sea between Dunaverty and Ireland.

Alexander Brus

OCTOBER 7th 1306
RATHLIN ISLAND

A month passed since the daring galleys smuggled Robert's "army" to the tiny island of Rathlin, a mere dot of less than eight square miles set in the hostile sea barely six miles from the northern coast of Ireland. Upon arriving, the thankful men had set about gathering firewood, and raised their tents inside the large, sheltering caves on Rathlin's northeast coast.

The sparse inhabitants helped with trade goods and in other ways that would prove to allow the Scots to survive the winter. The Irish were, in general, allies of King Edward, but the Bruses had lands and other investments in the north of Ireland and held strong sway there. Queen Elizabeth came from Ireland, and was well liked by the locals. Her father, the Earl of Ulster, was also well liked and was one of King Edward's most trusted lieutenants.

Edward Brus, the oldest of the king's brothers, was left on Rathlin as commander of a small contingent stationed there in accordance with King Robert's confidential plan.

"When do we leave?" asked Alexander as he, Edward, Thomas, and James Douglas sat on a bluff above the caves where the men were bivouacked, for here they were assured of secrecy. They looked down on the three galleys sent from Islay by King Robert and Donald Macdonald to bring much needed additional supplies for the men hiding out on Rathlin. The vessels had arrived only the day before, and were anchored and bobbing on the relatively calm water in the shallow cove.

"The captains of the galleys agree that, on the morrow's dawn, the tides should be favorable," said Edward. A gust of cold wind whipped their necks and caused them to tuck deeper into their cloaks. The day was dark and drear, and the omnipresent fog and drizzle often turned to sheets of rain with howling winds.

"Each of us is to take six or eight men," said Edward, "so pick as ye like for travelin' companions. The rest will remain here, with Douglas and Haye, perchance 'til spring."

"Aye, Sire," answered James Douglas who then turned back toward the sea. "Reckon from up here ye could see a sail comin' from Kintyre at almost the first minute it left.

"There are many sails in these waters... how would ye know they were comin' for ye?" asked Thomas.

"Leopards on 'em, I guess," answered Douglas, grinning.

"They think we're still in Dunaverty, yonder," said Edward with a frown, growing impatient with the often expressed notion that the English would know where to come after them, even if they found out the Bruses were not holed up in Dunaverty.

"Who's first to be loaded?" asked Thomas, changing the subject.

"Alexander," said Edward. Turning to the youngest he said, "Ye will go to our lands around Coleraine, then over to Derry where James Stewart has lands."

"And next?" asked Thomas, anticipating the answer.

"Aye, ye are next, Thomas," said Edward, slapping him on the knee. "Ye will go to our coast lands along Antrim. And I will go to Olderfleet where the Brus name is also well respected. We must talk to everyone who seems fit and has cause to hate the English and the Comyns."

"Don't worry about the Irish, brother," interrupted Alexander. "They need not hate to fight."

"Aye," agreed Thomas, "A bit of ale and a hint of a cause..."

"Sounds a lot like the Scots, to me," laughed Alexander.

They all laughed, then Edward added, "And it don't hinder our purpose that Brother Robert married an Ulsterwoman, neither. Our fair queen may be our greatest advantage in this Irish gamble. So, let's go down and have a drink to toast our queen, and ask the Lord God to be with her, that we may win our wager."

"I'm for that," agreed Alexander through chattering teeth. Again they all chuckled, and maintained a good humor as they picked their way back down the steep hill to a warm fire and a warmer cup.

. .

The next morning, the three galleys were loaded with hope for the continuation of the rebellion. They sailed around to the southern tip of the island together, then separated, each to a different direction, but all destined for the mainland of the north of Ireland.

Only when they gathered back on Rathlin Island, would they know how successful they had been in raising enough men, weapons, supplies, and money to continue the fight.

OCTOBER 10th 1306
LANERCOST SANCTUARY

After his capture, Sir Nigel Brus, with the help of the skilled hands of the English physicians, barely survived the abdominal wound he received at the battle of Kildrummy. Being borne to Berwick, the venue of his trial, in terrible misery on a litter across rough terrain was certainly torture enough for any rebel. But then, that was by wicked design on the part of the young Prince Edward, who was sorely jealous of Nigel's brave heart and resolution to survive.

The Prince of Wales had personally sat in judgment, not only of Sir Nigel, but also of some one hundred twelve other Scots taken prisoner at Kildrummy. Of all those captured, only one single exception to trial was noticed and promptly forgotten by the Prince: Sir Robert Boyd, who, it was said and duly noted, by some "devious means of witchcraft," had managed to escape along the road to judgment.

Now, the trials at Berwick were over.

The winds of winter were testing their potential as King Edward, in his ever worsening illness, sought to relieve his agony of body and soul by changing his surroundings, and so had moved his residence from the town of Carlisle to Lanercost Sanctuary, about six miles to the east.

It was late morn and King Edward was lying in bed, more asleep than awake, when visions of Robert Brus leading scores of mighty warriors came across his delirious mind, threatening him with broadswords and morningstar maces. The king awoke with a jolt, sweat oozing from every pore to soak his sheets and surround him with a peculiar odor.

"God damned, I am!" he shrieked. "Why have I been forsaken?"

The monks nearby clapped their hands over their ears and feigned deafness as 'Longshanks' ranted for more than a quarter-hour against the rebellion and the cursed and treasonous Robert Brus.

"Bring me Fulco Ballard!" he demanded, reaching an intermission in his curses.

Sir Fulco immediately appeared by the king's bedside. "My Lord," he said as he bowed, before straightening the old king's pillows.

The king looked at his steward for a full minute before he spoke, as if to reassure himself of his servant's reality. "You would never run against me, would you, Fulco?"

"No, Sire. You are purely my heart and soul, and my total devotion," returned Sir Fulco, who had been with the king for many years and truly loved him. The kindly knight was greatly saddened to see the devastation being wrought by the illness on the old sovereign's body and mind, as would be anyone who regarded him with barest affection.

"Help me to the chamber pot," requested the king weakly as he did his best to rise from his pillows. Sir Fulco took the king by the arm and helped him to sit on the edge of the bed, then held the pot for him. When the king was finished, Ballard called a servant into the room to dispose of the waste, and sent for the king's valet to begin the morning's routine of dressing.

'Longshanks' moved slowly and was suspicious of everyone who entered or left the room.

"What is the agenda for the day?" asked the king from behind a screen as the valet removed the sweat-soaked nightclothes and helped the old man into fresh linens.

"The Prince of Wales arrives today from Berwick," said Fulco, "and wishes to consult with you on the disposition of rebels taken at Kildrummy."

"Have they been tried and found guilty?"

"They have been tried, Sire, but I know not the outcome," returned Fulco, positioning himself at a small desk in the room and pushing the papers there into a neat stack in front of him.

"What more?" prodded the king.

"There is still the question of the women, and the Earl of Atholl, who are now held in Carlisle," answered Sir Fulco.

The king's face twisted in anguish at the thought of more people nearby who prayed not only for his departure from this earth, but also for the destruction of his desire to have Scotland under his domain when he so departed. He sighed.

"I shall meet with my son when he arrives, and we shall then address the issue of the ones we hold here," he answered, and, the promise of sweet vengeance spinning in his mind, displayed a devious smile. He stepped from behind the screen fully clothed and shod for his day's activities. While the king and Ballard continued their daily business, the valet made up his bed and departed quietly.

A servant from the kitchen arrived with bread and porridge for the king, who examined the man's face for signs of treachery. Would he be capable of poisoning the food?

"This man's been in your service for many years, Sire," offered Fulco as a level of confidence for the king, though the sovereign continued to study the servant to a degree that grew uncomfortable for the man.

"Put it down," he said at last, waving the man away.

The servant quickly laid out a cloth on the table in front of the king and put the plates of food on it, then backed away, bowing. The king ate meagerly as he and Sir Fulco continued their discussion of the day's planned activities. Fulco committed everything the king said to paper in note form, even though he knew that the king only had energy sufficient for the accomplishment of a small portion of these desires. Then the fully-clothed king lay back upon his freshly-made bed to rest for another three-quarters of an hour.

Suddenly, the king exclaimed, "You are not to leave me alone while I rest!"

"Of course not, My Lord, I shall be at work right here until you wake," the good steward assured him. Fulco then continued to fill in the gaps in his notes while the king napped.

. .

It was early afternoon when the Prince of Wales arrived at the sanctuary. Accommodations there were relatively sparse for the king and his entourage, much less the newcomers, so the Prince's contingent of soldiers bivouacked in the wood a short distance away. Young Edward came directly to his father, bowed low, and sat in the chair next to him.

"Your trip from Berwick, how was it?" asked the king, more to understand his son's mind than to know the answer.

"I hate lyin' about in the wood," growled the prince. "Castle living is my thought for good times."

"You held court in Berwick on the treasonous scum of Kildrummy?" said 'Longshanks', changing the subject.

"I did," he answered, "but I've another bone to quarrel over."

The king glared at his son. What manner of black trade has he in mind, he wondered silently, then took one of his spells of coughing. Young Edward watched as the king finished coughing and spitting, then wiped his mouth on his sleeve before quaffing a goblet of water.

"I have done as you have bade me," continued the prince after the interruption. "I have captured Kildrummy, slain your... *our* enemies, captured many..."

"Out with your desire!" shouted the king. "Prologue bores me!"

"Piers Gaveston!" said the prince sternly. "I want Piers returned from exile! And this time for all time!"

King Edward's eyes knitted in deep furrows as his anger grew. "My own son turns against my will?" he snapped, and slammed his fist as hard as he could on the arm of his chair.

The king winced not, yet young Edward knew the hand was aching as he coldly bargained with his father. "You need my help to accomplish all that you desire before your death, which we both know grows more imminent with each bloody coughing spell. Do as I ask... and I will finish this deed for you." He smiled the patronizing smile of a man in control.

'Longshanks' knew the younger man to be right about his needing help, for his trust of those around him grew less each day. But he was not so quick to give in as that, and so counter-proposed a bargain of his own. "Rout Robert the Brus himself from his bastion at Dunaverty, where he lingers with only a handful of men, and your wish for your friend will be forthcoming. And not one moment preceding."

The Prince of Wales was angered by his father's tenacious will and reasoning ability, persevering yet in this debilitated frame. He fumed and squirmed in his chair, but when his anger cooled to logic, he agreed to the pact.

"Now, enough of this petty bickering," suggested the king, smiling, "We should be agreeable to one another! After all, you, one day... soon," he paused, "will be the king."

The prince knew he was being patronized but chose not to take issue; he simply grumbled a bit instead.

This one is so malleable, thought the king to himself, that I worry for his worth as a monarch. Yet, he is all there is left to me. Examples, he needs, to understand how to be king. Then he motioned to Sir Fulco, who was never far from the king's presence, to have wine sent for them.

"Tell me, my son, of the proceedings at Berwick."

"The most conspicuous among the captives," he started, "is Nigel Brus, whom we caught, down and bloodied, as we triumphantly entered by the castle gate after only... perhaps a fortnight's siege. My suspicions tell me that he botched the taking of his own life as we entered, to save himself from English justice."

The king smiled approvingly, then asked, "And what be the outcome for now?"

"Tried and condemned," he replied. "I am here to consult with you on the method of his execution."

"Did he whine in his prosecution? Did he beg mercy, as all such cowards do in the end?" asked the king, prying for a bit of titillating gossip to spread to his abbreviated court.

"He was barely alive," the prince dismissed the question lightly, misreading the king's intent to know.

King Edward frowned once again, then passed the thought by for additional information on the other prisoners. The wine arrived and the two men sat quiet for a long moment, sipping before the prince spoke again.

"There were one hundred and nine other rebels still alive who submitted to your will, father," he said at last with a nod of deference to the king. "Then there were the other two, of course, the women, whom I sent here for *your* disposition."

"Afraid to send women to the gallows?"

"I think it would be best if it were your decision, Milord," cautiously replied the prince, who knew political death when it was as plainly laid out as this.

The old king began another round of coughing; his wine cup fell wildly to the flagstone floor from the king's flailing hand. Sir Fulco moved closer to assist the king but was motioned back. The king did not want to appear in a weakened position before the prince. When he had at last recovered, he accepted a fresh draught of wine and returned his attention to the nub of the meeting.

"Of the one hundred and nine," he paused in thought, then ordered, "hang the lot of them, save the knights, whom you will hang *and* behead," said the king in a manner not unlike ordering a leg of mutton for the evening's supper.

"No exceptions?" asked the prince. "No ransom for the landed knights?"

"No ransom... no exceptions," he said emphatically as he drew in a deep swig of wine, "These Scots curs need to be mannered!"

"And of the Brus?"

"Let him be the sharpest prick in this bramble bush of thorns," replied the king. "For him, we reserve the execution of Wallace. With no exceptions!"

"And his head?"

"Piked above the castle gate at Berwick, of course."

The Prince of Wales cunningly agreed. On the morrow he repaired to Berwick to carry out the will of King Edward, his stalwart and prudent father.

OCTOBER 12th 1306
LANERCOST SANCTUARY

In the monk's dining hall of the sanctuary, a somewhat stronger King Edward held court for the trial of Sir John Strathbogie.

"Do you wish an advocate, Sir John?" asked Fulco Ballard in the absence of a full accompaniment of legal and clerical persons.

The king was feigning disinterest as he sat in the most elegant robes he had with him in these reduced circumstances, behind a long, paper-strewn table upon the dais built especially for him.

Atholl sat before him, dirty and unkempt, on a low, three-legged milk stool. His body sorely ached from wounds and broken bones that would not heal, caused by the beatings received during and subsequent to his capture at the Sanctuary of Saint Duthac at Easter Ross, and at the hands of the guards in the dungeon at Carlisle. The worst were from Carlisle, where he had languished for over a month in constant jeopardy of ill treatment.

"Nay," replied Atholl in a gravelly, deep-toned voice brought on by the continual suffering. "It will change the outcome not a jot."

King Edward dropped the paper he held in his palsied hand. He could not resist this opening: "And pray say, in what outcome do you see these proceedings culminating?"

Atholl knew the king was up to trickery, but with a deep breath answered all the same, "I shall be found guilty," replied Atholl.

"And are you guilty?"

"Ye choose to condemn me from my own mouth?" he returned.

"If you choose to wag your tongue, you can surely hang by it," gainsaid the king with a snicker.

"Then I speak neither for nor against myself except to remind ye, Edward Plantagenet... that we are cousins through our mothers, and with due consideration to that, a wee bit of leniency could be shown."

"The Bible says, 'Cousin', that if your own eye offends you, you must pluck it out," quoted the king. "And *I* say that if my own earl attempts to kill his king, I shall pluck *him* out!"

Atholl sank even lower on his stool, knowing that his fate was nearly played out. The only shred of hope he had left was the fact that it had been more than two hundred years since any earl had been executed by his sovereign, and of this the king himself had informed him, once upon a time.

Edward sat looking down on Sir John and a great sadness fell across his face, and he lowered his head as in mourning. Finally, he raised his head and asked, pitiably, "Why do you hate me so?"

"Hate ye?" returned Atholl, brashly. "Does not a bird hate its cage? We came not to take possession of *yer* life and lands. We want only that which is rightfully ours."

"But... Scotland... is... *mine*," the king laid his right hand against his breast as he spoke slowly and emphatically. "And you are trying to take it... from... *me*!" He paused and looked glaringly at the Earl of Atholl. "You have only that which *I*... grant to you. Is that not so?"

"Ye grant me not my God-given right to freedom!" said Atholl with as much passion as he had shown since his capture.

"And God gives me the rights to all that I conquer as king," Edward said smiling and thinking to create his own bit of homespun philosophy.

"How do ye argue with such a wit-tangle as that!?"

At that insult the king became enraged, and suddenly spoke to Ballard while wagging his bony finger toward Sir John, "Read the litany of charges, for the record!" Then he coughed several times, but otherwise remained in control of himself.

Sir Fulco read the charges for near a quarter of an hour.

As they were being read, the afflicted earl's mind wandered back to his days with King Robert, and the battles of Methven and Dail Righ, and how he had tried to save the Brus women. He hated failing at that task most of all, for they, and Robert, had entrusted their safety to him. He also knew this was the end of his participation in the rebellion, but knew not what he must do to survive. The worst, he thought, would be having to swear fealty to King Edward.

The loud words being read by Sir Fulco came back into Atholl's mind as he was being asked, "Do you confess these high crimes against your king and the people of England?"

"I submit... to the will of the king," spoke Atholl almost meekly, knowing that to say otherwise would serve only to incur the king's wrath all the more.

King Edward was pleased with the answer. "On with the sentencing then," he said.

With great effort, Atholl sat up, as straight as his crippled body would allow from the low position on the stool, to hear his fate pronounced. As he did, the chains on his hands and legs rattled. Sweet sounds, thought the king, who felt a resurgence of sovereign power that his sickly body seldom allowed him to enjoy, and he reveled in it.

"Sir John Strathbogie, earl of Atholl, since you are of royal blood..."

started the king, "...and of *my* royal blood at that... you shall be taken to London, where those of high order who think to oppose me," he coughed again, "will witness your punishment."

Atholl knew now that he was in direr trouble than he had expected, but refused to show the least emotion before the court.

He stood.

The king went on at full tilt, "You shall not be drawn on a hurdle, as a common peasant... but you shall have the tallest and mightiest horse in the crown's stable... as is suitable for a kinsman of your king, to ride to your place of execution. There..." the king paused and availed himself of a sip of wine, to enjoy the moment and to prolong Atholl's agony.

He cleared his throat.

"And there," he repeated, leaning forward in his chair for emphasis, "you shall be *hanged,* on a gallows especially constructed for you, *'Cousin!'*"

He settled back in his chair and smiled before continuing. "Said gallows will be no less than thirty feet higher than the gallows on which *all* the others have been hanged. Then, ere you are dead, you will be hauled down from said gallows, and your head will be severed from your body by ax, to be then put on a pike and displayed at London Bridge... beside the clean-picked skull of the traitor Wallace!" the king said viciously.

Playing at irony to its fullest, he then added, "*Your* pike... of course, shall be the higher."

He could not help a smothered snicker, thinking himself clever in his deliverance of the sentence and enjoying his toying with the earl, who wavered on his feet. Whether from the moment's emotion or his physical exhaustion, the earl's slight faltering was much to Edward's satisfaction. An excellent example he will make, he thought, and I shall show my son how to be king by *my* example.

Then forthwith, and in a growling voice the king said, "Take this vermin-ridden traitor from here; he fouls the air with his stench!" Edward pulled a perfumed handkerchief out of his tunic and waved it about in front of his nose.

The soldiers took Atholl by the arms and half dragged him as he hobbled away. Atholl spoke not at all, nor did any other in that place.

The king turned his head and closed his eyes that he might hear the sounds of his captive's chains all the more clearly until the great door out of the dining hall closed behind him and all was silent.

"Bring in the women!" commanded the king in an unusually buoyant mood, having savored the moment to its fullest.

"Perhaps a respite first, Sire?" suggested Sir Fulco, knowing how tired the king must have been.

"Then, after the midday meal," returned the king following a thoughtful pause.

"Milord," replied Fulco, bowing. "I shall make it so."

"My helpers, Fulco," ordered the king, suddenly feeling weak. "I shall lie down for a while and rest before eating."

Sir Fulco motioned the two strong men who stood by the side of the dais to come to the aid of the king and repair him to his bed.

. .

In the early afternoon, the five women captives were brought into the dining hall. They were told not to talk, and to stand in front of the dais until the king arrived.

After an hour or more of waiting, young Princess Marjorie grew tired and started to waver. The queen, moving close to her side, propped her up, and Lady Mary Campbell also helped to keep her standing straight. Lady Isabel MacDuff stood sternly beside Lady Christian Seton, as all had the resolve to take the punishment without so much as an uncomfortable squirm.

This was the first time the five women had been together since before the siege of Kildrummy and the queen and her party's move north with Atholl. They were each happy to find the others still alive, for they knew all had been in the gravest danger for the last month.

Now they stood before the person of their most terrible foe, King Edward. They all knew him from his court, and all had been his guests on many social occasions. But now they were the enemy, and they knew he was prone to fits of passing rage when he had been crossed.

Whether by design or by weariness, the king was extremely late to the proceedings. Even the guards and servants were getting fidgety before he arrived.

Suddenly, trumpets sounded, shocking everybody to renewed life as the two muscular servants carried the gaunt ruler to the large chair that temporarily served as throne for the king of mighty England. He settled himself into the chair and, without a word, started shuffling the warrants of indictment to and fro in pretended study.

Then just as suddenly, he looked up at the women and noticed they were all yet standing. "Sir Fulco!" he mockingly scolded, "Where are your manners? Have these… females… be seated." Sir Fulco gave a signal and five chairs were instantly brought up to where the Brus women stood. They sat, and secretly were thankful for the permission.

Finally, the king laid the papers on the table and said in a voice as loud as he could manage, "A family of malcontent miscreants… and a horse thief... whose own *husband,* a proud and honorable man, placed a bounty on her head."

The women said nothing to the accusations but let the old man continue.

"Perhaps the bounty money on your head should fall into my treasury since you were seized by my soldiers?" smiled the king shrewdly at Isabel, who gazed without emotion into his eyes.

When he realized he was getting nowhere in the needling of the accused women, he turned his head as if to say to himself that it was, of course, a rhetorical question.

The women sat perfectly composed and without a word. They all knew they would be found guilty and none wanted to be convicted from their own words. Even the child Marjorie had a strong sense of the weight of the situation and played her part as well.

Fulco Ballard came forward and, calling each woman by name, asked if she wished to confess. Each knew the penalty for confession and prudently spoke not.

"Women's tongues that don't wag?" chided the king. Several onlookers in the court chortled at his jibe.

He feigned reading for nearly another half-hour, until even Sir Fulco was himself exasperated, but, from a long association with the king, had learned well to hide his true feelings.

Then suddenly, as if he had been stoutly shaken awake, he ordered Sir Fulco to read the indictments against the five.

The papers were dutifully read. Elizabeth saw the king's head nod in light sleep as the readings went on, but said nothing.

"Anything to say in your own defense?" asked the king when the papers were at last laid before him.

Elizabeth stood. "Milord Edward."

"Yes, Milady?" spoke the king.

"I would ask two boons," she started. The king nodded permission for her to continue. "The child," she said, laying a hand on Marjorie's shoulder, "is but twelve years old, and, though the daughter of my husband, yer sworn enemy, should be treated differently than the rest of us, who willingly chose our fate."

"The court will consider your request, Milady," replied the king, coldly. He felt primarily that his having snared these women would flush out the elusive Robert Brus. Secondarily, he still did not wish to send these women to the gallows, thinking that their executions would possibly have a negative effect on the subsequent pacification of the Scottish population. Then he added, "And your second request?"

"I wish to know the fate of Earl Sir John Strathbogie."

"The Earl of Atholl, Milady, should be naught of your concern. You should fear for your own collective necks, not for the life of one who failed you in the field," answered the king.

"I would know, nonetheless," spoke Elizabeth as she held her head high and ignored the threat.

Perhaps to brag or perhaps to watch her reaction, the old king told her in exacting details of the earl's sentence, noticing that, as he did so the queen wavered only slightly, and the others reacted not at all. None satisfied the king with the shedding of a single tear, though they did fear the sentences he was about to pronounce upon them because they understood the extent of the cruelty of which he was capable.

"And what have ye planned for the five of us?" asked Elizabeth, who remained standing and was now showing some of her Irish temper.

"As you wish to rush the proceedings, Milady," said the king, "I now find each of you guilty of high treason in a time of a... so-called... uprising, and all accused are considered a part of it! You, each and all, have caused good people to go against their rightful king! By so doing, you have brought much misery upon those you pretended to help. So... guilty it is, for you, each and all alike."

"And also for the child?" asked Elizabeth defiantly.

"Guilty!" he pronounced, then added in patronizing tones, "but the court is not without sympathy in this matter..."

To what manner of sadistic devilment are we being subjected? Elizabeth wondered. Why does he dangle the fears of our fate so playfully on a string before us?

"...and has," he continued in his old, droning voice, "therefore decided that your lives will be spared."

There was a hushed sigh of relief, and not just from the women, when the five heard him say those words. But, he had not finished.

"Isabel MacDuff," he decreed, "once Countess of Buchan..." He paused a moment to cough, and Isabel stood to receive her sentence, "... for having stolen your husband's fine destriers and run off with that scoundrel Brus... *and* for having *crowned* him 'King of Scotland' at his pathetically inane coronation..."

At that he paused, watching Elizabeth's face while he added a bit of scandal, "...*And* my spies have it that you were also his concubine..." There he struck a nerve, not with Elizabeth, but with Isabel, who gasped. He continued, "...which is not a matter for this court, but simply added to illustrate the poor character of your person..."

The king waved Ballard to his side. "Where are those sentences?" he whispered. "They were here somewhere."

Sir Fulco retrieved the correct paper from the midst of the mass of documents in front of the king and quietly pushed it to his attention.

"Yes... here. Isabel MacDuff, for your crimes... you shall be installed in an iron cage, which will be suspended on the outer wall of Berwick castle... there to be gawked at, night and day, by passersby, as a reminder to anyone thinkin' to join this childish rebellion... that it will cost them a great sacrifice. No doubt it is more than any reasonable soul might be willing to pay." He smiled as he signaled the guards to take possession of their prisoner.

A hanging cage?! What a twisted mind he must have, thought Elizabeth.

Two armed guards took hold of Lady Isabel's arms and started her toward the exit. "I am not and have not been his mistress!" she screamed at Elizabeth as the guards forced her toward the door.

"I know," answered the queen in a firm, loud voice that Isabel could hear, but she remained facing toward the dais.

Marjorie began to cry, but the queen hushed her and held her tight.

The sentencing continued, "The widow Christian Seton shall be repaired to the convent at Sixhills where she may forever mourn her late husband... seeing no other man... and rue her decision to follow her rebel brothers!"

"Mary Brus... who, as I understand it, recently wed Neil Campbell... and that he, to this moment, is in the company of the traitor Robert Brus... shall also be put into a cage, to hang on the wall of Roxburgh castle, for all to witness the justice of her punishment! But, who knows? We may have an unusually mild winter or two!" he added dryly, then commanded, "Take them away!"

The sisters walked proudly from the dining hall, prodded from behind by the blunt, clumsy knuckles of the guards.

"And for us?" asked the queen who yet had her arms protectively around Marjorie. "A cage for us have ye also, Edward Plantagenet?"

"Enough insolence, woman!" cried the king, rising up and leaning across the table toward her. "You are enough to strike pity clean from my heart."

Can't strike what's never been there, thought Elizabeth but, for the sake of Marjorie, kept it to herself.

"For the daughter of Robert Brus..." he started, ruffling his papers, again.

Marjorie squeezed Elizabeth's hand and closed her eyes in fear.

"... A cage on the Tower of London wall. A charming place, where she will be compelled to speak to no one and, like the others, may find seclusion only while availing herself of the privy."

"She is but a child! Ye must be mad!" protested the queen.

King Edward ignored the insult and ordered Marjorie's removal.

"Mother! Mother! Don't let them take me!" she screamed as Elizabeth made a vain attempt to hold on to her but was held fast by two guards as the child was wrenched loose and taken away in hysterics by others.

After the child's shrieks were lessened by distance and the closings of successive doors behind her, King Edward asked, "Why does she call to you 'Mother'? You are not her mother."

"She was not born of my body, but I *am* her mother," argued the queen in great anger.

"So what cage have ye for me?"

"You are Elizabeth de Burgh, and I, a good friend of your father." He used her father's loyalty to contrast her disloyalty. "Richard de Burgh has in the past provided me with great service, and even yet does so against the French, where he has greatly distinguished himself. Out of respect for *his* loyalty and friendship to me, I have decided to show leniency to his daughter."

The King sipped from his cup and, clearing his throat, continued. "Therefore, you will be repaired to Burstwick-in-Holderness and kept under house arrest! You are permitted to dwell there with but two ladies-in-waiting, they of my choosing... and I promise you, Milady, they will be as old and joyless as can be found, and completely without wit."

He grinned with the pleasure he enjoyed at the saying of it.

Elizabeth nodded, then spoke in a quiet and determined voice, "Ye send my child to a cage on London Tower and me to house arrest... Ye send a family hither and thither to be locked in cages in fair weather and foul, like animals in some royal menagerie? My husband, Robert de Brus, *King* of Scotland, will have ye skewered on his claymore for this injustice!"

The King laughed at her, quickly joined by others in the court, and waved for her removal from his presence, "You Bruses are now but gettin' that for which you set your sails... disaster, for yourselves and your followers!" he shouted as she was escorted through the door, the humor gone from his voice.

As his words echoed in the darkening hall, the door closed and only a few guards and Fulco Ballard remained with him. Momentarily, he fell back in his chair with a great feeling of exhaustion. Though delighted with having been able to inflict great pain upon the traitorous Brus clan, he felt somehow saddened by the events, as if a major portion of his life had suddenly come to a close. He shook off the feeling and called for his bearers.

• •

Later, in the early evening, as the king awoke from a long, restless nap, the windows shown black and burning candles were the only light in his chamber as the deep shadows played jokes on the old man's mind.

"Ballard!" he cried out. Such a brave man was the king at one time, but now, fear of approaching death crept into his very being.

Sir Fulco appeared beside the king's bed. He carried a candle lantern that illuminated his face in strange ways, or so thought the king.

"Sit," commanded King Edward.

Fulco drew a chair to the edge of the bed. He was accustomed to these evening hour moods and knew the king simply wanted another soul nearby.

"I understand life not," confessed the king.

"Few men do, Sire," replied Fulco. "What troubles you?"

"I have the daughter of my mortal enemy tight under my thumb and vengeance says I did the prudent thing in sending her to the tower." He paused in reflective thought for a long moment before voicing the nub of his concern, "But, her child's face haunts my every glance."

"My Lord," said Fulco, "if I may... offer an observation?"

The king raised his hand a bit to give Fulco permission to speak.

"This decision of the child... may go badly with the people. They may say that their king's cruelty outstrips his wisdom... that his hatred outweighs his love."

"I understand your point," returned the king in a true revelatory tone. "The child would become a symbol of my hatred toward the Scots, for whom I profess to care!"

"Yes, Sire," replied Fulco who then let the king weave his own reasons for granting mercy.

"Ballard," said the king.

"Yes, Sire."

"On the morrow, have the child sent to a nunnery somewhere."

"A prudent... and loving, decision, Milord," said Fulco as he stood, "Will that be all?"

"Yes," answered the king, yet in thought. As Fulco was leaving the bedchamber, the king smiled. That night he slept well, and the next morning he felt better than he had in many days.

Donald Macdonald

OCTOBER 23RD 1306
FINLAGGAN CASTLE ON THE ISLE OF ISLAY

Donald Macdonald and his brother, Angus Og, were both adventure seeking men and passingly enterprising businessmen, trading in and smuggling most commodities of the day, including slaves and mercenaries. They owned a great fleet of galleys that constantly plied the seas along the western coast of Scotland and connected with the many inhabited islands in those waters.

Sir Donald was one of the Lords of the Isles, who many times had met in the great hall of Finlaggan castle. The lords, to a man, had one thing in common with Robert Brus: they each had a blood feud with the Macdougalls, their own discontent going back half a century, and were most willing to help King Robert in any way they could, so long as it did not interfere with business.

Thus it was that, while the brothers of the Brus sailed west toward Rathlin Island before splitting up and going to various destinations in the north of Ireland, Robert and Donald Macdonald went to the Isle of Islay.

A nippy chill permeated the air as the two men rode far beyond the castle walls of Finlaggan. Lord Donald Macdonald and King Robert Brus dismounted their horses and wandered into the wood. They each carried a bow and a quiver of arrows. Robert was never separated from his claymore, and he had it on this day, strapped to his back. Donald was smaller in stature than Robert, but with a physique of equal proportions, and a neatly trimmed beard and a mustache that curled up on the ends. He and Robert had been acquainted with one another for some time, but now they were spending days of enjoyable semi-leisure together and becoming fast friends.

For a lengthy distance up and down the rugged hills, the two crept quietly through the underbrush, barely making a sound. They came to a clearing surrounding a small pond. In several places along the tarn's rim they saw fresh boar tracks and decided to linger nearby until the boar showed himself.

Separating to cover as much of the clearing as possible, each man took up a spot and settled down to wait. The wind blew cold around them but they soon heard, in the near wood, the sounds of boar hooves picking their way through the dry leaves.

They nocked their arrows and patiently waited.

Before long, a large boar sniffed the air at the edge of the clearing, before moving with a grunt toward the water to drink. A sow followed close behind as Robert fully drew his bow and waited for Donald, who was closer, to strike first.

The arrow from Donald's bow slashed the air and hit the boar full force, but rather than laying dead, the pig rolled over and broke off the arrow shaft.

Blood from the wound poured as the angry beast spied Robert in the thicket.

Having seen the boar drop, Robert had stood to deliver his own deadly arrow on the sow, but just as his arrow was loosed, the wounded boar charged Robert.

The wild pig's eyes were red and his yellow-white tusks were spattered with a mixture of saliva and blood.

Robert realized the beast would be upon him before he could load and loose another arrow and so threw the bow to the ground and drew his dirk.

No sooner had the blade cleared its scabbard than the pig reared and squealed in pain, and fell dead at Robert's feet.

Donald's second arrow had found its target with no time to spare.

In his excitement, Donald yelped loudly. Robert walked calmly down-slope to the tarn. The Macdonald came grinning to Robert, who dropped and stretched out face down in the grass at the edge of the quiet, clear lake and put his mouth into the cold water to quench his immense thirst.

"Great shot, Robert! You caught the sow clean through the heart!" he exclaimed as he joined the king in having a drink.

"Thought I would never taste water again," teased Robert as he stood, having drunk his fill and dried his chin and beard on the edge of his heavy cloak. Then he added, "Ye've got the skills of battle yerself. Putting two arrows into a target moving that fast is fair marksmanship, I'd say."

Donald grinned as he also rose from the ground, but he said not a word, for he knew better than to admit his skill to a man who was in such dire need of fighters.

The two walked along the edge of the pond toward the killed sow. Donald, somewhat guiltily, felt he was shirking his duties to his beliefs and his country by not accepting what he considered his king's obvious offer to join the army. Circling the lake he thought of the boar as a man of war and, although he had been in many battles to protect his own family and friends, he found it difficult to think of killing as a way of life.

"My King," he said at last, "my greatest value to ye can be far more than just another sword and bow."

Robert turned to him somewhat confused, "What say ye?"

"Were ye not suggestin' that I join yer army...?"

"I was but complimentin' yer shootin', man," said Robert in all sincerity. "'Twas passin' good, to my thinkin'...saved me from gettin' gored, or worse."

Donald smiled in return, a bit discomfited at his mistake, and said, "Well, I do want to volunteer, but not as a soldier. Give me a bit of time and ye'll see what I can do for yer cause, Robert."

"I take all help that comes my way," remarked Robert as they reached their quarry, "but, for now, we need to get these two pigs back to Finlaggan, where they will be the main course for the Lords this night."

"Aye," said Donald, smiling broadly. Each one grabbed a hind leg of the sow and, with great effort, dragged her back through the woods to where they had left the horses. Even in the chilly air, the exertion had worked both men into a sweat.

After catching his breath, Robert got a length of rope from his saddlebow.

"Ye hangin' her here?" asked Donald.

"Nay," answered Robert, "but my horse is draggin' out that big boar!" Macdonald laughed as Robert mounted his stallion and rode off to retrieve the kill.

• •

That evening in the great hall, where many of the lords of the various islands around Islay had been holding council meetings, they now relaxed and ate of Robert's freshly killed swine, and enjoyed the meal.

"Not often do we have meat kilt by our king!" announced one of the lords in a loud voice, before he washed his mouthful down with a large gulp of wine from his goblet. They all laughed and looked at King

Robert, who had the seat of honor, mid-table on the dais. They were seated on both sides of him and when they all stood and cheered him, he was overtaken with gratitude for their comradeship.

Robert stood before the men and declared, "Ye have done me great honor, and 'tis the least I can do to return to ye meat for yer table."

The men raised their cups and drank to King Robert.

Robert raised his own chalice and drank to the Lords of the Isles, to the beautiful island of Islay, and to freedom for Scotland.

Rousing cheers permeated the hall, for the people of the Hebrides admired and supported him, and well knew that his success would keep King Edward from their waters and shores with his taxes on trade.

. .

Later, most of the lords had had their fill of food and wine and had gone their separate ways. One, at the end of the table, had passed out from overindulgence, and his wardrobe man and squire were having a tough time getting the heavy fellow up and to his sleeping quarters.

Robert and Donald remained at the table and talked into the night.

"Ye plannin' to continue this rebellion?" asked a very relaxed Donald between slow, small sips of his wine.

Robert, leaning forward over the table and resting on his elbows, slowly nodded. "What else would I do?" he responded with his own question, to which Donald shrugged.

"Ye and yers could have a good life on the continent. Take King John, for instance," reasoned Donald. "He lives well there, entertaining, hunting..."

Robert interrupted gruffly, "Balliol was born to that life! Surely not of the stuff of kings, was *he* made."

"Perhaps not, but he *was* Scotland's king."

"Scotland's king? Edward's man on a string!" gainsaid Robert.

Donald nodded in approval.

"'Tis my fate that I shall be king," said Robert, more thoughtfully. "In '97, the people rose up against England with Wallace because he had successes! And the people thought he would protect them, so they fought for him! And they will rally to us as our successes grow!"

"But, ye've not had successes, only defeats," said Donald, who would not have been so bold had he drunk no wine but, alas, he had. Robert took it not well, frowning and snarling at Donald, and brusquely standing to leave his company. Then, as suddenly as he had stood, he sat back down beside his friend.

He sipped his wine. Donald sat in silence.

"Ye are right," the king flatly said at last.

"Ye're goin' to live on the continent?" asked Donald, mild surprise in his voice.

"Nay," replied Robert shaking his head. "Ye are right about our lack of success. We were forty-five hundred at Methven, and now we're split up and gone to everywhere, and less than... than a hundred!"

"Ye'll come back." encouraged his drunken friend. "We'll find many to the north... willin' to follow ye, for they are mightily fearful of those who rule there."

Robert sat in a long, black silence, thinking of why he should go on. At that moment he could think of little reason. The people of Scotland certainly cared little. Would it not be better that he give it up and gallivant around Europe as his father and John Balliol had done? Or, he could go to live in Norway, where his sister was queen. He could do whatever he wished to do! He just could never again do so in Scotland. In spite of that, abdicating the throne and the revolution seemed to be a reasonable decision, until the thought solidified in his mind: He'd be just another whore to the elite! Not likely! Thus, was the decision made.

"I need two things, my friend," said Robert, at last.

"If they are within my power," nodded Lord Donald.

"These things are easily within yer power," returned the king.

"Then, say yer needs and it is made so," Donald concluded.

"First, I need six trusted men to go to Carrick and collect the Martinmas rents due me. I desperately need the money," confessed Robert.

"Lay out yer tenants on paper and I'll have my kinsmen 'complish the chore," the Macdonald assured his king, adding, "and... I am *not* a poor man. I will add to yer war chest," he offered.

"I'm not beggin' of ye."

"Ye begged not, I gave freely," returned Donald with a smile.

Robert studied Donald's face and saw true generosity there, and so nodded acceptance.

"And the other need?" asked Donald.

"I would have ye take me to my kin."

"Kin?"

"Aye, Christina of the Northern Isles," spoke Robert.

"In Garmoran?" asked Donald, sitting up straighter. "Yer kin? I ne'er thought yer kin to be in Garmoran."

"My first wife's sister-in-law," explained Robert.

"Aah," he nodded in understanding. "I can do this, also, but we must leave soon, for the weather will go bad in a hurry now."

"As soon as yer agents are dispatched to Carrick," agreed Robert.

NOVEMBER 12th 1306
The Misty Isles of the Inner Hebrides

Lord Donald Macdonald and King Robert de Brus went from island to island seeking the elusive "Christina of the Isles," a thirty-year-old widow and kinswoman to Robert through his first wife, Isabel de Mar. Christina had dominion over many large and small lands and islands in this region, and was wealthy and powerful. Her people were relatively well-to-do artisans and farmers, and her trade routes extended from Norway to the Middle East. She was as shrewd in her business transactions as she was in governing her lands and people.

At last, the two galleys of Donald's fleet came to an island where a castle on the eastern shore appeared to rise straight up to a stirring height from the depths of the misty sea. It was set firmly upon a pinnacle of solid rock that, itself, rose some eighty feet above the water.

"How magnificent!" exclaimed Robert as it suddenly appeared before him out of the thinning fog.

"Aye," agreed Donald. "This Lady of the Isles knows the life, she does."

"First, ask if she abides within," said Robert. "Ye know how many of her lands and islands we've visited only to find naught of her."

As the galleys rounded the sheer rock cliff, Donald directed the oarsmen to make for shore in a small shallow cove below the castle, where several other galleys laid about with furled sails. When they reached the shallow water, Robert and Donald jumped into the freezing, foaming waves and heaved their craft onto the shore. The oarsmen did likewise and the boats were pulled up the beach, farther from the water. Runnels in the stone beach ran deep, for the keels of many galleys from earliest times to that moment had worn impressions in the stone from identical beachings.

Adventuresome Vikings! thought Robert, whose blood ran directly to that hardy people through his de Brus lineage.

"Damned cold!" shivered Donald, wet to his waist.

"Damned cold, for sure," said Robert as he secured the bowline of the galley to a stub of protruding rock.

The second galley came ashore in the same manner and tied up alongside the first. The newly arrived seamen all climbed from their vessels and joined the others as they started up the pathway to the top of the cliff and the mysterious, majestic castle there.

Robert and Donald, leading their twenty-five or so followers, drew near to the castle gate and shouted to the guard. The winter wind whipped violently off the water and tore at the seafarers, and those who were also unfortunate enough to be wet from the landing were quickly all but frozen and in much pain.

"Who ventures forth on such a day?" shouted a guard from the ramparts of the castle wall.

"King Robert de Brus of Scotland!" shouted Donald into the moaning gale, "and Lord Donald Macdonald of the Isles."

There was a loud roar of laughter on the wall as the pickets thought they were being joked by insane men. The laughter suddenly stopped, and within a moment a woman's face appeared over the ramparts to look down upon the newcomers.

"Is she the one we seek?" asked Donald who had heard much of the lady but knew her not by sight.

"Aye, 'tis," replied Robert still shivering but now not knowing whether it was from the cold or the excitement from finally finding her.

The gate was immediately opened, and the cold men rushed briskly inside the walls to be sheltered from the wind. They were then shown directly into the guards' quarters, where a most welcome fire roared in the fireplace. The chilled newcomers drew close to the hearth to thaw out, as their wet trews were freezing to their stiffening legs.

Robert and Donald, though equally wet, were diverted from their men to enter the great hall, where they were greeted by the Lady Christina.

"Lord Robert de Brus," said Christina with a teasing smile, "or is it, as I have heard from some, King Robert?"

"'Tis indeed the latter, Milady," replied Robert with a bow of courtesy, "though 'tis a title of dubious distinction at this point."

Christina smiled and curtsied to her kinsman, who now carried the fate of Scotland upon his shoulders. She then turned her attention toward Lord Donald, who thought, from this distance, that she must have been the most beautiful woman he had ever seen. Her heavy winter robes were designed to be quite revealing of her handsome form, and to add to the infatuation, she thought much of the two men who stood before her.

"Donald Macdonald, of Islay," said Donald with a smile, a bow and a noticeable shiver.

"Ah, forgive me! Ye men must be frozen," she said apologetically, and with a sweep of her arm in the direction of the enormous fireplace added, "Please, to the fire."

Robert and Donald sat on stools near the blazing fireplace and warmed themselves, removing their icy shoes and stockings and rubbing their nearly frozen feet with their only slightly warmer hands. At their hostess' direction, maidservants brought warm, dry cloths on which they dried themselves, and warmed wine in jeweled goblets to warm them inside. The two men sat mostly in silence before the fire and sipped the wine, absorbed in their own notions for most of a half-hour, as their hostess had disappeared elsewhere.

"Expect we made a poor entrance, don't ye think, Robert?" said Donald at last and somewhat wistfully.

"Ye cannot be what ye're not," philosophized Robert, who was feeling almost normal again.

Donald sneezed and sniffed. "Damn!" he lamented. "'Tis illness comin' on me, bein' out in the cold and wet!"

"Ye'll live through it," laughed Robert, knowing that, on other occasions, they both had been at least as cold, and far wetter.

Donald laughed, too, but was not quite sure he was in full agreement with his king. It was then that a maidservant silently entered the room and curtsied.

"Lady Christina asks that ye ones be fetched," she said in a quiet, unassuming voice. "Come with me, please, My Lords."

They arose from their comfortable stools by the fire and followed her as they had been instructed.

"I've never seen a castle such as this," remarked Donald in a whisper as the men walked down a heavily tapestried hallway.

"Nor I," confirmed the king, "but I like it well."

They were led into a room not far from the solar that had a great tub of warm water in it.

"My lady hopes that this pleases ye," said the maidservant, gesturing toward the tub.

Donald looked at the tub, full of steaming water and festooned with ornate art works of intricately carved ivory on a par with its sumptuous surroundings, and whistled softly.

"Is this how they live in the upper isles?" he asked, obviously impressed.

Robert shrugged, "My first trip here, too." The young woman asked for the men's clothing. "We'll manage our raiment," said Robert. "Thank ye, and leave us, now."

The woman curtsied and left, closing the door behind her, and Donald asked, "Why'd ye throw her out?"

Robert looked at Donald quizzically then said, "Modesty, my friend."

"Hah! Well, *I'm* not shy," said Donald as he sneezed again.

"Ye had best jump into the hot water ere ye catch somethin' bad enough to kill ye," said Robert, throwing his last bit of damp clothing in a heap on the floor.

"After ye, My King," teased Donald with a large grin and a low pretentious bow.

"I'll certainly not wait for the likes of ye," the king said, slipping gingerly into the warm water. Soon, he was up to his neck and enjoying every drop of it.

"Robert?"

"Aye," he said, soaking in the physical luxury.

"Ye think the lady had the notion we stink?" And he sniffed under his arms.

"Nay," said Robert, "She no doubt thought us cold. Now, come for yer bath." The combination of the warm water and the warm wine had made Robert more relaxed than he had been in his current memory.

As soon as Donald slipped into the water opposite Robert the door again swung open. The two men could say nothing as four maidservants swept in upon them, two to each man, and commenced scrubbing them briskly from their heads to their toes.

"They know hospitality passin' well here, Robert," quipped Donald to the embarrassed Robert as the women held up large towels for their exit from the water.

When the men were about dry, two of the women left and returned with fresh clothing. These things more suitable for a social occasion than those they had abandoned, still laying where they were doffed, in heaps on the floor. There being no need for modesty at that point, the two men allowed the servants to help them dress. As they silently gathered up the soiled castoffs, the women curtsied crisply and exited as they had come, and before the door closed, another maid entered.

"Supper will be served shortly in the great hall," she said, after which she curtsied. "If ye would, please follow me to yer quarters."

Again the two men looked at each other, shrugged their shoulders and followed as they were instructed. The room into which they were ushered was exceedingly large, with a window of clear glass overlooking the sea. A single oversized bed stood against one wall. Candles were lit to compensate for the dwindling light of the short winter day.

"Milady offers her wishes that ye will enjoy yer accommodations," said the woman.

"Ye can be most assured of that," said Donald as he toured the room and was taken by the many intricate works of art that made the room luxuriant beyond his ken.

"Ye may tell yer lady that we shall be quite comfortable here, and that her hospitality is greater than we could have wished," said Robert more formally.

"I shall return for ye at the supper hour, then, My Lord," she curtsied to Robert, then smiled at Donald and gave him a much briefer curtsy as she left the room and closed the door behind her.

"Well, Donald, looks like ye've made a conquest already," teased Robert as he threw himself across the bed.

"Aye, it happens all the time," bragged his friend with a swagger. He went around inspecting the fine tapestries and carpentry in the room for a few minutes, and when he turned to say something to Robert he found that the exhausted king had fallen sound asleep.

. .

As promised, the young woman returned and led the two men into the great hall, where there were only three places set on a long table on the dais.

"Expectin' much company, she isn't," remarked Donald.

"Looks sparse, it does," returned Robert.

Then, Christina entered, dressed in a magnificent gown overthrown by a beautiful dark blue robe, both garments embroidered lavishly with gold and silver threads. Her emblem of a single white swan on an island placed on a shield, was repeated throughout the designs.

I'm in love, thought Donald, exceedingly excited by the lady's appearance.

After pleasantries were exchanged and wine was poured into the three goblets, they sat down to an exceptionally fine dinner of pheasant and boar's leg, delicious breads and grain pudding, all laid out on the table by maidservants of unusually attractive appearance, the men noticed. Their cups were not allowed to fall to half empty, and their plates were continually adorned with more meat or some delicacy of exquisite taste.

Robert, not wanting to be distracted from his mission, spoke, "Milady, if I may speak to ye of my purpose here at this time..."

Christina interrupted by raising her finger to her pursed lips, then said, "Let us enjoy the evenin', good king, for perhaps there will be none other like it for the remainder of our lives.."

Two brown-skinned servants sat nearby and, in unison, played exotically sweet melodies on their lutes.

"They look the same, and play the same," commented Donald.

"They are twins of unusual talent. I rescued them both from slave traders of the Mediterranean region," offered Christina. "Their songs, 'tis said, will take ye to a place of yer choosin' that makes ye happy."

"Right now, that place seems to be here," said Donald, as graciously as he could manage.

Christina returned his smile and replied, "Most kind of ye, Milord." Then she closed her eyes to absorb the music more clearly.

This place borders on fantasy, thought Robert. He continued his meal of more than he had eaten since they left Finlaggan two weeks earlier. As for its preparation, he could not remember ever having eaten better, though many of the flavors were unknown to him.

Donald closed his eyes and rested his head on upturned palms to see if he could hear what Lady Christina was hearing. Somehow he thought she must be hearing more but he tried all the harder.

"Do ye dance, Sir Donald?" asked Christina when she noticed he was enraptured with the music.

"Nay, Milady," replied Donald, truthfully, but quickly added, "perhaps ye could teach me a step or two."

Christina stood and stepped off the dais to the main floor area of the great hall and held her hand toward Donald.

Donald was all but agog, for he had never known a woman of this magnificence. He stood and smiled, and met her on the floor. She took his hands in hers and moved to the music, showing him how to move his feet in the formal dance. After a few moments he caught on to the simple steps, and as he followed her lead they moved lightly across the floor in time to the music, gazing intently into each other's eyes.

Robert turned in his chair to watch the two for a moment. He grinned and shook his head before turning back to the table to continue his meal. No need to let good food go cold for the likes of new love, he thought.

When Christina and Donald returned to the table some quarter of an hour later, he pushed his plate to her side of the table and stepped over to sit beside her.

"Abandoning yer king?" asked Robert with a smile.

"Nay, My King," answered Donald in good cheer. "I am but a sword's length away."

"Ye'll be more than that presently," said Robert, "for I'm seein' to the men. Then, I'm thinkin' about that warm bed, I am." Robert graciously took his leave, kissing Christina's hand.

Late into the evening, she and Donald ate little, and talked much, of many things. Donald was completely intoxicated by the Mistress of the Isles and she, in turn, thought much of him.

· ·

For a fortnight, the two men remained in the company of the lady and were treated with the most pleasurable care. In those times, Donald slept little in the room that he and Robert were assigned, as he often spent away his days and nights with Lady Christina.

One morning Robert sat alone in his room, staring out the window at the gray winter day. Over the sea he could barely catch a vague outline of the neighboring island, so easily visible in clear weather. Donald casually strolled into the room with a large towel around his body. He had been bathing in the heated tub and was looking for freshly cleaned clothes to wear.

"Hail, King Robert," teased Donald when he saw the king sitting alone.

"Hail yerself," replied Robert with a taste of anger in his voice.

Donald sensed the tension and came to Robert, "Where be yer wit, Robbie?" he asked.

"Elsewhere. Across the sea," replied Robert tersely. He returned his stare toward the vast, undulating form as it ebbed and swelled against the cliff beneath the castle.

"Ye want to leave this paradise?"

"Nay," said Robert truthfully, "I want not to leave... for we are visiting a pixilated world not of our ken. I rest easy here and long for my queen who winters many miles to the north. I lose sight of the battle, and the faces of our enemies grow shadowy and vague." He paused a moment and then asserted, "We must be on our way! We must escape this enchanted paradise ere we forget our purpose!"

"Ye may take whatever of my galleys and men ye desire and leave, My King, and go with my blessing and, I pray, success in yer endeavor," said Donald. "As for me, this enchantment has become my glory. And I will not leave the lady, for I love her, totally and forever!" he added, soberly.

Robert suddenly kicked the footstool on which he had been resting his feet into a table, which in turn knocked an ancient urn to the floor. The lovely and valuable Celtic vessel shattered into a thousand smashed pieces. Donald instantly jumped back not knowing the king's mind.

They both focused on the shattered pieces on the floor and Robert said, "Ye see... formed rightly together this was something of great beauty and worth. Now it is but useless pieces."

"Ye broke the urn to make yer point?"

The king shook his head. "It was an accident that the urn was broken. Even so, it served to say what I was having difficulty putting into words, my friend," he said.

"Ye have a way with expression, Sire," said Donald who then understood that even though Robert was his friend, he was first of all, the king.

"We need my kinswoman's help... for money, and supplies, and ships to carry an army to the enemy. We need her permission to visit her islands and solicit men in arms from among her vassals, and we need her introductions into Ross and Sutherland. That's what we need," pleaded the king for his friend's understanding and remembrance of who they were and what they were about.

"I will secure these things for ye, Robert, for I promised I would do well by ye," replied Donald at last. "But when ye continue yer war, I will return here with the Lady of the Isles, for it is here, with this woman, that I... have found true happiness."

"Agreed," answered Robert. "Ye help me in this way and I will fight for yer freedom to maintain this manner of life... fantastic though it may be," he said with a grin.

The two men pledged their parts in the bargain with a handshake and rowdy backslapping.

. .

Within a week the two galleys of Lord Donald Macdonald, and three more from Lady Christina, made their way toward the first island in their planned journey. The weather was bitterly cold and the men grumbled, but Robert knew what must be done and they set icy sails to accomplish the task before them.

"I have escaped the enchantment of the Misty Isles," confessed Robert to Donald as he sniffed in the fresh, cold air of the sea.

"Ye may have, but I remain the Isles' most willing prisoner," said Donald.

Robert smiled at his friend, then yelled vigorously into the wind. It howled back with an equally vigorous force. King Robert de Brus was on the high crest of the world again.

Reginald Crawford

JANUARY 27th 1307
DUNAVERTY CASTLE

Two hours before dawn, Angus Og Macdonald was roused from his sound slumber by his wardrobe keeper, who had been first awakened by the captain of the guard.

"Sire, ye are wanted on the wall," said the servant in a loud whisper.

"What?" shouted Angus, groggily, "Who comes into my bedchamber before the day is yet broken and to what intent?"

"'Tis I, William, yer keeper, Milord," he said as he pulled the flickering candle closer to his face so that Angus could see him more clearly.

"Oh, 'tis ye," replied Angus, releasing his grip on the dirk he kept under his pillow and sitting up. Rolling his head and flexing his shoulders to work out the stiffness, he finally asked, "What word have ye, then?"

"They want ye on the west wall, Sire."

"Harrumph!" the sleepy master of the castle growled, then hoisted himself to the edge of his bed and scratched, taking a moment to awaken.

He then went to the foot of the bed, where William had placed a pile of clothes, and dressed in as many of them as he felt comfortable. Considering the cold, he wrapped his stout cloak about him before leaving for the courtyard and the wall. He huffed laboriously as his overweight body worked its way up the stone spiral stairs of the tower to the wall walk.

"What be yer trouble?" asked Angus as he came to the captain of the guard.

"Sire," returned the captain, pointing into the inky void where gleamed a small point of light, "Off yonder, on Rathlin, a signal fire of sorts. I know not its significance."

Angus leaned over the wall and stared into the cold blackness for more than several minutes to catch a clear view of the signal through the blowing snow and wind.

Smacking his fist down upon the stone battlement he ordered, "Captain, take the royal standard and the Brus banner from their staffs!" He started to leave, but turned back to add, "And have me awakened as the sun is a full four fingers above the horizon into the dawn."

"Aye, Sire," answered the captain, and he bowed on Angus' exit from the wall. He then pivoted to face the two pikemen standing nearby and shouted, "Ye heard him, take 'em down!"

. .

The next morning, on the land side of Dunaverty Castle, Lord John Menteith arose from his roughly made pallet and emerged from his tent shivering with the cold and the snow. Every morning at about the same time, as he rounded the back of his tent to take care of first things first, he would think of Robert de Brus having such a restful winter in the warmth of yonder castle, while he and his men froze their arses in the field. As he urinated on the freshly fallen snow, he thought about, and hoped he could, soon be pissing on the grave of that 'counterfeit king.'

Walking to the front of the tent to stir the fire as he had done for these past many weeks, he looked up at the castle and cursed the Brus and royal standards just before crouching to blow the fire hotter prior to adding fuel. It was at about the third long blow that he suddenly realized something was wrong. He abruptly jerked his head back to the wall to see only the Macdonald standard! The other two staffs stood bare!

The objects of his curses no longer flew!

"Sound the alarm!" he wailed, "Awaken this whole godforsaken camp! Robert de Brus has escaped as we slept!"

Within moments, the clamor of mustering men and horses and armor and weapons echoed and re-echoed in a most chaotic manner.

Sir John de Botetourt approached Menteith, who yet stood in front of the fire bundled tightly in a hefty wad of woolen blankets, trews, and boots.

"What be the stir?" asked Botetourt, seeing Menteith only half dressed for almost any kind of occasion.

"The Brus has escaped!" exclaimed Menteith, pointing frantically toward the flagstaffs on the wall of Dunaverty castle.

"Great God in Heaven!" shouted Botetourt. "We've spent our winter here to catch him, and he's slipped from our grasp as we slept!"

"My words exactly!" replied Menteith with a snarl. "Now, not only shall King Edward *not* give us lands for the capture of Brus, but he will have our heads on pikes as well!" he shouted, as if Botetourt were leagues away rather than at arm's length. "Send word to our galleys layin' off yonder that we will be leavin' this damned place... immediately... this morning."

"How do we know it's not a cagey trick to get us to leave?" asked Botetourt, at which thought Menteith was genuinely surprised.

"Damn me!" he exclaimed. "Ye could be right!"

"Why not go and ask the question?"

Menteith froze. His eyes stared blankly and his jaw dropped at Botetourt's question. "Why not, indeed," he finally replied, and he, still bundled as before, strode boldly off, down the narrow spit of land separating the castle bluff from the mainland, where camped his army.

The walk took but a minute.

"The laird of the castle!" screamed Menteith in great billowy breaths to the sentry on the wall. "I demand to see the lord of the castle! *Now!*"

The guard's head disappeared from Menteith's view as the sentry left to report to his captain that a half-dressed, insane man from the enemy camp was demanding to see the laird at the front gate.

"Appears right frozen, too," he snickered.

The captain smiled and said to the guard, "Tell him the laird of the castle will be there, presently." The captain then left the wall to awaken Sir Angus.

A half hour passed, and Menteith and Botetourt huffed chilled vapors and stamped the length of the strip leading to the castle gate, time and again, trying to keep warm until, at last, Sir Angus appeared over the ramparts and looked down on the two fuming men.

"May I be of service, Milords?" asked Angus in a patronizing manner.

"Is the Brus and his gang of murderers within or not?!" blurted Lord Menteith without thinking of courtesy or protocol.

"Robert de Brus, King of Scots," said Angus, pausing for effect, "has dwelled not within this castle for quite some time," he stated truthfully, adding sarcastically, "D'ye wish to leave a message for my lord, the king?"

The two men in front of the gate cursed and argued, one blaming the other for the slip King Robert had given them.

"Well, I _still_ don't believe the bastard has left," argued John Botetourt.

"Ye yet think it a trick, do ye?" asked Menteith.

"Aye," replied Botetourt, "I do! These sneakin' rebels will do and say anything to keep their worthless necks from bein' axed. Not a jot of chivalry amongst the lot of 'em!"

"Can ye prove the Brus is not within?" shouted Menteith to Macdonald.

"Ye two, alone and unarmed, may come within and inspect all ye will," said Angus. "It matters not to me."

"It's a trick," whispered Botetourt. "He but wants to get us alone and unarmed within the castle where we will be butchered... or held for ransom!"

"Now ye're thinkin' all manner of things are tricks," said Menteith, scowling as he prodded the chest of his companion with his index finger and added, "Ye've been in bivouac too damned long and lost yer nerve. The camp whores have crazed ye, man."

Botetourt was angry but said nothing more as Menteith shouted back to Sir Angus that they would accept his offer, and would return directly to enter the castle for a search.

. .

Later in the day, the two men met, dressed in their finest armor and weaponry. Having thought it over, Sir John Menteith, prime commander of the troops and directly under the command of King Edward, decided it was too dangerous for both men of command positions to risk being taken prisoner touring the castle. He thus ordered Sir John de Botetourt to disarm and go alone to inspect the premises and report back to him.

"Afeared of trickery?" asked Botetourt with a smirk as he turned toward the castle to attend to his inspection.

Sir John Menteith answered not, but only sneered and cursed under his breath and wished John Macdougall were here with his "blue devils," and fantasized how that would be the end of the Macdonalds and the Bruses.

When Botetourt returned to report that the mostly spent army of Robert de Brus was to be found in neither "nook nor cranny," Menteith went into a terrible rage and threw blame for the rebels' escape on Botetourt. He then ordered his men to break camp and haul their remaining supplies to the galley transports. They were to return immediately to Ayr, where they had begun their journey to lay siege to Dunaverty more than two months earlier.

From the wall walk, Angus watched with glee as the ships made their way east in the late afternoon dusk. "Prepare a single signal fire on the southwest wall and set it ablaze upon the midnight hour," he instructed the captain of the guard. "Then seek a fire from the shores of Rathlin as yer answer."

"Aye, Sire," said the captain.

"But, awake me only if ye get no reply," said Angus smiling.

"I understand, Sire," replied the captain. As Angus withdrew from the parapet, the soldier returned to his duty post and ordered his men to the task of setting the firewood for the midnight signal.

. .

At the designated time, miles across the frigid, black sea, a cold and shivering lookout on the high bluff above the caves of Rathlin shouted to his counterpart, "Pass the word, the fire from Dunaverty is sighted!" The second lookout, lower down the hill on the island, signaled to a third, who stood guard nearer to where Robert and his men were gathered in planning their invasion of the Scottish mainland.

Within moments a fourth man in the communication chain, Robert's young squire Andrew, reported directly to his king, who sat cross-legged beside a fire at the mouth of the cave, talking with several men gathered around. "Signal fire from Dunaverty is showin', Sire," the youth said.

"Good! Order our signal fire to be set right quick, as we planned!" returned the king.

"Aye, Sire," said the squire, leaving the cave at a trot. Robert and the others continued to be engaged in a most high level planning council.

Having arrived on Rathlin the day before, King Robert and Sir Donald Macdonald were in high spirits. Because of Robert's brothers' success in the north of Ireland, the rocky ledges at the mouths of the caves had been lined with many men, shouting and waving to the king's single galley in welcome.

Robert and Donald had also been successful, securing numerous galleys, men, and money from, not only Christina of the Isles, but many of her neighbors as well. In Ross and in Sutherland, where the earls were not his allies, many who wanted social change, and others who simply wanted adventure and glory, had joined Robert in Scotland's cause.

The king was excited and well encouraged to see the hundreds of men greeting them, and could now visualize the next round of war shaping up in his favor, even though he was pitting this mostly ragtag army against the military might of England.

In the midnight meeting, Robert pulled a log closer to the fire and sat upon it. The smoke followed drafts in the ancient caves, and in certain places on the bluff, the snow-covered ground seemed to be alive and exhaling wisps of smoke from the fires that warmed the wide-mouthed caves.

"What be our count?" asked Alexander de Brus as he sat on a stone nub with a pen and a tally sheet on his lap, ready to write.

Edward de Brus spoke, "'Bout seven hundred, twenty-five from all Ireland was the reckonin.' Ships from them parts were less than twenty and each can transport 'bout twenty-five, includin' weapons and victuals."

Alexander dutifully committed the figures to the paper before Robert asked, "If ye brought over seven hundred to this island, how is it that ye made it on those few ships?"

"'Tweren't far, Sire. We stood them all upright and lashed them to the masts. There was some pukin', but we made Rathlin without havin' to throw a single one of their sorry Irish arses overboard," chuckled Reginald Crawford, a large Irish chieftain with a great red beard and long curly hair. He had volunteered to help forge the Irish conscripts into a cohesive fighting force.

The men in the council laughed at Crawford's humorous comment, and Robert said, "We got more than a thousand gatherin' up. Some here now will go on to Dunaverty in the morn with Edward and me, and others will come directly from the north in a few days."

Alexander wrote this down to add to the tally.

"What's yer notion 'bout strikin'?" asked Black Douglas as he massaged his shoulder to ease the stiffness from his wound at Dail Righ.

"We're sendin' Alexander and Thomas, and Crawford yonder, and as many Irish as will fit into his boats... without havin' to stand them up... to Galloway," explained Robert with a grin in Crawford's direction.

A large somber man, Malcolm MacQuillan, lord of Kintyre stood. He was dark in complexion and had black hair, but no social graces that were memorable. "What be my part in this fracas?" he asked, as gruff as it was brief.

Robert stood to look at him eye-to-eye, then smiled a bit and said, "I but met ye in person this morn, Sir Malcolm, and know ye by reputation as a fierce and brave warrior, but I know not the one who sits so quietly at yer side."

The big man looked down at the man Robert made reference to as if to make sure it was he before stating, "My cousin, Sir Patrick MacQuillan."

Sir Patrick stood and bowed dutifully, saying, "At yer service, Sire."

"He's young, and not yet battle proven, but he has a fine wit for doin' spy work and such as that," said Malcolm as he put his long arm around his smaller cousin's shoulders to show family support.

Sir Patrick grinned with shyness.

"He helped Sir Donald, here, spy out the garrison in Ayr," bragged Malcolm as he pounded the young man hard upon the back. Patrick regained his balance but nearly fell headlong into the fire. Sir Malcolm had grabbed him by the neck of his chest armor and pulled him again upright just in time.

Patrick recouped his composure and, being embarrassed by the episode, sat quietly down.

There was a roar of laughter around the meet from all but the king.

"That might change the plan for the better," said Robert as he sat back on the log and warmed his bare hands before the fire.

Malcolm MacQuillan returned to his rough rock edge and sat as Robert again spoke, "The notion strikin' me now is to send Sir Patrick and a few others to Galloway in a single boat so that he can see the array of the English there 'bouts."

"I could do that," said young Patrick enthusiastically.

"Aye, he could," agreed Sir Malcolm.

"Then," continued the king, "when we send Thomas, Alexander, Sir Malcolm and Sir Reginald to Galloway, we will know better how to spread out and stay in the field so that we can do away with as many English messengers as can be found. If Edward's lieutenants in Ayr can't get their orders through from Lanercost, they will do nothin'... out of pure fear."

"I am well enough to fight, Sire," remarked Gilbert de la Haye who had been slowly gaining his strength through the fall and winter months. He had always had enough to eat while he convalesced, for King Robert had seen to it that the small struggling band of hard core survivors was well supplied from Finlaggan while they lay hidden outlaws.

Sir Gilbert had been placed in the hospitality of one of the island's families. They had a warm hovel, which had provided more shelter from the harsh winter weather than the tent structures pitched in the dank caves. To one who hadn't known him before his wounds, Sir Gilbert looked truly fit and strong.

"Ye can go with me, then," returned Robert. "From Dunaverty we'll move on to Arran, then to the mainland of Carrick. There I will be at home and can perhaps increase our number and supplies." And I can have my queen fetched from the Orkneys by March, he thought with a smile, for the mere idea of seeing Elizabeth again excited him mightily.

"Let us all get some sleep now," suggested Thomas de Brus, who had already been most nearly put to sleep by the warm fire.

The men agreed by a round of "ayes" and the meet was ended.

. .

By mid-morning the next day, the galley of Robert de Brus appeared along the shores of Dunaverty Harbor from Rathlin Island.

"Ye can run up the royal standards once again, Captain," instructed Sir Angus who watched the approaching galleys from the ramparts of the castle.

"Aye, Milord," he replied with a smile of satisfaction from the trick they played on the English who had left Dunaverty's "park" in shambles when they departed their winter camp.

"King Robert! Welcome!" said Sir Angus, bowing low as the king came ashore.

"Ye takin' care of my business?" asked Robert in a most friendly manner as he clasped the hand of his host.

"Aye, Milord," returned Angus, "ye will find all things in perfect order, as to yer wishes."

"As I expected," replied the king, who then turned to see Angus' brother, Sir Donald Macdonald make his way up from the sea.

"We came in almost the same manner as we left," added Robert.

"Except its not a'stormin'," reminded Angus.

The remaining men beached the galley on the ice-laced shore and tied it to a nearby rock. They then followed the path taken by King Robert and Lord Donald, across the narrow strip of land, into the castle gate and up the narrow, rough cut stairs through heavy stone walls and into the fortress.

The three men laughed and cajoled each other as they walked straight to the great hall.

Angus excused himself to retrieve a strong box from the solar. In a moment, he had it brought into the hall and placed before the king and his brother Edward, who warmed themselves at the hearth. When the box landed on the table, Robert could tell it contained coin of the realm.

"Got my rents, I see," he remarked.

"There were a few stubborn sorts who feigned English fealty," explained Sir Angus, wagging his head as he sat across the table from the king," but others have taken over for them now," he said, smiling and running his finger across his throat to indicate their method of demise.

"What's the tally?"

"Five hundred, sixty-one pounds," answered Angus proudly, and his pudgy fingers pushed the box across the table.

Robert shook his head and sighed, "Thought t'would be more somehow."

Donald looked knowingly at his brother and said, "This is not a business deal. This is survival."

"I had ...certain expenses," lamented Sir Angus, tossing his hands aloft and twisting his face as if to say he had acted honorably in his duty to collect and amass the rents according to the king's orders.

"What was the percentage ye calculated?" asked Donald.

Robert looked puzzled.

"A mere ten, brother," was the response.

"Bringing the total to...?"

"Six hundred, twenty-four pounds," said Angus without further hesitation.

"'Tis well," said Robert, satisfied, as he opened the box to inspect the contents closer.

"Ye will have this and the ten percent more," demanded Donald.

"As ye wish, my brother," returned Angus. "Ye are the head of the family. There is no further argument," he added in resignation.

"Thank ye," replied Donald, sardonically. "We do have a war to win here. Then tradin' will be much more profitable."

"Aye," said Angus somewhat appeased.

"We'll take a portion with us for immediate expenses and leave the remainder here in yer care, Sir Angus. I shall, from time to time, send messengers for certain sums and ye will turn over those sums to the men who bring ye the messages," ordered the king.

"I understand, Sire," returned Sir Angus. "I will send for my factor now to set all the figures to paper... includin' ten percent additional."

Donald smiled approvingly.

"Good," said Robert, adding, "We have another two hundred twenty-seven pounds in coin and bar gold to add to our war chest."

"Most interestin'," replied Angus, almost salivating at the thought and unable to resist a bit of wheedling. "Would ye be of a mind to invest some of this largesse, say... in slave tradin' from the east, Milord?"

Robert laughed heartily at the little round man, "Angus, ye know the world, but ye know me not!"

"I am not offended," said Angus as his factor entered the hall.

"No offence intended," said the king, "only a kind of compliment."

"Then I am honored," returned Sir Angus with a smile and a courteous bow.

"One other item," said Robert.

"Aye, Milord?" replied Angus.

"Ye need to set another signal fire toward Rathlin to let them know all is well for more to come ashore on the morrow," said the king.

"Aye, Sire," again replied Angus with another bow. He then turned his full attention to the factor, to explain the administration of the small fortune on which so much depended.

Gilbert de la Haye

JANUARY 30ᵗʰ 1307
THE ISLE OF ARRAN

'The Black' Douglas and Sir Gilbert de la Haye, commanding a small force of thirty-five battle-hardened men in two galleys, kept close to the shore of Kintyre for most of the day so the lookouts on the Isle of Arran could not see them approach. As the gray day turned into the blackness of night, Douglas ordered the captains of the two galleys to row them around the southern shore toward Brodick Bay on the eastern side of Arran, where the English governor of the island held the castle.

The wind was so horrific that the sails were worse than useless, and the oarsmen had to row all the way through the huge swells. It took masterful piloting skills to maneuver around the rocky shore in the gathering blackness, but the Macdonalds' smugglers had traversed this shoreline many times before in equally harsh squalls.

This venture was King Robert's first step in his return to the mainland of Scotland and he left it to two of his most trusted captains, while he remained temporarily at Dunaverty with the Macdonald brothers, waiting for more men to come from the northern islands.

"If we had not the needle and a lamp, we would have been sore put to find this place on such a dark night, I'm thinkin'," remarked Sir Gilbert as he struggled to maintain his balance on the pitching boat.

"Aye, but they would have caught sight of us quick enough in the daylight," returned Black Douglas. The two galleys dropped anchor just off shore under cover of a blowing murkiness and a large cliff, a few hundred paces south of the governor's fortress. The water was icy cold and the warriors were truly thankful that the boats each towed a tiny esquif in its wake. An esquif held only a few Scots each trip, but all eventually made it ashore safely, and much drier and warmer than if they had swum to the pebbly beach.

By daylight, the winds and the ocean were greatly calmed, but a thick fog remained as the small Scottish band made their way to the dock below the castle. There, three large English cargo galleys lay ready for offloading, having just beaten the blustery gale to the somewhat sheltered bay.

"Ye think we could pirate those vessels, Gilbert?" asked Douglas when he realized what was at hand.

"I know nothin' of masterin' a ship, and I wager ye'd come up shy on that one yerself," whispered Haye. They crept closer for a better look.

"What's to it except rowin' and twistin' the rudder?" returned Douglas.

Haye smiled, "Ye're daft man."

Suddenly they heard voices coming from the wooden steps that zigzagged to the castle above.

"English!" exclaimed Haye too loudly, causing the English troops on the steps to stop talking and listen. The two Scotsmen froze in place and the English, hearing nothing more, continued on down the steps, thinking it must have been a gull they heard. Haye and Douglas slipped back into the fog amongst the shadows of the large rocks to signal their waiting men to come forward.

The thirty or so unsuspecting English soldiers got to the waiting galleys and began hefting the large sacks of flour, meats, small barrels of molasses, wine, and other victuals, clothing, and weapons, and started to climb the steps.

About the time the sun would have been breaking the horizon, had it been a clear day, the Scots jumped upon the working party from hiding places among the rock formations along the path.

The English soldiers, thinking they were there alone, were initially terrified into immobility by the screaming war cries that emanated from the grayness surrounding them, and before they regained their senses they were suddenly under attack, seemingly from all sides.

Once the voices were accompanied by human form, the English instinctively dropped their loads and tried to draw their weapons, but it was too late.

The moment of surprise was all the Scots needed to take the day.

James Douglas was on the big man leading the line up the steps, his broad sword finding the man's belly even before he could drop the sack he carried.

Sir Gilbert hit his man with a body throw that sent the man tumbling off the stairs and into the snow-covered grass bordering them. He hacked the man's throat once.

Haye quickly moved to the next, who came toward him with sword in hand and great fear in his eyes. That man had not a chance, for another Scot swung his broadsword to the back of his neck and Sir Gilbert simultaneously slashed his chest.

It was all over within a hundred breaths of air. Every English soldier lay dead or near death on the crimson steps of the dock.

Not a Scot lay among them.

"Good morn's work!" congratulated Douglas letting out a mighty war whoop. He repeatedly slammed his sword on his shield, holding it toward the castle wall. His men followed suit and the pickets on the wall soon took notice of the tumult below, but could not tell the source through the layer of thick fog.

"Report to the governor what we hear!" shouted one of the pickets to his companion, who ran pell-mell to awaken the master. To another the first picket ordered, "Shut the gate! Be quick about it!"

But the Scots had gathered up some of the scattered supplies and retreated to the cliffs to have a wee bit of contraband breakfast.

As the fog intermittently cleared on that cold January morning, the entire English garrison of Brodick Castle was armed for war and looking out in all directions for the enemy, who seemed to have vanished with the mists. The Scots remained hidden among the rocks and brushy grasses, thinking that they might draw out more from within the walls.

Suddenly, a guard on the seaward wall pointed to the stairs to the dock and shouted, "My God! Do ye see!?" just before he became ill and ran off to retch. A second man froze in horror to recognize his compatriots' bodies scattered helter-skelter amidst their own gore.

"What?" asked the governor as he came hastily to the guard's side and looked over the wall. But there was no need for the stupefied man to answer, for the governor saw plainly enough; his thirty-man detail lay cut to bloody ribbons on the steps and in the snow.

"Sound the alarm!" he shouted.

"We're already at battle posts, Excellency," said the governor's second in command. Coming to the governor's side to see the carnage for himself, he gasped and turned away from the scene in revulsion.

"Were you not to command that work party?" asked the governor through clenched teeth.

"And I was right ready to join them when I heard them down there screamin', but..."

"Right ready, eh?!" interrupted the governor, who took note of the nightclothes beneath his subordinate's hastily donned cloak.

"Yes, Excellency," weakly returned the underling.

The governor glared with disgust at the errant man and in increasing volume placed full blame upon his head. After a moment's pause, he more calmly, but no less disgustedly, said, "You will personally take a contingent outside the walls to investigate what manner of man is our enemy, if he remains hereabouts!"

The underwarden sighed and went about gathering thirty men more to see to the governor's bidding.

A short while later, the gate opened and English troops in chain mail and upper body armor carefully emerged and moved stealthily toward the dreaded staircase.

"More fodder for our blades," whispered Black Douglas with a resolute smile.

"Aye," returned Sir Gilbert, "Jamie lad, ye like my new uniform?"

"Aye," replied Douglas lightly, "it looks a bit like mine."

"Aye," agreed Gilbert with a smile, for among the grabbed items from the galley were ten English uniforms, possibly destined for new recruits to the English garrison. Instead, they had been distributed to whichever of the hardy Scots they fit, including de la Haye and the Douglas.

As the cautiously searching English approached, the ten Scots disguised in the seized uniforms joined with the English troops by nimbly falling in behind them.

Once ready, James Douglas signaled his raiders with a great war cry and the searchers became surprised victims, attacked from the rear by those they thought were their own, and from the front by screaming banshees who sprang from nowhere and everywhere.

The English watching from the wall were confused at seeing their fellow soldiers fall upon and slay each other, and indistinct spirits jump out of the mists and join the attack.

The governor ordered the gate, already shut and guarded, be barred tight against anyone, English or spirit, who might wish to enter. Sanctuary of the castle, for those outside its walls at that point, was denied.

The soldiers within the castle now looked upon each other as possibly being bewitched, and they soon began to gather in small groups for mutual protection from each other.

"Oh, God," prayed the governor aloud as he watched the battle's end, "save us from this great band of evil spirits who have us in their power!" Then he thought, I have but forty men left; I dare not risk them to be slaughtered by such a superior force.

And so, he remained fully alert and shut tight in his castle, with his only defense being soldiers who didn't trust each other.

There were no prisoners taken that morning and again, not a Scottish life was lost.

"Send a message to the captains of our galleys to return to Dunaverty and report to King Robert that the Isle of Arran has been secured and we are well provisioned," ordered James Douglas to Haye.

"Aye," said Sir Gilbert with a smile and a slight bow, "with the utmost pleasure. We takin' the castle?"

"Nay, I want it not," replied the Douglas, "we'll stay in yonder wood 'til King Robert comes, no doubt getting' fat by the time he arrives."

. .

And so, in the copse on the gentle slope behind the castle, the thirty-five Scots took the pirated provisions from the three ships and set up winter camp, keeping the affrighted castle under siege.

Sir James Douglas had many more fires lit at night than his few men needed, to give illusion to the watchers from the castle that there were many more of them.

Cuthbert

FEBRUARY 1ST 1307
DUNAVERTY CASTLE

"Good news, brother," said Edward de Brus as he approached the king, who stood on the edge of Dunaverty Castle's western wall. This was the precipice from which Robert and his men had descended to the waiting boats in their escape from Lords Menteith and Botetourt the previous autumn. Then, his men numbered less than a hundred, and Robert had not known how he was to come back; he simply had known he must.

"What is yer news?" asked Robert introspectively, without taking his eyes from the sea.

"Douglas' galleys have returned with news that he has Arran subdued," answered Edward with a smile as he came to the side of his brother. Robert did not respond or change his mood, but continued to survey the ocean.

Edward, too, looked into the distance and enjoyed the magnificent view before adding, "Ye lookin' for more galleys today, Robbie?"

"Six more are due on the morrow, and yonder, twenty-five rest at anchor," said Robert pointing below him to Dunaverty Harbor.

"Where we puttin' more?" asked Edward as he pulled the hood to his surcoat tighter about his head in the stout northeast wind. "We've got men scattered about the castle like cord wood for the fire."

"Just keep them warm and fed, and busy gettin' prepared," replied Robert. "We'll be leavin' here for Arran in a week to match Thomas and Alexander's landin' in Galloway."

"Aye," replied Edward.

"We need to be landin' in Carrick about the ninth of the month," said Robert, and for the first time he took his eyes from the sea for a moment and looked at his brother. "And I need for ye to handle a task for me, and quietly." His brother nodded acceptance. "I want ye to scout among the lads to discover a clever one who knows the lands of Carrick, and can move among them without hesitation or arousing suspicion."

"I know one now, name of Cuthbert," said Sir Edward, "grew up in our parts and is quick-witted and prudent."

"Cuthbert... Somehow I know that name. Then the next question is easy," said Robert.

"Next question?" asked Edward.

"Can he be trusted to keep his own counsel?"

"As well as any man not put to the rack," returned Edward.

"I guess I mean, has he a penchant for greed?"

Edward thought a moment before responding, "He has been with us since before Methven, and seems a reliable sort to me in that respect." They both then turned toward the great hall wherein to warm themselves.

"Fetch him to me, and send word to one of our more ingenious smugglers to ready his vessel for a dark run to Carrick, tonight."

"Aye, Rob," replied Edward as he went to search out Cuthbert.

The king went into the great hall where his squire, Andrew, sat polishing the king's new breastplate, heavily festooned with gold and silver and given to him by his sister-in-law, Christina of the Isles. Robert instantly recalled her presentation speech. "Ye'll be needin' this when ye triumph over yer enemies," she had said matter-of-factly, as if it were assured.

Andrew suddenly realized the king had come into his presence and jumped hastily to his feet, dropping the heavy breastplate to the flagstone floor with a loud clang.

Robert winced and shook his head. "Now ye're dentin' up my new armor quicker than the English are havin' a chance at it, lad."

"Uh... I'm... I'm sorry, Milord," he stammered, reaching to retrieve the heavy armor.

As the boy heaved the breastplate onto the large wooden table, Robert came to inspect the damage, saying after a cursory examination, "I guess if it won't hold up to such a droppin', I surely don't want to wear it in a fight."

Andrew unwittingly giggled and, realizing he shouldn't have, put his hand over his mouth. As the king glanced sternly at the startled boy, the youth was so merry-eyed that Robert had to laugh out loud. Andrew joined with him so that the two of them made the whole hall ring with laughter.

In the midst of the high spirits Edward came into the hall with another, less imposing man, and was amazed at the laughter. Robert had been so serious of late that it seemed all the merriment had left his soul. Thus, when he realized the laughter emanated from his brother, and though he had no idea the nub of the fun, he began to laugh also.

"My Lord King," addressed Edward at last.

"Aye," said Robert controlling his chortle as he saw Edward was not alone.

"This be the one ye seek," returned Edward.

The king stood to greet the man. "Don't I know ye?" asked Robert, his eyes brought to bear upon the newcomer.

"We had a... a... wee chat, in the wood after Methven, Sire," stammered Cuthbert.

"Aye, I remember," the king answered, though his memory was faint.

The three sat at the table, causing Andrew to move down to the end to finish his polishing chore. He licked his thumb and rubbed it briskly upon a new scratch he noticed on the edge of it, and immediately went to burnishing it with his yellowish chamois skin while the men continued their talk.

Robert abruptly recalled seeing the fellow, rough hewn and agile, climbing to their hideout in the forest a year before, and it brought back the whole conversation. He asked, "How be yer son?"

"I've not seen him since his birthin'... Ye remember me, My King?" the surprised man asked.

"Red plaid sash," replied Robert." Where's yer sash?"

"No doubt 'tis layin' rottin' in one of them winterin' caves on Rathlin, Sire," he replied, scratching his head.

"Tough winter, for sure," said Edward though he had spent only a small portion of the winter there.

Robert observed the man a moment before saying, "Cuthbert, I need a special man for an important and secret job... and my brother, Sir Edward, thinks ye are the only man up to the task."

Cuthbert said not a word but looked left and right before leaning in closely to hear his special orders from his king. "Aye, Sire, I'll not fail ye!" he whispered.

"No goin' off to birth another bairn," cautioned Robert.

The man flushed red and said quietly, "If the woman has a babe now, Sire, she'll have to birth it all by herself... for she got it all by herself!"

Edward turned away to keep from laughing, and Robert had to strive to keep a straight face. Finally, the king said, "I mean ye must not abandon yer mission for any reason."

"So I swear before God, My Lord King," he whispered, solemnly.

Robert now also whispered, to show that he too considered the task vital and clandestine. "A galley will take ye to the shore of Carrick, this night."

"I am ready," hissed Cuthbert.

The king continued speaking cautiously, "There, ye will move amongst the citizenry and spy out the minds and hearts of the people, to puzzle whether they will support us when we come to liberate them from English rule."

"But... ye are their lord... and their king! Why would they not honor ye in welcome?" asked Cuthbert somewhat confused.

"That's exactly the question I need to have answered. Thus you must let them not know ye are from me, but only that ye are a caird, or a pilgrim, and know few in the area," instructed Robert.

"And the ones what do know me?" asked Cuthbert.

"Tell them naught of our gatherin' or of what I have told ye. Say only that ye have lost interest in the war and are makin' yer way to yer home," said the king.

"Aye, Milord," said Cuthbert, his eyes wide with the import of his mission.

"If the people are ready to rise up in our favor, then in the early afternoon on the ninth day, today being the first, light a blaze on the rise just north of Turnberry. It must be big enough that the smoke by day and the glow of the flame by night can be seen from the Isle of Arran," instructed the king.

"Done," he assured King Robert. "But what if the answer be no? What do I do then?"

"Then, Cuthbert," the king paused but a moment and looked the man directly in the eyes, "I suspect that ye had better go home to yer wife and sons, and never mention this to a soul." The man's eyes filled with tears and Robert knew that the man had read his meaning.

"I will do this right smartly, Sire. And I will wait for ye to come ashore that I can join up with ye again," added the patriot.

"I know ye will," said Robert, slapping the fellow on the shoulder. "Now go, and find yerself some rugged clothing, that ye may be warm and fit for the important part ye are about to play."

The proud man stood up to reach his tallest height, then bowed low before leaving the hall to prepare for his spy mission.

"Ye reckon he will do right?" asked Sir Edward quietly after the newly appointed spy had left the room.

"I reckon ye picked him for a reason... and I know him to be loyal and trustworthy, if not exceptionally clever," replied Robert. "I expect he will get the job done rightly enough."

Both men sat thinking about Cuthbert's question, "But what if the answer be no?" and neither wanted to mention it to the other, though the question would haunt the both of them for seven nights and seven days more.

"What about Alexander and Thomas?" asked Edward trying to dispel the notion.

"Send word to them by galley on the morrow that all remains set for the ninth," quietly ordered Robert.

"I shall see to it personally," said Edward equally as hushed.

James "The Black" Douglas

FEBRUARY 8ᵗʰ 1307
ISLE OF ARRAN - EARLDOM OF CARRICK

With Sir Patrick MacQuillan, cousin to the Lord of Kintyre, spying out the shore lands of Galloway for the landing of Thomas and Alexander Brus' mostly Irish army, and Cuthbert spying out the earldom of Carrick for King Robert's invasion of the mainland, the die was soon cast for the immediate determination of the fates of many.

Robert had assembled nearly five hundred fighting men and thirty-three galleys for the Carrick assault, and they all set sail in the early morning of February the eighth from the harbor at Dunaverty.

He would first join James 'The Black' Douglas and Gilbert de la Haye who, with little effort from their small band, were keeping the English garrison at Brodick castle drawn up as tight as a frightened turtle in its shell. It was late in the day when the thirty-three Scottish vessels were pulled ashore in Brodick Bay, and Sir James and Sir Gilbert came down to the water's edge to greet their king.

The wind was biting cold and the sky, gray, making the daylight wane even earlier in the winter afternoon.

Many of the new arrivals had surcoats with hoods, and tightly woven wool kirtles and trews to keep them warm. Others came with motley rags tied around their heads and hands, for that was all they had. None of them were much for fancy armor or clothes, but they were fierce and well-armed island and highland warriors, all of them hoping to profit from their adventure in one way or another.

"Trimmin' the time a tad close, ye reckon?" asked 'The Black' Douglas as he approached the king.

"We'll get no signal 'til the morrow," replied Robert as the men piled out of the galleys to muster on shore and await orders. "Where are ye bivouacked and who is in the castle?"

"Fearful English, Sire, but under whose command we know not," chimed in Sir Gilbert. "We've been livin' in the wood on the hill behind the castle, just keepin' an eye on things."

"I see ye survived that Dail Righ fracas," said Neil Campbell as he came up behind Sir Gilbert to join the group.

"Neil!" shouted Gilbert with delighted surprise. "Ye're still with the livin'!"

"And why not?" returned Campbell, grinning broadly.

"Hain't heard from ye in quite a spell, that's why," Gilbert answered as James Douglas greeted Neil with a nod of his head and a slap on the back, and Neil nodded and smiled in acknowledgment.

"Been off collectin' up Campbells for the fight is all," said Neil throwing his arm around Gilbert in comradeship.

Gilbert winced slightly.

"Hain't quite got yer sword arm full back, have ye?" bantered Sir Neil, sounding lighter hearted about that subject than he felt.

"Near 'nough to whip the likes of ye," returned Sir Gilbert with a smile and an elbow jabbed into Neil's ribs.

"What's stinkin'?" asked Sir Edward as he arrived to join the others.

James explained, "Aw, that's fifty or sixty English we killed when we first got here. If ye think the smell is bad now, ye should wait 'til they warm up, again.

"The scavengin' sea birds feed off the carrion, but they've not yet done away with 'em entirely."

He wagged his head in the direction of the castle and added, "The others won't come out and bury them for fear of gettin' dead themselves. Don't know where they got such a notion!" he laughed, as did the others.

Ignoring the stench, Robert looked up the hill to the walled fortress. "What are ye doin' to them on the hill to keep them cowered so?"

"Swear," said James Douglas shaking his head, "we've done nothin' since the first day, save sit on yonder hill so's they could see that we're still about."

"Humph!" said the king, eyeing the fortress above them, "whoever commands must be the timid sort."

"Aye. I cannot figure him," returned the Douglas.

"Some of our men seem to be scantily dressed for the weather," said Sir Gilbert as he watched the new arrivals continue to pile out of the boats and onto the shore.

"Aye," returned Edward, "we stripped all we could from Dunaverty and came up a wee bit shy."

"Well, there's three galleys along the dock yonder, still with considerable stores of victuals, and clothin' and such, if ye can get yer lads to bear the stink 'round and about," Gilbert pointed.

"I think we can manage," said Edward, and he walked away, grabbing several men close by to form a work party and gather the booty before complete dark set in.

"Leave aboard what ye don't need right away," ordered Robert. "We'll sail them with us on the morrow."

Robert set night pickets on the fleet, for he did not trust the fearful occupants of the castle, who had been so well behaved under the past circumstances. His faint-heartedness to the contrary, the English commander possibly would not elect to continue his quiet behavior with such an enticing target as this row of galleys laying easily within his grasp.

As it turned out, the pickets might as well have lain asleep all night.

. .

The next day, the gray overcast broke allowing some patchy sun to shine across the landscape, but the blustery winds remained, and the water in the bay became choppier than it had been the previous evening.

In spite of the weather, the men generally seemed to be in a rowdy mood, with their bellies full and their backsides covered in English-made clothes. And they were cheered even more when Robert and Edward walked among them to speak of small matters and size up their potential for the coming fight.

. .

About the noon hour, the two brothers left the camp and went toward the south, near the abandoned castle of Kildonan, to hold vigil on a bluff overlooking the sea toward Carrick, that gray line of gently sloping hills upon the horizon.

For more than two hours the two men sat and waited. They built a fire in a cave below the bluff to keep themselves warm. The sun helped, but it was the cave's shelter from the western winds that provided the most benefit.

"I can almost see Thomas and Alexander takin' their galleys across to Loch Ryan," said Edward pointing across the sea toward the south.

"Even at this height, ye can't see twenty miles seaward," replied Robert quietly.

"I know, but I also know they're on their way right now," responded

Edward as he sat to re-warm his hands by the fire.

"Aye," agreed Robert, "if the plan's runnin' smooth."

Then suddenly, as they sat huddled near the fire in the cave Edward jumped up and shouted, "There 'tis!" An occasional puff of smoke could be seen on the Carrick shore in spite of the wind.

"That's smoke a'right," agreed Robert as he stood for a better look.

"Cuthbert came through for us on this one, he did," cried Edward excitedly, pounding his brother on the shoulder. "The people *want* us to come to them... they'll join and fight with us. Our seven hundred will become a thousand, perhaps even five thousand and..."

"And yer wit is gettin' ahead of what ye have in yer hand, little brother," interrupted Robert with a laugh that belied his protest. "Let's see for ourselves what's what when we get there, tonight."

"Aye," agreed Edward, realizing his brother was right in his prudence and caution, but they both stood, smiling, and watched the struggling plume of smoke.

. .

Daylight was failing when the Scottish army at last finished embarking on the thirty-three galleys in which they had come with King Robert, plus the three they had taken from the English garrison at Castle Brodick.

Setting off with high hopes, they rowed eastward toward the trail of smoke that drifted on the wind from a small pinprick of light across the darkening channel. To give themselves something to occupy their thoughts and hands, many of the warriors filled in as oarsmen, spelling the regulars.

Hard and heavy and deep into the night, the Scots rowed in the choppy waters, not using their sails for fear of easy detection by the enemy, ever following the light from the fire until it died out, just before they reached the shore of Carrick, north of Turnberry Castle.

Cuthbert waited in the bush not far from the smoldering embers. When the half-frozen man was about to leave the shoreline and seek shelter, he heard what he thought were oars being pulled through the oarlocks of many boats.

"Hail in the boats!" shouted Cuthbert from the bush, his heart pounding so hard that he could hear the blood rushing through his ears. What if he were mistaken and hailed a band of English? How would he explain his presence on the beach at such an hour?

Nevertheless, he strained to listen for a response.

Robert could not be sure he heard the voice across the hundred paces of lapping water, the wind, and the rhythm of the oars.

"Hold yer rowin'" ordered King Robert quietly to the captain.

At the captain's signal, the oars were shipped and the order was silently passed along to the other vessels.

Then it came again, faint but audible, "Hail in the boats!"

"Sounds like our man, it does," remarked Edward perking his ear shoreward.

"Row for shore," Robert ordered the boat captain, adding, "Tell the rest to hold at sea 'til we get to the nub of this."

He had become suspicious that all was not well ashore and drew his great claymore, just in case things were not as they seemed. Edward and the other twenty or so warriors likewise prepared for possible trickery.

Robert was the first to pitch himself overboard as the galley's bottom grated against the shore. His boots splashed as he walked cautiously onto the beach toward the dying embers, trying to locate his spy.

At the sound of dry grasses being parted and brush cracking beneath another's tread, the wary king, every muscle tense and ready to fight, turned to face whoever approached.

At once he recognized Cuthbert coming down to the water's edge from his hiding place.

Damned spooky, thought Robert as Cuthbert came out to greet him.

"Cuthbert!" he called, "be ye alone?" Robert had hoped there would be at least some Carrickmen with him and ready to join his army.

"Aye, Milord..." started Cuthbert, as he drew near. The man opened his mouth to say something, but he knew not what more to say. Instead, he threw himself to his knees before the king.

"Yer signal fire served us passin' well," the king congratulated his agent, though he was somewhat mystified at his groveling.

"I... uh... I..." stammered Cuthbert.

"Out with yer thought, man," commanded Robert as he sheathed his sword.

"I... was not... the one who set the fire," said Cuthbert sheepishly.

Sir Edward came to the side of the two men with a lit torch and the others from the boat crowded the beach at a respectful distance to catch the news. The oarsmen remained aboard their craft and the other galleys lingered offshore as ordered.

"The fire was set on the day and time we agreed it would be set! What do ye mean that ye set it not?!" Robert said angrily as he took the small man's clothing into his large hands and lifted him up from the ground.

In the torchlight, the two men's faces were so close that the breath vapors from their noses and mouths mixed midway betwixt them. "If not ye, who? Who signaled us here from Brodick?" the king demanded.

"They... they meant not to signal ye... they were merely serfs workin' under another's orders," explained the terrified infiltrator. "They set and kept the blaze with underbrush cleared from yon new field... they prepare it to be cultivated in the spring! That's all... Sire."

Robert let go of the man's garment and Cuthbert stood shivering, whether from cold or fear mattered not. The three men stood mute for a moment, until Cuthbert tried further to explain what had happened. "I was alarmed when I saw the smoke coming up from this place, and ran to see what was its cause. When I arrived and saw the workers clearin' the field, I could think of no way to stop them, or the fire, without giving us all away to the English." Tears rolled down his weathered cheeks.

Finally, Edward spoke. "So, if ye set not the fire, is the mood in Carrick against us?" he asked.

"The... the people of Carrick will not... give aid to ye, or yer cause, in any way," answered Cuthbert. "Lord Henry Percy is earl of these lands of Carrick now, and he has English troops layin' about 'most everywhere, waitin' for ye to return, though he expects ye in the spring, he does."

"The damned bastards have taken yer lands, Robert!" cursed Edward.

"Did ye expect different?" asked the king. "Edward already had taken Annandale. Why not Carrick as well?"

"Damn his eyes!" the frustrated Edward spat upon the stone strewn beach.

Robert continued to query his spy. "The English troops, how many and where are they?"

"'Bout two hundred livin' amongst the people in Turnberry village, and another hundred or so in the castle itself... and many more... I know not their number... scattered across the land a'keepin' watch," said the man.

"And the people of Carrick?" asked Robert. "What of them?"

Shaking his head the informer said, "They be sore afraid of Sir Percy... and they be scared of ye, too, Lord King. Broad and large of it is, they care not for yer cause, and they see ye have no wins on the battlefield... and for a people who want only to be safe and live a life without fear, they see ye not as their savior, but as a danger to them. They'll go with whoever has the uppermost hand, Sire, and right now they see that as bein' the English," the sorrowful Cuthbert grew silent.

It was hard news for Robert to take, worse than that his lands and properties had been taken and given to another. His own people, who knew him well, had not the courage to strike out with him to rid their lands of the invaders and become free Scots again.

"And they prefer the English as their overlords?" asked the king pushing for enough information to make a decision on whether to continue into Carrick or reconsider the plan.

"Nay! Nay, they like them not! But, 'tis about as much as they like ye not, Milord," said the spy.

Edward spoke up through gritted teeth. "I know not what ye have in mind, brother, but for my part, I am ready for the fight to begin, here! We have our men waitin' out there in the galleys and ready to fight, and I'm not for tellin' them that we will just slink away with our tails betwixt our legs! Whether for good or for ill, I stand here on our fathers' land, ready to live on it once more, or be buried in it! Aye, *this* is where *I* remain!"

"Well said, brother," agreed King Robert, though his disappointment was obvious. After a moment, he took a great breath and began anew, "As ye have spoke, so shall it be. Have the rest of the men put ashore and we'll serve up Lord Percy with a wee bit of a surprise this night."

"Aye, Robert, we will!" swore Edward, and he turned to go signal the other galleys to put in.

"Ye are well right," returned Robert, but the fresh thought of failure bade him alter his orders. "Edward! When the men are disembarked, order all the galleys, save one, back to Dunaverty to drop off any supplies they have remaining. From there, they are to be returned to the ones that lent them to us. We'll have no further need of them, for with God's help, we will not leave this mainland, again!"

And almost in the shadow of his own Turnberry Castle, Robert de Brus' small liberation army came quietly ashore and stood in a freshly cleared planting field.

As King Robert gave them their orders, the half-moon shown brightly betwixt the swiftly moving clouds on that cold February night, giving everything about them a silvery gleam. This was the only light they would use to carry forth with Robert's plan.

. .

The English troops garrisoned among the populace, either in their homes or in tents surrounding Turnberry Village, had retired early, as they had come to do as a matter of course since occupying the village and castle months ago. Some of the more fortunate ones had arranged for sexual pleasures of an evening, while others went to a sound sleep after a rowdy time at the tavern. Only the scant pickets were alive to that part of the world, and they, merely because it was too cold to stay still for long.

Robert and Edward led the retaliatory raid on the English that night. Learning the sentries' movements in short order, the Scots were soon able to sneak up to each one and silently do away with him. No quarter was given, and they knew none could be expected if they were caught. So, in the crisp winter moonlight, while millions of stars shone in the heavens, the throats of the hapless pickets were quietly sliced and their bodies eased softly to the ground. The Scots then went from house to house and tent to tent, slaying the enemy in his bed as he slept. No English soldier or Comyn Scot in the town lived to see the morrow's light, for the Scottish and Irish troops of Robert Brus were most efficient at their task.

FEBRUARY 9th 1307
GALLOWAY AND LOCH RYAN

Meanwhile, some twenty miles to the south, the English in Galloway were a far different matter, as the Scots came to the designated place on the northeastern shore of Lock Ryan.

The moon's light continually changed from bright to dark as the clouds moved swiftly before it. Most of the eighteen galleys of the Scots' southern flank rowed quietly to the shore.

"Ye see Sir Patrick's lantern aglow?" asked Malcolm MacQuillan from aboard the lead galley.

"Nay," replied Sir Thomas Brus, "nary a beam."

"Well, naught's landin' 'til we see a light along the shore."

The men in the lead boat strained their eyes into the gloom. Thomas leaned out over the bow of the galley and into the darkness so far that he lost his balance and, had it not been for Alexander, would have fallen overboard. As it was, Thomas' brother caught the back of his belt and prevented his going all the way over the side, but his arm and shoulder got soaked in the freezing water. It was all the two of them could do to wrest his weight back aboard.

Alexander shook his head in disbelief. "Thomas, ye're big, but yer brain goes beggin'!"

Thomas smiled sheepishly as he wrapped himself in a cloak, but it was lost to the exasperated Alexander in the darkness.

"Look... *Look!*" shouted the Irish Chieftain Reginald Crawford, as restrained as he could manage in his excitement. He stood bolt upright in the galley and pointed toward the shore, "A light!"

"So it is," agreed Alexander and he motioned for the captain and the oarsmen to move closer to shore.

The four leaders were the first to step out of the vessel into the shallow water as the keel grounded itself on the shore.

They were straightaway followed by the men in the first ship, and as the others beached, the Irish warriors on board rushed onto the shore with drawn weapons. Once gathered, the entourage made its way into the thicket toward the small flickering lantern.

After picking their way through the scraggly winter underbrush, a surprising distance toward the light, Thomas de Brus stopped and, drawing his claymore, looked about in all directions.

"This hain't suitin' me, brother," he whispered to Alexander, who did likewise. More cautiously, they continued leading their company of warriors into the wood, their senses keenly alert to anything unusual.

All but two galleys had come ashore, they having fallen behind the others while still a good distance off. The two vessels were only just reaching the landing site and found their comrades had completely disappeared from their galleys and the woods beyond.

They tried to find their trail, but could not follow it far because of the intermittent moonlight, and they dared not try to yell or otherwise signal.

The Brus brothers and their hardy band of nearly three hundred and fifty Irish came to a clearing, whereupon they saw the twinkling light still farther beyond them, on the edge of the far side.

"Ye know," said Alexander softly to Thomas, "seems to me like that light has been movin' and drawin' us deeper into this open ground."

"Seems so, brother," agreed Thomas, and he turned to warn the followers who were strung out through the woods behind him.

Only one syllable escaped his bearded lips when clan Macdougall Scots, mixed in with a greater number of English, screamed their bloody war cries and attacked the Brus band mercilessly.

Mostly, confusion characterized the slaughter that followed.

Swords, battle-axes, and daggers flashed wildly in the moon's temperamental light.

Many on both sides were slain by their own men in the chaos.

Screams of agony rent the air, and savage and angry war cries combined with the rumblings of numerous weapons cleaving flesh and bone and clashing with other accoutrements of war, until most on both sides lay dead and dying.

Those in the two galleys that had not made landfall with the others, heard the screams and din of battle emanating from the blackness of the wood. Their eyes widened and strained to see any hint that might let them know the situation.

But, there was not a commander among them to give orders to go 'hither or thither,' and so, fear drove them to move hastily away.

As the latecomers pushed their ships off the shore and rowed as arduously as they could to get away from that place, archers from the woods made the shore and shot fire-tipped arrows at them as they receded.

Most of the glowing missiles flew over the heads of the fleeing Scots or, falling short, landed harmlessly in the water, hissing as the cold water extinguished them.

The oarsmen were strong and frightened, and they rowed to the maximal limits of their strength until they felt their arms would separate from their shoulders. The vessels, which had found it impossible to keep up with the others, now moved quite rapidly away from the shore.

In spite of their haste, several arrows from the archers found the galleys' hulls, and the craven laggards had to lean over the low gunnels and scoop water with their hands to extinguish the fire before it spread. Then, they disappeared into the pre-dawn darkness.

In the bloody clearing, Dungal Macdouall, leader of Clan Macdouall, came forth with the tiny candle lantern he had used to lead the ill-fated mission into the debacle. As he moved through the mass of flesh and weapons he stopped and leaned down to see the faces of any who yet moaned or otherwise exhibited signs of life.

The apparent dead he viewed not, for he was looking for specific men who might be alive, men who could be identified on sight only by himself and but one other who accompanied him in the grisly search.

Neil Campbell

FEBRUARY 9ᵗʰ 1307
TURNBERRY VILLAGE - CARRICK

At the village of Turnberry, even before the first light of dawn the next morning, wails and lamentations were heard, first from one, then another, and soon the town was filled with cries from women who awoke to find their lovers killed beside them in their beds. Then, it was not long before cursing and screaming arose from those of 'some means' who found they were to surrender their horses, cattle, edible stores and such, with or without their consent, to the devils who had struck in the night.

The whole town was soon in an uproar and the people frightened out of their wits. Responsible men of the village drew their swords and, carrying torches, began traveling from one calamity to another in search of the murderers and thieves. The Brus forces managed to avoid some of them, and those who happened upon the bloodstained and rugged Scots usually threw down their weapons and ran. It was just after daylight that the town was declared to be in the hands of the Bruses.

Hearing all the commotion from the village, the alarms sounded early within the castle. The huge gate was closed and barred, and the wall sentries reinforced by threes, but they merely reported what movements they saw in the town below them, and made no attempt at rescue.

Robert strode through the little village of houses and tents to review the booty of livestock and foodstuffs and valuables assembled by his men.

"What about them in the castle, Robert?" asked Neil Campbell who stood with Turnberry Castle as his background.

"Who's within?" asked Robert.

"Sir Percy may yet be, but we can't be sure. He is said to have been there last night before we arrived," Neil answered.

"Wonder why they didn't come to save their own?" said Robert.

Sir Neil shrugged his broad shoulders. "Didn't know it was happenin', I reckon."

Robert looked past Neil to the castle. "Reckon."

"One other thing," added Sir Neil.

"What's that?"

"A messenger may have slipped out to the east, presumably toward Lanercost and Edward."

"Damnation!" said the king as he shielded his eyes from the early sun and searched the eastern horizon as if he would be able to see the long gone messenger.

"Thought ye should know," returned Sir Neil.

"Aye," agreed Robert with much irritation. "I should have known when it happened!" he barked.

. .

By noon that day, the two galleys that had escaped the others' doom as part of the ill-fated attack on the southern flank, came looking for King Robert along the shore.

They hadn't known exactly where he was to land, only that it was somewhere in Carrick. At last they spotted the one remaining galley King Robert was holding there as a possible messenger ship. The Irishmen came ashore running and sought out the king.

When the small representative group had been directed to and entered his newly commandeered tent, Robert jumped to his feet, knowing something was gravely wrong, and searching the faces for a familiar one without success. James Douglas stood at his side.

"Why are ye here?" demanded the king of the weary Celtic rabble. "Why are ye not with my brothers and yer chieftain to the south?" His attitude and demeanor quickly sapped the newcomers' courage.

"We...We were attacked, Sire! The whole of our band was set upon by a great host which fell on us out of the darkness," said the self-appointed spokesman.

"My brothers?" entreated the king with fearful, glaring eyes, "What of them!? What is their fate!?"

"I... I cannot say, Milord, what happened to yer kin," stuttered the man. "All I can say is that they were l... la...layin' in wait for us when we got there last night," said the man as he bowed his head, adding, "They knew we were comin', a'right."

"Knew!?" queried the king in anger, "How!?"

"I know naught, S... Sire, s... sa...save we ones here barely skinned out with *our* lives," he explained, then added more softly, "But, with all the screamin' and yellin', I'd say they were all... dead!"

Anger masked Robert's fear and sorrow for his brothers as he pounded the small table before him with his fists and lowered his great head to his chest.

James Douglas, his heart also grieving for the misfortune that had fallen Alexander and Thomas de Brus, whom he had come to know so well, ushered the group out of the tent and left the king to his sorrow and anger.

"What do ye think he will do with us?" asked the spokesman, timidly.

"Do?" replied Douglas. "Nothin' to ye, but a'plenty to them that did him and his brothers wrong." Then he pointed all around him at the bodies of King Robert's slain enemies being laid out in great numbers like cord wood in the cold, until sufficient thawing made easier the digging of a large grave.

Soon after, Robert sent for his brother Edward, to tell him of the news of Thomas and Alexander.

"Send a man to Galloway to find out if our brothers are still alive," instructed Robert, "and if they are, we'll go and get them... stealthily!"

"Aye," agreed Edward despondently as he patted his brother on the back. "I will see to it within the hour."

Edward had turned to leave him when Robert said, "We wanted to make our stand, brother. This may be the price we pay."

Edward, his eyes brimming with tears, paused, then said simply, "Aye," and went on.

. . .

That night, after the news of the apparent disaster in Galloway, there were about a hundred and twenty men who had come in the company of King Robert and now became fearful that his leadership would lead to their own destruction. And so, banding together, they decided to take their fate into their own hands. They grabbed what booty they could without arousing the suspicions of the others and abandoned the Brus camp at Turnberry.

Some of the deserters confiscated the three galleys that lay on the shore and went sailing back to their homes, while others simply disappeared into the countryside.

When King Robert was informed of this the following morning, he asked only one question, "Did they take any horses?" and was satisfied when the answer was no.

Later that day, he gathered his captains in his tent. They all stood about him as he forced himself to go on. "We have captured all of

Turnberry save the castle, and have no siege equipment to scale the castle walls..." he started. He looked at the faces of the handful of bright and courageous young men who had followed him into "his" war, and could see Thomas and Alexander standing among them, in his mind's eye. His heart told him to give it up and save these brave men and his remaining brothers, and perhaps Thomas and Alexander, too, if they yet lived. And while he argued within himself about this, he sat in silence, until the rugged knights before him became uneasy and somewhat restless. Hearing their discomfort, he emerged from his reverie and spoke again.

"Damn it to hell! This is the crux of it! We've bare pulled together twenty horses from this village. They, our swords, and ourselves is what we possess. All else we must dig from the earth with our very fingernails, and not shirk from our bloodied fingers. 'Tis not goin' to be ours to have anything come to us in an easy manner."

He stood and looked at them directly, moving from face to face as he said, "I have spoke it before and I repeat it now... Ye want yer leave, take it! No blame will I have against ye, I swear!"

With that he walked around and through the group and out of the tent into the cold wind.

He did not want to hear them talk among themselves, which he knew they would do, and he walked but a short way from the tent ere he sat on a step before a thatched cottage to await their decision. It surprised him that they soon followed him to where he sat and again gathered before him.

Then 'The Black' Douglas spoke, "None here had such mind as leavin.' We are with ye to the end, where'er and whate'er that end might be."

The others agreed, most adding a steadfast, "Aye," to Douglas' words.

Robert looked each man in the eyes until subtle tears welled up in his own and he could no longer see theirs plainly enough, and he cast his eyes down.

What brave magnificent comrades. God grant me the wisdom to guide them aright from here, he prayed silently.

"Robert, my brother, my king... we will not fail!" said Sir Edward determinedly.

Without trying to speak through his emotion-choked throat, Robert reached into his tunic and retrieved the thin band of gold that had served him as crown at his coronation. It was somewhat misshapen, and Robert fingered it to make it straight before placing it, once again, on his head.

The men were momentarily awe struck with their patriotism and their admiration of the man beneath the crown.

"Aye," said Neil Campbell at last, "I would that we had a piper among us, now!"

All present gave a rambunctious cheer!

Robert was humbled and pleased, and with a solemn but more hopeful heart, continued talking to them of the way things would be in the near future as they strode back into the tent to continue their advisement by their king.

Once inside he said, returning to the original subject, "Turnberry we leave today, without a fight! As I have said, we have not the means to lay siege to yon castle, and the messenger who escaped from there the night before last is no doubt nearing Lanercost by now, and will tell 'Longshanks' that we are here. If we stay, he will have troops here upon us ere we kill our first man from inside the castle walls."

The men were disappointed but none objected. Robert went on, "Nay, lads, we're headin' for the highlands! Edward and I know these mountains passin' well. We know all the secret passages and caves here 'bouts. Our only aim now must be _survival!_"

He stood awaiting comment from his faithful captains.

"We will make ready," said Sir Gilbert, simply.

Agreement was echoed throughout the tent, and the men left to tend to necessary arrangements. It had started to snow, large quiet flakes that covered the frozen corpses. Time to move on.

FEBRUARY 12th 1307
LANERCOST SANCTUARY

The messenger that Robert feared had escaped from Turnberry had indeed made a direct path to King Edward in Lanercost Sanctuary. The message was certainly garbled, having been written by Sir Henry Percy in his own hand under much panic and duress. The short of it was that, as far as Edward was concerned, he read only five words, "Robert Brus... back on... mainland." Nothing more was needed!

"Fulco!" Edward screamed from his bed with the high-pitched squawk of an old crone.

Within half a moment Sir Fulco Ballard showed himself at the king's bedside. "You called, Sire?" he responded.

"We have writing of letters to do," explained the king, agitatedly.

"Milord," Fulco said with a courteous bow, then walked to the small desk across the room to take dictation from the king.

"No, no!" snapped the monarch waving his scrawny arm about in Ballard's direction. "Draw the desk and chair close by me that I need not shout my lungs apart for you to hear my words."

Sir Fulco did as he was bade, dragging the heavy furniture noisily across the cold, stone floor and placing it near the king's resting place. He then sat and, after opening his small, gilded inkstand, picked up his pen and dipped it into the black fluid.

Pen poised, he silently waited his liege's pleasure.

The king, meanwhile, stared at his long, hairy toes, standing out from under the bed quilts. Amid all the flurry of excitement he had caused, his mind wandered from the crisis at hand. He aimlessly wondered why the toenails had turned yellow in his old age. He then noticed the one nail he had lost in some battle or other, so many years ago that it was no longer possible to put a name to the incident, though he remembered it well. It had eventually grown back, but quite crookedly. As suddenly as he had gone into the meditation on his feet, he began to dictate the contents of the first letter.

"This is to Aymer de Valence, earl of Pembroke. 'My *Dear* Cousin and *Most* Loyal Friend,'" his dictated words of affection oozed sarcasm. "I have it from Sir Henry Percy, and from a true eyewitness, that the traitor Robert de Brus, who feigns the royal Scottish crown, has returned to the mainland with a force of thousands of horse and foot, and has most heinously butchered most of the garrison at Turnberry while they slept in their comfort.' You have all of that, Fulco?" asked the king of his scribe.

"Yes, Sire," said Fulco who but took notes at these sessions and more elaborately stroked a final draft afterwards, "every word."

The king continued, growing more abusive and excited with every utterance, "'Since you command all military action in Scotland, Cousin, why have I not heard that you have this accursed scoundrel in irons, awaiting the kings pleasure?!'" His voice was unusually shrill. "And it would be a great pleasure," he added under his breath before continuing his dictation. "As we have not yet received word of his death or arrest by your hand, or even of your attempt to apprehend the murderous traitor, it is woefully obvious to us that you have failed your king!'"

The king waited for Sir Fulco's quill to finish scratching on the paper, then went on, "'As you are of our own blood, we have decided to grant you the opportunity to redeem yourself. Another three hundred pounds sterling awaits you when I have Robert de Brus within my grasp!'" The king watched in momentary fascination as his bony fingers closed into a tight fist. "'You are to hold Turnberry and Ayr at all cost! You will allow him no sanctuary under my purview, whether in castle or piggery! To make damned sure of this, we will bring Sir Dungal Macdouall to the southern borders of Galloway, and Sir John Macdougall from the west to flush them out of the highlands!'" The king punctuated his words by slamming down his fist upon his bed. "'Make sure these goddamned lines of communication remain open betwixt *thee and me*!'" He paused to mentally recapitulate his words and see if all that was needed was said, then added in an off-handed manner, "Sign, et cetera."

"Shall I put this into the usual diplomatic form, Sire?" asked Ballard.

The king waved his hand to indicate his approval, then began a new thought, "We have a few swan knights here..." He paused again and coughed into his loosened fist and wiped his hands on the bedclothes, "...have orders drawn to send them to Turnberry, immediately! Then, send to Berwick, a message to my son to take what's left of his army and push into Carrick from the east with all haste!"

"It will be done, Milord," assured Fulco. The old man having paused in his wit once more, he rose to leave, but the king once again signaled his servant with his hand. Fulco, understanding the frail old man wanted him to remain by his bed, did so.

After a long reflective the king slowly spoke, "You think, old friend, that our strong-handedness with this rebellion has turned upon us?"

Sir Fulco thought long and hard ere he answered, for he knew the vengeful moods to which his monarch was capable.

"I know not how to answer you, My King," said Ballard, "But there has been spiteful gossip."

"Court gossip about my domestic policies?" asked the king raising one eyebrow and glaring over at his steward. "What?"

"There are some who have misgivings, and wag their tongues to match their wit," said Sir Fulco.

Throwing the pillow that had propped up his back onto the floor, the king slid deep under the covers like a child who didn't want to hear what his father was about to tell him. In these wintry days, he depended on his almost constant companion for far more than writing letters and managing his ordinary and privy affairs. It was his prudent advice, existing only between them, that Edward cherished most now, for although his wit was mostly within his command the old tyrant knew well that it slipped from time to time, and Sir Fulco was always there to see and hear what he lacked.

Fulco continued, "They say... that you leave no field of grace to those who have sided with Sir Robert de Brus, My Lord. They say that one who has done so is condemned to die ere submitting to the king's pleasure... and, knowing beforehand that he will be drawn, hanged and axed, he would naturally figure to throw in his lot whole heartedly with the rebels rather than submit to a certain and most horrible death... or so the court gossip goes." He paused, then added, "Of course, Milord, it is but idle gossip of some in the court."

King Edward had turned his back toward Sir Fulco, who sat motionless for a full moment before he heard the peaceful snores of his sovereign.

Glad to be able to provide such a delightful bedtime tale to woo the sandman to your eyes, Lord King, thought Fulco sarcastically. He extinguished all but two of the lit candles and left the bedchamber with the dictated notes in hand.

The door closed softly and the eyes of the king slowly opened on the dim room. "Twaddle," he said to himself, "just driveling poppycock."

Then he slept.

Christina of Carrick

MARCH 3RD 1307
THE HILL COUNTRY OF CARRICK

It was three weeks since Robert and his struggling band returned to the mainland of Scotland, and he had chosen a site for his patriot army to build themselves makeshift lodgings. Now, roughly made but sturdy stables built of sticks for the few appropriated destriers, and lean-to type shelters for the men dotted the several hills upon which they were bivouacked. King Robert wanted a loose configuration of his camp so that his forces could not all be surrounded and attacked, unawares and unarmed, by wandering bands of their enemy, purposefully and methodically searching for them.

Spies informed Robert of the vise King Edward was drawing tighter on him each day, and he knew he would need to move soon, and keep moving until his army was large enough to fight effectively.

He also knew his army of patriots was shrinking rather than increasing. The mass desertion after Turnberry was a devastating reduction in their numbers, and almost every day a trickle of deserters diminished them further.

The confiscated stores from the three Brodick Bay galleys were running low on such staple foods as bread flour and oatmeal. On the other hand, they still warmed themselves in the cold and wind with the English uniforms taken at the same time.

Every day a hunting party was arranged, and usually bagged whatever small game was about. That, at least would serve as meat for the hungry men. At first, a pair of hunters would be sent to the hunt and they would cook their first kill on the spot because they were so hungry. Soon, there were many volunteers to be hunters. Men who barely knew how to nock an arrow would come early to Sir Edward's side for a chance to be in on the day's hunt. Shortly, they learned to use the weapon well enough to survive, a skill that would serve them well in battle.

King Robert spent much of his time in a small cave near the top of a tor that had a commanding view of the valley below. Edward Brus, his stalwart brother and second in command, conferred with him constantly on the next move to make, since the plan that was laid out at Dunaverty Castle dolefully failed to materialize.

They also sent several more spies to Galloway seeking any shred of information about their brothers, Thomas and Alexander.

English messengers from east to west were still getting through and it was thus that he knew for certain that something terrible had happened to his brothers and his southern flank.

• •

In the middle of the morning, King Robert sat on a ledge near his cave contemplating the situation, trying to figure his way out of the conundrum, when he saw far into the valley, a train of riders coming straight for his camp.

He hastily raised his horn and gave a quick, short blast to call in his pickets and alert the camp that strangers were near. Quickly his warriors girded themselves with whatever scant armor they possessed, and their weapons flashed in the rare bit of sunlight.

With thin snow on the shaded sides of the hills, it was easy to keep an eye on the entourage of forty or so riders following the three obvious leaders.

"What ye seein'?" asked Edward as he trotted up to Robert's side.

"One thing for sure," returned Robert calmly, "they hain't sneakin' up on us."

"That's a good sign," replied Edward. "Want the men to lay back?"

Robert turned to see his meager army hiding among the rocks and the bare winter trees, ready for the kill. He had not seen this level of alertness since they arrived in the hills, and he liked their demeanor as they stood at the ready.

"Let them puff a wee bit more," answered Robert as his own claymore dangled from around his neck and over the ledge between his overhanging legs.

"Aye," returned Edward as he sat down beside his brother to watch the meanderers come closer.

"Who ye reckon they are?" asked Edward after a few minutes.

"No notion," replied the king, "but I've noticed that the horses they're ridin' are takin' this terrain passin' well... and I don't recall e'er seein' one quite like 'em... e'er. Have ye?"

"Now that ye've said it, Rob," said Edward as he stood, "I hain't ne'er seen one quite like 'em either."

"Have half the men go about their business and the rest remain at the ready until we figure who these visitors are, Eddie lad," instructed the king. "After all, it could be one of King Edward's foul tricks afoot."

"Aye, Rob, I'll dismiss the cooks and stock keepers. Nearly a quarter of the rest are out on the hunt." Edward de Brus turned and carried out his orders back in the command camp.

It was still quite a while before the train of streelings met up with the patrol sent to greet them and asked to speak to King Robert de Brus. Cautiously, the sentries instructed the train to hold where it was until they were permitted to continue. Someone from the camp would come to meet them.

One dour faced sentry, who obviously trusted the newcomers not one bit, scrambled up the hillside and once out of sight, went to the camp. As the three leaders of the array waited, they dismounted to put the sentries at their ease. Soon Sir Edward appeared, seemingly out of nowhere, and, gladly recognizing the three, took them immediately to Robert's cave dwelling.

"King Robert!" shouted Edward, full of ebullience, "we have guests!"

The new arrivals stood looking toward the mouth of the cave in anticipation of the emergence of the king, when he walked up behind them and spoke, "What manner of men have we here?"

Even Edward was caught off guard, and he with the other three turned in united surprise to meet the king's voice.

The shortest of the three callers suddenly rushed upon the king and kissed him full and passionately upon his bearded lips before he could retrieve his dirk. Pulling away from his attacker, the king withdrew a step to get a better look.

"D'ye not recognize me in the clothing of a man?" The voice was sultry and low-pitched, but definitely not that of a male. He knew its owner at once.

"By God! It's Christina!" he shouted with glee and hugged her warmly, fairly smothering her in his great arms. He then returned the favor of the kiss. This time, she was the one who withdrew from the embrace.

"I am not accustomed to havin' such betwixt us, Robert," said Christina of Carrick as she pushed Robert's claymore, still suspended around his neck, to one side.

Christina was a beautiful, lusty kinswoman of Robert's, and during the earlier wars with England, before Elizabeth had come into Robert's life, Christina had been greatly in love with him.

And she loved him still.

As for Robert, his entire demeanor instantly changed at just the sight of her.

Robert had a reflection of earlier days when Christina and he were lovers. During their years together, she had given birth to two children, a boy and a girl. Though a sweet and pleasurable time for them, it was an unlikely love affair from the start, especially considering the ambitions of the young Robert de Brus. After they parted, he had seen that she was well provided for with lands and animals. Now she stood smiling at him once again, and he grinned broadly in return.

Finally his reverie broke and he asked, "How are the children?"

"Growin' tall and strong. Neil is takin' on the appearance of ye, and the girl... somethin' of me."

"I must see them soon."

"We would like that," she returned with that smile of hers that tugged at his heart.

After another moment of embrace, Robert said, "And who travels with ye?"

Christina turned to look at them, "Ye recognize them not?"

He studied the faces of the two men and then realized he knew them both.

"'Tis Sir John Wallace," said Christina. The large man stepped forward and bowed respectfully to Robert. He was not as tall or otherwise as large as was his late brother William, the late Guardian of Scotland, but he was fully King Robert's height.

Robert acknowledged the man with a reserved nod, then spoke, "I know Sir John well. We fought the English together many times in what seems now as 'olden days'."

"Aye," said Sir John, "and I have come to continue that fight with ye, King Robert."

"We certainly welcome ye to our side, but yer kin lie with the Comyns," said the king, somewhat surprised that Wallace would go against his family.

"And they lie with the English, who are and ever shall be my sworn enemy," replied John Wallace, his face grim and forthright.

"Makes two of us," replied the king, and he reached his hand out to shake Wallace's. Then he turned his attention to the second man, "How's yer deportment, these days, Sir Robert?" he asked in a teasing tone.

"Bein' chased by too many English to notice," returned Robert Boyd in the same manner.

"Why are ye not in Kildrummy with Nigel?" asked the lighthearted king. "There ye'd be safe enough from the English." Robert Boyd's mouth went agape at the question, for he then realized that the king did not know of Kildrummy's siege by Lord Pembroke and the Prince of Wales.

"I... I was there, but I escaped, Sire," returned Boyd, not knowing what else to say.

"Escaped? Escaped from what, pray?" asked King Robert, his heart pounding as he realized something was amiss at Kildrummy.

"Sire... Kildrummy... fell to an English siege... some five or six months ago," replied Boyd.

Robert was stunned and stepped back from Boyd. Kildrummy was the strongest and best supplied castle in the realm! That was why he had sent Elizabeth and Marjorie there with his brother Nigel and John Strathbogie! How could it be that Kildrummy had fallen so long ago, so soon after they had arrived there? And why have I not been told ere this? His heart suddenly fell, and he simply asked, "The queen...?"

"She and the princess Marjorie and yer sister Mary left ere the siege began, Sire," hastened Boyd.

The king's eyes brimmed with tears, and he hesitated to ask the next question. Christina came to his side and linked her arm into his for moral as well as physical support. He seemed struck dumb, so Boyd volunteered the answers without the questions.

"Sire, 'tis apparent that we were betrayed from within," he started in a quiet, almost monotone voice. It was plain his heart ached at what he had to say.

"We were well prepared and holdin' our own, as we expected, but in the early morn about two weeks into the attack, a great fire, set by the smithy, destroyed a large part of the curtain."

He grew silent for a moment and took a deep breath before starting again.

"When last I saw yer poor brother, he was barely alive and in English hands. I had bartered our escape with one of the guards, but Nigel refused to go. Wounded as he was, he knew he would jeopardize my chance... and so ordered me to flee without him. He was an exceptionally brave man, especially for one so young,"

"Was... ye said 'was'... is he dead?" Robert's eyes were large and wide as he tried to see through his tears to read the man's face.

"I ... don't know for certain, Sire, but they were to be takin' him to Berwick for 'trial,' at King Edward's court. And... I heard Edward's 'whelp of a son' swear to Sir Nigel as he lay wounded, that he would live just long enough to feel the headsman's ax." Boyd, his own eyes growing watery, paused and hung his head, wiping his nose on the back of his hand.

Robert was so stunned that he grew numb. Nigel, the youngest of the de Brus brothers, the one with the best sense of laughter, and fun... dead! "And what of my sister Christian? What of her?" asked Robert as he turned downhill and sat upon a snow-laden stone, his legs suddenly tired and unsure.

Robert Boyd walked around to face his king, whom Christina hunkered gently beside and put her arm around to comfort him as best she could.

"She and Isabel MacDuff were both captured alive, and hard fightin' to the end, but they were sent elsewhere after their capture," said Boyd, trying to put the easiest edge possible on the bad news.

Then the king asked, "And my queen?"

At this Christina took a deep breath and interceded, almost in a whisper in her deep, charismatic voice, with her lips close to Robert's ear, "They were captured, Robert, in Easter Ross with Atholl, and from there sent to the King in Lanercost for him to deal with. And that's where the Prince of Wales sent sister Christian and Isabel MacDuff after Kildrummy fell."

"Surely he murdered *them* not?" Robert whispered through his tears.

"Nay," replied Christina, her own face wet with the sorrow she felt for her old and intimate friend, "they killed them not. But 'Longshanks' has separated them and decreed that they be imprisoned around the countryside as pleased him, so ye could not capture them back."

"And Atholl?" asked Robert.

"To London, and death, to show others hereabouts what happens to them, even earls, who would join yer rebellion." She held tight to his arm and lay her head against his as he silently wept.

"What have I wrought on so many?" he asked himself in a whisper. "What have I wrought?"

"Ye have yet to hear the whole of it, My King," whispered Christina tenderly.

"More? How could there be more?" he asked.

"The many ye sent to Galloway," she said softly as Edward, weeping silently at the news, pushed in tighter to listen. "They too are betrayed. I heard from my kin there that, after being tricked into a trap, yer army was set upon in the dark by Dungal Macdouall and his gang of murderers. One from yer ranks, named Patrick, turned them in for favors from the king. Few survived the attack, but an Irishman by the name of Reginald Crawford, and Malcolm MacQuillan, lord of

Kintyre, were decapitated on the spot. All but their heads yet lay in the soil of Galloway. Both of yer brothers, Alexander and Thomas, were severely wounded, but not killed in the fight. They were not able to resist capture, and were sent straightaway to Carlisle and King Edward's justice." She paused, knowing that his and Edward's sorrow was far greater than her own, and that was greater than any she had ever known. "By Edward's command, they were put to death."

The King of Scots wept bitterly for his lost brothers. Thomas, tough as an oak, but with his great heart and humble manner, he belied his ferocity in war. Never had Robert seen a man with greater courage on the battlefield or in any kind of fight. And Alexander the scholar, the Dean of Glasgow, his great intellect and pious demeanor, his calm voice of reason now silenced, his Cambridge studies all for naught. What treasures Scotland had lost at King Edward's bloody hands! How could God have allowed this to happen to them, when he, the eldest brother, was the one responsible for this horror? Why had God not allowed him to die before leading his family into such catastrophe?

When he could stand the ache in his midriff no longer, he stood and faced into the beautiful valley below and screamed. A howl as savage as any demon's erupted from the depths of his sundered heart and echoed back from the highest tors across the way.

Again, and again, he roared, the same agonizing lamentations, shaking his two great fists in anger for his loss, and for the imprisonment of his wife and child and sisters.

When his voice would no longer scream, he fell to his knees and groveled in the dirt, so great was his sorrow.

He was sore defeated.

Let the English come.

It mattered not.

Edward rushed to his brother and gently pulled him to his feet. Robert and Edward looked at each other's red, swollen eyes and tear-stained faces, and each knew his brother's anguish. The two embraced each other for a long moment, until Robert's crushed spirit could take no more.

Had it not been for Edward's great strength, all in camp would have seen their king collapse to the ground in a faint.

With the help of Christina and Robert Boyd, he remained on his feet, and was retired to his pallet of heather covered with deerskins in the cave.

Boyd returned to comfort Edward in his great sorrow.

Christina bathed the king's heated face and great head with cool water, then lay alongside the king and comforted him as best she could for a long while, into the evening hours.

His eyes would not stop weeping, and his wounded voice remained speechless in his grief for the devastating murders of his brothers and the capture of his family.

Neither would he eat, and Christina could get him to take but a sip or two of water, and eventually he fell into a restless slumber from sheer exhaustion.

As word of the losses spread among the men, a melancholy quiet fell across the whole of the camp. Some now said they had all made a mistake by going along with King Robert. Others simply wondered how the poor monarch could rise above the crushing loss and continue the pursuit of the war.

Emerging from the cave in the evening, Christina of Carrick saw that the forty men in arms she had brought with her to this place were fed and bedded down for the night. She then returned to Robert's side and at long last, slept.

Though he slept, depleted of all reserves, Robert did not rest. The images of his wife and daughter and sisters, and his poor betrayed and murdered brothers, played themselves before his mind. They would not let him have a moment of peaceful slumber.

In waking moments the king bore upon himself the blame for all that had happened, finding no solace in any mitigation he tried to persuade himself to accept. In short, he was done, and he knew it. He could see no avenues of action that would have any positive effect on the war that he, so damnably cocksure and overly impressed with himself, had started.

Finally, he sat up and, leaning against the cold stone of the cave wall, watched the flickering shadows thrown about by the fire at the cave's mouth.

The prayers to Saint Fillan had pleased the people, but somehow... they reached not the ears of God, he silently wept. God surely has forsaken so many due to my conceit... all those brave, brave men and women, and children, who died at Methven and Dail Righ, and... only God knows how many hamlets and towns.

And now, Kildrummy and Galloway! He moaned aloud in despair. Then, praying in a hoarse whisper, his sorrow and guilt poured forth. "Oh, God in heaven... would that Ye had taken me in the stead of any other, and perhaps thousands of those slain would yet live in peace... including my poor brothers. And all of those now in prisons... and in cages... for having followed my lead... would now be free to live their lives." Tears again flowed abundantly from his eyes.

"John Comyn! ...It was the murder of John Comyn on holy ground that has cursed me and mine. But, Father in heaven, if Ye hear me not, how can I stand in grace again? If absolution is held beyond my reach, who is safe who follows me? How can I undo a knot that I have tied so complex, and so tight?" he sighed and turned on his pallet once again, agonizingly sick in heart and soul.

"Perhaps, Oh God, if I were to take my good lieutenants and go to the Holy Land, I could earn Yer mercy, at least for those I have sacrificed in my folly, though I burn in hell for my great sins against Ye. If it be Yer will that I follow my father's and grandfather's holy path and wield my sword for Ye against the heathens in Jerusalem, I pray that Ye will give me a sign. Lord God, I pray for Yer guidance as to what ye would have me do, that I may right the great wrongs I have wrought against Ye in my pride!"

As he lay wallowing in his great sorrow and guilt, he became aware of the slow, peaceful breaths taken by the warm Christina, lying dutifully beside him in his hour of wretchedness. As he had done on many other, more joyous occasions, he reached out and touched her silky curls, splayed upon his pillow.

Even the gentle Christina have I unjustly submitted to torment. She must have hated to bring me this news, he thought. She must carry love for me still, to bring me such terrible tidings and bear my sorrow willingly.

The dwindling fire continued to play shadow images across the ceiling of the cave.

Strange, he thought, how many nights I have spent holed up in this cave without even noticing the beauty of the firelight. The images now seem stronger, somehow more meaningful than before, though the fire grows weak. Perhaps it is because I have given up the fight. Perhaps the shadows are tellin' me to go to Ayr on the morrow and plead for the lives of my remaining family and followers in exchange for mine. Damn him! I believed I could outlast 'Longshanks' at this tourney, but he has bested me... and I have paid with almost all!

As he gazed across the darkening cave, his attention was caught and held by the movements of a small spider as it dangled from beneath a rock ledge. It was barely visible in the dying firelight, but Robert became fascinated by the tiny creature's struggle to reach another prominence along the cave wall. He quietly put more wood on the fire the better to see the tiny creature's efforts.

Climbing up its delicate lifeline, the spider then crawled along the wall to a spot from where it flung itself into space toward the point it was trying to reach. Falling short, it swung like a pendulum in the void. It climbed up the filament again, only to repeat its failed attempt.

While Robert watched, no matter how many times the spider tried, it was unable to swing itself to the opposite knob and attach the end of its thread, instead swinging silently back to dangle in emptiness.

"Sometimes, it's just not in yer stars to build yer web, though ye try as ye might," the king, feeling strangely akin to it, whispered to the spider.

But, as the first light of day seeped into the cave, the spider at long last succeeded in catching hold, and was able to attach the second point of support for its web.

Robert watched in awe as the tiny weaver systematically attached a third and a fourth fiber, and from there the intricate design grew quickly into a work that glowed in the morning's first light as if it were lit from within. He sat and stared at what seemed an exquisite miracle.

"If such is a stubborn Scottish spider, should it not be so for the King of Scots as well?" He spoke as loudly as he could with his strained vocal chords, and that awoke Christina, who sat up beside him.

"Robert," she asked, "are ye a'right?"

"Nay," he responded, quietly, "but better, I think. Perhaps I may live a while longer, though last night I thought not."

"It was a terrible blow, nay, a number of terrible blows to be suffered all at once, dear Rob." She leaned her head upon his strong arm, again.

"Aye," he agreed, "but a needed beating. I just wish..." his voice trailed off into his regrets. "Ye know," he continued after a long pause, "I think I've been given my answer." He said it so quietly, not boastfully as one might say if he had received a message from God, that it caused her to shiver.

"For true, Robert?" she asked, her eyes wide.

"Aye." He would have showed her the completed spider's web, but he knew that she wouldn't understand it as a sign from God, for it was the creating of it that was the true miracle.

Suddenly, he stood and, taking her hand, pulled her to her feet. He held her close to him and kissed her gently on the forehead, and she thought she detected a wan smile on his resolute mouth.

Little did she realize the thoughts that were roiling in his newly inspired mind, but it was not long before she found that he was no longer awaiting his fate.

As they ate from the skimpy breakfast the camp shared, he asked Christina in his throaty growl, now slightly louder than a whisper, "What manner of horse is that ye and yer men come mounted on, woman?"

She smiled. She knew his appreciation of good horseflesh would soon have him ask. "'Tis our own crossbreed that comes out of local mares, but sired by some magnificent, quick-footed stallions brought back from the Holy Land by my uncles."

"Are they as strong as they look?" he queried

"Aye, and nimble-footed, too. They can near go anyplace a goat can!" she bragged.

Robert ignored the boasting and asked, "And the men ridin' with ye, are they fit?"

"Dear Robert, they are fit and also, my gift to ye. I place them in yer service. They are well-trained highland warriors. They were placed in my service by one who... once... admired me," she said smiling, "and as I now greatly admire ye, so they are yers."

"Not as slaves!" he protested. "I'll take the horses as a gift, but not the men. Any man who fights with me now, knows what he's up against, and must make his decision to be with me of his own free will. I'll have it no other way!"

Christina placed her hand gently over his mouth and said, "Their hearts, each and all, are with ye, my Robert."

John Wallace

march 26th 1307
the hills of carrick near the galloway border

No more was King Robert to be drawn into pitched battles. That kind of warfare, for which he had trained all his life, benefited the well-equipped multitude of English troops, not his ill-equipped handful.

Obviously, since classical combat was not practical, something different must be tried. And so, for the three weeks after Christina of Carrick and Sir Robert Boyd brought him the tragic news about his family, King Robert attacked both English and Comyn faction troops with regularity as he could find them, but in small groups.

His forty conscripts from Christina, with their quick, sure-footed horses, had proven most valuable in his new concept of waging war stealthily, and taught his other highland lads much about striking quietly and fast. The Scots had already displayed talent in such.

Sir Henry Percy, named Earl of Carrick by King Edward after Robert was crowned, had taken up residence in Robert Brus' own domicile of Turnberry castle, and had then suffered the greatly humiliating loss of his men in the village.

He grew so fearful of Robert's wrath that he refused to sniff the air beyond the thick stone walls. At last, a personal guard of one hundred knights, one hundred foot soldiers, and fifty or so squires, escorted him body and baggage back to his English estates, where he remained, never to return to the hills and glens of Carrick again.

From a craggy rise across the valley, Robert watched him and his retinue go. He had no thought of risking one man to the taking of that miserable, pusillanimous life.

At about that same time, England's Edward sent two thousand additional troops into Carrick.

Lord Pembroke had specific orders to use whatever means necessary to subdue the rebellion. He ordered Mowbray and de Umfraville, then commanding the castle in Ayr, to spread out along the coast surrounding Ayr and all the way to Turnberry.

John de Botetourt and John Menteith, they who had held the fruitless vigil at Dunaverty Castle for much of the winter, patrolled inland and around to the east of the hill country where the king and his men lurked.

Dungal Macdouall, he who had ambuscaded Thomas and Alexander at Loch Ryan, was ordered from Wigtownshire on the southern side of Galloway to push north through the hills toward Carrick. John Macdougall of Argyll, purely out of revenge, came gladly from the north with his wild men.

Thus was the obsessive plan enacted as laid out by King Edward, who desperately needed to succeed before he died in order for his "legacy" to be fulfilled.

Thousands of armored and fully-equipped troops were pitted against Robert's less than six score, most of whom were his own highland lads, barely alive, poorly clad, and poorer-equipped. They chased Brus through the rocky terrain but were unable to catch him. Robert was always one or two steps ahead, and many times would turn and strike where he was least expected.

The lightning strikes and disappearances of the "rebel king" and his raiders shook Aymer's entire army. The ragtag band seemed to be everywhere at once and nowhere at all.

As their newfound success gained momentum, more fighters, by twos and by fours, secretly came to join Robert's ranks, and the people began to share news of English troop movements with his spies.

. .

Under increasing pressure from King Edward and, driven by the offer of his added reward of sterling, set a plot in motion with John Macdougall.

Having found out approximately where King Robert camped in the hills, the pair formed a contingent of but two hundred men, with knights, squires, and soldiers of foot in the mix. A size and composition of this sort was supposed to be tempting for the Scots and their "king," especially if he thought he had surprise as an ally. Their theory was correct.

When news of such a force approaching their area reached the Brus camp only days later, plans were quickly made to capture the commander and kill as many of the soldiers as possible. Were they successful in the capture, they could thereby draw an admirable ransom.

"If we swoop down in small groups of, perhaps, twos and threes, we can be on them before they're set for the fight," suggested Douglas. "Their not having our sure-footed ponies, and the ground being unfamiliar to them and still scattered with ice and snow, I imagine bein' on horseback could be a disadvantage. And... and we could roll under the horses' bellies and cut them with our dirks, like those quick little bastards did against us at Dail Righ!"

"Ye mean, attack on foot *under* the horses and get drenched with horse guts?" asked Gilbert de la Haye distastefully.

"A man can hide behind a tree, but not if he's astride a horse! He can get under a horse if he hain't ridin' one, too!" interjected Edward Brus.

"I like the notion," said King Robert, "but we need to be quick."

"Aye," the men said in almost unison.

"And *very* quick not to get caught under a fallin' horse," said Gilbert with caution, still not enamored of the idea.

The English soon followed the well-traveled road at the base of the hills where waited Robert and his men. The Scots seemed to have virtually melted into the sparse winter landscape, biding their time behind practically every rock, tree, and patch of tall grass along the route.

Suddenly, Cuthbert came running from over the hill behind them. In his haste he tumbled down the hill into dead leaves. Raising his head, he looked farther down the hill to see King Robert standing behind a small pine near the road, his claymore in his hand and tucked against the back of his leg.

Glancing north, he also saw the English array coming up the road. He dared not scream out an alarm, but he had to get the king's attention, so he rolled and tumbled and ran down the steep hill, landing with a thud within fifteen or so feet of the hiding king.

At the noise Robert turned around and saw Cuthbert lying in the grass, flat on his back. He knew then that something was amiss, for Cuthbert would not otherwise jeopardize them thus.

Robert rushed to the exhausted scout who lay with the wind knocked out of him but otherwise sound. "Are ye a'right, man?" asked the king.

Cuthbert replied with his warning, in short, quick breaths, "Them blue... woad-stained ones... big bunch of 'em... comin' at us... t'other side ... hill..." he pointed.

"Damn!" said Robert, his eyes flashing.

It was all a trap!

He searched for a way out. This was just too reminiscent of Dail Righ. He looked up the hill. John Macdougall's bunch had not crested the top. Then he looked down to the roadway, where Pembroke's well-arrayed army was just coming in sight. It seemed too late to get away.

He gave Cuthbert a muscular arm and pulled the still panting messenger to his feet.

Robert hastily signaled for his lieutenants to join him, and just as quickly gave them orders. "Edward, 'tis a trap! Ye, Wallace and Boyd take most of the men and horses and skitter off in that direction," he said pointing to the south. "Avoid a fight if at all possible!"

"Aye," replied Sir Edward.

"Douglas, ye and Gilbert go yonder with half of the rest, and I'll take the others..." Robert said, glancing at the hillside and the roadway, "Meet at the little stone farmhouse beyond yonder ridge on the morrow morn... now, go!"

The men with Edward raced for the horses they had hidden in a nearby hollow and made away at a gallop. Douglas' men were mostly on foot, but each of those mounted hoisted another man behind him and charged off. Robert had no time to reach his horse and he, Cuthbert, Andrew, and the last thirty-plus men, raced on foot for the evergreen wood.

John Macdougall, the first in his column to reach the top of the ridge, looked down between the trees at the scattering men and recognized the king dodging into the greenery. His war whoop could be heard over the valley, and he then screamed, "Yer head will be hangin' o'er the door of my keep *this day*, Robert de Brus!"

Down the hill a blue wave of the small, fierce, painted warriors swarmed on foot, going in all directions, chasing whomever they thought they might have a chance to catch. The fearless painted horde had on more clothing than their boots this time, but not by much.

John Macdougall waved for some of his men to follow him as he spurred his horse toward the green wood wherein he last saw Robert. On horseback, it was a dangerous ride down the steep and slippery hill, and he lost some of his soldiers when their horses fell and rolled over them, but still he spurred his own mount forward.

"Bring up that damn cur!" he shouted to one of his men as he reached the edge of the forest. Robert's dog was brought forward on a leash. His scars showed he had been badly treated, and even now was nearly dead, but his instinct for the trail and his loyalty to Robert, whom he faithfully tried to reach, did not fail as he picked up his master's scent.

Robert was running hard when he first heard the familiar barking of his hound and knew it was only a matter of time before they caught up to him and his men.

Poor old dog don't know when to lie down and die, thought Robert.

The king's only armor was the chest plate given to him by Christina of the Isles and though he wanted to rip it off to run faster, he dared not.

Winded as he was, he told his runners to scatter, and where to meet the next morn, but took young Andrew with him.

"We've got to get the dog off my scent," he said as they reached the ice-cold creek. Robert re-strapped his sword from his waist to his back, wrapped his long cloak around his arm to keep it dry, and the two walked into the freezing stream, nearly up to Andrew's waist. Robert knew they would not last long in the frigid water, so he moved as swiftly downstream as they both could manage. The hound's baying and Sir John's men were getting closer.

"Can't move no more, Sire," soon lamented Andrew, out of breath. "Ye must save yerself!"

Robert looked at the shivering stripling in the dreadfully cold water and picked him up and threw him onto the bank, "It's me the dog's got the scent of. Ye walk along there a ways, and I'll get out directly."

As they progressed downstream in that manner, the boy glanced uphill from where he trotted along the bank. "Sire?" he said.

"Aye?"

"I may have an idea that will stall them a bit." Robert kept walking, but asked what it might be that the boy thought he could do to save them. "As ye said, Sire, the dog seeks only yerself, and if we could set him off at the wrong trail, it could give us more time to put distance between us."

"And?" Robert still had not slowed.

"Well, Sire, if ye would give me yer sash, I could show ye quick enough," the agile youth held out his hand.

The king shook his head. He did not want to endanger the boy more, and if the English caught him with Robert's sash, they would make quick work of him. "I'll not have ye leavin' them a false trail so that I can get away and leave ye to face my enemies alone."

He kept slogging through the icy bath though his legs ached beyond bearing.

"Oh, they'll not catch me, Milord! Please, I know what I'm about!" He thrust his blue fingers out to beg for the sash, again. At this, Robert paused and looked him in the eye.

The confident boy would be no worse off if he were caught with the king's sash than he would if he were caught with him in person, and the royal legs could not take the freezing water too much longer. So he relented and handed the youth his bright red and gold sash.

"Ye must go on yer way, Milord! I'll find ye downstream, don't worry!"

With that the boy turned and ran up the hill toward the wood, dragging the sash along the ground and through the brush. As Robert continued on down the stream, the boy entered the woods and ran hurriedly to a grove of ancient pines. There he dragged the sash around and around several of the trees' great trunks, wiping the bark of each with the now disheveled fabric.

Finally, he picked a particular tree and, after rubbing it at ground level with the much-abused cloth, climbed with great agility high into its branches. There he tied the brightly colored sash and, climbing out on the branch as far as he dared, reached across to a sturdy branch in a neighboring tree.

He managed to find his way a goodly distance through several tree-tops that way, as he had often done when playing with the other squires, until he heard the dog and its attendants approaching. He climbed down quickly, then, and returned to the bank of the burn to seek his master.

Robert had slogged through the water for about another five hundred paces, at which time he was no longer able to feel his legs.

He pulled himself from the water on the opposite side from where they had gotten into the creek and found he could no longer walk, much less run.

His knees would not bend. As he stood there trying to get his legs to work, he damned himself for allowing the boy to lay a false trail. Andrew was, after all, just a child, and knew not in what danger he had placed himself.

He sat on the bank and rubbed his numb legs, hoping to get the feeling to return, but having limited success. Then he heard a sound of someone or something running along the edge of the stream from whence he had just come.

Struggling with all his might, Robert managed to pull himself to his feet with the aid of a tree, and, drawing his sword from its sheath around his neck, braced himself to meet his adversary.

"I hate runnin' from a fight, anyway," lamented Robert through gritted teeth.

"Aye," returned Andrew as he trotted up the creek bank toward the crippled monarch. "Hain't much of it to pleasure a man," he added as he drew close enough to whisper.

"Andrew!" Robert was more than a little surprised at not seeing any English or the dog on the boy's heels. "How did ye ... the... never mind for now, but one day ye must tell me what trick ye played on the tailed villains!"

Either fear of freezing or the fear of John Macdougall's gang forced Robert to move his numbed feet, and he and his squire helped each other up the hill with great effort. They moved onto a sill overlooking a large area below, where they saw John Macdougall and his men, still a ways back, trying to get the poor dog to pick up the scent once more.

The animal, having lost the scent at the edge of the creek, ceased baying and roamed along the creek on first one side, then the other, as the handlers cursed him loudly and urged him onward with the points of their blades.

"Chasin' me with my own dog, again," commented Robert as the two shivering Scots eased back from the edge of the precipice and left to hide deeper in the wood.

Whether or not the Macdougall band picked up the trail and came after them, they were not about to wait to see.

"I thought we were kilt, for sure," whispered Andrew through blue lips and chattering teeth as he and his king moved around to the opposite side of the ridge. There the welcome spring sun was shining brightly and warm, and helped the two thaw somewhat as they made their way down the steep incline.

Along the creek, John Macdougall cursed the dog incessantly and complained that he should have known that a damned Brus dog couldn't find stink on scite. He was almost ready to send out his human scouts to find Robert's trail, when the dog again began baying excitedly and took off up the hill toward a stand of trees, their graceful boughs swaying gently in the wind.

"Follow him, men!" he ordered and kicked his own mount hard while jerking its head toward the dog's lead.

The dog howled and sniffed at the first tree he came to, and circled it around and around, then hurried to the next one on which Andrew had laid Robert's scent. Finally, he came to the last tree the boy had scented, and being unable to find a track going away, scratched at the bottom of the ancient tree and howled piteously.

"We've got him! We've got him!" screamed Macdougall, racing up to the tree.

Stretching his neck in all directions and trying to find Robert in the tree, Macdougall caught sight of a moving flash of red and gold in the upper branches.

Pointing to the spot, he screamed maniacally, "Kill him! There he is! Bowmen, bring him down! Ten... no... five shillings to the man whose arrow first finds his heart!"

The air was instantly filled with multiple flights of lethal barbs as each archer tried for the bounty. Pine needles and small branches fell from the target area, but the fugitive did not.

After a few moments, Macdougall called a halt.

He thought, surely, the Scottish 'king' was dead after such a barrage. The only reason that the body of de Brus had not fallen out of the tree must have been that so many missiles, having run him through, had then lodged solidly in the trunk of the tree, pinning him in place where he had hidden.

"Captain, put two men up that tree to fetch the body," he ordered, almost gleefully. "And if he be not dead, be careful not to kill him! Methinks King Edward would prefer to witness that when we present 'King Robert' to him at Lanercost."

Two men stood in their saddles and boosted themselves up into the stout old tree, reaching the site within seconds. When they saw what had been riddled with dozens of English arrows, they hesitated to bring it down, but there was no recourse with John Macdougall at the base of the great trunk yelling, "Is he alive? What say ye? Is the damned son-of-a-bitch alive or dead?"

Pulling the fabric loose, they brought it down in shreds and handed it to an officer, who passed it to Macdougall.

As the Macdougall soldiers searched the vicinity for a sign of the vanished Scottish 'pretender,' Robert and Andrew were well away from that place.

Macdougall himself was in a grand fury, cursing and abusing the men and the dog, which he had the foot soldier kick at every opportunity for a quarter of a mile along the trail back. He cursed the men for being cowards, as they had failed to capture, not only Robert de Brus, but any of his men! Yet, his own forces had lost several horses, two of the riders were dead, and others injured!

He remained livid and foul the whole of the day.

When Sir John met up with Lord Pembroke a little while later, the two commiserated over the failed plot, and on their way back to Ayr to ponder the error of their method, they got themselves so drunk they could hardly sit their horses.

Thomas Randolph, riding immediately behind them, chortled to himself as the two told each other lies about what they would do when they finally caught up to Brus.

Wonder what they will do for adventure and glory after that, pondered the bemused Thomas to himself.

• •

Robert and Andrew, both cold to the bone and miserably wet but having escaped Macdougall's trap, found a cave nearby. It was less than comfortable, but warmer than being out in the early spring wind in their wet clothes. Leaves and twigs littered the cave floor near its mouth and Andrew made a small pile of them deeper in the cave.

He then took out his dirk and with trembling, bluish hands pulled a small piece of flint from one of his pockets and struck spark after spark into the dry tinder. Soon a small fire was going, fed with scrounged dead branches from the forest floor.

On Robert's order, Andrew stripped out of his wet clothing, which he then hung near the fire on sticks jabbed into the ground, and wrapped himself in Robert's great woolen cloak. Soon the brave squire was comfortably warm again.

Robert's legs and feet were his greatest concern, and he and Andrew kept rubbing them, trying to undo the harm that had been done them by the icy cold stream. They were aching and stinging fiercely.

"Suppose that Argyll gang sees our smoke," said Andrew, checking his damp trews hanging on sticks before the fire.

"Then, have a fight on our hands, we will" said Robert with a slight smile, knowing that their small fire deep inside the cave wouldn't be seen unless the English were already close onto them.

"I'm right ready for them, Sire," Andrew smiled in return with a nonchalant air, waving his dirk in the firelight.

"Cock sure in yer long tooth!" teased Robert, and they both laughed, as much in their relief as in good humor.

"If they're around," said Andrew, sniggering," they'll hear us laughin' ere they see the smoke."

"Aye," agreed Robert.

With some evergreen boughs for cushioning and Robert's cloak for cover, the cave for shelter and the fire for warmth, the two fugitives made themselves comfortable as they could manage that night.

• •

At the earliest dawn, they arose and cautiously set out for the small stone farmhouse on the other side of the vale. It was a painfully long walk on Robert's sore feet, but Andrew found a fairly straight tree branch and cut a stout walking stick for his king. The squire, however, seemed to be none the worse for his chilling.

As the dirty boy and the limping knight neared the dwelling about midday, an old woman carrying a broom came out the front door of the low thatch-roofed hovel.

"What ye want?" she asked, gruffly, looking them over as they approached.

"Nay, nothing,' good woman," said Robert now wincing at each step, "...save to 'bide and rest for a short while." Then looking at his somewhat skinny young squire, he turned back and said, "Though if ye had a bowl of porridge for the lad here, I'd be willin' to pay for it," and he brought out half a copper coin from his pouch and held it out to her.

Cautiously taking the English coin, the old woman looked it over and, setting a small stool outside the door, said, "Sit here. I'll find somethin' for him. Maybe ye, too," she said as she turned to re-enter her home.

"I don't trust her, My Lord King," frowned Andrew, not liking the looks of the snaggle-toothed old biddy. "Maybe we should just wait yonder, where we can watch for the others."

"Lord King?" asked the woman as she stepped back outside, having thought she heard Andrew call him so. "And what king are ye?" she demanded most unpleasantly.

"I am Robert de Brus, King of Scots," he declared straightforwardly, "though I have naught to prove it to ye."

"Prove it? Ha!" she cackled. "Naught but a damned fool would falsely claim to be ye, these days, and by the look in yer eye, ye air no fool. Come 'bide inside, Sire, that I may fix ye a bit of a poor woman's food," and as she waved them to enter her humble, dark dwelling, she awkwardly curtsied.

Andrew looked at Robert, who heightened his eyebrows. "I'm well famished," said the king.

"Aye," agreed Andrew as they both accepted the old woman's offer with no further ado.

Warmed bread with rendered hog fat spread inside, and large wooden bowls full of steaming hot porridge were all she could offer, but it tasted delicious to the old woman's two guests.

They were like hungry wolves.

Once they had finished, she put the coin back on the table before Robert.

"Nay, Mother," he picked up the coin and put it back in her hard, withered hand, but she insisted.

"It certainly is my small gift to my king," she said, "and if I don't act rightly in yer presence, then ye're to forgive an old woman, for ye're the first of royalty ever to suffer these eyes to fall upon ye."

Robert stood on his aching feet, took her peasant's hand and kissed it, smiling, "Good woman, I have dined with the crowns of Europe, and

I say to ye now, that ye are the most gracious host I have e'er known."

The old woman was greatly pleased and blushing visibly, even in the darkened interior, and made another attempt at a curtsy.

"Me three sons," she said after regaining her composure for a moment. "They must go with ye!"

"We saw them not as we came," said Robert.

"They're off tendin' livestock and whatnot," she replied. "Left early this morn, but they'll be back directly."

At that moment the woman was frightened by a sudden, threatening commotion outside the house. Men's angry voices rose in almost violent conflict with one another. Robert tried to allay her fears.

"Sounds like some of my men have arrived, Mother," he said, recognizing the contentious voices of his brother Edward and the Douglas.

"And my boys, too," said the woman with a relieved smile as she went to the door, Robert and Andrew following.

"Boys! Boys! Ye can leave them strangers in peace, now," she shouted. "They are here as our guests. They fight for Scotland, and yer king stands behind ye."

Her three large and husky men that she only referred to as "boys" turned to see Robert standing before the doorway with their mother.

Immediately, they lowered their weapons of pitchfork and staffs, and the eldest knelt to one knee. Looking sideways and glowering at his younger brothers, he soon had them kneeling beside him.

Robert's men sheathed their weapons, and those riding, dismounted. Robert told the three "boys" to rise.

I hain't got 'nough for that bunch, thought the woman and so ordered her oldest son to slay a ram straightaway, and another she ordered to bring in firewood for the oven.

"Nay, good woman," said Robert, stopping her from such a sacrifice. "We cannot expect ye to feed the lot of us. There will be near a hundred twenty more arrivin' ere long, the Good Lord willin', and we are used to feedin' ourselves."

The woman and her sons were awed to think that the king's whole army would soon be on their humble plot.

"Would that I could feast ye all," she said with tears in her eyes, feeling that she had failed her country's army by being poor and unable to do for them as she would like.

"Perhaps one day we shall be back this way, and then things may be better for all of us." Robert hugged the small farmwoman, though he had to bend 'way down to do so.

All afternoon until nearly dark, the warriors ambled into the growing encampment, many, knowing their fellows would probably be ravenous, brought wild game they had killed along their routes, including numerous birds, squirrels and rabbits, and a large wild boar.

Their hosts were invited to partake of their victuals, and all had their stomachs filled by the end of the evening. That night Robert's men slept anywhere they could find or construct shelter, but the woman insisted that the king sleep in her hovel on a bed of fresh straw.

. .

The next morn the men were better rested. As the army prepared itself for departure, the old woman again offered her three strapping sons to fight the English with King Robert. He resisted, not wanting to leave the poor crone to fend for herself out in the wilderness, but finally agreed to "test their mettle" by giving them the opportunity to show their prowess with their bows.

"What would ye have them target?" asked the woman.

"Have them pick their own," the king replied.

"Murdoch!" she ordered, "Show yer king how ye would handle Englishmen, Son."

Without a word, the eldest of the three nocked an arrow onto his bowstring and, walking down the wash about ten paces, scouted the trees around the edge of the field. He stopped and casually brought his bow up to a high angle and with no delay, loosed his arrow into the branches of a bare tree where sat a pair of ravens. The shaft pierced the one and, passing nearly through, impaled the second, dropping both from their perch on the same skewer.

A low whistle escaped Andrew's lips.

The second son stepped readily forward and, determined to outdo his brother, drew back his arrow and sent it almost straight up, drilling a raven flying above their heads. As it tumbled end-over-end to the ground, the second son turned and grinned at Robert.

"His name is MacKie," boasted his mother.

The youngest of the three brothers next stepped forward and, perhaps in too much haste, drew back his bowstring and threw his shaft also at a raven on the wing, but he gave it not enough of a lead and the arrow passed just behind the bird, clipping its tail feathers. The man turned and looked at his mother sheepishly.

"That one be MacLung," she said quietly, shaking her head only slightly.

Robert was well satisfied with the performances of the three and said so. The first two sons he chose to go with him, to bring down the foe as they had brought down the ravens. But, he instructed the youngest to stay at home and serve his aged mother.

This, the man pledged to do with his life.

While Murdoch and MacKie gathered their belongings to carry with them, Robert thanked their mother for her hospitality and kindness. Climbing aboard a dappled gray mount, he gazed down upon her and bound himself to her with his word, "Some day, when I am able, I shall repay yer generosity, Mother."

"All who fight for the freedom of Scotland are welcome in this house, My Lord King," she returned.

Her two sons came out with their weapons and sundries, and each asked his mother's blessing.

"Do right by yer God and yer king, Murdoch, and they will do right by ye," she said as she kissed her eldest.

As his brother stepped aside, her middle son stepped before her and removed his wide-brimmed hat. The old woman repeated her blessing to him, "Do right by yer God and yer king, MacKie, and they will do right by ye."

Then she kissed him as well, and, placing her gnarled old hands on her two sons' heads said, "May God save ye to come home and live in Scotland as free men."

And when they looked up she smiled at them through a mother's tears.

Robert nodded to Edward, and together they turned their horses up the trail and left the little farm, the old woman's sons falling in with the other foot soldiers and, perhaps for the last time, leaving the place where they were born.

She stood where they left her as they passed below the ridge, beyond which they could no longer see their mother. They were quiet on their journey then, not knowing whether she would be in sunshine or in shadow when they returned.

•   •

Later that afternoon, having traversed a considerable distance, the small army came upon a bluff overlooking the valley below.

"I smell English," said James Douglas as he sighted a large assembly of well-ordered soldiers bivouacked there.

"What say ye, Robert? Shall we rout them from their beds tonight?," said Edward with a grin.

"Too many of them. We'd have the devil's own time tryin' to get away," observed Robert. "But I would like to get them back for yesterday."

Staying well away from the edge of the bluff, they continued moving away from the large English encampment. It was not long before they spotted more troops through the trees.

"Look yonder," said Wallace, and he dismounted and crawled across the ground to the edge of the promontory, laid himself flat and peered over the rim.

Robert alighted, and also moved beneath the sight line from below, to locate himself beside Wallace.

"Ye can barely see through the trees, yonder, in the village," whispered Wallace, pointing toward a deployment of mounted troops. "Must be the command position. They've commandeered the softest pallets to sleep on."

"Now, that's a tolerable-sized host for us to whittle on," replied Robert, his eyes discerning the details of the situation below.

The king chose his brother Edward, James Douglas, Gilbert de la Haye, John Wallace and twenty-three of the mounted highlanders.

That evening and into the night, the rebels quietly maneuvered into position around the tiny village that the English soldiers had virtually taken over.

"Twenty-eight against two hundred," whispered Robert to Edward as the men waited excitedly for the dawn. "Hain't bad odds."

Edward smiled and stifled a chuckle.

At earliest light, King Robert moved into position.

Every man knew where to strike his mightiest blow.

The village buildings lined both sides of a common area, where the camp folk were starting their chores for the day.

Few soldiers were awake with the exception of several pickets, and, de Brus having been so thoroughly run from the field of battle only two days past, the camp commanders did not consider there was need for heightened alert.

'The Black' Douglas crouched behind the town well when a man needing water for the morning porridge came to fetch it.

Douglas squeezed tighter to the ground as the man lowered his bucket into the water.

The water splashed and the bucket was withdrawn full.

"Tired of bein' a slave to them son-of-a-bitchin' lazy dogs," muttered the man.

Douglas smiled and thought, 'Bide only a few minutes longer, laddie.

The man shambled away to the cooking fire.

The Douglas' estimate was correct, for moments later, Robert stepped into the open.

The common folk paid no attention, for warriors with great swords came and went regularly. But, Robert's men knew the signal and went to work at once dispatching the enemy.

Chaos shattered the dreams of sleeping minds, and the lives of the

English were casually snuffed like so many candles as the swift dirks and swords of the cat-footed highlanders did their deeds with cunning and without mercy.

Some awoke in alarm as they heard the muffled cries of comrades, dying in abrupt agony. They unsheathed their swords or grabbed a close battle-ax to fend off the attackers but it was too late for most. The ones who could escape did so in all haste; others were killed as they fled.

The highlanders moved through the village with ease and, very shortly, the enemy was either killed or on the run toward the main body of their force. With no soldiers within reach, the Scots came into the commons with swords drawn, prepared to kill the camp workers.

"Hold!" shouted Douglas. "These folks are ours if we let them be!"

Robert came to his side and immediately saw the situation, while in the distance, trumpets of alarm began to sound from the main English camp.

"Let these locals abide!" ordered Robert. "They be not our enemy... but yonder our enemy wakes!" he shouted, pointing down the valley. In the main camp could be heard much commotion.

The Brus men melted into the long shadows of the dawn as easily as they had materialized only moments before. Robert and the others followed suit as the English trumpets blasted nearer and nearer.

"That was King Robert de Brus!" exclaimed the man from the well. "I swear, that was King Robert de Brus... God bless him!"

"Then we must flee!" said a friend who was standing close to him. "I fear if it *was* the king, and we're left alive and standin' bold-like here, the English will think we had a hand in the killin's."

"Aye," said the man, his eyes grown suddenly wide with panic. "Ye're thinkin' rightly! Run! Run! Hide in the wood!" he shouted to all the Scots. "And if caught, say we was run out in fear of our lives by what we figured was bandits!"

This sounded agreeable to the twenty or so villagers, who scrambled for the thicket. Two others, running hard to reach cover and being sturdy young men, tired of a peasant's life, were inspired by the raid and agreed between themselves that the rebels' lives were better. At least there was no tyrant's boot on their necks.

Within an hour the English army was thoroughly mobilized and riding against the insurrectionists, but as they had no notion of which way the rebels went, they searched in all directions, finding them in none.

Thus, Robert's renown grew.

Dungal Macdouall

April 14th 1307
Ayr Castle

Aymer de Valence peered from the solar window. It was a cold, drizzly morning, and the earl's mood matched the dreariness of the weather.

He wistfully wiped condensation from the glass with one hand while the other fingered the pommel on the sword strapped to his waist, though he yet wore trews and a long baggy shirt from his night's restless sleep.

The elder of his two captive sisters stoked the fire as the other slipped quietly into the privy. He had thought that, once he had taken Kildrummy, he would get shed them, but that had not happened.

He had grown fond of their company and had taken to dressing them in expensive clothes, elaborate gowns and handmade shoes of exact specifications, and now delighted in introducing them to visitors as his 'dear cousins from Aberdeen.'

Aymer's doleful eyes roamed from the many English galleys, laying at rest in the harbor for use of the army, to beyond the wetlands opposite, to the little town of Ayr. At his feet lay the latest of numerous dispatches from King Edward, again demanding the capture of Brus.

"How far does this madman think a thousand pounds and a fancy goddamned box will go?" Aymer whispered to himself.

He left the window, flopped himself unceremoniously onto the bed, and stared up at the ceiling. "The might of the great English army... damn!" he shouted in frustration.

The one sister, who had been stoking the fire, came to him. She sat on her knees on the bed beside him and caressed his genitals, for she knew no other way to communicate with him. He brusquely pushed her hand away and looked at her.

"What is your name?" he suddenly asked.

She looked at him with her clear, green eyes, and with some hesitation answered, "Lela."

"I never knew that before," he replied running his fingers through her red curls, then along her breast line to the nipple under her luxurious robe.

"Ye ne'er asked afore," she said bluntly, but in her shy manner.

Her sister, wrapped in a large winter robe, emerged through the inside door of the solar and stood before the fire and warmed her hands. Then she opened her robe to expose her naked body to the warmth.

"What be her name?" Aymer asked, propping himself up on one elbow and looking at the younger sister.

"Ye would not believe how we were named, Yer Grace," remarked Lela, smiling.

He laughed... truly laughed, perhaps for the first time in many months of his long and arduous trek of trying to break the rebellion. "And what is the name I won't believe?" he asked.

"Lula." she came back.

"Lula?" repeated Pembroke, "*Lela* and *Lula?*"

"Aye, Sire," she answered with a giggle.

There then erupted from the throat of Lord Pembroke an uproarious laugh that suddenly filled every fragment of the solar.

Startled, Lula turned suddenly toward Aymer and Lela, her bare body framed on both sides by the dark blue of the robe. Fear clouded her eyes, for since they had been coerced into the bed of Sir Aymer, she had heard no one speak her name, save her sister in personal moments. Just as suddenly, she realized her exposure and hastened to pull the robe closed.

But it was too late.

Aymer stopped laughing and grew quite serious, pulling himself to a sitting position. Only the crackle of the burning wood was heard for a long, long, awkward moment.

"Ye're with child," said Lela at last, the color drained from her face.

Lula started to cry quietly and sat on a small stool near the fireplace. Lela came to her and comforted her as best she could.

Aymer sat on the edge of the bed, blinking wide-eyed in wonder.

Then he exclaimed, "I'm havin' a bastard son!"

The sisters shrunk back at his abrupt declaration, fearing retaliation from their huge captor, whom they knew to be cruel when displeased.

Then Sir Aymer smiled and repeated himself, "I'm havin' a bastard son!"

"Ye are pleased, My Lord?" asked Lela incredulously.

"I am!" he said enthusiastically. "By God, if the King of mighty England can have bastard sons, then so can I!"

The sisters smiled meekly. This new attitude of Pembroke's was disconcerting and they felt uncomfortable being friendly with one who had so often treated them shabbily. They trusted him not at all, for now he was strange to their knowledge of him.

Then Lula asked meekly, "How do ye know, Sire?"

"Know? Know what?" he prodded, smiling at the pregnant girl.

"That 'twill will be a son," she said timidly.

"By God it came, and by God it *will* be a son!" he declared sternly then said, "I'll have a drink on it! Bring me a cup of whisky, Wench... Lela!"

Lela jumped to fetch her master a cup of the liquor. Aymer could not resist going to Lula and gently reaching his hand into her robe and rubbing her belly. She was again shy.

Lela came to him with his drink and he held his cup above his head as if to announce to the gods that he demanded a boy child and none other. Then he drank and said, "Perhaps the only things worth havin' in this whole damned country is this here whisky... and you two, with my son."

The whisky surely went quick to his head, thought the sisters as they looked at each other.

He made straight for the table and poured himself a second.

"Great day in the morn!" he exclaimed enthusiastically after he bolted back that cup. "Let's have breakfast! I want a big platter of roast pig and chicken eggs and hot breads and wine... and... I'm as hungry as a three-peckered billy goat is randy!"

The young women giggled at his sudden change in character, but were in agreement with his thought, for they were hungry, too.

. .

Pembroke sent his wardrobe keeper to the cookhouse with his breakfast order as the threesome dressed in silks and jewels for the occasion. They arrived thus formally attired in the great hall, where there was much activity, as the food was just being placed on the table.

"Sit, sit, my pretties," said Pembroke, "you here," he said to Lela and pointing on his left, "and, you with my son, sit on my right," and he patted the chair.

They sat as Sir Aymer had instructed, and the food was piled high in front of them.

As they began to eat, an unkempt Thomas Randolph came into the great hall seeking his morning repast.

"Sir Thomas! You look like dog shit this morn!" greeted Aymer with a broad grin.

"And a great goddamned morn to ye, Lord Pembroke," returned Thomas, giving as good as he had gotten.

Aymer laughed merrily.

Thomas picked up a goblet and a wine bottle and approached the table, taking a seat across from the three and looked at them. Something was different, even peculiar. He poured himself about half glass of wine, then said in a raspy voice, "Ye three look like the barn cat what nabbed hisself a bird."

"We're havin' a bastard son!" Aymer announced proudly, carving a substantial portion from the side of the pig on the serving trencher and taking a large, greasy bite before dropping the rest on his plate.

Thomas frowned in disbelief. But he was hung over from the night before and didn't really care. Without comment he swallowed most of the wine he had poured.

"Ye havin' brains and eggs?" he asked, his smarting eyes glancing at the food.

"Roast boar and eggs," returned Pembroke between bites, "and most delicious, it is, too. You et, Thomas?"

"Nay, but if ye have a mind to share, I'll put some down," replied Thomas, grabbing a plate and a knife. Then, again, he wasn't sure that greasy boar's meat would settle on his stomach, and so started with bread and just a bit of butter.

The large wooden door to the hall opened once again and the steward of the castle entered. "My Lord," he addressed Sir Aymer with a respectful bow, "the Lord of Galloway is within the walls and begs an audience with ye."

"Sir Dungal Macdouall? Here?" questioned Pembroke between bites of meat smeared with gravy and egg yolk.

"Aye, Sire," he returned, and would have spoken more but the door swung open hard, knocking the slight frame of the steward onto the flagstone floor.

Aymer fairly leapt to his feet, not at all pleased.

There stood Dungal Macdouall before him, a man of might and madness wrapped as one.

Thomas turned in his seat to see the great warrior who had beaten the Irish army of Thomas and Alexander Brus in a dark fight, though it cost as many of his own men as of the Bruses.' Sir Patrick stood behind Lord Dungal, and a large man stood beside Sir Patrick.

"What is this untoward intrusion upon my breakfast?" demanded Pembroke angrily.

The head of the Macdouall clan strode brashly toward the table and took a position opposite de Valence, looking him and his pair of opulently bedecked concubines.

"Now I see, Pembroke! We're left to do the bulk of the fightin' with the Brus while ye set about in yer finery havin' victuals with yer trollops," snorted Dungal in derision.

"Have a bite, Lord Dungal," invited Pembroke crisply, squelching his urge to respond to the slur, and instead passing his hand over the table of food in a gesture of sharing. "Perhaps it may improve your rotten disposition."

Dungal's two minions closed behind him, malignantly fingering the hilts of their swords.

Lela and Lula started to move from their seats, but Pembroke grabbed them and held them fast, saying, "Bide with me, My Ladies, Sir Dungal will cause no harm to you... will you, Macdouall?"

As the sisters relented and nervously sat again, Aymer placed his hand on the grip of his own sword as a caution to Dungal and his two companions that he would not be intimidated in a castle under his own command.

Thomas remained seated, nibbling bread and quietly observing, hoping he didn't have to go to Pembroke's aid, considering the hangover he carried.

The tension fairly crackled in the air as both sides glared at each other, until a side door quietly opened and a stream of some twelve armed knights entered and stood behind Pembroke and the women.

Pembroke sat down again, and picked up the meat from his plate to continue eating, a smug smile on his face. Thomas turned back toward the table with his crust of bread.

Pembroke said again, this time more menacingly, "Sit and have a bite, Dungal, and your two bootlickers, too. Besides, you bring fear to the bosoms of these ladies," he added, kissing the hand of each with his greasy mouth.

The three men sat ill naturedly beside Thomas, and Pembroke ordered plates for them and for more food to be brought. Seeing that they were there to place blame, he also ordered a servant to fetch Sir Ingram and Sir Phillip.

"Who be your toadies?" asked Pembroke, curious.

"There's Shaw," said Dungal pointing to the large man, "and this here's Sir Patrick, from Kintyre, who was most helpful to us in a recent fracas.

"Ah, yes," said Pembroke, coldly, "the traitor."

"Patriot!" barked Dungal. "A Comyn patriot, supportin' our great King Edward, I like to think!"

Pembroke continued eating without pause until he had both cheeks full, then said, "There was a 'patriot' like him at Kildrummy, too." He chewed and took a large gulp from his goblet before completing his thought. "For a few stone-weight in gold, he sold out. Right, Thomas?" he asked his silent and hangover-ridden knight across the table.

Thomas nodded slightly and continued to down a bite of bread with his wine. "We showed our 'patriot' at Kildrummy how we appreciated him, too, didn't we, Thomas?" prodded Pembroke with a cunning smile.

Thomas realized that some of the meaning of that speech was aimed at him, but he ignored it.

As the group finished their meal, the two lieutenants that Pembroke summoned arrived. The dirty trenchers and food were removed, and more bottles of wine and cups took their place.

At Pembroke's inquiry, Dungal started the tale of events that prompted his visit. "Ye all know that the Brus is terrorizin' Galloway for the shamin' his brothers got at my hands…"

"Aye," interrupted Umfraville. "A great service to the kingdom."

Dungal looked at him, trying to figure why the popinjay was patronizing him, then went on with his story. "We have spies over the whole of northern Galloway, and one lately spotted the Brus army, and not too far from us."

He paused to take a long sip of wine as if seeking courage to continue the story. "So, out we went for them. The moon was near full, and we were wanderin' along a path beside a wide burn, when all on a sudden… we saw him!"

Dungal now had the attention of the full table, and the knights standing behind Pembroke, as well. Umfraville, perhaps the man at the table most anxious to put an end to Robert Brus, urged Macdouall to continue.

"There he was, Robert Brus himself, just standin' calmly across the stream from us, and wavin' his great arm, beckonin' us, nay *commandin'* us to come for him! And not another soul around but him and us! So, I sent ten good men of horse into the burn to get him. I shouted curses for his name. Then, as my men were fordin', he raised his hands, like this!" Dungal raised his hands to demonstrate the way Robert Brus had done. "And he made the ford narrow down to but a strip so wide, and most of my men were near swept away and fell off their horses into deeper and swifter water than was there before."

"So he made the stream bed change its course with a wave of his hand?" asked Pembroke, his eyes grown wide.

"Aye," returned Dungal. "I swear, it happened exactly as I am speakin' it to ye at this very moment."

Randolph smiled and sipped his wine and thought, What merriment Robert would get from hearin' this ol' woman's tale.

Dungal persisted with his story. "So, one of my men got across the ford to him. The king neither blinked nor ran, but sudden-like, a stout staff came magically to his hand, and with it, he struck the horse dead! Then he drew his great claymore that glimmered as bright as the moon, and his eyes glowed the devil's own red, like… like hot burnin' coals from the furnaces of hell! I swear it! And he likewise dispatched my man with a single blow, and he did the same to the next four men I sent acrosst the narrow ford after 'im!"

"Ye'd been into yer wine flask a wee bit too much that night, I'd say," commented Thomas, who could no longer tolerate the fantasy of the story.

"Nay, man," Macdouall said with widened eyes, "'Tis all the God's pure truth!" Pointing to the large man he said, "Shaw, here, will tell ye the exact, same story, as I just spoke it to ye, he will."

Shaw nodded in agreement.

Pembroke smiled, but refrained from an out and out belly laugh, though it would have been his second good laugh for the morning. Instead, he asked, "So, did lightnin' bolts fly out of his red eyes?"

"Nay, now ye mock me!" said Dungal, knitting his brow in anger and hotly reaching for his dirk as he stood to confront his host, sending his chair crashing backward.

The tensions around the table were suddenly alive again with fear and bold anger.

The sisters screamed in terror.

"Sheath your dirk, Macdouall, for you will have not a target you can best for long," said Pembroke calmly.

Dungal, affronted, grudgingly sat back on his seat, after which the others eased their guards again.

"Tell us what happened, then," urged Sir Phillip Mowbray, he having been most interested in the story.

Dungal yet thought he was being made a fool of and said. "Ye bastards laugh, but I see ye not makin' for Galloway to catch this pack of evil fiends."

"We're not makin' a fool of you," said Pembroke, thinking, Though, you're makin' plenty the fool of yourself. However, he said that part not.

"Well then," Sir Dungal sniffed and drank to the bottom of his wine cup, then filled it again. "I'll tell ye the end of the tale. We was about to send the whole of our two hundred to meet this one, single devil... when, on the ridge above the burn appeared hundreds of his men! Again, 'twas magic! The moon was at their backs and they stood for a quarter of a mile hither and thither on that bank, and each of them had that same look of red-hot embers in their eyes!" His voice had trailed off to a whisper.

The table sat in silence, each for a different reason. Thomas just wanted to get it over with, though there were others whose imagination held them speechless.

"So, was that the end?" asked Umfraville, having found his voice at last.

"'Cept for us, high-tailin' it while our souls were still in our skin," he said.

"This devil-man must not be allowed to go further!" exclaimed Umfraville. The cups and bottles of wine all around jumped as he emphasized his words with the pounding of his fist on the table.

Pembroke took a long breath and pondered the situation. Then he excused the sisters, who had taken to fidgeting in their chairs at all the talk of devils and magicians' evil tricks.

"You, Sir Dungal," started Pembroke after the sisters had left, "return to Galloway and seek out the place where Brus is holed up. Sir Thomas and I will be along directly, with as many knights as we can muster, to clean up this mess."

"Ye know not what ye say, Lord Pembroke," warned Dungal. "If ye come, ye best bring a witch to ride at the head of yer army and ward off the evil placed in this one who proclaims hisself King of Scots!"

Thomas quietly shook his head in amusement, but Dungal was totally convinced of the supernatural powers of Robert Brus. Were it not so, he knew, the rebel would already be firmly in his grasp.

. .

Sir Dungal and his men left Pembroke in the great hall, departing Ayr castle and repairing to Galloway with the intention of following the earl's orders and sending spies into the countryside.

Once Macdouall had left, the twelve knights were dismissed, and Sir Ingram and Sir Phillip retired to their quarters to write letters to King Edward regarding their own ideas on how to bring the rebellion to a swift and victorious conclusion.

No doubt, their letters were full of the details told by Macdouall.

Aymer sat deep in the same chair in which he had breakfasted only an hour earlier. Sir Thomas, in a mellow mood brought on by the wine he still sipped, sat across the table from him.

A bowl of dried figs imported from the Holy Land sat on the table between them. Aymer took and chewed one of the sugary fruits, thoughtfully bargaining in his mind the best way to extricate himself from this deal he had struck with King Edward, this deal that was now gone sour from his viewpoint.

After all, he wanted not the glory, but the power and the money that would garner him greater stature in his homeland.

He had believed he would have this war won within a half year, but it had gone on far longer. As a matter of fact, it had made many a turn on which he had not counted. With the expense of maintaining and provisioning the armies he led, the thousand pounds had run its length and still he had not succeeded, nor did it appear that success was near. But, if fate altered its recent course, he could yet catch Robert Brus and receive the added reward the king had promised him.

The only other way out that Aymer could gauge was for the king to die of one or more of his several afflictions, a perhaps not too distant event in any case. Then, he could simply return home.

Absently, he spoke aloud. "Glory is God's... There is much to learn about yourself in failure."

Thomas looked up from his cup and replied, "Don't expect too much, then failure hain't so bad."

APRIL 22ND 1307
BOTHWELL CASTLE

It was slightly less than a week since Lord Pembroke left Ayr and repaired to Bothwell, one of the grandest castles in Scotland and the earl's chosen headquarters. He had turned Ayr over to Sir Ingram de Umfraville, with Sir Phillip Mowbray as second in command. Since Bothwell was more north and east, the troops were divided rather equally between the two venues to make for a wider line of defense, running generally along the northern border of Carrick.

de Valence had been in residence at Bothwell barely four days before a messenger arrived from the nervous Dungal Macdouall in Galloway.

The young messenger was ushered into a large, opulent room on an upper level in the donjon. Pembroke sat behind a massive, intricately carved oak writing table, and before a stained glass window, which framed his bulky and impressive person. The boy was so taken by the lavish surroundings that he gawked at the luxurious furnishings and the richly woven tapestries without coming straight to the earl.

"Have you a message for me?" barked the impatient Pembroke angrily.

The messenger smiled a sort of one-sided smile that showed missing teeth, probably as a result of confrontations with barnyard bullies.

"Aye, Milord," he said all but inaudibly as he fumbled in his bag, then handed a small paper across the desk to Pembroke, who only grunted in reply.

"Ye have a word to go back, Milord?" he asked. He had grown a bit uncomfortable while the earl broke the seal on the message from Sir Dungal and began to read.

"No," said Pembroke, and waved his hand to dismiss the youth.

"As ye wish, Milord," spoke the messenger, bowing. He backed toward the door, bowing again before he turned and left the room. However, his immediate exit was halted when the tail of his surcoat caught fast in the massive door as it came shut.

Hearing a peculiar sound, Pembroke became amused as the messenger tried to pull the pinched material through the narrow slit, but the weighty door would not yield its prize.

Pembroke wondered how long it would be before the lad opened the door to retrieve his coat. It was one extended, agonizing moment for the intimidated messenger, but an entertaining one for the earl, until, at last, the door opened and the fabric disappeared, and running footsteps receded down the hall.

Pembroke chuckled to himself at the messenger's ineptitude, but his mood changed quickly enough as he reread the message: "Robert Brus has been seen in the woodlands of Glen Trool and his evil army lays about there taking its ease. Hurry with troops for he abides nowhere for many days."

Aymer pushed court documents to the front of his large desk, retrieved a map from a drawer and spread it flat, trying to understand how best to catch the rabbit in his own terrain. He sat thus, studying the pen lines on the parchment and sipping whisky until near suppertime.

. . .

The next morning, after a night of grand feasting and drinking and taking his sexual pleasures with Lela and Lula, Pembroke was ready to set off for Glen Trool.

He had ordered Thomas Randolph to hand-pick fifteen hundred armored and horsed knights from some of the finest the English army had to offer, sent by King Edward for the expressed purpose of flushing out Robert de Brus and his rebels and end their days on earth.

The array looked grand and powerful as it exited the castle gates and, flags flying, fairly cascaded down the hill amid much pomp and blowing of trumpets. Going before the parade, Aymer de Valence and Randolph rode amidst the splendor.

"Ye know ye'll not catch Robert with all this folderol, don't ye?" cautioned Thomas.

"I know that if I do get to him, I'll have an army that will win on my terms, Sir Thomas, and the king will get off my arse," said Pembroke with a smile and a wink.

Knowing he had a far greater force and more weaponry and armor than had de Brus, Earl Aymer was unconcerned about vanquishing the Scot and his ragtag hooligans. His only doubt was whether or not he could get to Glen Trool before they once again faded.

Thomas shook his head and uncorked his wine flask for a quick drink, saying nothing further.

"We'll see how it all plays out." Aymer smiled again.

Thomas shrugged his huge shoulders and rode on.

APRIL 25th 1307
GLEN TROOL IN GALLOWAY

Glen Trool was a hostile, and thus infrequently traveled, wilderness full of rough terrain. There were many hiding places for a mere three hundred men, most of whom had grown up in this environment.

The rebel camp was on land that was boulder-strewn and fairly devoid of trees, protected on one flank by a sheer mountainside, with a more favorable space surrounding it to the edge of the distant wood.

King Robert was up early.

"Ye of a mind to hunt?" asked Robert, kicking the upturned soles of James Douglas' boots.

James squinted up at the seemingly giant silhouette standing over him. "Ye makin' off again, today?"

"Game's a'plenty," replied Robert, cheerfully, "and we've men to feed and meat to dry for when we leave here. Besides, I enjoy the hunt."

"Ye would," moaned James, and he sat upright and stretched his arms and neck. "I hope to be sleepin' in a feather bed somewhere, soon. This livin' in the wild is killin'."

He scratched his head and, discovering a mite in his hair, pulled it out and squashed it between his fingers. Rubbing his fingers in the grass, he asked, "The Campbell goin' with us?"

"Aye, he is." said the king. "He's behind yonder rock at the creek … takin' his ablutions... he'll be back directly." He turned to meet Murdoch and MacKie, the widow's 'boys' who had shown such prowess with their longbows.

"Ye two have full quivers?" he asked.

"Aye, My King," said Murdoch, " but, we'll need not near so many to bring down the deer ye want."

"Save one or two for the king," said James. "He'll be takin' somethin' for a trophy."

Robert laughed at the jest. "No trophy here, save survival."

"I got some bearers for the game," said Neil Campbell as he approached the group.

"Good," returned Robert, and added with a wink, "Soon as laziness, here, gets to his feet, we'll be gone."

"Damn!" swore James as he jumped up with a frown. "This good 'nough for ye?"

Robert and Neil laughed and headed off for the woods, just a few hundred paces away. Murdoch and MacKie were right behind them, and the twelve or so bearers followed with plenty of rope. James strapped on his claymore, picked up a longbow and walked fast to catch up.

The entourage passed the small group of fletchers, who sat in a huddle around a morning fire, enjoying an herbal brew made by one of the group. His recipe was secret, and he was relishing the vexing of his comrades about the main ingredient.

"Ye men make us a great store of straight arrows with an appetite for English arses," said Robert, grinning nonchalantly as he passed.

"Our fingers are numb from the makin' of them, Milord King," teased one of the arrow smiths, who scrambled to his feet and bowed to the king.

"Bring us a good-sized goose or two, Sire," said another, "we need the feathers!"

The king laughed and promised he would. Farther up the trail he said, "I do like to hear the men in an agreeable mood. It bodes well for the day."

APRIL 26th 1307
GALLOWAY NEAR GLEN TROOL

That evening, some three miles north of Glen Trool, Pembroke and Randolph had their tents pitched for the night and were rearing back on leather-seated chairs, just taking the ease of gentlemen and enjoying more than one stiff drink of straight whisky. The fifteen hundred knights, and attendant squires and servants of various descriptions, bivouacked around on the nearly flat ground, straddling a cold stream that provided ample water for the camp.

"Fire's a delight on this cool of an evenin'," remarked Pembroke, far out of character.

"Had yer full measure of whisky this night, ye hain't," remarked Thomas, he pouring Aymer another cup.

Pembroke sniffed and sat pensive for a full moment. Then he said, "Lookin' forward to the endin' of this Brus chasin.'"

"Not near as much as King Robert looks toward it, I'll wager," replied Thomas.

Aymer mused as he took a sip from his liquor. "You think much of him, Randolph?"

"Aye," Thomas replied in mellow tones. "Greatest man I ever knew." He paused and looked at the liquid in his cup before whispering, "And I hate me for goin' against him."

"As I recall, I gave you no other choice, 'cept to die," said Pembroke, slurring his words, "You do r'member that, don't you?" His head wobbled as he turned to look at Thomas.

"I remember, and I swore... ye have me," admitted Randolph with a frown and a growl.

"I knew we were much alike," said Aymer, smiling. "Hell, we were friends b'fore this fracas came about... we'll be friends aft'rit."

"Maybe," grunted Thomas, "if we live beyond the length of Robert's claymore."

"Surely, you *can't* believe... that *all* these knights layin' about hither and thither," said an incredulous Pembroke while pointing his sword in a broad sweep, "won't fetch that little batch of rebels to our gallows!"

"I believe nothin' no more," returned the forlorn knight, "'cept the silence from weary notions... I get from whisky or ale." He tilted back his head and drained the fiery liquid from his cup before pouring himself another. The two sat in silence, staring through blurred eyes at movements in the camp.

"There's always bastard sons!" exclaimed Aymer suddenly, surprising Thomas with the sudden shift of subject. "Let us drink to bastard sons!"

"Ye know what belly yer bastard son grows in," lamented Thomas, refusing to be cheered. "I know not where my bastard sons lay their heads. But, I'm sure I have aplenty."

"Then let's drink to the notion of it," announced Pembroke, holding his glass above his head.

"Why not," said Randolph, adding under his breath, "I'm fixin' to take my next drink, anyhow."

The two men drank on into the night, but from there, they did so mostly in silence, for both were too inebriated for the wit to say more.

. .

"This the one ye wanted?" asked Randolph, the next morning, as he presented an old camp woman, raggedly dressed and mostly toothless, to Aymer de Valence. The hag had long ceased struggling against the iron grip with which the knight had dragged her to this spot.

"That is the one," replied Pembroke as he emerged from his tent into the incessant drizzle of the spring rains.

Her eyes gazed downward. Fear was conspicuous with her every shaking breath as she stood before the great Earl of Pembroke, for she knew not why he had singled her out.

Aymer pulled her head up by the chin so that he could see her face. She blinked as the rain, however gentle, fell upon and near her eyes. He studied her countenance from this direction and that, to see how she would appear to Robert de Brus, when that time came, and decided she would evoke in the Brus exactly the response he desired.

His instructions to her were quite simple and specific in what he wanted her to do for him. At the end of the tutelage the old woman nodded shyly and returned to her forest shelter to prepare for her involuntary journey.

"Let us see for ourselves," spoke Pembroke as he waved his arm to his groom to fetch his horse, "what manner of defense these rebels have."

Thomas Randolph pulled himself aboard his coal black Friesian stallion and waited as Aymer's horse was brought to him. The rain played softly on his armor in a rhythmic tone that took his mind back to when he and Robert were the best of friends. Now, he thought, *I'm* the hunt dog on his trail. Dejectedly, he realized that this meeting could be the end of his old 'crony-in-arms.'

There be no possible way that Robert can withstand these many knights and barons warrin' upon his small coterie, he concluded.

"Where's the old hag?" asked Pembroke, riding up to Randolph.

"She's fixin' to leave. She'll be here directly."

"Then she can catch us up!" the earl said, spurring his large horse and heading south toward the budding wood at a trot.

Thomas hesitated, seeing the old woman hurrying in his direction, then he followed Aymer southward. The woman hastened on foot as fast as she was able, but soon lost sight of them. Fortunately, the wood called for a slow pace for horses as they picked their way among the branches and undergrowth, and the woman again caught sight of them, but she was out of breath from running and was holding her side when Thomas looked back and saw her, again.

He stopped his horse and waited for her to catch up.

"Sorry, Milord," she said between gasping breaths, "me legs hain't what they once was, I'm a'feared."

Thomas dismounted and hoisted her onto the back of his huge steed, then pulled himself into his saddle again. She held tight to him as he kicked the horse's flanks, and they soon caught up to Pembroke, who peered back at them.

"She lose her legs?" asked Pembroke sarcastically.

"Nay," answered Randolph, "but I didn't figure ye wanted her dead in the mud, neither."

Pembroke said nothing more, but rode on, Thomas and the woman following. Up the hill they rode to a low rise that overlooked the whole of Glen Trool.

The men dismounted and stood on the back edge of the ridge.

Loch Trool lay below them in the mist, reflecting the grayness of the sky. Across the loch was the rocky, mostly flat area where they saw three tents, and smoke from at least seven or eight small cooking fires.

"What do you make of it?" asked Pembroke at the end of a long breath.

Seems like the dog's got the rabbit trapped and wants the easiest way to make the kill, thought Randolph, but instead he said to Aymer, "Them boulders won't let the horses get around in there with the necessary speed, and not without givin' plenty of warnin.'"

"Then we'll have to sneak up on foot," observed Pembroke.

"How many, ye reckon?" said Thomas.

"I reckon we have the old hag for the figurin' of that," said Pembroke with a smile. Then he motioned to the poor woman, who neared and looked cautiously over the edge of the precipice.

Pembroke pointed across the lake to the other side of the rocky valley. "You see the camp of Robert Brus yonder?"

"Aye, Milord," she said through blue, shaking lips.

"Go there and do as I bade you," he said, pointing again, this time at the edge of the forest nearest to the Brus camp. "We'll meet you right there at the first light on the morrow, for you to tell us of your findings. You have the wits for that chore?!" asked Aymer roughly.

"A- aye... Milord," she replied, still shaking. "How must I get from here to there, Milord?" asked the fatigued spy.

"Why," said the astounded Pembroke, "you walk, woman!"

"Aye, Milord," she whispered.

Then Pembroke came back with, "Do this well, for if Robert Brus has the slightest suspect that you've been sent from us, he will blind out your eyes and cause his men to use you for target practice."

The old woman shook all the more. "I... I will do the best I'm able, Milord."

"Good! Else you know what will become of you with that bunch of wild heathen," sneered Pembroke as he waved her on.

The woman started off down the hill via a rough pathway that seemed eventually to lead around the loch.

"Your kindness near spoiled our spy," Pembroke admonished Thomas as the woman disappeared into the mists below. "We need her worn to the bone so that Brus will believe she is but a wandering peasant."

"And ye have struck her dumb with fear," returned Thomas.

"Fear, Thomas, is the driver of folk's wits and souls," said the earl in the manner of a philosopher imparting a great wisdom. "She *will* do her part," he assured his companion, adding, "or I shall use her for a target myself."

Thomas grunted and walked down the hill toward their waiting horses. Pembroke grinned with self-satisfaction and followed.

. .

It took hours and numerous periods of rest, but the old woman arrived, drenched and weary in the camp of King Robert. She was seen approaching by one of the pickets, who straightaway took her to Sir Edward. He ordered her to be fed and drawn into a warm shelter, for which she was truly grateful.

As she became warmer and her stomach ceased to growl in hunger, she began to spin her web of lies, as Pembroke had instructed, all the while holding the vision of her frail, limp body being used for target practice.

Then, her fearful imagination conjured a vision of her flesh and innards being eaten by the soldiers in a demonic ritual, and she forgot all else that she was to say.

"Have ye seen any English soldiers here 'bouts in yer travels?" asked Edward.

"Nay," lied the old woman, "only well-wishers for yer cause," she improvised.

Well-wishers! In Galloway? thought Edward suspiciously. He left her then and went for his brother, who was resting on a bed of green heather in his tent.

"Ye speak to this woman, Robert?" asked Edward. "Her wit seems misplaced, and her story rings false."

"Perhaps she is but addled," suggested the king.

"Could be, but I think ye should hear her tale for yerself."

"Bring her to me," said Robert as he sat on the edge of his heather pallet.

Within the tent was a wide, protruding rock that Robert sometimes used as a chair, and when the woman was brought to him he instructed her to sit on the flat stone.

"Ye're a lost wanderer, Mother?" asked King Robert.

"A poor widow, what's been cast out, Sire," recited the nervous woman, keeping her eyes angled toward the ground.

King Robert stood to offer her a dram of whisky, and she immediately felt threatened with his huge presence towering over her. She was awestruck as her gaze slowly followed his body upward to his piercing eyes, set deep in his tanned face and surrounded by his auburn and unruly hair.

Frightened nearly to death, she lost her nerve and collapsed at his feet sobbing, "Please don't eat me, Lord King... please, please I beg ye... eat me not, for I am old and my flesh, no doubt stringy... and me wee ones will miss their dear grandma and..."

"Enough woman!" commanded Robert, frowning in his puzzlement. "Wherefore did ye get the notion I would have ye for food?"

"From Laird Pembroke," the woman blurted as she remained at his feet crying and mewling in fear.

Robert, who now knew her to be an unwilling spy, reached down and firmly took her by the arms, standing her up to her full height. "Where are the English, Mother?" he asked calmly.

Surprised at the question, she swallowed hard, her freightened eyes darting about for an escape. Seeing none, she unburdened herself of her secret, "There are a great host of knights in armor, and on great horses, comin' for ye on the morn, Sire... King."

"From which direction?" asked Robert.

"I know not. But they were across the loch this morn, and I was to meet them in yonder wood nearest yer camp on the morrow's morn," she exclaimed, "in the early, *early* morn."

"How many?" again he asked.

She shrugged her shoulders and replied, "I know not how to count them, but many, many more than I've seen are here with ye."

"So be it," sighed Robert. "Edward!" he called toward the tent opening, and Edward stepped inside. "Take this woman to rest in one of the shelters."

"Ye'll not be a'eatin' me?" she asked in a whine as she was being escorted from the tent.

He smiled, "Nay, good Mother. Here we eat only from the wilderness, what we cannot take from the English."

She was relieved to hear so, and angry at Lord Pembroke for "settin' the fear of Satan" in her bosom.

Robert immediately called a meeting of his lieutenants to plan what they must do for the next morning. At last, perhaps we have a change in our stars, he thought, watching his subordinates hurry toward his tent.

. .

The early light broke on a day that had lost the drizzly rain of the day before, and, save for what lay in puddles and rivulets on the ground, would be dry.

Pembroke and Randolph had led the knights to the wood across the lake from where the woman had been sent to the Scots' camp, and there ordered them to abandon their mounts as they would make their way forward on foot. The wood was but a short distance from the camp, which could be reached relatively quickly at a brisk run.

They amassed in full numbers just over the rise and waited for the appearance of the old spy. The two leaders remained on horseback, as their plan was to let the knights do all the dirty work.

"Where you reckon she is?" asked Pembroke as the sky grew brighter and the birds took to wing.

"No doubt dead on the path from yonder to here," remarked Randolph dryly.

"She had more gumption than that," returned Pembroke.

"Sometimes, gumption just runs out," said Thomas, raising his eyebrows with a smile, and laying the matter to fate.

"Damnation!" cried Pembroke, louder than he intended.

"That was probably enough to wake the camp," remarked Thomas with a low groan.

"I don't give a goddamn!" scowled Aymer. "Where's my old hag!"

"She hain't a'comin'," said Thomas matter-of-factly. "She hain't a'comin 'cause she's dropped dead on the path."

Pembroke grumbled and cursed, more quietly than before. As he realized that his darkness was fleeting, he came to the conclusion that Thomas was probably right, and he was sacrificing valuable time on the slim chance the old camp woman was still alive and able to report back to him.

"Proceed," ordered Pembroke reluctantly.

The captain of the knights waved his sword and the fifteen hundred knights quietly moved through the trees until they came to the edge of the copse. There, before them some few hundred paces, was the Scottish camp. It was gray through the mist, but they could see it well enough to advance.

The dying fires from the night before made wispy, lingering smoke trails. They saw men yet asleep in their shelters. A single man carried a bucket of water up the hill from the loch. All seemed as it should, so the captain yelled the order... "ATTACK!!"

The energized knights ran headlong over the boulders toward the sleeping camp, screaming war whoops all the way.

The camp was not disturbed by the approaching warriors, as men remained asleep in their shelters.

None wriggled or looked about.

King Robert was the first the charging knights saw to show life as he rose from behind one of the boulders closest to them.

Other boulders soon relinquished more rebels, who emerged as if by some witch's spell.

They were neither asleep nor unprepared for the battle.

Suddenly, nothing was what it was supposed to be.

The captain attempted to stop the assault, having been taken with fear as he realized he had led his men into a rebel trap.

The running knights fell over each other in their confusion.

Robert stood at the forefront of his band of three hundred, facing a well-trained army some five times his number. MacKie stood beside him, his bow at the ready.

"Target their leader yonder, Lad," said Robert, pointing toward the man obviously commanding the English knights.

MacKie adroitly drew back his bow and loosed the arrow.

The first strike of the battle found its way into the throat of the captain, who fell dead before one of his knights had struck a blow. Panicking, many turned and fled toward the wood they had just left.

Robert, swinging his great claymore over his head, signaled for a counterattack, and, whooping his most fearsome, led the charge.

Twenty-one de Brus bowmen loosed their five flights of arrows, the last ones being launched as the first ones found flesh under armor. The other Scots rushed forward, their round shields and bucklers held high, some with spears and swords, some with battle-axes and maces, and some with just sharpened, fire-hardened sticks.

The roaring voices of the attacking Scots that early morn would have struck fear into the heart of any man who thought he might have to answer to their wrath.

Even the most stalwart of Pembroke's knights were shaken and most turned and ran in disarray, back across the broken plain toward the woods.

The Scots were hot after them.

Edward, Neil, Gilbert, Robert Boyd, John Wallace, and 'The Black' Douglas, each and all, followed the king up the hill among their ragtag army.

Pembroke awaited with Randolph at the top of the hill. Hearing echoes of the war cries reverberating off the hills, he knew it would be but a short while before it was time for his victory entrance. He envisioned the long-desired capitulation by the illusive Robert Brus, when they heard the panicky cries and the crashing of men running up through the wood from downhill.

"What you make of that?" asked Pembroke, spurring his mount over the hill's crest.

"Hain't good," replied Thomas, following, "whatever else my notion might be."

"GOD DAMN!" exclaimed Pembroke loudly, upon seeing his men emerging from the fog line and scrambling up the hill toward him.

"Time to withdraw," said Randolph, turning his horse and riding swiftly back over the crest of the ridge, with Pembroke near behind.

Within minutes, the knights were also over the ridge and mounting their horses in terror. Their armor had greatly slowed them, while most of the Scots had none, and so had the clear advantage of maneuverability.

The Scots breached the ridge in time to see the knights scattering in all directions below them. Some retreating men were satisfied with being dragged along, hanging from their saddlebows, not taking the time to hoist themselves and their armor into the saddle.

The woods were full of dropped weapons that Robert's men would gleefully pick up on their way back to camp.

But for now, King Robert could not help laughing as his men stood at the top of the ridge making their terrible noises, hooting and defaming their retreating enemy.

Surprise and their boldness had paid off.

The English ran from the mountain as fast as horse and foot would allow. Some forty-three knights died at the hands of the Scots in their hasty flight.

The spider's first strand is affixed to the wall, thought Robert. He then announced to his gathered men, "Glean from the dead what ye can use, and fix to leave Galloway today, for they will be back, I'm thinkin', and better arrayed, too, once their manhood has returned to them!"

MAY 3RD 1307
CARLISLE

After the stunning defeat at Glen Trool, Lord Pembroke sent his beaten knights back to Bothwell to heal their bodies from their wounds, and their spirits from the trouncing. He and Thomas Randolph went not with them, but reported to Carlisle, there to await an audience with King Edward, still laid up in Lanercost.

Aymer was not pleasured by being summoned to the king's side. Rather, due to his continued failure to put down the rebellion and bring Robert de Brus to justice, he terribly feared Edward's wrath.

The morning dawn brought rain again, and that added to Sir Aymer's already miserable disposition. His hands shook as he poured himself a goblet of breakfast ale. Thomas sat across the table from him and, with squinting eyes, shared his ale pitcher.

"Ye need to rouse me so early in the morn?" asked Randolph, as grumpy as Pembroke was glum.

"If you had the notion that this would be the last day of your life, you'd want drinking company, too!" replied Aymer, and he took a great draught of the ale. He next pulled a chunk of bread from the loaf and, having no appetite for food, gnawed timidly at the edge.

"Edward hain't a'goin' to kill ye today," said Thomas, who sipped his ale and chose to drink without any bread.

"Brus is not within my hands," lamented Pembroke. "My poor bastard son will grow up without a father."

"That's why he hain't a'goin' to kill ye," teased Thomas.

"Laugh if you like... but you just might be hanging along side me," grunted Sir Aymer.

Thomas grunted, too, and became sullenly quiet, for he knew it could easily become fact.

"WITNESS!!" shouted Pembroke slamming his cup onto the table.

Randolph jumped, his hand reaching for his claymore, his eyes at least twice as open as they were before. "What the goddamned hell was signified by that?" snarled Thomas, having seen no danger.

"Witness... seein' your own head in the noose... is not so goddamned hilarious! Aha!" he topped Thomas.

The two men drank in silence for the next little while, both deliberating on their possible futures.

Finally Thomas again spoke up, "Well, as ye have often reminded me, ye, yerself would have hanged and axed me almost a year ago, had we not been friends."

Pembroke smiled, "We've had a grand time of it on occasion, we have."

"Aye," replied Thomas. They sat musing over the recent events, prompting Pembroke to speak his mind.

"If I'm hanged and axed this day, will you take Lela and Lula back to Aberdeen for me?"

"And see to yer bastard son, too, I reckon?" questioned Thomas.

"It would be well for the boy to grow up within sight of a real man," said Aymer, nodding.

"And ye think I would do as much for yer son?" he asked.

"I'm... asking," said Aymer awkwardly, and recovering his dominant attitude added with more than a little ire, "...as one who spared your sorry life upon a time... out of *friendship*!"

Thomas paused and looked at his friend, the old despot; they were much alike in many ways, yet he hated the earl for making him choose between Robert and his own life. And he hated himself more, for having chosen as he did. But what did he owe Pembroke that would cause him to want to repay this dubious debt?

Aymer, taking Thomas' silence as meaning the answer was 'no,' sullenly returned to his cup, that was soon emptied.

"More ale!!" shouted Pembroke. "The Earl of Pembroke and Warden of all Scotland wants more ale!"

The kitchen servants scurried to his table with another pitcher of ale and another loaf of bread. "Will there be more, Milord?" one servant nervously asked.

"Not from you," snarled Pembroke, pushing him away.

"Settle yer bowels, man," said Thomas as soon as the servants were out of earshot, "I ne'er said 'no.'"

Aymer blinked. His eyes moistened, "You ne'er said 'aye,' neither."

"I'm sayin' 'aye' now," he quietly spoke.

Pembroke smiled broadly, and overcome with emotion and perhaps with the ale, uttered, "You have the soul of a full-winged angel, my good friend!"

Thomas was somewhat embarrassed and quickly peered around to see if they had been overheard.

"Well, I surely hain't ne'er been tol' that afore!" He sipped at his glass.

"You have never said you'd see to my seed after I'm gone before, neither," replied Aymer, teary-eyed.

"Well, ye hain't hanged yet, neither!" gainsaid Thomas with a smile, and Aymer roared with unruly laughter and lifted his goblet towards Thomas in salute. Thomas returned the gesture and the vessels crashed hard against one another, splattering the air between the two men with ale and pouring it forth down their sleeves and upon the table. They both laughed loudly and drank the remains of the libations down.

"Time to go see that son-of-a-bitch king!" said Pembroke, slamming his vessel to the floor.

"I'll go with ye," said Thomas as he shattered his own cup on the floor and sent pieces skittering to the farthest corner of the room, "...just in case I'm needed to carry yer ugly head somewhere in a basket!"

Again, they both laughed heartily at the macabre jest.

Pembroke sent for his groom and ordered him to saddle both their horses for their visit to the king.

• •

Within a quarter hour, the two men left the great hall and went into the courtyard. There, their lavishly saddled and armored horses were waiting in their finest accoutrements. The rains had subsided for the moment, but the gray skies remained.

The two knights mounted, and while Lord Pembroke's attendants adjusted his raiment for their best appearance, Randolph clucked at his mount and, walking him into the courtyard, looked casually about.

As his gaze wandered, he saw a blackened and rotting head on a pike over the main door to the keep. Somberly gazing upon the relic, he mused on the bad luck the poor bastard had suffered to wind up so, when he was struck dumb by a bone-chilling realization.

He pointed it out to Pembroke, who also took a moment to recognize the all but decomposed face.

It was the head of Thomas de Brus.

The groom, seeing what had piqued the interest of the two men, offered, "There's more of them rebels piked over the gates. You can see 'em as you're goin' out."

Aymer and Thomas said not a word, but wheeled their horses and headed for the main gate of the walled town of Carlisle. Both were mute as they exited the castle, and Randolph was sorely pained that his kinsman, friend, and fellow carouser was dead, and his head, so quick to throw itself back and laugh, was now displayed on King Edward's pike.

Passing beneath the portcullis, the two could not resist turning in their saddles and looking up to see whose head was piked above the gate. Immediately, this time, they recognized the countenance of Alexander de Brus.

Neither Thomas nor his companion could believe that even

England's Edward could have killed such a brilliant scholar as Alexander de Brus, but there, dripping with rainwater, was all that remained of the Dean of Glasgow.

"Damn the blaggards... *damn them all that had part in this!*" uttered Thomas in disgust.

Pembroke's spirits again sank.

They were a doleful sight riding toward Lanercost, in spite of their resplendent mounts and personal finery.

Randolph caught sight of Pembroke as they slowly progressed toward their fateful parley with their king, the same vengeful man who had ordered the deaths of Thomas and Alexander de Brus.

Pembroke was hunched over in his saddle, looking older and feebler than Randolph had ever perceived him to be before. "Seein' yer own homely dome on one of Edward's pikes, are ye?" he asked the earl.

The truth of the question brought tears to Pembroke's eyes, but he acknowledged it not.

Thomas rode along a ways and then, striking the earl on the shoulder, tried to encourage him with humor, saying, "Aw, ye worry too much, ye ol' fart blossom. Ye'll not be seein' yer head above the gate at Carlisle... even if the rest of us do!"

Pembroke smiled a weak smile, then scowled and dug his spurs deep into his horse's belly. The horse reared and galloped off.

Thomas followed.

Theirs was a gloomy ride the rest of the way.

Arriving at the sanctuary, they were greeted by Sir Fulco Ballard, who welcomed them into the king's corner of the building with all the pomp that he could muster, so far from his true bailiwick. They were then offered a seat on a bench along the wall outside the king's bedchamber, from where he conducted most of his business affairs at that time. They included the masterminding of the plans for the war against the Scots rebels.

For what seemed the entire afternoon, they waited. They could hear the tirades of the king coming from inside the chamber from time to time. But no audience for Pembroke was forthcoming.

"What you reckon is keepin' the king from callin' me in?" asked Aymer, picking lint from his tabard and slumping on the hard bench seat.

"Longer we sit about... the longer ye keep yer head," teased Thomas.

Sir Aymer frowned and looked down the hall, away from Thomas.

"Well," said Thomas angrily, "*I* hain't a'gotta see Edward!" With that he stood and walked away.

After ten or so paces he turned back. Despite two pikemen guarding Edward's door, Aymer was the epitome of being alone, his great bulk humped over his lap, elbows on his knees to prop up his arms and hands, which held up his down-turned head. A more miserable sight Thomas could not imagine, though he really did not think Pembroke would meet the de Bruses' fate.

"Aw, scite," murmured Thomas. Then he went back and assumed his place on the bench beside Pembroke.

The two sat in silence for at least another half-hour before the door to the bedchamber opened and Sir Fulco came into the hallway. He walked straight-backed and purposefully, and came before Pembroke, who stood as he approached.

Sir Fulco looked up to see Pembroke's eyes, for he was a much smaller man than the earl, in height as well as girth. "The king will see you now, Milord Pembroke," he said, and turned to lead the reluctant Sir Aymer to the king's bedside.

The door closed behind them, and save the two who stood guard, Sir Thomas remained alone.

"Do you yet know the pain!?" started King Edward, who was in his bedstead leaning against several pillows.

"Pain, Sire?" replied Lord Pembroke, swallowing hard.

"Yes," said the king. "Waiting pains. Not knowing when the door would open to you, or what you might find on the other side."

"I purely hain't got the notion," returned Pembroke as Sir Fulco pushed a chair near to the bed for him. Aymer ignored the offer and went straight to his knees. "If I have offended you, My King, I pray that you forgive me," he cringed, sobbing and groping for the king's hand to kiss it, as further proof to the king that he was truly sorry, though for what he wasn't quite sure.

"You keep your king waiting!" snarled Edward. "I am a dying man, and do you not keep *me* waiting for Brus' head!?"

"Forgiveness, My Lord King, I beg your forgiveness," groveled Pembroke the more.

Edward looked down upon his 'Warden of Scotland' and smiling cruelly thought, He looks sufficiently pummeled to do as I twist him to do, now.

Pembroke sniffed and quaked.

"Sit," commanded the king at last.

Pembroke crawled into the chair, "What be your pleasure, Lord King?" he asked as he regained his composure somewhat.

"I want... *not* to wait," replied Edward as he shuffled through many letters laid out on his large bed.

"You will wait no more," said Pembroke with his eyes to the floor.

"You don't know what you answer," said the king, having read Pembroke perfectly. "You grieve for your life, that I have not yet taken."

Aymer was careful how to answer the king, for he knew him to be a wily fox who virtually danced with his thoughts and changed partners as whim dictated.

"Robert Brus, My King," he said, "is within a hair's breadth of bein' in my hands." He held up his big hands, palms upturned, and snapped the fingers shut.

"Is that a fact, Lord Pembroke? Spies have it that you, and my *bold* knights, were routed in Glen Trool by less than three hundred ragged beggars armed with little more than pointed sticks," chided Edward.

"It was much worse than that... there were many more... a well armed and well trained army," lied Pembroke, "and... and we counterattacked to find they had vanished into what appeared to be misty air."

"You must have been into your spirits, Lord Pembroke!" accused the king.

"We were surprised, I admit... I thought it would be a common arrest, but I miscalculated the might of King Robert's army!"

"KING!? You dare use the word 'king' when you speak of Robert de Brus in my presence!?" screamed Edward, his eyes large and fierce.

Aymer's eyes were large, too, and round with fear, "I .. I ...only meant that...".

The king interrupted him by raising one bony hand, his mood having suddenly changed, "Think nothing more of it, dear Cousin," he said with a smile. "A kinsman is entitled to one slip of the tongue."

Pembroke sighed and sat back in his chair, sweating copiously.

"Enough about the Glen Trool debacle. Let us move on to how you will serve the crown from here forward," said Edward, again shuffling through the papers. From amongst them he retrieved a bejeweled ceremonial sword and impaled a paper at the foot of his bed, holding it out at sword point to Sir Aymer.

"This missive is only hours old, and says that Robert de Brus holes up in Galston, not far from Bothwell and Ayr, where we have many knights and soldiers of foot right handy."

"I shall lead your great army to his defeat... I'll... I'll leave with the morn's sun," replied Pembroke nervously.

"You'll be undone once again with that trick," returned the king, glaring in disapproval.

Pembroke sank back again. What manner of wit does he require of me, he wondered.

The king continued, "Why is it that Robert de Brus lurks about in hill and dale and jumps out at the most inopportune moments to murder great numbers of our brave forces?"

"I know not," shrugged Pembroke.

"You and I both know of his youth. He was trained to be a chivalrous knight, yet he sneaks about and lurks in hiding, and falls upon our men when they cannot easily defend themselves, and murders them in cold blood. Will he not come out and engage us on flat ground as he was schooled? Do you not see... that with our superior numbers and weapons we can easily win such a proper battle?"

"I have tried, Sire, to coax him from his hills. I have tried trickery and he ran away a coward. I know of nothin' that will bring him to the fore in a chivalrous contest," lamented Pembroke.

"I do," said Edward quietly.

"Sire?" queried Pembroke.

"Fulco, take a letter to Robert de Brus!" commanded the king. Fulco picked up his pen and held it ready.

"We offer Robert de Brus all of Scotland balanced on a single battle at Loudoun..." dictated the king.

"I've lost my reason on this," interjected Pembroke, completely bewildered.

"Keep listening to my letter," Edward said, and continued, "If he has the decisive win... we shall abandon all of Scotland to him! And if *we* are the victors... Robert de Brus shall forfeit his life... and his fortunes to us... on the tenth of May... in the year of our Lord, etc ... Have you got all of that Fulco?!"

"Yes, Milord," replied Sir Fulco, still scribbling with his quill.

"Fix it so's it reads rightly," the aged monarch instructed.

Sir Fulco nodded and bowed, to withdraw a few steps back.

"You are offerin' Brus a chance to win all of Scotland in a single fight!?" exclaimed Pembroke.

"I'm offering *you*, my cousin, a chance to win all of Scotland in a single fight," gainsaid the king.

"Send that today, by our fastest herald," he further commanded. "It must be announced and posted in prominent places throughout the region surrounding Galston, Bothwell and Ayr."

Sir Fulco bowed and left, and Sir Aymer listened as the king finalized the plan to take Robert Brus at Loudoun on the tenth of May.

. .

When Pembroke finally left the bedchamber, his faithful friend Thomas Randolph sat waiting on the same hard bench. The guards had changed but he held steadfast.

"See ye still got yer head," he quipped, standing up and stretching out his back.

Pembroke smiled, "Come, my friend. We have mighty works to perform!"

"Sure puffed out yer sail, he did," replied Thomas as the two men left the sanctuary and headed back to Carlisle for the night.

Then, it would be on to Bothwell Castle in the morn.

MAY 6th 1307
ROBERT'S HEADQUARTERS AT GALSTON

The old woman who had been used by Lord Pembroke as a spy at Glen Trool perhaps became Robert's greatest confederate, for she wagged her tongue in his favor so fully, that the news of Robert's victory over the grossly superior English army flew far and wide. With word of his successes, hope, long dormant in the Scottish heart, began to smolder.

As tales of his exploits, some true, some not, spread across the countryside, that faint ember of hope glowed more brightly. Then it began to flicker with added courage, and the ranks of Robert's army, still smaller and poorer by far than that of the English, grew by fives and tens.

To aid in this effort, Robert's brother Edward and the other lieutenants had been dispatched to various parts of Carrick and to lands north, including Cunningham and Kyle, to lay a foundation of truth beneath the rumors and tales that were circulating about Robert's triumphs. As a result of their efforts, many of the outlying areas were handily and easily brought under King Robert's peace.

Robert had established his headquarters near Galston, where he abided when he received the message from King Edward. Though it came bearing Pembroke's signature, the Scottish king knew that only the old fox Edward could promise an end to the aggression against Scotland. Thus, the Scot had studied and vacillated over the paper's contents since its arrival.

His instincts told him immediately that this 'all or nothing' offer was a trick, for both Lord Pembroke's and King Edward's word slipped easily around, as if on winter's ice, to fit their momentary convenience.

In spite of the missive's promise to do so, Robert was certain that Edward would never relinquish his hold on Scotland if beaten, and that, if the Scots failed to carry the day, Edward would put him and his army to death and doom Scotland forever to English suzerainty.

Yet, he could not refuse the meet.

Pembroke and his king knew well their quarry.

Fully familiar with the topography of Loudoun, Robert realized that his small force held no chance against Pembroke's army.

Except for a single high outcropping of rock, Loudoun was a plain, broad and mostly flat, with a thousand-year-old road, laid down by the Romans, passing through it. Loudoun totally lacked any kind of sheltering vegetation or other natural protection for his men.

It did have boggy areas on either side, but the center ground was open and firm, and wide enough for more than half a thousand English knights to charge abreast, nearly the total of his own forces. And there would be line after line of charging knights. He would be easily outflanked; there was simply too much open space there for him to defend.

The English had chosen well their battleground.

At last he called a meeting with his brother and laid out a plan to him, with which Edward de Brus concurred, and without delay they set about bringing it to fruition, for the battle was called for merely days hence. They had little time to gather at Loudoun Hill and prepare for one of the greatest and most dangerous engagements they had ever fought against the English.

And if Robert's plan failed, it would be their last.

Ingram de Umfraville

MAY 7th 1307
CASTLE BOTHWELL

The morning of the seventh Sir Ingram de Umfraville visited Lord Pembroke in Castle Bothwell to discuss the layout of the battle scene. Lord and knight sat opposite each other near the middle of a long wooden table. There was laid flat a large map, held at the corners by various small pieces of crockery.

Surrounding the map were many small papers listing men and weapons and supplies needed for the annihilation of the de Brus forces.

"I have sent several spies to scout Loudoun and its environs," declared Pembroke. "I don't expect to see hide nor hair of them for a day or two, for the Brus will only now be receiving the challenge and has not had time even to plot a strategy… *if* he will stand and fight."

"I would not depend on that, Milord," answered de Umfraville disdainfully. "The rebel has ne'er faired well in chivalrous encounters, but only when he can murder his enemies whilst they slumber in their beds."

"I hear that he has near six hundred in his company now," chuckled Pembroke as Thomas Randolph came to the table and took a seat beside him.

"What's *he* a'doin' lurkin' here 'bouts?" growled Umfraville in a deliberate affront.

"Who?" asked Aymer looking around for another save Thomas. "Of whom, pray, do you speak?" He looked bewilderedly back to Umfraville.

Sir Ingram frowned and gestured toward Thomas.

"You distrust Randolph?" the earl asked.

"Aye," replied Umfraville more testily. "I knew him to be against us at Methven and I thought him against us at Kildrummy! And he did ye no good at Glen Trool, neither!"

"Randolph stays," stated Pembroke, bluntly disregarding Umfraville's opinion of his friend.

Sir Ingram's anger seethed as Thomas grinned at him in a childish way as if to say, "I won and ye lost."

Pembroke returned to his battle plan. "Sir Ingram, you will take the first waves with your thousand knights and five hundred foot. The field is plain... and the road leads straight through the middle."

"Aye," replied Umfraville, "I know the area somewhat... but I expect the Brus to be lurkin' somewhere like the scurrilous dog he is, and attack us unawares."

"If you feel so, you will be wary at all times, never a bad notion for an army, anyway," dryly commented Pembroke as he attempted to move on. "After your troops sweep in with its first wave..."

"Do ye not hear me? He'll not wait for us to arrive at Loudoun plain, but will attack us ere we reach the agreed battle site!" interrupted Umfraville.

"Then?" said Pembroke in a loud, sharp voice. He was unaccustomed to being so interrupted by his underlings.

"Then, yer plan of battle will not work," cried Ingram.

"If ye are jumped elsewhere... fight," interjected Thomas, "Yer forces outnumber his by near three to one!"

"Thomas is right," returned Pembroke angrily. "Engagement is engagement!"

Umfraville's anger boiled all the more. "Why in God's name do ye sit with maps and such layin' about if ye care not for the plan?" With that he picked up a handful of papers and threw them at Thomas, who grinned again, knowing he was pricking at Umfraville's prideful nature.

"Great battles have oft been won once the map was thrown to the dirt," snapped Pembroke, growing tired of Umfraville's whining. "We'll not fully know how to act save when we get there!"

Sir Ingram's hands tightened to fists. His narrowed eyes glared at Thomas, who warily reached for his dirk.

Umfraville jumped to his feet, his dagger in his hand, to which Thomas responded in kind.

Pembroke also stood and, pressing the palms of his hands toward the two men for peace, talked all the while. "Your hatred for the Bruses is rightly strong, Sir Ingram," he stated. "Your desire for revenge for your kinsman, the 'Red' Comyn, could ne'er be hidden in your face when you heard the name of Robert de Brus spoken, and such will serve you well in battle. Yet it serves the kingdom poorly to display your rage at *this* table, for we are all of the same wit and will!"

At Pembroke's chiding, Sir Ingram slowly sat back in his chair, but somehow his scowl refused to wane.

Thomas, rather than returning to his chair, left the table and went to the door to tell the guard to send wine. A looser wit is what we all could use now, he thought.

The three talked on for another hour and a half, during which the plan of attack was adjusted and agreed upon. As the time fled, the wine poured more frequently and that served as oil on troubled waters. de Umfraville returned to Ayr Castle that same day to prepare his troops for their role in the upcoming battle at Loudoun Hill, set for three days hence.

BEFORE DAWN - MAY 10ᵗʰ 1307
BURSTWICK-IN-HOLDERNESS, ENGLAND

Elizabeth awoke early, yet imprisoned as King Edward instructed. Her accommodations in her confinement were sparse. Her bed was a pallet of straw and her table and chairs no more than rough boxes to sit upon when plain foodstuffs and drink were brought to her and her two ladies-in-waiting.

These were endless days for the formerly vivacious Elizabeth de Brus. The old women Edward had confined with her had become more of a chore for her to take care of, than ever it was the other way around. But, on the other hand, their survival had become a daily occupation that kept her from becoming imbecilic with boredom and vexation.

"What so pricks at my soul this morn?" Elizabeth queried herself as she entered the guarde robe for the beginning of her ablutions.

A strange, haunting sensation poured over the entirety of her being as she went about the remainder of her routine task. When she finished, she attired herself in the same dress she had worn every day for the past year.

"Think I'll petition Edward for a new dress," she teased herself as she danced a step, pretending she was in court at Westminster. She imagined the gaiety of the court at tourney times, with its splendor and colors and, most of all, the plenty and exotic variety of things to eat and drink. God in heaven! She could fair taste the succulent meats and smell the aromas of the fresh-baked breads and sweet rolls. Her mouth watered hungrily, for it had been far more than a year since any such delicacies, or any but the barest fare, passed her lips.

"Ol' 'Longshanks' owes me at least a dress," she reasoned. "After all, I am the daughter of the Earl of Ulster, his most loyal captain…"

Her speech awoke one of her ladies-in-waiting. The crone grumbled at being so inconvenienced.

"Back to sleep," said Elizabeth in a quieter voice, "I'll not wake ye 'til full light."

The old woman soon was snoring deeply as before and Elizabeth, still agitated, began to pace the length of the narrow room.

"Holy Mother, must I continue to be tortured this way?" she whispered solemnly as she stopped and stared out the single window afforded her in the chamber. Then she immediately felt the pangs of guilt, for at least she was warm and dry, while Robert and his men, and

Marjorie, Isabel, and her sisters-in-law, were in far worse straits than she, if they yet lived.

The wan light offered barely distinguishable silhouettes of her only luxury, the gardens beyond her window. As she searched out her favorite spots within it through the undulating surfaces of the small glass panes, a single tear traversed her cheek.

"Robert," she whispered into the darkness beyond as she ran her fingers across the cold glass, "dear Robert, I long dearly for ye this day... as I have 'pon all others. But, now... I suffer a trembling dread I ne'er have known before."

She covered her face with her hands and closed her eyes tightly. Her loose dark curls fell over her hands.

"Back to yer worldly senses, woman," she scolded herself, trying to shake the cold, overwhelming fear.

It worked but momentarily.

She sighed deeply with a hint of quavering in her breath as the unstoppable tears rolled one upon another down her lovely, stoic face.

"Where are ye this day, dear Robert," she spoke again into the blackness.

The blackness answered not in return.

King Robert

MAY 10ᵗʰ 1307
LOUDOUN HILL

It was almost light, but before the sun rent the seam between earth and sky, King Robert was perched on the edge of the great rock known as Loudoun Hill and looking northward, from whence the English troops would approach the field. His feet dangled over the edge of the precipitously sloped rock, and a few small, loose pebbles rolled off the edge and bounced down the side to the plain, far below.

As he watched his Scots milling about beneath him, shafts of light made their first vivid streaks across the landscape, and his mind flashed back to the last day he and Elizabeth had been together in their solar at dawn.

"Elizabeth... my sweet Elizabeth... this very sun arises on ye as on me, my darlin' ...and what will this day give rise to," he said aloud as if she were there. "Will my actions help me regain ye to my arms... or remove ye from me, fore'er? Will we meet again in God's warm sunshine, or will I this day enter into the valley of the shadow... for that is the only way I'll not come for ye. But, if I live... then woe unto them that try to keep ye from me!"

He took a deep breath and closed his eyes, feeling the wind in his hair and on his face. It was almost as if Elizabeth had breathed upon him in her closeness. "May ye be with me in spirit, Elizabeth, as I meet the challenge of them who took ye from me." He held his arms out to his sides and up, lifting his face toward heaven in supplication. "I pray

Almighty God be with us both... for though we may be far apart and I know not where ye dwell, I love ye still, and with all my heart."

With his jaw set tight, he reached into his loose fitting makeshift tabard and drew out the royal standard, wrapped about his coarsely made crown. "A crown that mostly is not, my love," he smiled, still talking aloud to Elizabeth, and placed the gold band on his head, adding in his own thoughts, ...but I wear it as if the jewels of the world shone from it.

He completed unfolding the red 'Lion Rampant' centered on the yellow field. The edges blew a bit in the light breeze as he fixed it full out upon his lap. This was the same standard that had flown so proudly at Methven. The browned stain, yet smeared across the middle, especially touched Robert's heart, for it was the lifeblood of the courageous Alexander Scrymgeour that flowed upon the flag as he fell in battle, mortally stabbed by Sir Ingram de Umfraville. The blood of many other brave souls also splattered upon it as they tried to hold the banner above the carnage.

He watched the whole of the battle play again before his mind. Little brother Nigel, jousting at Umfraville with the broken end of the staff and the standard furled about it... just for the sport of it. Dear Nigel, silently mourned Robert. Oh, that I would have ye all, Thomas, and Alexander, and Christopher, and Randolph. And the many others who fell at Methven and Dail Righ... I would that ye were all at my side for this day. Aye, if ye were but with me now, the winning this day would not be in question.

Young Andrew climbed to the king's side to see to his needs and saw the valiant cloth across Robert's knees.

"Andrew! Come lad, enjoy the pleasures of this fine morning with me," beckoned the king, as much to boost his own spirits as to talk with the boy.

"I knew not that the flag had been saved," said Andrew, his eyes affixed to the large flag fluttering in the soft breeze.

"Indeed it was, lad," the monarch replied, smoothing the bloodied cloth with his hand. "Indeed we have our flag, consecrated with the blood of courageous countrymen who bled their lives away for the freedom of the realm!" He grew quiet a moment before adding, "Indeed... we have our royal standard."

Andrew sat beside the king on the rock, "May I touch it?" he asked.

"Aye," said the king as he offered the flag to the squire.

Andrew's hand moved slowly across the flag with a sense of reverent awe.

Watching the boy's respect for the relic, a thought occurred to

Robert and he so spoke it. "Andrew, I would be greatly pleased for ye to be my new royal standard bearer."

Andrew's hand jerked back as if struck by a viper.

"Me?" he asked.

"Ye, lad," he said with a smile much akin to that of a proud father.

"But, I am but a squire, My Lord," he protested mildly, for though he feared the honor was not deserved, at that moment he wanted it to come to pass more than anything else.

"I have witnessed how ye showed yerself in perilous times," the king went on, "and though yet a lad, ye are of the same cloth as that of which brave men are made."

They sat for a long moment, then Andrew hugged Robert and wept at the praise he received from his lord.

Robert returned the hug and smiled to himself.

In a moment more the king ordered, "Get ye a sharpened and sturdy staff and affix this standard to it. Then tell Sir Edward he is to give ye armor from the booty of Glen Trool, for ye are the new standard bearer."

Andrew wiped his eyes and said, "What must I do, My King?"

"Let this cloth fly free and not be captured. Other than that, our God and I will instruct ye as the times for the doin' come," said Robert, who folded the bloodied red and yellow cloth back to a small bundle as he talked, and when finished, handed it to his squire.

"Aye, Sire," returned Andrew. He stuffed the sacred emblem into his shirt and climbed nimbly back down to the plain.

The king followed soon after, to see to the readiness for battle of men and gear, and to their deployment in the anticipated run of the day. He first set 'The Black' Douglas to watch from the pinnacle of the up-thrust rock. No sooner had he done so than a lookout from Little Loudoun, several miles to the east, rode into the camp and hastily dismounted, kneeling when he came to the king.

"They're a'comin', Sire," he said with quickened breaths.

"How many?" Robert asked.

"Well over a thousand armored knights... comin' down the road from Ayr!" gasped the man excitedly. "And at least five... maybe six hundred foot soldiers."

Robert turned to Edward and ordered that the other lookouts from around the camp's outskirts be brought in, for they would be needed now for defense.

A few moments later, Gilbert de la Haye came raging abruptly to the king when he heard the news of the size of the approaching enemy force. "Ye must be a madman to stand against three-fold yer own number! How can ye expect a win!?" he fumed loudly enough for half the camp to hear.

His emotional display caused the king to become annoyed at his apparent cowardice. Rather than so accusing him, Robert took Sir Gilbert aside and said firmly, "Sir, ye are discouragin' those amongst us who may already be afflicted with faint-heartedness."

"I speak only God's truth, Sire," worried Sir Gilbert.

"If ye fear the combat, ye must withdraw," spoke the king softly.

Gilbert stood back a full pace, "Ye callin' me a coward, Sire?"

"Nay, Sir Gilbert," replied Robert coolly, "a coward, ne'er!"

"Then why do ye reproach me so," returned Gilbert, "when I but speak plain sense?"

Robert looked at him for a long moment, before saying sternly and soberly, "This day *will* be ours, Gilbert! Now, take to yer horse, either to help us win our freedom... or to hie away from Loudoun plain."

Gilbert looked Robert eye-to-eye and, believing what he had said, felt a sudden calmness envelop him. His pounding heart ceased to throb in his ears and his breathing came more normally as his gaze was held spellbound by the sincerity of his king's.

"As we planned," he said bowing humbly and, mounting his destrier, placed his helmet on his head. With a sturdy war whoop, he then unsheathed his claymore and, swinging it around his head, rode to gather his command.

Sir Gilbert had gone not ten paces when 'The Black' Douglas yelled an alarm and pointed to the north. They all turned to look, and Robert quickly estimated that at least fifteen hundred more of the enemy were maneuvering through the trees at the far end of the road and arraying themselves along the tree line.

As they poured into the valley to face the rebels, it seemed to the out-manned Scots that the line of warriors had no end.

In their ever-widening line, the English knights were a beautiful, but terrible sight in their polished armor and astride their fine horses, which were also dressed in brightly colored array. Each man held a shield with his family's contrivance painted on it, and many had affixed plumes of feathers or sprigs of evergreen to their helmets. Some had colored cloths festooning their lances or their helmets, in remembrance of special ladies they left behind. Above them flew banners and flags of every description and color imaginable, led by the royal standard of King Edward, and the dragon banner declaring "no quarter."

Douglas was soon on the plain again and came hurriedly to Robert. "They make a fine-lookin' bunch, do they not, Sire?" the young knight excitedly asked his king.

"Aye, Sir James, they do, but appearances mean little once the battle is joined." The king looked about him at his motley band of less than six hundred and smiled.

God bless them, he mused, they will teach their smartly dressed foe a lesson or two before the day ends.

"Ye, each and every one, know yer work. Let's be about it," said the king with great calm, and he climbed aboard his huge Friesian.

He wore proudly his crown, and over his shirt and trews, a chain-mail coat and upper body armor, overlaid by his tabard. His legs were covered up to the knees by animal skins, fur sides out and laced with narrow leather strips.

Except for his crown and tabard, he could have been any one of his sturdy soldiers, and yet, with his claymore by his side and a battle-ax affixed to his saddlebow, he was magnificent in appearance and in demeanor.

Young Andrew arrived, bedecked in armor slightly too big for him, but he looked as fearsome as the others upon his spirited, rearing horse as he stalwartly attended his king to the battle lines, holding high the royal standard.

Edward and James Douglas followed, after whom came the forty horsed highlanders of Christina of Carrick.

The specially trained phalanxes of Gilbert de la Haye, Neil Campbell, Robert Boyd, and John Wallace were next in the lines of defense, and trotting to their places after them came the three hundred soldiers of foot.

The main knot of the combatant body, those better armed, stayed steady within approximately fifty paces of open ground in the middle of the valley, their line strung across the cobbled roadway and equally on either side.

The other brave souls filling the ranks wielded antiquated swords, knives, and battle-axes, such as had seen service some hundred or more years earlier, or sharpened sticks and similar makeshift weapons.

Area farmers, armed with pitchforks, scythes, and other farm implements, stood shoulder to shoulder with them, creating at least the illusion of a battle-ready line when seen from the enemy's viewpoint.

But the enemy could readily discern that there was not a second line of rebels, and they laughed at the Scots as being unfit opponents.

Hearing the deriding laughter and shouts from the magnificently arrayed English, the Scots stood stoically in position, the king in the center front with the royal standard, carried tall and proud by young Andrew, waving wide in the breeze behind him.

The highlanders flanked the king but were back a pace or two.

On the other side, Pembroke's forces, aligned in the trees, waited as the men from Ayr under the command of Sir Ingram Umfraville lined up in front of them.

"Those who just came," explained Robert as he turned around in his saddle toward Andrew, "will be the vanguard wave."

"Aye, Sire," said Andrew with a toss of his head indicating he understood.

Then he swallowed hard as stark reality sent a tingle up his spine.

One of the farmers began it, and others joined in, a jeering chant that was soon picked up by nearly everyone to tantalize the English: "Tail-ed dogs, Tail-ed dogs, Tail-ed dogs, Tail-ed dogs," and they shook their shovels and hoes in the air to stir their enemy's anger. The English troops yelled insults back until there was hardly anything heard on either side but a great roar and clamor.

Umfraville drew his claymore and swung it wildly in the air. Betwixt the jeering and the sight of Robert Brus quietly standing less than a hundred fifty yards away, his blood boiled with the hate of his self-declared feud and he started his charge.

His well-trained men remained waiting however, for the battle signal from the trumpeters.

Umfraville realized he was alone before he got halfway to the Scots.

He reined up his beast and turned toward his men, who wondered what manner of man would alone charge a waiting army, even this puny one.

Impatient and embarrassed, he screamed curses at them for failing to follow him.

The Brus Scots laughed contemptuously as he stood furious between his men and them.

"Ye'll taste of hell-fire this day, Robert de Brus!" screamed Umfraville as he shook his claymore in the Scots' direction.

They laughed all the louder and continued their jeering.

Umfraville turned his horse and dug his spurs deep into its belly, tearing the flesh and opening bright red streaks along their paths. The animal cried out in pain, rearing and whinnying, and shook its great head so that it nearly unseated its rider.

Umfraville gouged his spurs again into the horse's flanks and the creature bolted hard for the English ranks.

Pembroke came to his side from the ranks of the second array, which he had led from Bothwell Castle. They were the very ones that had been with him at Glen Trool and had acquired a healthy respect for this rabble, this Scottish band of unlikely soldiers.

"You holdin' together?" asked Pembroke.

"Aye! Aye! Aye! Goddamned well, I am!" screamed Ingram as he glared down the road at King Robert. The King of Scots had not so much as drawn his sword during Umfraville's charge, but he and his army had stood solid as God and fate would have it.

Pembroke, dressed in all his glory with gold and silver armor plate and jeweled dagger and sword, pranced his well-armored horse to and fro before the center of the front ranks as he sized up the competition. Then, he returned to Umfraville to confer and to bolster Umfraville's courage through his sense of logic.

"I see it thus, Sir Ingram: They have a weak position and their flanks are poorly arrayed with untrained riffraff. Further, they have left themselves much room behind for retreat... They do not expect to win."

"Then why are they here?" asked Umfraville from the back of his yet smarting and unsettled horse.

"Chivalry, perhaps, or plain and simple pridefulness!" he adjudged with a smile. "This day will be the last on God's green earth for 'King' Robert de Brus, I assure you."

Among the Scottish farmers was one who played the pipes, and at that moment he stood behind the center of the Scots lines and began to play a merry tune. Those few who had been with the king at Methven looked to the bloodied royal standard and heard the pipes 'a'windin',' and their hearts stirred wildly for their cause. The feeling was contagious as patriotic boldness impassioned every Scottish soul there, waiting for the English assault to unleash itself.

Pembroke then gave the order to trumpet for the charge.

Umfraville licked his lips and gritted his teeth as he slammed his helmet shut. He again swished his claymore wildly and spurred his horse, still bleeding from the previous vain charge.

The vanguard started their roll as over three hundred knights moved out in a single line, the main and rear ranks launching themselves at the proper times to be close behind.

The ground shook with the vibrations of a thousand large destriers, thundering to meet their enemy of barely six hundred poorly armed Scots, including no more than three score and five horsed knights and a like number of untested squires.

King Robert, the sun at his back, waited until the attacking force got halfway to his line before he gave the signal for his men to retire to a less advanced position.

The English knights lowered their lances and positioned their strong shields for combat as Robert's knights retreated twenty paces, through the ranks of the phalanxes.

Seeing the maneuver, though the sun was in their faces, the proud

English understood it not, for it was expected that the relative handful of free Scottish knights would come and meet them in one last chivalrous onslaught.

Umfraville, leading the charge, became emboldened by the apparent retreat and was even more eager to reach the Scots' line.

The Brus is mine, he thought. I have revenge for the killin' of the Red Comyn at last!

He encouraged his troops onward all the more.

As the magnificent charging horde drew nearer to the Scots' paltry number, the farmers fell back, some gripped with such fear that they turned and bolted in panic.

That was well, for it gave the galloping warriors the desire to chase down the running rabbits, and they had no thought of there being trenches ahead, dug by those same farmers, until that first imposing wave fell headlong into them.

On either side of the old road, and stretching two hundred yards across the plain to the boggy outlands, Edward and his hastily recruited farmers had labored for days, from first light until after dark, digging three successive ditches in the tall grass.

Each was deep enough to ruin a horse when it fell in, and wide enough not to be easily jumped. Should one trench be jumped, the next was placed to be inescapable.

Even the warriors had lent a hand to these preparations. As Robert instructed, they left untouched only the fifty paces in the center to be accessible by a charging foe.

Now, they were seeing compensation for their labors as the enemy hurled itself into their waiting traps.

Umfraville, who many thought allowed the vanguard force to overtake him so that he personally would not suffer the first round of conflict, exulted in hearing the screams of men and horses to his right and left, and the awful crashing of armored bodies thrown to earth.

The Scots were being taught their lessons, Umfraville thought.

Turning to watch the carnage he expected was being inflicted upon the hapless Scots, he was stunned to realize that the noise he heard came from the vast majority of his vanguard line, falling victim to the well-placed ditches.

He reined in his horse when he saw the toll they had wreaked upon his grand army and screamed, "God in Heaven! We've been mislead!"

A handful of the vanguard wave, still to his rear, immediately fell over top of Sir Ingram, and his bewildered and panicky horse threw him across several others before he sharply collided with the ground, leaving him badly shaken and momentarily disoriented.

The second wave, close onto the first, soon joined them in the morass of flesh and metal. Only those in the center of the charging line were spared the ditches, and their expectations were far from the Scots presentation.

Instead of having horsed knights fight horsed knights, Robert had sent forward his companies of spearmen, fronted by several lines of stalwarts carrying shields of varied descriptions, including round wooden ones, metal ones of various shapes, mostly captured as booty, and others, made merely of wattle smeared with clay.

The men behind the shield bearers were the largest and bulkiest of Robert's foot soldiers. Wedging the butt ends of long, wooden shafts into the mud, they held low the sharpened ends and waited.

"Steady, lads!" shouted Robert, facing the onrushing first wave from behind the bristling formation.

Gilbert de la Haye and John Wallace commanded the forward-most detachment and anxiously watched as the approaching cavalry lowered their lances to accommodate the heights of the defenders' shields.

Please God, that their wooden spears are longer than the lances of the advancing knights, Robert prayed.

In only a few pounding heartbeats, the tale would be told.

"For Scotland!" shouted the phalanx commanders.

Instantly, the fire-hardened points of the long, stout spears rose up in unison to the height of the horses' chests or their riders' groins, and those wielding them pushed the butt ends deeper into the dirt and leaned hard upon them to hold them fast.

The advancing knights had no escape by the time the shafts shifted, and they and their horses were impaled upon them by the score.

About twenty Scots fell, wounded or killed in the first onslaught, either by hurled English lances or the shattered vestiges of their own weapons.

"Retreat!" ordered Sir Gilbert when he saw the damage his relatively small group had successfully inflicted.

John Wallace instructed his men likewise, and both commands dragged their casualties with them to safer ground.

They were replaced by the commands under Neil Campbell and Robert Boyd, who quickly set up their defenses for the next phase of the battle.

As the main wave came rushing close onto their position, King Robert gave a loud whoop and drew his claymore.

Ingram de Umfraville stood some thirty paces back from the engagement, cursing the name of Brus and looking over the field for his claymore and his mount.

Umfraville's knights of the vanguard wave who were yet able, had been trying, hampered by their heavy armor, to climb out of the ditches and get back to their own lines, when most had been trampled or crushed by their fellows in the main wave.

Reining in their steeds with all their might, the ill fated knights could not stop their charging mounts, and, like the vanguard, tumbled one upon the other into the trenches.

The farmers forestalled with hoe and shovel any escape by English soldiers who tried to crawl out of the deathtraps on the Scots side.

Lord Pembroke and Thomas Randolph were puzzled by what little they could see.

"You tell what's happenin' Thomas?" asked Pembroke, frowning.

"Too many men on the field," replied Randolph, squinting into the sun as the two men sat astride the horses in front of their waiting army.

Seeing their peers in the throes of destruction, those nearer the center of the main wave turned their horses toward the small opening in the center, and suddenly hundreds of knights were trying to squeeze onto a very narrow strip of land.

Those brave English knights became their own worst enemy, for as more of them crowded in upon each other, they were killed and wounded more often by their own swords and horses than by the Scots.

Pembroke's horse whinnied and jumped as the cries of dying men and horses filled the air.

Pembroke gently patted him and watched intently.

As the rear wave passed in the attack they could see Umfraville standing in the middle of the field, shaking his fists in the air.

"Son-of-a-bitchin' idiot!' exclaimed Sir Aymer. "Go save that little bastard's arse!"

"Aye," said Thomas Randolph, spurring his horse toward the melee.

"And see what else is about in that pile!" shouted Pembroke as Thomas rode off.

Many of the knights had turned and were heading back to their ranks, the field being too narrow for them to join the fight.

The Scots had done the maximum damage possible with their tightly packed stationary pikes, and abandoned that technique for some old-fashioned sword work, at which they had become proficient under the tutelage of their king.

Thomas had his horse in a trot and at first passed Umfraville by. He had caught sight of King Robert in the thick of the battle, with a claymore in one hand and a battle-ax in the other, taking lives and limbs with both.

He grew fascinated watching Robert and Edward fighting together, side-by-side, dispatching all who approached them. To him it seemed a dance of grace and beauty, in spite of the horror.

In a brief moment of respite, King Robert looked beyond the immediate fray to see what the enemy had next in mind to do and caught sight of de Umfraville, running helter-skelter around the rear of the English line like a madman.

Nearby, a single English knight sat his horse and watched the Scot king over the slaughter.

Who is he that looks so familiar, Robert silently queried himself. He knew the man, he was sure, but viewing him at a distance and amidst the confusion, could not put a name to him.

Just then his attention was drawn toward a frenzied enemy, nearing his left and prepared to strike. Robert deftly turned away the blow with his claymore, and followed with a single blow from his battle-ax that caught the attacker in the unprotected underarm, slicing well into the ribcage. The man fell between their two horses and was trampled underfoot.

It suddenly occurred to Robert who the English knight was, so calmly sitting his horse just beyond the battle's reach. But Robert's horse turned this way and that, trying to maintain his footing on the increasingly treacherous ground, and Robert was unable to catch sight of the knight right away.

"Thomas!" he yelled several times, but Randolph could not hear him over the cacophony of battle, and Robert failed to glimpse his nephew before he was again involved in dispatching the foe.

Several hastily retreating English knights nearly ran Umfraville over.

None stopped to pull him aboard his horse. Thomas, at last, turned his horse and approached Sir Ingram, "Ye had 'nough?" he asked.

"Go to hell!" screamed the livid Umfraville. "And wait for yer friend Brus to join ye! I'm seein' Brus flung into hell-fire this day, by God!"

"Wouldn't count on it," returned Thomas.

"Is he dead a'ready?" said Umfraville, tugging at Thomas' leg armor.

"Looks plenty lively to me," said Thomas with a smile, glancing over his shoulder.

"Why are ye so goddamned happy?" screamed Umfraville, stomping the smooth stones of the old road in frustration.

"'Cause ye hain't." Thomas grinned. With that he reached his strong arm down to give Ingram a hoist up to the back of his horse.

The two rode the one horse back to where Pembroke sat his fine steed, and upon reaching him, Randolph unceremoniously dumped the still ranting de Umfraville on the ground before the Warden of Scotland.

"Cursed both my ears off," remarked Thomas, chuckling.

"Looks like you have the most of both, still," teased Aymer.

Umfraville then had a full-blown outburst of profanity. Pembroke nudged his horse down the line to get somewhat out of earshot, but it didn't work.

Umfraville followed Pembroke and Randolph around screaming, "I knew ye couldn't trust that Robert de Brus for a fair fight!"

Meanwhile, the battle for the narrow stretch of land began slowly to wane as the survivors of the English lines extricated themselves from the mess as best they could. Many deeply resented Umfraville and blamed him for the poorly planned attack.

The majority painfully pulled themselves and their dead and wounded comrades from those horrible ditches, where struggling horses yet inflicted broken bones and mortal wounds upon those who could not flee.

Sir James Douglas lost his horse to an Englishman's sword, barely jumping clear when the beast hit the ground.

"Damn!" he cried, getting to his feet just as another enemy, also unmounted, came to meet him.

They fought until Douglas finally wrestled his opponent to the ground and pushed his dirk through the man's helmet visor. The stab was deadly, the scream, brief.

Realizing Douglas was on the ground, Robert glimpsed a riderless horse running toward him and grabbed its reins. He managed to maneuver the beast through the struggle, with some help from his ax and boot, and handed it over to Douglas. "Ye'll be likin' this English one," shouted Robert over the din, and he wheeled his own horse to counter an attack from his rear.

James Douglas climbed upon the saddle of the well-armored horse and proceeded to battle the next knight, who came rushing to meet him.

There was yet a bloody jumble of English knights and Scots rebels standing toe-to-toe and hoof-to-hoof, and fighting with every breath of life in their bodies and souls. Brave men, they were, every one fighting for king and country, each understanding the cause as he saw it.

It soon became apparent to all within the knot of the fight that the Scots were getting the better of the English, who continued by ones and twos to yield ground or leave the fight entirely.

Some hoped the Scots would make the mistake of following them, because Pembroke had yet to unleash his troops from Bothwell. Pembroke's stalwarts would have relished a return engagement with those who had, only a fortnight ago, made such a mockery of them.

As the English vacated the narrow strip, Robert reformed his men and again stood in the forefront of the configuration, his claymore and his raiment bloodied and his head, encircled in the small band of gold, held high.

Andrew Stewart, himself bloodied in combat, moved forward in the group of nearly exhausted, panting soldiers, to display the standard closer to the king.

He had not let his banner down and had one-handedly slaughtered two individuals who seemed determined to cause the royal flag to slip to the mire underfoot. He was shaking with excitement and overtaken with a sense of valor he had not experienced before.

Instinctively, he screamed loudly and whooped along with the other Scots. They knew that it was not over, but they had undeniably won this first clash.

Across the field, Thomas Randolph saw King Robert and his men and a swell of contrition and admiration came over him that he could no longer resist.

Lord Pembroke watched with growing suspicion as Thomas unlashed his wineskin from his saddlebow and offered it to his lord with one of his ingratiating smiles. Pembroke took the skin and drank deep.

"Don't do this Thomas," begged Pembroke as he handed the skin back to him.

Thomas drank the wine and corked the spout as he replied, "Ye know I have no choice, my friend."

"You *do* have choices," returned Pembroke, somewhat angered, "and as you make choices, so must I."

Thomas made no objection or comment, but slapped Aymer on the back and smiled.

Pembroke turned in his saddle. "Bring me a crossbow and a bolt!"

"It matters not," said Thomas.

The crossbow was handed up to Pembroke by a squire from within the ranks. It was loaded and cocked.

Thomas, still smiling, clucked at his horse and headed at a walk for Robert's line.

Pembroke drew the weapon to his shoulder and aimed it straight at Thomas' back.

Thomas slowly rode on, expecting a quick death at Pembroke's hands. 'Twould be more deserved, he philosophized to himself, than leadin' the sorry life I been livin.'

Sir Aymer reluctantly placed his finger on the trigger and started to squeeze it, slowly.

"Shoot the traitor, ye son-of-a-bitchin' bastard!" screamed Umfraville, realizing what was happening. Pembroke turned and looked disapprovingly at de Umfraville, who grew temporarily silent, knowing that his outburst had harmed only himself.

"I will deal with you later," was the earl's only comment, and he looked again toward Thomas, little more than twenty paces away. He re-aimed the crossbow and placed his finger again on the trigger.

Thomas stopped his mount and turned. He smiled and waved merrily to his drinking comrade.

Umfraville, for the second time, screamed and cursed Randolph, and Pembroke for not shooting the Scot.

Pembroke, incensed at his subordinate's ill-considered outbursts, turned and trained the weapon on him. He thought hard for a minute about how he had really rather shoot the now quaking de Umfraville, for whom he cared little, than Thomas, for whom he cared much.

His nostrils flared and his jaw clenched, the earl dropped his aim and fired the deadly missile to thud between de Umfraville's trembling feet.

And Umfraville, at last, shut up.

Handing the spent weapon back to the squire, Aymer then looked to Thomas and yelled, "Don't forget you'll be standin' for my bastard son, Randolph!"

"I hain't forgot," returned Thomas, and with a last wave, he swung about and rode on toward the Scots.

Aymer walked his horse and followed him a few paces.

He found it hard to release Thomas.

In a way, he thought of him as his only confidant in the world.

Across the field, Edward saw the English knight approach and said to his brother, "Here comes a messenger, wantin' us to surrender."

"See what he has to say," replied the king, paying little heed to the approaching figure. Even though Robert glanced up and saw Thomas coming, he discounted the notion that it was he, for it had been said that Thomas was executed with Christopher Seton the previous summer. Besides, when Robert had earlier called his name, Thomas had failed to answer.

"Looks like Thomas Randolph!" said Edward as the knight grew closer.

Now Robert studied the form on the English horse and his heart beat faster with pure joy. It *was* Thomas!

He yet *lived*!

"Aye! 'Tis!" loudly exclaimed Robert, who then spurred his horse over the carnage into the field to meet him.

"Ye're not yet dead?" questioned the laughing king as he neared his old friend and kinsman.

"Look dead, I might," exclaimed Thomas with equal excitement, "but, so far, I hain't!"

Robert reached across to Thomas and hugged him boldly. Thomas awkwardly returned the gesture.

The king whooped and Thomas cleared his ear with his index finger and shook his head, grinning. "Ye are purely good at hollerin'," he exclaimed with raised eyebrows.

"If ye are alive," asked Robert, "is... is Christopher, also?" Robert asked, hopefully.

Thomas shook his head sadly.

"Nay, Sire, I saw him die with my own eyes."

The two grew solemn and quiet.

At the other end of the battleground, Pembroke watched the 'homecoming' and sighed, dejectedly. Best nothin' happens to me lest my son be raised a damned Scot, and my women be taken to Scottish beds, he thought, then resignedly chuckled to himself and walked his destrier back to the line.

Ingram Umfraville fumed yet, though he was silent. Not only was Robert Brus still alive, but he had defeated de Umfraville, once again.

A wounded captain of Umfraville's command passed Umfraville by and came directly to Pembroke. "They have broken us, Milord," he reluctantly admitted as he sank lower in his saddle and faltered in pain and blood loss from his wounds.

"But you were so many!" remarked Pembroke, disgruntled, adding, "Ditches be damned, you *still* greatly outnumbered them!"

The captain raised himself in his saddle only enough to answer. "They knew just how much ground they could rightly defend... and forced us to fight within it. Their light armor allowed them free movement, whilst, once we were unhorsed, we were but clumsy fools, unable even to defend ourselves against them."

The captain grew faint, slumping all the more in his saddle, and would have fallen had Pembroke not caught him.

"He is a brave man... see that he lives to fight another day," the earl said to the men who gently lowered the captain from the saddle.

"Aye, Milord," replied one of the men, and four stalwarts took the unconscious fellow away to treat his wounds.

Pembroke summoned a squire to wipe the felled captain's blood from his hands and armor.

The captain's pained words had been a cold slap in the face to Umfraville, sore and headachy, and smarting severely from the disdainful glares of those around him. Desperate to overcome their scorn, he walked straight to one of Pembroke's constables, astride his horse only a few paces away.

"Get the hell off yer goddamned mount!" screamed Umfraville in his usual ill temper.

The constable frowned and started to kick the wretched looking Umfraville back into the mud, but he first looked to Lord Pembroke.

Aymer shrugged and, being curious about Ingram's intentions more than anything else, signaled for the constable to dismount. He did so, however reluctantly, and handed the reins to Umfraville, who grabbed them in haste and climbed aboard.

He gouged muddy spurs into the horse's flanks and galloped impetuously across the field to where King Robert and Thomas Randolph calmly sat astride their chargers.

Umfraville paid little heed to his wounded and retreating English troops, most of whom were admirably trying to help each other out of the murderous pits and back to their lines.

All across the field men of both sides wondered what was afoot and stopped to gawk.

Umfraville swung his claymore above his head and screamed curses, ending with a challenge to the Scottish king: "I claim the right of single combat with ye, Robert de Brus!"

"Who is this muddied brigand?" asked Robert, puzzled.

"Ye know him, Sire," explained Thomas, grinning. "It's Ingram de Umfraville, and he's plenty unhappy ye've thrashed well his command."

"Then, where was he when the fightin' was a'plenty?"

"Flat on his back in the midst of yon field," laughed Thomas.

Robert stifled a laugh as Ingram's impatience got the better of his tongue and again he screamed his demand.

This time, Robert drew his claymore without another word, and nudged his horse forward to face Sir Ingram. The self-declared Comyn avenger could not abide the wait and spurred his horse to meet his enemy all the sooner.

In his haste he disregarded the fact that he rode across bloody, carnage-strewn mud, and reining in his mount as he approached Robert, caused the animal to slide at the critical moment.

Taking his first swing at Robert, Umfraville felt his mount's footing giving way, and as he tried to recover, the claymore went astray and cleft one of the frightened beast's ears clean asunder. Screaming in pain, the horse reared and dumped the off-balance Umfraville, who fell backward into the gory mud, yet again.

The Scots' troops, observing the fracas from their positions, cheered as the knight fell to earth.

Some of the retreating English troops who had stood and watched cheered as well.

It was clear they had no respect or affection for their commander.

"Seems he addled himself, Robert," commented Thomas, riding to where Umfraville's limp, fully armored body, sans helmet, lay unconscious. Dismounting, he picked up the muddy, pompous ass and threw him across the saddle of the constable's horse, turned it toward the English lines, and slapped it on the rump.

Robert and Thomas returned to the Scots' lines to await attack.

The piper began to play anew as the warriors reformed their array, knowing they would not have the element of surprise on their side this go-round.

"They've got right smart more to come at ye," said Thomas as he prepared to don his helmet.

"Appears so," said King Robert, taking a long draught from his water skin, "but we're standin' ground."

The bewildered horse carrying Umfraville's unconscious form had run off at such a pace that the knight slid off onto the ground, just short of the tree line where waited the earl and his army.

Pembroke laughed so hard that his eyes teared up, and he uncorked his wineskin and toasted Umfraville's heaped carcass.

"He's muddied my horse and fairly cleaved his poor ear!" complained the constable, once he had caught his abused mount and walked it back to where the earl sat. Pembroke made no comment, and the constable, wishing not to provoke him, simply mounted and asked, "Form up for the attack, Lord Pembroke?"

Pembroke again shrugged, and, looking at de Umfraville, chortled.

The constable frowned, thinking Sir Aymer was poking fun at him or his one-eared horse, to which he objected nearly inaudibly, "Hain't funny!"

"Hain't... but 'tis," returned Pembroke, taking no offense and glancing at the field before him. He again opened his wine flask and thought to drink, but first, he looked at the constable.

A small witful smile crossed his heavy-featured lips.

"Care for a bit of the vine?" he asked.

Pembroke hated to drink alone.

"Mindful proud to partake," the constable remarked, licking his parched mouth.

Taking the skin from the earl, he measured a great swig into his mouth, so that his cheeks were expanded to the fullest. After all, he might not get an offer of a second drink.

He handed the flask back to Pembroke, who also drank a mighty swig.

They looked across the battlefield. The earl laughed sardonically and shook his head at the Scots preparing to oppose another English line.

He saw Robert and Thomas sitting their horses, proud and ready.

Though the Scots had been bloodied, they had not been hurt badly enough for Pembroke to send his elite force to meet them, and perhaps to be so direly battered as was Umfraville's.

No. God is with the Brus, this morn, he thought. The fortunes of this war have turned.

"Back to Bothwell," ordered Pembroke, peeling off and leaving the field.

"Who's fixin' this mess?" protested the constable.

"Umfraville... when he comes to himself," replied Pembroke without turning around. His horse pranced gingerly over top of Sir Ingram, with the constable falling in immediately behind. They filed off through the mounted knights, who followed.

From across the crimson plain, the Scots could not believe that Pembroke was abandoning the fray. Not when his knights were so near to annihilating all that remained of the Scots army. Yet Aymer's beautifully costumed and powerful array continued to ride out after him, without having struck a single blow.

Robert and Thomas and Edward sat upon their mounts and gaped.

Lord Aymer had quit the field!

"Send someone to the top of the hill to see for sure that this isn't some English trick," ordered Robert to 'The Black' Douglas.

"Ye want these wounded English kilt?" asked Sir Edward, looking at those being left behind by the departing Pembroke.

"Nay, let 'em be," ordered Robert. "And, leave the camp folk to scavenge weapons and bury our dead." The three then rode out upon the battleground to assess the number of English killed.

"I heard that Aymer had sent spies to report yer actions before the battle, but they ne'er came back. Did ye meet up with any of 'em in the last few days?" asked Thomas.

"Aye," answered Edward, "we met 'em."

Thomas passed his wine flask to Robert and waited for a continuation.

"We dragged 'em back here... behind a fast horse... and threw them into one of the trenches. I 'magine they're still down there, some-where," grinned Edward as he received the flask from Robert and took a drink.

The friends stayed in position, sharing the wine and talking until James Douglas confirmed that the English had withdrawn.

Only then did Robert wheel his horse about and leave the battle-field, the 'Lion Rampant,' held high by its young bearer, following closely at his heels.

JULY 8th 1307
LANERCOST SANCTUARY

Hearing of Loudoun Hill and the subsequent successes of Robert of Scotland in the days following, Edward of England was whipped into a mighty diatribe of hate, and again became strongly bent on revenge against Robert de Brus and the Scots who followed him. He was sorely disappointed in Pembroke's performance as Warden of Scotland, and in the other lords that he had sent to Scotland to lead his expensive armies, as well. All had failed him miserably, and so he resolved to place himself at the head of the greatest army he could muster, and prevail where others had so dreadfully blundered.

He sent summonses to every lord that owed him service and demanded they repair to Carlisle on the Eighth of July 1307, for the purpose of subduing the rebellion, once and for all. Most responded as they were bade, and a grand army of knights and many accompanying folk gathered in and camped around the town.

"Has my son arrived as yet?" growled King Edward, now but a shadow of the once physically powerful monarch.

"No, Lord King," replied Sir Fulco as he watched the valet meticulously dress the feeble king, sitting most impatiently on the edge of his huge and ornate bed. The papers of the kingdom remained strewn about, intermixed with the bedclothes.

"See to it that he is sent to me immediately!" huffed Edward as the valet fitted his chest armor in position and affixed it to the back plate.

Sir Fulco bowed and left the room to seek current information on the whereabouts of the Prince of Wales, who was due from Berwick that morning with at least two hundred of his 'swan knights,' and another two hundred fifty squires, archers, and soldiers of foot.

Sir Fulco returned to the king with no definitive word on the arrival of his son.

"Help me to stand," demanded the king, and two guards hastened forward to hold the king until he managed to will himself to his feet, albeit unsteadily.

"Aha!" he shouted. "Did you, Fulco, think I was not spry enough for the task?" asked the wobbly king in the shrill voice of an enfeebled man.

"You have been badly laid up for many days, Sire," replied Ballard. "I *am* purely amazed at your strength."

The two stalwarts aided the king to the high altar of the sanctuary on the other side of the structure. Two servants carried the empty litter that had borne the king for these last months.

Edward slowly sat in the chair placed before the altar for his purpose, and the litter was placed betwixt him and the altar. The priests arrived on cue to thank God for the return of their king to health, and to bless the campaign he was about to mount against the rebellious Scots.

Between incense and prayers, nearly an hour was spent, and Edward grew weary of the "babbling priests" and called an abrupt halt to the ceremony. The priests seemed to melt away, once they were interrupted with no word of apology or regret.

The king ordered Sir Fulco to repair to the courtyard and seek news of the prince's ever later arrival, while he sat frowning and in silence, running his skeletal fingers in the grooves of the intricately carved, Viking-inspired design on the arms of the ornate wooden chair.

"What manner of son would not hasten to his father's side in his greatest hour of need?" wondered the king aloud.

"Fulco!" he screamed in his loudest voice. High and strident, it echoed about the cavernous hall.

Sir Fulco heard him not, but a servant who had, came to the king's steward and told him of the king's bidding.

"Yes, Sire?" said Fulco, rushing to his side.

"The prince?" he asked.

"Good news, Milord! He is but an hour away, according to a herald sent by the prince to announce his arrival," answered Fulco.

"I shall await him here," returned Edward.

"I will have the doors opened that the cool breeze from the outside may come through, Sire," said Fulco with a bow.

The king waved his hand in approval and Fulco did as he had said. Then, he who was long accustomed to waiting for no man, waited.

Soon, there was cheering and loud clamoring without, and the king knew his son had finally arrived. He ordered his two guards to hoist him to his feet and help him to the door. Beyond the portico stood his old destrier, large and magnificent in its festooned armor, surrounded by colorful flags, with fully bedecked knights standing honor guard.

Edward Plantagenet, king of England, was awed even for him, for he remembered his former glory and this fared well in comparison. Old battles replayed in his mind. Real or imagined, the sound of trumpets filled his senses and he was swept with excitement.

The Prince of Wales came to him and bowed dutifully.

"You look in perfect health, my father," he lied.

The old man, showing the courage and determination with which he had carried himself throughout his life, cast off the strong hands of his supporting guards. Though his courage and stubbornness had served him and his country fittingly, his tired, weak legs went akimbo for a moment, and it was only through sheer grit that he straightened them and, accompanied only by the prince, slowly walked toward his waiting mount.

Waiting crowds, alerted by minions of Fulco Ballard, boisterously cheered to see their aged sovereign once again on his feet. Small children were hoisted up to sit on shoulders, that they might see their mighty king ride away on his valiant mount to conquer Scotland.

Edward managed a weak smile, though the sun's brightness nearly forced his eyes tight shut, making him all but blind. Still, he rallied to the crowd's enthusiasm and managed to raise one withered arm, which the multitude saw not beneath his kingly armor.

Fulco had also had constructed a portable platform to be used whenever the king mounted or dismounted his steed. It was equally as high as the royal stirrup, to ease the king's settling into the saddle, for Ballard knew full well that his heavily armored king could not otherwise manage to straddle the poor beast.

The prince helped his father's foot find the stirrup and the grooms steadied the already overtaxed king on his perch.

More cheers arose as his horse moved slowly forward, that Edward might take the lead of this portion of his gathering army, but the king did not acknowledge the throng's presence further.

Now, it was on to Carlisle, where there awaited at least four thousand more to join in the hunt for Robert de Brus.

The procession went only as speedily as did the king who led it, and thus they were until the last of daylight getting to the walls of Carlisle.

The king was past exhaustion, and Sir Fulco ordered that he be taken to suitable quarters, immediately.

.   .

The next morning, in the solar of the keep in Castle Carlisle, King Edward awoke and, knowing not where he was, called for his steward, who came immediately to his side and bowed fittingly.

"Yes, My Lord King," spoke Fulco feigning cheerfulness. "Your morning repast?"

"Where in hell's name am I, Fulco?" worried the king, his old eyes nearly lost in their sockets.

"Carlisle, Sire," replied Fulco, "Your army awaits your continued journey."

"Humph," returned the king, and after searching his memory for a moment replied crossly, "Of course. I knew that!"

"I knew, you knew, Milord," patronized Fulco as he motioned for the king's breakfast to be brought in to him.

"We havin' sausage and eggs this morn?" the king asked upon seeing the tray coming toward him.

"Your nose has lost not its sense of smell, Sire," answered Fulco with a smile.

The king smiled in return.

It would be a good day.

He was at last about to eliminate the Scottish rebels, which apparently none other could manage, and Robert de Brus, their "king," would soon join his brothers and that other traitor... what was his name? It escaped him for the moment, but no matter. The pillows were propped and puffed, and he laid back on them to enjoy his leisurely meal, while in the courtyard the army of the king sat in full armor and in full array astride their mounts.

James Airth, the Swan Knight who had wounded Nigel Brus in the battle of Kildrummy, was one who waited. Will this king ne'er come for his men, he wondered, as the morning dragged slowly by.

He was no exception, for metal armor fitted with leather and sheep's wool felt comfortable in every season save summer, and was literally enough to cause heat stroke on a day as unusually hot as this ninth of July.

After at least two hours of their standing thus in the grueling heat, the king at last appeared at the door of the keep. Trumpets blared and all the army hailed their king. 'Longshanks' was again inspired, and, yet again, he threw off the guards propping him up. And, again through sheer will, he made his way to his horse, standing patiently beside the ubiquitous mounting platform.

The army cheered appropriately.

James Airth wondered if the hurrahs were for the king or for the anticipation of cooler breezes, which would surely be found beyond the walls of the town.

The king assumed his position at the head of the army and his son, the Prince of Wales, rode at his side.

Slowly toward Scotland did they journey, for the king refused to be borne about on a litter, and could not stay mounted at a faster gait.

. .

On the eleventh of July, four days after leaving the sanctuary, they were encamped near the village of Burgh-on-Sands, a mere six miles closer to Scotland than he had been while virtually bedfast in Lanercost for those many months.

The king had a larger tent than all the others and was furnished with a comfortable pallet and chairs, carried on accompanying wagons. As was his custom, he slept well beyond sunup as the army busied itself with feeding and caring for the animals, and readying itself for the day's journey.

"Reckon, ol' 'Longshanks' will be ready ere noon?" asked a companion to James Airth.

James threw up his hands, "Damned if I know," he said sourly as he watered his horse from a leather bucket.

"Fulco!" said King Edward in an almost lost voice as he realized he was yet among the living.

"Yes, Milord," replied his dutiful servant, who stood close by the king's pallet.

Two physicians entered. The king's eyes rolled to meet their entrance.

"What business have these 'blackbirds' here!? I am cured!" he exclaimed as strongly as he could.

"Sire," explained Sir Fulco, "you have soiled your bedclothes during the night and I felt it prudent to call on the physicians to ascertain your fitness for the day's ride."

"I'm damned well fit enough!" he asserted, and he tried to prove his words by arising to his elbows. "What!" said the startled king. "Who restrains me on my bed?"

"Naught save God, Sire," sadly replied Sir Fulco, whose suspicions, gleaned from his all night vigil, bore true.

The men of black robes inspected the limp body of their king and found their skills and knowledge ruefully lacking. Privately, they told Sir Fulco the prognosis he had already guessed.

Fulco Ballard went immediately to inform the Prince of Wales of his father's condition.

"He can speak and turn his head, all else fails his commands," he explained in suitably calm and hushed tones. "He will surely die within the course of the day, My Prince."

The prince sat quietly in his tent for a full moment and then commented without emotion, "At last, I will know what I have wanted to know for half my life."

"Milord?" said Fulco, not understanding.

The prince raised his brows and smiled pleasantly, "How it will truly feel to view him dead."

'Tis a cold thing to contemplate, thought Fulco, sadly, but knew better than to pursue the conversation further, for the prince would be king as soon as the last breath of his father was drawn.

"I shall return to attend the king, Milord," he said, adding, "... with your permission."

Young Edward shrugged his shoulders, for he cared not, and his mind fleetly went to the morrow and the fulfillment of *his* prideful agenda.

Fulco hastened to the king's bedside and sat quietly in a good-sized wooden chair to await the king's awakening from his doze. Within moments, the failing monarch's eyes opened and Sir Fulco found it his duty to tell his king and lifelong friend, of sorts, that his moments on earth grew short.

"Send for my son," said the king weakly after a moment of disbelief, then resignation to the truth.

Fulco left the tent in search of the prince while the two physicians stood worthlessly at the foot of the bed, wondering what bit of knowledge they could glean from their failure.

The prince arrived shortly, and sat in the chair next to his father. A priest also arrived and stood beside the physicians, and began mumbling a prayer for the dying old man. Sir Fulco stood back and, eyes brimming, silently watched the drama evolve.

"I am here, Father," said the prince unemotionally.

The king opened his eyes and looked upon his son for a lengthy spell. The prince became uneasy, being reminded of the many times in the past when his father had made him feel thus, and he liked it not.

At last the king spoke, slowly and feebly. "I am dying, my son, and you must..." the king paused to cough weakly, then continued, "...you will be king on this day." The king paused again to notice the almost undetectable smile on his son's face and said, "I know, you shall be gladdened by this event," the king frowned, "but I shall not."

"I shall be saddened, also," replied the prince.

"'Tis too late for lies," said the king, shaking his head, "for within mere moments I am off to glory... and you will be fulfilling my legacy." His breath came more strenuously, now, and he often choked upon it.

"Of... being king?" asked the prince.

"Of killing Robert de Brus," frowned the sinking monarch as well as he could.

"'Tis done," said young Edward, casually.

"Not so soon are you unburdened, my son," replied his father, "for you have not heard my last requests as yet."

"Last requests?" questioned the prince, impatient, now, at the old man's ramblings.

"Last requests... first I would that my heart ... be removed from my body... and carried to Jerusalem, that I might... at long last... share in the 'holy wars' that domestic concerns... ne'er allowed me to join..."

Tears ran freely down Sir Fulco's face as he overheard the discourse.

The king continued, now in an extremely vengeful voice. "I further charge you to take my vacated body... and, by boiling, separate it... bone from flesh! The bone to be properly interred... and the flesh, placed in a large urn... to journey at the head of this army 'til Robert de Brus is killed... by stealth or in battle, I care not. Or, captured and executed... in the vilest manner you can dream about... like Wallace..." and his face brightened momentarily. "Yes! That was his name... Wallace!" The king's face then collapsed in its expression, from sheer exhaustion. All grew motionless and silent.

One of the physicians stepped forward to place a mirror under the monarch's nose and watch for signs of breath. There were none, though he waited patiently.

"Is he dead?" bluntly asked the prince, finally.

The physician indicated that he was, and, bowing low, backed away from the dead king. The prince, however, stood and leaned urgently over the still form.

"Say something more, Father!" implored the prince, concerned with posterity. "Those cannot be your last words!"

But they were his last words.

Edward I, king of England, had died as he lived, demanding of others that which he had found beyond his own ability, and being blunt about it. Perhaps one of England's greatest kings, he had let his obsession of conquering Scotland and wreaking revenge on Robert de Brus precede all else. Now, in death, he wanted to continue his obsession in the embodiment of his son.

"I am now the king!" whispered young Edward as the physicians retired from the bedside. "I am now king!" he shouted unreservedly. Then he looked longingly at his father, lying dead before him. A corpse at last! No more toadying to this black heart's will, he inwardly rejoiced.

Sir Fulco retired for a moment and the physicians went to their knees in prayer as the priest moved closer to the old king's head and continued his rites of absolution, drawing with his thumb the sign of the cross on the motionless brow.

Fulco returned to unfold the three leopards flag and reverently lay it across the body of his old friend. The faithful servant then knelt at the side of the deathbed with head bowed and tears flowing down his face.

He was not allowed to be long at his grief, for the new king soon arose from his chair and grabbed Sir Fulco by his arm, literally dragging him to his feet and outside of the tent.

Sir Fulco straightened himself, trying to regain his dignity.

"You, steward, have three last requirements to fulfill, and if you do them well, I will grant you a pension, that you and your family may live out your days in the country with no cares, save perhaps your own health."

"Name them, Lord King, I will do as I am bade," said Fulco bowing.

"*Lord King*!" said the new monarch, temporarily distracted. "How good that sounds to my ear!" he laughed, his relief finally emerging.

"Milord," reminded Sir Fulco, "your requests?"

"For sure, Ballard," said the new-made king as he returned to his purpose. "You know where my father sent my good friend, Piers Gaveston?"

"I do, Sire," the steward replied.

"Send for him!" ordered young Edward. "Tell him that... he can come home now... the mean spirited one is dead!"

"I will word it appropriately," quietly replied Fulco.

"'Word it'... *exactly* ...as I have spoken it," said Edward, frowning menacingly.

Fulco sighed and said, "And the second request, Sire?"

"You will accompany my father's body to Waltham Abbey. There, they will know what to do with it 'til I can figure a royal entombment... befitting his greatness."

"And the last?"

"Hmmm? Oh, yes. The last is that you utilize your abilities as true author of my father's recent papers... to prepare a more fitting statement for his 'last words.'"

"These things I will do, Sire," said Fulco, and he bowed and took his leave to return inside the tent to continue mourning the old king's death. He was saddened that the last requests his sovereign and... yes, his friend... so strongly demanded would be ignored.

Fulco knew that, for him, life would certainly be faint-witted beyond this day.

King Robert was in no way saddened to hear of 'Longshanks'' passing, for the arduous trek of recent times had more than decimated his family and close friends, and certainly had placed himself and his homeland in mortal peril. Indeed, at Edward Plantagenet's death, both Robert's surviving family and his country were left widely separated by 'Longshanks' machinations.

The mastermind of the war against Scotland was gone, as was the power behind its prosecution. King Edward II lasted but six weeks more before returning to London and dispersing his army to the four corners of the realm from whence they had come. He had other agenda to contrive, other desires to fulfill.

The Hammer of the Scots was dead.

For further reading about Robert de Bruce and The Scottish Wars of Independence we recommend the following works:

Barrow, G. W. S. *Robert Bruce and the Community of the Realm of Scotland.* London, England: Eyere & Spottiswood, 1965

Barron, Evan Macleod *The Scottish Wars of Independence.* First published 1914. Current publisher: New York, USA: Barnes and Noble Books, 1997

Scott, Ronald McNair *Robert the Bruce – King of Scots.* First published 1982. Peter Bedrick Books. Current publisher: New York, Barnes and Noble Books, 1993.

Duncan, A.A.M. (translation and notes by) *John Barbour – The Bruce.* Edinburgh, Scotland: Canongate Books, Inc., 1997

Bingham, Caroline *Robert the Bruce.* London, England, 1998

McNamee, Colm *The Wars of the Bruces.* East Lothian, Scotland, 1997

Video

(Simon Schama, *A History of Britain,* The History Channel, February 28, 2001)